BE A GOOD SOLDIER:
CHILDREN'S GRIEF IN ENGLISH MODERNIST NOVELS

JENNIFER MARGARET FRASER

Be a Good Soldier

Children's Grief in English Modernist Novels

UNIVERSITY OF TORONTO PRESS
Toronto Buffalo London

ISBN 978-1-4426-4313-0 (cloth)

∞

Printed on acid-free, 100% post-consumer recycled paper with
vegetable-based inks.

Library and Archives Canada Cataloguing in Publication

Fraser, Jennifer Margaret, 1966–
Be a good soldier : children's grief in English modernist novels / Jennifer
Margaret Fraser.

Includes bibliographical references and index.
ISBN 978-1-4426-4313-0

1. English fiction – 20th century – History and criticism.   2. Children in
literature.   3. Grief in literature.   I. Title.

PR888.C5F73 2011   823'.912093523   C2011-903216-3

This book has been published with the help of a grant from the Canadian
Federation for the Humanities and Social Sciences, through the Aid
to Scholarly Publications Program, using funds provided by the Social
Sciences and Humanities Research Council of Canada.

University of Toronto Press acknowledges the financial assistance to its
publishing program of the Canada Council for the Arts and the Ontario
Arts Council.

 Canada Council Conseil des Arts
for the Arts   du Canada

 ONTARIO ARTS COUNCIL
CONSEIL DES ARTS DE L'ONTARIO

University of Toronto Press acknowledges the financial support of the
Government of Canada through the Canada Book Fund for its publishing
activities.

For Thomas George Brown, son of a good soldier,
who chose to be a good father

Contents

Acknowledgments

Peter Nesselroth introduced me to the writings of Jacques Derrida, and he also shared with me his own haunting childhood story; both of these gifts have shaped this book. Wendy O'Brien-Ewara, dear friend and brilliant scholar, has greatly influenced this study. Carola Kaplan's initial reaction to, and support of, the development of the Conrad chapter inspired me to continue pursuing this project. Claire Battersill commented helpfully on the Woolf chapter. Anne Fogarty's invitation to lecture at the James Joyce Summer School in Dublin provided opportunities to pursue my work on the *Finnegans Wake* chapter. Funding for that trip was generously provided by a professional development grant from St Michaels University School.

When I first began this book, I received remarkable support from my colleagues and friends Jennifer Walcott, Karrie Weinstock, Jennifer Levine, and Julia Thompson in Toronto. Now in Victoria, Janice McCachen and Terence Young are an invaluable professional, literary, and intellectual support.

R. Brandon Kershner's reading of, and suggestions about, the completed manuscript were exceptional. Richard Ratzlaff believed in the project and advised adroitly throughout the publication process, and I am very grateful to him, to the readers of the manuscript, as well as to Barb Porter and Catherine Frost at University of Toronto Press. My parents' untiring belief in, and support of, my scholarly work has always been a crucial foundation.

This book is dedicated to my husband, whose father, George Brown, was a gunner on a Lancaster during the Second World War. His father survived thirty-six successful runs until his plane was shot down. He parachuted to safety and kept the ripcord for the rest of his life in his desk drawer. Returning to Ontario, he taught his two sons to scan the sky and never let down their guard. They learned that grief meant a moment of weakness, exposing one to attack. George Brown was a good solider and his sons suffered.

We also have two boys, and my husband has strived throughout their upbringing to let go of lessons learned from his brave father and to allow our sons, privileged enough not to have to fight a war, to grieve. Watching my husband's struggle, between the lessons learned and the lessons one wants to impart, compares to watching someone shake themselves free of stone.

Jacques Derrida died while I was writing this book and when I speak of him and his remarkable mind, it is, to use his phrase, with 'tears in my voice.'

BE A GOOD SOLDIER:
CHILDREN'S GRIEF IN ENGLISH MODERNIST NOVELS

Introduction to Children's Grief: The Return from Exile

The Origins of this Study

In my early twenties, I went to Italy to study for six months and I called home to Vancouver, Canada, every week or two. I decided to call on a Monday; I had the uncanny feeling there was something wrong. As soon as I heard my mother's voice, I could tell she had terrible news for me. Very calmly, she told me to come home; my older brother had been stabbed in the heart and lung in a freak attack. The paramedics categorized him as 'dead on arrival.' The emergency doctors revived him. His lung was punctured. The knife went right through his back. The knife might have been dirty. They transfused him with pints and pints of other peoples' blood, which might be infected. He suffered two cardiac arrests. A specialist performed open heart surgery in the emergency department. Now he was in critical condition on life support.

The stabbing happened in the early hours of Sunday morning; no one expected him to survive. They knew his brain was still intact, yet he was hanging by a thread, hooked up to machines. My father was not allowed in the intensive care unit because he could not stop crying. The nurses told my mother that, if she wanted access, she was not to shed a tear; when her son pulled out of the morphine, she was to tell him to *fight*; she was to tell him he was going to be okay and to keep fighting. So my mother sat by my brother's bed and held his hand and told him, without shedding a tear, to fight for his life. And he did. And he survived. For years after, my mother still could not cry. It was as if she had turned to stone. Watching my mother struggle with various therapies and antidotes to her paralysed grief acted as a catalyst for this literary study.

I started thinking a lot about grief and the way in which it could jeopardize the need we have at times to fight for our lives. Watching my brother, a writer, script draft after draft of this event has left us all bleeding.

During the trial on the attempted murder of my brother, it was revealed that the assailant was eighteen and in the American navy; he had grown up in a violent home. Learning these details of the young man who wanted to kill, without motivation except for a driving need to wound the world, contributed to my exploration of grief, but it made the focus shift to childhood. The assailant used violence as a way to interact with others, as he had come from a home where he clearly had had to fight, not just fight back tears, but actually fight physically to survive.

A modernist, I became amazed at the recurring themes in the novels I first studied, and then taught, of hurt children and damaged fighters. There is a profound concern about the suppression of childhood grief and its return in the form of aggression in modernist fiction, but so far it does not appear to have caught the attention of scholars. Nonetheless, there are striking bonds, repeated tropes, comparable conclusions reached by novelists as diverse as Joseph Conrad, Jean Rhys, Rebecca West, Ford Madox Ford, Virginia Woolf, and James Joyce. Each one of these modernists establishes a relationship between the immobilizing of childhood grief and the mobilizing of an adult soldier-self (literal or figurative). Because *Be a Good Soldier: Children's Grief in English Modernist Novels* is a focused work, it only begins to describe what I believe to be a large and complex body of literature awaiting further investigation. I limit this study to six novelists and only certain of their texts; this is not to suggest that these are the only works that explore childhood's role in the modernist era. I have further limited my study of the child to his or her expression of, or suppression of, grief. The novelists and their specific works have been chosen because they share a sense that childhood grief is powerful and potentially dangerous if exiled by social dictum.[1]

All the novelists in this study have articulated, in one form or another, children's grief. This inclusion presents a literary hurdle because the expression of grief, especially childhood grief, challenges social mores and traditional narration. Grief is defined by being inarticulate. In the *Iliad,* Homer makes Antilochus responsible for telling Achilles that Patroclus has been killed and he is incapacitated: 'He stood there speechless a while, struck dumb ... / tears filling his eyes, his strong voice choked' (17.783–4). In a contemporary book on grief, the author stresses the 'overwhelming of our powers of articulation' as the defining feature of the emotion that therefore leads to 'the gestural language of tears' (Lutz 21). Paul Fussell highlights the inscriptions in First World War cemeteries that refuse 'to play the game of memorial language' and thus allow their grief to be inarticulate with such phrases as a 'sorrow too deep for words' (70). Samuel Hynes contrasts the rhetoric of the war exemplified by Rupert Brooke's sonnets of 'Holiness, Love, Pain, Honour, Nobleness, Glory, Heroism, Sacrifice, England' and the lack of language facing Ford Madox Ford, who has 'no words for the reality of war' (109). Adults struggle to find the words for grief, whereas children do not even know where to begin looking. Besides, children grow up in a culture that disapproves of their attempts to express grief.

Contemporary grief expert Grace Hyslop Christ explains that the inarticulate way children 'communicate their grief' makes it difficult for adults to respond. Notably, she begins to categorize children's reactions from the age of three, when they are beyond the 'infant' phase of not being able to speak. However, each phase of childhood that she focuses on is defined by being inarticulate when faced with expressing grief. Her research reveals that children from three to five years old may express grief by thumb sucking, bed-wetting, night terrors, and so on. Children from six to eight are more likely to express their grief by using 'magical thinking processes.' And children from nine to eleven are 'so overwhelmed' that they 'did not like to talk' and 'refused to express or experience their sadness'; thus, they resort 'to intellectualization' (235–6). Pam Heaney notes: 'Adults all too frequently think that children's losses are trivial, or that the lost objects are replaceable, and they chastise the children for "carrying on about it."' And yet, we 'grieve whenever we lose anything, whether it be someone or something.' Regardless of this 'natural, normal response to loss of any kind,' the 'majority of people are not comfortable seeing someone else distraught, so they try to avoid the situation.' This 'is especially so in many people's interactions with children' (20–7). Rather than trying to normalize, or silence by ignoring, the disruptive childhood voices of modernist narratives, my approach foregrounds their disruption. This requires a shift from Freud's psychological approach, which aims to cure and integrate, to Jacques Derrida's philosophical approach, which aims to understand and incorporate. Thus, this study of modernist novels draws on Derrida's exploration of the dissenting role of childhood and of grief. Notably, Derrida locates the origins of his deconstructive approach within his own childhood grief.

In *Circumfession*, Derrida writes the necessity and impossibility of his own and all childhood grief.[2] John Caputo notes that in this text

Derrida's words flow 'like the tears of a child weeping for his mother' (*Prayers* 235). *Circumfession* is as challenging to read as a Virginia Woolf novel or even, perhaps, *Finnegans Wake*. One of the reasons for this difficulty is that, on one level, all these texts strive to speak from within a child's tearful world. *Circumfession* takes as its central incision, circumcision, an act that Derrida says creates a 'wounded baby' (66). He acknowledges that this is the incision that generates his theories: "*Circumcision, that's all I've ever talked about, consider the discourse on the limit, margins, marks, marches, etc., the closure, the ring (alliance and gift), the sacrifice, the writing of the body, the* pharmakos *excluded or cut off, the cutting / sewing of* Glas, *the blow and sewing back up*"' (70). I have been unable to locate other scholars' work concerned with Derrida's presentation of his own childhood grief and the way in which it shaped his desire to collapse hierarchical relationships between not only parent and child, but also all other power structures.[3] Derrida's constant return to the 'wounded baby' forms the theoretical framework used to listen for the grieving childhood voices in the narratives of English modernism.

Grieving for Jean-François Lyotard, Derrida considers his friend's 'last writings on childhood and tears.' He defines this work as 'an immense treatise on absolute disarmament, on that which links thought to infinite vulnerability.' For Derrida, this is clearly one of Lyotard's great triumphs: his ability to bring together the usually separate realms of thought and vulnerability and his articulation of the seemingly inarticulate realms of childhood and tears. Derrida discovers in writing the eulogy that his friend's death, his loss, his grief, are comparably 'unthinkable' and 'beyond words.' However, rather than arming himself, he enters into Lyotard's realm of disarmament: 'I am going to take refuge in the texts that he wrote here, and I am going to listen to him, on the Pacific Wall, so as to rethink childhood' (*WM* 214–15). In a typically paradoxical manoeuvre, Derrida turns to words in order to find refuge from feelings that are beyond words. He does not arm himself against pending death; he returns to his own grieving childhood. He does not give up; he responds to the battle with the oceanic emblem for peace, the Pacific (pacific, *adj.* peaceful; making or loving peace; *OED*). He does not barricade himself behind a wall; he listens to the loss and discovery of friendship while positioned *on* the wall, reading.

In a study of modernism and mourning, Jahan Ramazani observes that poetry is one method of accessing the alienated self: 'The elegy thus afforded male poets the exploration of feelings publicly marked as unavailable and alien, permitting the social mask of the griefless male to slip a little' (20). Going beyond the adult need to grieve explored in elegy, modernist narratives seek ways to return to the inarticulate, grieving, exiled self of childhood. This return requires readers, despite the difficulty and disruption, to listen for foreign terms like those of Joyce's *Finnegans Wake*, where a voice is still calling: '—Stll cllng! Nmr! Peace, Pacific!' (502.11).

Modernist Children: The Return from Exile

As documented by historians, in the 1860s British society underwent a change in its concept of childhood and its response to children. According to historian Jean Heywood, this was 'the beginning of social justice for children' (56). An early Victorian culture of moral rigidity for the young, with its often violent discipline, shifted into the more liberal approaches of the 1870s and beyond, when children slowly gained status as individuals with rights. This is not to say, however, that cruelty, exploitation, and neglect subsided, as documented by Lionel Rose and as will be further discussed in this study. Nonetheless, the novelists of the modernist era clearly responded to the changing historical sense of what constitutes a child, and they expressed a concern not only with children's rights, but also with children's feelings.

The chapters of this study are arranged to reveal a developing sense in the modernist era that, although society may configure childhood grief as foreign, alien, and unnatural, in fact, it is resident, native, and innate. The arc traced by this book reveals novelists working to create a space, a textual home for the open expression of childhood grief. While society exiles childhood grief during this era, the novelists under discussion strive to allow it back home. The chapters of *Be a Good Soldier: Children's Grief in English Modernist Novels* are arranged to reveal a movement towards creating a fictional home for grieving-child narration. Thus, as we travel from the first writer to the last, the child becomes more and more vocal and the texts become more and more radical, more innovative, and more challenging to read.

In the first two chapters, the suppressed childhood self manifests itself in political movements: Russian revolutionaries for Conrad and the colonized for Rhys. Joseph Conrad's *Under Western Eyes* situates childhood grief as remote as Russia for his British readers. He uses an English translator for a narrative frame, yet has him stop short of translating the inarticulate language of grief found in the Russian diary of the protagonist, as if it is simply too foreign to share.

In Jean Rhys's five novellas, the child figure clearly resides within the stories, but is configured as alien. Read as a quintet, Rhys's stories move away from Europe, where she lived and wrote as an adult, and they travel back to the West Indies and the patois she would have heard as a child. Despite this clear movement, a sense that childhood grief belongs to an alien, tropical zone permeates all her texts.

Rhys reverses the immigration tale told in *Jane Eyre* of Mrs Rochester travelling to England and instead has Mr Rochester journey to the West Indies; thus, he travels back to the time and place when the story of childhood grief could be recounted in a language that comforted rather than suppressed it. This is the place where even Rochester can reflect on his requirement as a child to suppress emotions. However, at the end of *Wide Sargasso Sea*, the grieving Antoinette, dominated by childhood memories and moments, yearning for the lost landscape of her child-hood, is exiled to the attic of a British manor house (the site of the British nursery). With the exception of those who populate *Wide Sargasso Sea*, all Conrad's and Rhys's characters relegate childhood to the past; it surfaces as memories. A shift occurs in Rebecca West's and Ford Madox Ford's novels, where children become independent fictional characters.

In the third chapter of this study, on Rebecca West's *The Return of the Soldier*, the protagonist, Chris Baldry, has a son, but he dies at the age of two. For healing to take place in this novel, the exiled child of the protag-onist must be returned. This child is both a figure for Chris Baldry's own childhood, as well as the man's dead two-year-old. Neither child has been fully grieved. With terrible irony, the return of the child allows for the re-turn of the soldier. Now that he is cured, now that he is a psychologically fit man, Chris is returned to the trenches. Although the story is set in the English countryside, like Rhys's novellas childhood grief is imagined by the narrator as belonging to a remote tropical place. However, there is an intermediary landscape that marks the shift in the narratives to-wards further incorporation of the exiled, grieving child. West's 'Monkey Island' is nearby and is associated with a woman who does not require the suppression of grief and thus allows for a grieving, but also a loving, joyful, boyish side to Chris. She acts as a foil to Chris's wife, who requires her husband to be a hard soldier ready to fight in the war.

The fourth chapter is focused on Ford Madox Ford's *The Good Soldier* and the four novels of *Parade's End*. In the first novel there is an attempt by Americans to secure a British estate, as though it will be the home that they cannot find in America for childhood grief. Their attempts fail miserably, yet Ford makes clear that the powerful attraction in this novel is towards those who may allow for the connection to, or discovery of, one's suppressed grief during childhood. In *Parade's End*, like West's novel set during the First World War, there is an actual child character. Previously, with the exception of Rhys's opening narrator in *Wide Sargasso Sea*, children or childhood were only recalled. In *Parade's End*, Ford's protagonist, Christopher Tietjens, has a son who never speaks and thus has not been the focus of much critical analysis. Nonetheless, as I argue, this child is the driving force behind the events of the novel, most notably the fight to escape from the immobilization of grief.

Although children are actual characters, not merely recollections of adults, in West's and Ford's fiction, these children are kept silent. West has the child die and Ford has the child silent and out of reach for most of the novel. Nonetheless, these children are highly influential and significant to the development of the protagonist of each author's work. The grief of children in all of the narratives is configured as a fundamental component of the power structures explored. Conrad sets his story against the backdrop of a Russian dictatorship; Rhys sets her novellas on the stage of colonization of women and foreigners; West and Ford tell their tales right within the First World War. There is a disturbing conflation of the domestic home front and the military home front in West's and Ford's novels.

Not only do the final two authors in this study have children as independent characters in their fiction, but they give them voices. Virginia Woolf and James Joyce radically break with the past in having children express their grief and also in trying to recreate the way in which these children would speak. Hence, they create a fictional space that allows for childhood voices to narrate directly. In Virginia Woolf's *A Haunted House* and *The Waves* and James Joyce's *Finnegans Wake*, the narrative includes the distinct, at times seemingly inarticulate, language of children. In Woolf's two narratives, childhood grief finds a voice and speaks throughout. This grieving voice, distributed in *The Waves* among six narrators, rarely is spoken to others, but it constantly speaks within.

In Joyce's *Finnegans Wake*, the grieving childhood self speaks up and out, and thus in this final text the tragic underpinnings of the other novels transform into comedy. Childhood grief is only one side of the coin in the *Wake* and, if allowed its place in the social economy, the flip side is childhood and adult joy. At the wake for a dead man, one weeps and laughs, producing the 'laughtears' of the text.

Woolf and Joyce use a variety of techniques to create a home in which childhood grief can speak the unspeakable; as a result, their narratives overthrow our expectations for grammar, plot, setting, character, and narrator. One of Woolf's narrators in *The Waves* explains, 'for pain words are lacking,' yet these two authors paradoxically must employ words to tell the story of pain. Woolf uses a layered, poetic, fragmentary style to express what seems inexpressible, and Joyce uses a comedic, multilingual, accumulative style.[4]

A sustained reading of the requirement to suppress grief in the works of Conrad, Rhys, West, Ford, Woolf, and Joyce reveals that certain modernist narratives deconstruct the model of grief inherited from their predecessors, and that they do so by inserting into their texts a form of grief-language associated first with childhood memories, then with children themselves, and ultimately with child-narrators. The use of literary experimentalism and the shared metaphor of turning to stone by means of suppressing grief brings these novelists into dialogue. All of them strive in their fiction to break out of the stone-like pedagogical mould they have inherited.

At the start of this study, the child does not seem to belong and is certainly not comedic in the fiction. In historical studies of this era, one learns that the nursery was relegated to 'remote parts of the house'; it was a 'foreign territory,' and despite the house's opulence, the children were raised in 'spartan conditions' (Rose 223). Not only was the child's space in the upper-class home seen as a remote, almost foreign zone, it was also a place of suffering. Jonathan Gathorne-Hardy's research leads him to define the rule of the nursery as 'bullied despotism' (241).

In all six chapters, the bullies are configured as characters who have so successfully suppressed their own grief that they have become emotionally immobilized. The figures who behave cruelly, ranging from those who harshly treat children or spouses to those who officially rule others – teachers, police, judges, colonialists – are represented in these novels as those who have about as much feeling as stone or wood. They are presented as individuals who have successfully suppressed their own feelings of childhood grief and thus are able to take on positions of control and power.[5] Samuel Butler begins *The Way of All Flesh* with a description of the 'violent type of father' who, he maintains, is the norm at the turn of the twentieth century. The father's goal is to ensure that his children's wills are '"well broken" in childhood, to use an expression then much in vogue'; thus, the father 'thrashed his boys two or three times a week and some weeks a good deal oftener,' for, as he explains, 'in those days fathers were always thrashing their boys' (30–1). Offering a portrayal of the shift to modernism, Virginia Woolf imagines the Victorians departing and Butler coming out from 'below-stairs' with his novel in order to discourse on the 'family secrets' and she comments: 'the basement was really in an appalling state' (*Essays* 386). In order to bring the grieving child-self up from the basement, it is necessary to shift paradigms from Freud's hierarchical model to Derrida's collapsed binaries.

Paradigm Shift from Freud to Derrida

In his influential study, still the touchstone for studies on bereavement, 'Mourning and Melancholy,' Sigmund Freud argues that in the 'normal' process of bereavement, the mourner separates over time his or her 'libido' (capacity for love) from the lost love object. However, not letting go of the lost love object produces melancholy. As Julia Kristeva notes, 'the majority of literary criticism in the field tends to limit itself to the traditional form of elegy, and more often than not applies a Freudian-inflected approach' (151). Yet, as Joseph Zornado argues: 'As brilliant as many of Freud's observations were, his Oedipal theory inadvertently reproduced the dominant ideology regarding the nature of the child, and with the child's nature firmly established, the hierarchical relational structure of the adult to the child remained intact. The adult had to help the child redirect her energies, which meant to properly repress them if the child was to join the adult world as a functional member of the dominant cultural order of the Victorian era' (28). Thus, by resorting to fiction rather than elegy, by using a reversed position as seeing *through* the child's eyes instead of analysing the child from a psychoanalytic point of view, the novelists of this study provide a different way of thinking about the suppression of grief during childhood. Derrida's collapse of the hierarchy child / adult is exactly why his approach is crucial in order to open up and hear the unheard child-voices and grieving voices in these modernist texts.[6] Derrida, like the modernists of this study, finds that a return to a time before society ruled grief to be unacceptable is required in order to bypass grief's impossibility. Thus, the goal here is not to replace the Freudian model; rather, the plan is to build on it, look at it from alternative angles.

Freud sees Hamlet as possessing the insight of a melancholic (246). In contrast, the modernist authors, as will be discussed in detail later, do not look at Hamlet; they look *through* his eyes and see a social realm that demands he silence his childish grief. According to Freud, Hamlet is psychologically unhealthy. According to Derrida and the modernists, Hamlet's society is psychologically unhealthy.

We do not have a term that distinguishes the shedding of tears from the larger context of mourning or bereavement. A child or adult can cry for many different reasons: sorrow, anger, frustration, fear. One does not need to be suffering through a death in order to cry; yet all of the studies that work within the Freudian paradigm make mourning or bereavement their focus.[7] In this study, I nuance the concept of mourning by employing the terms 'grieving' and 'grief.' However, this nomenclature becomes further complicated, since we cannot underestimate how powerful grief may be for very young children. In observing children between the ages of one and three, John Bowlby observed: 'their responses to separation strongly resembled those of bereaved adults: protest, followed by despair, then apathy.'[8] Thus, it is difficult, when the focus is on children, to separate the tears shed in response to loss and the tears shed due to death.

William Watkin distinguishes three phases in mourning: 'Transition from the passive state of bereavement to the personal work of grief, and a public, published performance of communal rituals of mourning.' He then puts 'these three issues together – the crisis of materiality, the deconstruction of presence by the permanent and supplemental co-presence of absence, and the nexus between public and private emotions' (6). As a healer and a psychologist, Freud's interest mostly revolves around working through feelings effectively so as to reconnect the sufferer with society, manifesting the appropriate behaviour of what Watkin refers to as 'mourning.' Derrida and the modernist authors, in contrast, are more concerned with the second stage, which is 'the personal work of grief.' What sets modernist novels apart from the Freudian tradition is that they explore this in-between stage rather than strive to transform the inexpressible qualities of grief into the articulate forms of adult mourning or 'published performance.'[9] The novelists of this study engage with what Watkin calls the 'deconstruction of presence.'

The shift from Freud's ideas to those of Derrida and the modernist authors studied here is that the former imagines melancholy as the resultant reaction, an illness requiring a cure, whereas the latter group imagines social success demanding the suppression of grief, which causes emotional illness. When we use a Derridean approach as an alternative way of understanding childhood grief, then it is possible to move beyond the pedagogical and psychological models whereby the child or the mourner is talked about and analysed in order to affect a cure. Julia Kristeva makes the vital point that Derrida has turned 'attention away from those who grieve and towards those who have been lost' (199).

Within the context of this study, he has done what the selected modernist fiction writers do: turned attention away from the adult and instead turned towards the child who grieves and who is lost. Kristeva asserts that in grief studies Derrida is 'one of the most important commemorators of our age' (200).

Seeing through a Derridean lens, one can consider a more interactive, ongoing relationship whereby the lost child, what he imagines as a spectre-child (one's own past childhood), is the one who writes the adult self (in the present and future). In the novels under discussion, the spectre-child seems hurt and unable to speak, but instead of producing neurotic, socially unfit adults, this ghost-child, who has learned his or her lessons well, may well become a respected philosopher or a teacher or a war general as an adult. If society believes the suppression of grief is necessary and praiseworthy, then it will put into positions of power and influence those adults who succeed in crushing their grief. Derrida's most sustained analysis of this phenomenon occurs in *Specters of Marx*.[10] Hence, while Freud focuses on the maladaptive, Derrida and the novelists suggest that it is the hyper-adaptive in society, the very pillars of our modern world, who adhere to the suppression of grief and the silencing of the child within.

As Virginia Woolf asserts, during the modernist era, the way children were seen by adults changed: 'On or about December 1910, human character changed.' Then, she specifies: 'All human relations have shifted – those between masters and servants, husbands and wives, parents and children' (*Essays* 422).[11] Woolf sees as modern a movement away from the hierarchical structure wherein the parental position of power compares to the privileged gender position of husbands as well as the political and social position of masters. Many excellent studies have concentrated on the gender and the power shifts in modernism, whereas one is hard-pressed to find anything that investigates the shift in child/parent relations.[12] The focus of this study is the change that occurred between parents and children during English modernism, specifically in terms of the suppression and expression of grief in fictional narratives.

In the selected novels, the adult character can no longer operate under the belief that he or she has the upper hand over the child-self or children. In a variety of ways, the binary opposition adult/child collapses. Derrida explains why the dismantling of oppositions is vital: 'One of the two terms governs the other (axiologically, logically, etc.), or has the upper hand' and therefore the relationship is not one of mutual understanding; instead, it creates a 'violent hierarchy' (*P* 41). The modernists under discussion are highly aware of, and expose, the dangers inherent in this binary pair.[13] My emphasis, then, is on experience or process created by fiction and theorized in Derrida's responses to deaths that grieve him, his own childhood grief, and his analysis of haunting. Like modernist writers of fiction, Derrida uses *writing* to enter a grieving realm, and this is exactly why this study foregrounds the writing of fiction, as opposed to compiling data, facts, and figures for biography or history.

The writing of deconstruction, which does not demand the suppression of the neutrality between the binary pair, adult / child, reverses by means of a 'double-movement' the tendency to petrify. As Derrida writes: 'By means of this double, and precisely stratified, dislodged and dislodging, writing, we must also mark the interval between inversion, which brings low what was high, and the irruptive emergence of a new "concept," a concept that can no longer be, and never could be, included in the previous regime' (*P* 42). Derrida's description here of what happens in writing explains his affinity for modernist texts; as Niall Lucy imagines his attraction, it is to the 'force of dissemination' that modernists 'let loose' without any 'attempt to resist or suppress it' (*Dictionary* 29).

Derrida's exploration of grief resists stasis, hears childish sorrow, and accommodates haunting. As the chapters progress, there will be less and less theory, as Derrida's opening up of texts becomes clear in the initial chapters and would become redundant in the later ones if constantly referenced. For those interested in the theoretical underpinnings of this approach, Derrida's insights will be given in more detail in the endnotes. The effect parallels the subtext based on childhood that he supplies for the database of his work in *Circumfession*.

Derrida configures his approach as a kind of dream vision that suits this study. He imagines himself as pulled between three dreams: the first two are Freudian, but the last one indicates how he builds on and extends Freud's approach. The first Derridean dream is associated with the sex drive, 'dreaming of making love'; the next is infused with the death drive, 'being a resistance fighter in the last war'; and the final one revolves around his sons: 'I want one thing only, and that is to lose myself in the orchestra I would form with my sons, heal, bless' (*C* 208). Making the 'traumatic wound' to the child his focus, Derrida is no longer satisfied with 'the debate fixed around the figures of the father (Freud) or the mother (Bettelheim),' and thus he imagines himself here as a philosopher of / for the grieving child (sons) [*C* 135–6].

Discussing Freud's concerns about the belief that one might translate or transcribe the contents of the unconscious, Derrida imagines this idea belonging to the old regime as depending on or presupposing 'a text which would be already there, immobile' and he compares this text to 'the serene presence of a statue, of a written stone or archive' (*WD* 211). This statue stands at the centre of each of the modernist narratives and the ground beneath it is shaken until it topples. Building on the topos of turning to stone, and relevant to *Hamlet*, Derrida's grief makes him think of societal madness, which has the power to turn one to stone: 'Without such signs we are thrown into madness, into an accelerating thought that is nothing but immobility' (*WM* 100).[14] This sense of immobility surfaces frequently in modernist narratives and forms a key modernist trope.

Samuel Hynes records the reaction of artists to the pronouncement of the First World War as a 'paralysis of the imagination.' D.H. Lawrence writes that he lives 'in a sort of coma, like one of those nightmares when you can't move'; Edmund Gosse explains 'the passage of events ... has immobilized my mind' (*War* 11). In the novels of this study, the suppression of grief is continually linked to individuals who become unfeeling, rigid, and cold as stone.

Suppressing Grief and Turning to Stone

Julie-Marie Strange discovers that the inarticulate response to grief found in the poor of 1870–1914 forms a paradoxically eloquent contrast to the 'sentimental discourse' of the elite. She argues that 'expressions of bereavement did not depend upon verbal fluency,' and significantly for the modernist works under discussion: 'Grief could be articulated through a multitude of signs' such as 'fractured speech' (195). She discusses Jack Lawson's autobiography detailing his experiences during the First World War and explains that 'the sacrifice of soldiers during the war, for whom mothers had struggled, unleashed the "apparently stone hard" parents' emotional life' (272). All the modernists of this study use the trope of the stone-hard adult, the figure of immobilized grief.[15] Grief's power to transform the self into stone is first recorded in Ovid's *Metamorphoses* and thus belongs to the very foundation of western culture.

British poet Ted Hughes chooses to translate Ovid's myth of a proud mother, Niobe, whose children are killed by the gods. As she gazes at their 'corpses': 'Her face hardened / And whitened, as the blood left it. / Her very hair hardened / Like hair carved by a chisel. / Her open eyes became stones. / Her whole body / A stone' (223).[16] The mythological Niobe becomes a well-known symbol for suppressed grief in the modernist era by means of *Hamlet*, which is alluded to by all of the authors in this study and specifically in terms of grief by Conrad, Ford, Woolf, and Joyce. Shakespeare's play explores the mythic transformation from sorrow to stone.[17]

In Hamlet's first soliloquy, he likens his mother's grief to that of Niobe and then condemns the fact that she remains full of life as opposed to stone cold: 'A little month, or ere those shoes were old / With which she follow'd my poor father's body, / Like Niobe, all tears – why, she – O God, a beast that wants discourse of reason / Would have mourn'd longer' (I.ii.147–51). In contrast to Gertrude's opening scene, replete with elaborate speeches, the son's broken discourse expresses his inarticulate grief and anger. Although he seems to focus on the shameful lack of mourning for his father, the allusion to mother Niobe suggests that, for Hamlet, Gertrude's failure may well be compounded by the lack of concern she exhibits for her grieving son. Rather than turning to stone, she remains all too full of lustful life.

Shakespeare has Hamlet react against the societal expectation that he will suppress his grief.[18] Thus, in the first exchange with his mother he eloquently conveys his sorrow. Gertrude demands to know why Hamlet cannot end his mourning for his father when the rest of the court has accepted that the death of the king is a natural occurrence and they have moved beyond it: 'Why seems it so particular with thee?' demands his mother. The son responds: 'Seems, madam? Nay, it is.' He details expected mourning behaviour, 'solemn black,' 'fruitful river in the eye,' and claims they cannot 'denote [him] truly.' They are merely a show: 'they are the actions that a man might play.' He explains the depth of his grief: 'I have that within which passes show,' while his mourning expressions are 'but the trappings and the suits of woe' (I.ii.75–86). Hamlet distinguishes here between mourning, the theatrical display of what one feels, and his actual grief, which is beyond expression.

Grief lacks a stage where a man might play the mourning role; it lacks a language in which one might find relief; grief passes show. While grieving, Derrida maintains the term 'mourning,' but he specifies its distinction from socially sanctioned rituals: 'mourning that always has, unfortunately, as we know, a negative side, at once laborious, guilt ridden and narcissistic, reactive and turned toward melancholy, if not envy' (*WM* 221). He further exposes this ritualistic, if not theatrical, side: 'nothing is more unbearable or laughable than all the expressions of guilt in mourning, all its inevitable spectacles' (*WM* 44).[19] Mourning and melancholy have a certain ritual expression; hence, one might be a professional mourner or one might wear mourning clothes.

Mourning implies expression, whereas grief more accurately refers to the inexpressible.[20]

In the soliloquy following the players' exit, Hamlet raises self-reflexive questions about grief, its suppression, and our need for fiction in order to give voice to our silenced emotions. He is struck by the ease with which the actor can manifest intense sadness while he, destroyed by the loss of his father and betrayed by his mother, is powerless to express his own grief. He asks if indeed it is not monstrous that this actor with 'Tears, in his eyes, distraction in his aspect, / A broken voice, and his whole function suiting / With forms to his conceit? And all for nothing! / What's Hecuba to him, or he to her, / That he should weep for her?' (II.ii. 545–54)

The fiction of Hecuba is far more potent than the reality of his father's own death. The self-exploration and self-loathing posed by the protagonist applies in significant ways to us, the audience. Why are we at the theatre watching a tragedy? Alluding to Hamlet's self-reflexive questions about grief, Joyce wonders in *Finnegans Wake*: 'What's Hiccupper to hem or her to Hagaba? Ough, ough, brieve kindli!' (276.8–10). On the cusp of the Second World War, Joyce repeats Hamlet's question, but in a kind of childish language, and he blends it with Macbeth's despair as he extinguishes the light of the candle, as well as with German praise for a well-behaved child: 'auch auch brav' Kindli' (that too, good little child). David Bradshaw maintains that 'the umbilical connection between the fascist oppression of the late 1930s and the tyranny of the patriarchal Victorian family' is exactly what Virginia Woolf stresses in her final novel, *The Years*.[21] Bradshaw highlights a scene where the children of Woolf's novel, as they emerge from a basement where they sheltered from an air raid, speak 'distorted sounds' and 'unintelligible words.' Such language or lack thereof recalls the way in which readers understand Joyce's Wakese, and both novels thereby strive to acknowledge and 'give voice to what is ordinarily submerged and silent' (204–6).[22]

In contrast to the generation of young men in the modernist era, Hamlet's grief prevents him from acting like a good soldier: he does not have the decisive, active, warrior-like character of his masculine double, Fortinbras, who functions in the play as a man who has learned to suppress his grief and avenge his father. Shakespeare uses irony in the final unfolding of the tragedy in order to make this point: Fortinbras will play the role of King 'with sorrow,' at the same time as he honours Hamlet's final desperate acts as those of a man who has finally put grief away and hence become someone to admire, namely, a warrior: 'Let four captains / Bear Hamlet like a soldier to the stage, / For he was likely, had he been put on, / To have prov'd most royal; and for his passage, / The soldier's music and the rite of war / Speak loudly for him' (V.ii.400–5). Hamlet cannot express his grief 'which passes show' to his mother, let alone to this society. His whorish words, the equivalent of silence, are drowned out here, not by tears or an affective response, but by the music of soldiers that speaks 'loudly for him.' Shakespeare ensures that we do not miss the irony in this final scene with his use of theatrical terms: Fortinbras calls the 'noblest to the audience' of the dead prince and he wants Hamlet brought 'like a soldier to the stage.' This is Hamlet's final role: he will act the part of the soldier, a part as foreign to him as the role of a man without grief, but he must be a corpse to do it.[23] All the modernist works under discussion take this immobilization and relate it to the mobilization of a soldier-self or actual soldiers.

From Infant to Infantry

The novels' attempts to express the inexpressible in terms of both childhood and grief reveal a compelling relationship between infantry *and* infantry. In the present, the term means foot soldiers, but in the past infantry also meant infants collectively or as a body. Leading up to the First World War, the conflation of these two terms becomes more literal and less surprising, since, according to Mark Moss, 'parents in this increasingly regimented era now felt an obligation to bear children not just for personal or economic reasons, but for the state. They were producing patriots, citizens, and soldiers for whom the greatest honour was to serve their country as soldiers' (144).

In Rebecca West's autobiographical novel, *The Fountain Overflows*, the child-narrator notes how her teacher expects her to be 'brave like a soldier' (164). In *Eminent Victorians*, Lytton Strachey's portrait of the headmaster of Rugby, Dr Arnold, describes how 'the savage ritual of the whipping-block would remind a batch of whimpering children that, though sins against man and God might be forgiven them, a false quantity could only be expiated in tears and blood' (211). Philippe Ariès's research reveals that 'if the birch was retained, it was no longer simply as a punishment but above all as an instrument of education, an opportunity for the boy being flogged to exercise self-control, the first duty of the English gentleman' (265). What defines the nineteenth-century school system in Britain is the 'correlation of the adolescent and the soldier' with an emphasis on 'toughness and virility' (268). Rose's research of teaching methods from

1860 to 1918 reveals the same overlap between child-rearing and military training (134).

Parents who teach their children to be good soldiers, fight the good fight, and suppress feelings of grief may well be avoiding feelings of grief themselves.[24] Alice Miller exposes the vicious circle of such training: 'Almost everywhere we find the effort, marked by varying degrees of intensity and by the use of various coercive measures, to rid ourselves as quickly as possible of the child within us – i.e., the weak, helpless, dependent creature – in order to become an independent, competent adult deserving of respect.[25] When we reencounter this creature in our children, we persecute it with the same measures once used on ourselves. And this is what we are accustomed to call "child-rearing"' (58).[26] Conrad, Rhys, West, Ford, Woolf, and Joyce write novels that express in a variety of ways the weak, helpless, dependent child who haunts, narrates, acts, and otherwise fractures and opens up the independent, competent twentieth-century adult characters.

When we return to *Circumfession*, the text in which Derrida claims that the wounding done to a baby by circumcision is the central concern that has influenced his theoretical work in its various forms, we discover a way to understand the relationship between silenced children and silenced soldiers. Derrida writes: 'If I so much insist on circumcision in this text, it is because circumcision is precisely something which happens to a powerless child before he can speak, before he can sign, before he has a name' (21).[27] When we learn that during the First World War, infantry clung to 'childhood dolls and teddy bears' for protection against bullets and shells (Fussell 124), we must ask the question: how did it happen that the term we use for our youngest children is the same term we use for the young men we march off to war? Why do we expect children, like the child Rebecca West, to be 'good soldiers'? As explored in the novels under discussion, the answer to these questions may well revolve around silencing or suppressing the grief of children.

Derrida provides a way of listening for the silenced children who are written into modernist fiction. He describes the position of the young philosopher who is ready to speak out and challenge his master: 'Starting to enter into dialogue with the world, that is, starting to answer back, he always feels "caught in the act," like the "infant" who, by definition and as his name indicates, cannot speak and above all must not answer back' (*WD* 31). Derrida conveys a sense of the danger inherent in taking a different position from that of one's teacher, who represents the articulate world facing the silenced child. Stressed by Derrida, the infant is not only one who cannot speak; more provocative is his sense that this child 'must not answer back.'

Modernist authors take up the challenge of inarticulate infantry, children, and soldiers. They challenge the status quo established by teachers. However, they must contend with a double bind, for 'the experience of childhood is unutterable and thus lost to the adult: the child goes through it, but lacks the language to convey its reality to others, while the adult writer commands the full resources of language but is largely cut off from children's consciousness' (Goodenough, Heberle, and Sokoloff 2). In this study, I entwine this double problematic of the child / adult divide with the suppression of grief and the construction of a silently serving soldier-figure.

The words *infant* and *infantry* stem from the Latin *fari*, to speak and both are defined by the negating prefix 'in.' Both phases of life, being an infant and being a foot soldier, appear to be defined by the suppression of speech: the former is unable to articulate, cannot speak, and the latter must serve silently, must not answer back. Wilfred Owen, in a letter to Osbert Sitwell written in early July 1918, describes his instruction of a new recruit: 'I see to it that he is dumb' (Fussell 119). Likewise, in the *Cambridge Magazine* of 1916 Siegfried Sassoon responds in poetry to a critique about his need to 'defile' the concept of hero: 'And it was told that through my infant wail / There rose immortal semblances of song.' He takes the inarticulate wail of the infant and the infantry and transforms it into the new language of modernism.

In his study of the cultural milieu surrounding the First World War, Modris Eksteins records a dying soldier's words at the Somme: 'After the blessing his hands went together, eyes closed and he said "Gentle Jesus meek and mild, look upon a little child etc" – God bless father, mother, grandfather, and make me a good boy – then the Lord's Prayer' (174). The soldier who dies on the battlefield strives to be 'a good boy'; likewise, the child who suppresses his grief strives to be a good soldier.[28]

In *Moments of Being*, Woolf describes the act of writing as taking the 'blow' one suffers as a child and identifying it as a 'revelation': 'I make it real by putting it into words. It is only by putting it into words that I make it whole; this wholeness means that it has lost its power to hurt me; it gives me, perhaps because by doing this I take away the pain, a great delight to put the severed parts together.' From literature, Woolf then singles out *Hamlet*, which she describes as 'a truth about this vast mass that we call the world' (*MB* 72).[29] She imagines entering the world as an infant as a kind of blow that hurts; however, by writing this childhood revelation, and thereby overturning history, Woolf's writing becomes wholeness, togetherness, vastness – a time that precedes oppositional differences, what Woolf calls 'severed parts.'[30]

What brings together the modernists under discussion in this book is that they all explore in fiction the way in which the suppressing of grief may well produce a generation of willing warriors. What has been silenced these authors make resonant; what has been buried these writers exhume. Comparably, Jacques Derrida's mode of grieving yearns for the dead to speak, for silenced childhood selves to be articulate, for buried selves to be humanely returned. Echoing his friend, Jean-François Lyotard, whom he has lost, Derrida exclaims: '"there shall be no mourning" which keeps silent [*se tait*], mute, and keeps it down [*se terre*] between humus, inhuman, and inhumed' (*WM* 233).[31]

The Spectral Child

Questioning society's requirement to suppress grief, the shift into modernism surfaces in the work of Oscar Wilde, who chooses a surprising genre for a celebrated dramatist and poet: he writes a children's story, the ironically titled, 'Happy Prince.' In contrast to the boys' books of George Alfred Henty, which tutored two generations of readers with the lessons of the 'quiet action of personal control' and 'self-abnegation' (Moss 17), Wilde encourages a modern generation of children to feel grief and compassion.

Perhaps it seems careless to skip over the fact that Wilde is gay, in the light of the training he may have received as a boy to become a 'man.' However, as noted above in terms of Rebecca West's girl-character expected to be a 'good soldier,' both sexes were expected to suppress grief and were encouraged to do so in comparable terms. For a more thorough focus on gender, one can turn to Jane Potter's discussion of boys, in particular, but also of girls who were encouraged to serve British imperialist adventures in popular novels (10–12). Potter also examines the periodicals aimed at girls that 'devoted many pages to war themes' (15). Before the First World War, the *Girls' Empire Magazine* ran a ten-instalment feature, 'How to Be Strong,' since girls and women would 'play a no less important part in the future progress of the British Empire than their brothers' (37). In the modernist novels under discussion, I do not find a great deal of gender differencing in how boys and girls, men and women, feel grief or feel compelled to suppress it. There is a vast body of excellent scholarly work on gender concerns in all of the texts being analysed; thus, I will note gender distinction when it contributes to the study at hand without striving to make a sustained treatment of the different ways in which children were gendered during the modernist era. When I use the word *childhood*, unless there is a reason to distinguish within a particular moment, I mean both boys and girls.[32]

Anticipating modernist authors whose narratives are haunted and disrupted in complex ways by child figures, voices, and images, Oscar Wilde tells a tale to children and to the spectral children within adults. He undermines the pursuit of happiness and reveals the way in which society instructs the child to mature into a petrified adult who resembles a statue. Michael Levenson sees this focus as a fundamental tenet of modernism, which he describes as 'the shift in attention from large things to small, from public responsibility to private expression, from an "adult" earnestness and self-seriousness to "childlike" intimacy, sincerity, and amoralism' (*Genealogy* 57).

The hero of Wilde's children's story is a statue whose tears fall upon a swallow. The tears awaken the swallow to the suffering of others. The statue commemorates the adult ideal of living a life of happiness, whereas the bird is an ideal emblem of the social dictum to 'swallow your tears'; it also carries an echo of needing to 'swallow the lump in one's throat.' In the story, Wilde describes a parent teaching a child the importance of suppressing grief: '"Why can't you be like the Happy Prince?" asked a sensible mother of her little boy who was crying for the moon. "The Happy Prince never dreams of crying for anything"' (12). The gilded statue, who represents a prince who lived his life without compassion, begs the swallow to bring all its decorative gems and gold to suffering children, with the exception of one adult, a hungry young man whose desk is 'covered with papers,' for he is 'trying to finish a play for the Director of the Theatre, but he is too cold to write any more' (19). Those who must learn about grief are the children, before they fully learn to suppress it, and the writers, who, like Wilde himself, script plays. Wilde's writer is literally turning cold with poverty; however, he is figuratively becoming stone cold, a man without grief, a statue.

Derrida's distinction between speech and writing assists us in understanding how it is difficult, if not impossible, to speak grief; yet one can express grief by tapping into the realm of writing or *différance* (difference / deferral).[33] Grief, by definition, wells up; it is excessive to the point of prohibiting speech. If speech is our ability to differentiate and distinguish words so as to make sense, then a mode of communicating that tends towards supplementary meanings, a dissemination of possible significances, multiple traces, and plurivocal openings may well be effective in conveying the unspeakable.[34]

With his term *différance*, wilfully misspelling a word and making it the centre of his argument, Derrida speaks from a childlike perspective by definition as 'cannot speak, must not speak'; yet he rebels against this dictum by writing. Like the supposedly well-behaved child, he makes his 'a' seen and not heard. The seriousness of what he has done wrong would be fully appreciated by any student in the school system: for his rebellious idea is 'intersecting with a kind of gross spelling mistake, a lapse in the discipline and law which regulate writing and keep it seemly' (*MP* 3). Peggy Kamuf exposes the 'pedagogical convention' at work here: 'the convention of moral education, a whole tradition of reading (as) discipline' (introd. xvi). In an exploration titled 'Violence and Metaphysics,' Derrida writes powerfully of the war between the adult and the child: 'Language is indeed the possibility of the face-to-face and of being-upright, but it does not exclude inferiority, the humility of the glance at the father as the glance of the child made in memory of having been expulsed before knowing how to walk, and of having been delivered, prone and *infans*, into the hands of the adult masters' (*WD* 107).[35] The binary opposition is language (being articulate) and *infans* (being a non-speaker). However, as Virginia Woolf explains, in the modernist era the relationship between masters and servants and parents and children changes. Thus, the modernist authors in this study explore in a variety of ways how each speaking adult carries, within, a non-speaking child who shapes and impacts, perhaps distorts, adult speech and acts. This position of 'inferiority,' the inner child, haunts the 'father' who transforms into an 'adult master' in response to the glance of the humble child. In every adult, the child is not dead or gone; rather, it is real and unreal, is present and absent, is and was like a ghost.

Like Oscar Wilde, Marcel Proust acts as one of the pre-war modernists who uses grief as a way to access the changing relationship between parents and children. Aware of the Proustian child, James Joyce, in *Finnegans Wake* evoking the childhood scenes in *À la recherche du temps perdu*, imagines this highly influential modernist work 'as staneglass on stonegloss, inplayn unglish' (609.15).[36] Plain English becomes an in-play in non-English. Joyce follows with a list of place names that have magical associations for the child of *À la recherche* (609.16–18). Gazing at and through the figures and stories depicted on stained glass, as the Proustian child does in the church in Combray, suggests the idea of seeing with the eyes of the childhood self. Joyce couples this vision with the need to write a gloss on the stony-selves demanded by a society deeply uncomfortable with grief: 'staneglass on stonegloss.'

In 1919 the anniversary of the end of the First World War was marked by the immobilization of England: 'the entire country is to be simultaneously immobilised – trains, factories, traffic, even pedestrians, arrested in mid-stride – at precisely 11 a.m., Greenwich Mean Time, on 11 November, at the request of the King' (Stevenson 125). Grief would be experienced by turning still as a tombstone to mark the armistice. This is the gloss we strive to read, and as Derrida anticipates: 'This stone – provided that one knows how to decipher its inscription – is not far from announcing the death of the tyrant' (*MP* 4). Fiction writers in the modernist era generate a gloss to assist us in deciphering those socially approved figures who have successfully suppressed grief and thus turned to stone.

Proust foregrounds childhood grief as one of the catalysts to his modernist epic À *la recherche du temps perdu*: 'But of late I have been increasingly able to catch, if I listen attentively, the sound of the sobs which I had the strength to control in my father's presence, and which broke out only when I found myself alone with Mamma. In reality their echo has never ceased' (40). Proust's description of the child suppressing his grief in front of the father finds echoes in all of the modern novels under discussion; children are taught at an early age to be good soldiers, hold back their tears, suppress their sadness.[37]

In *Circumfession*, discussing 'the origin of tears,' Derrida presents himself as a Proustian child: 'the always puerile, weepy, pusillanimous son that I was, the adolescent who basically only liked reading writers quick to tears.' He remembers himself as 'that child with whom the grown-ups amused themselves by making him cry for nothing, who was always to weep over himself with the tears of his mother.' The child reads fiction in order to grieve freely, because the adult world, except for his mother, insists that his tears are nothing and for nothing. He seeks 'the other nongrammatical syntax that remains to be invented,' but this rebellious thought fills him with fear (118–20).

The Suppression of Grief

Jahan Ramazani's recent study of mourning focuses on the effort of modernist poetry 'to defy the social suppression of grief and to create new languages for its articulation' (362). Modernist fiction expresses a parallel defiance. The word *suppress* conveys on a series of different levels the societal reaction to grief. According to the *Oxford English Dictionary*, in its earliest use, *to suppress* meant 'To put down by force or authority; to quell; to vanquish, subdue. b. To withhold or withdraw from publication (a book or writing); to prevent or prohibit the circulation of.'[38] Political and military leaders suppressed writing in a way comparable to the suppression of children at home and at school. Instructed in the care of children by Victorian pedagogues, the parents and teachers who use their force and authority to quell, vanquish, and subdue the emotional reactions of their children and students are shown by the modernists to create ideal adults for marital oppression, colonial rule, and war as they transfer the lessons learned into a political arena.

Modern novelists see the act of writing grief as threatened by a society that seeks to withhold and withdraw the publication of such feelings. Therefore, putting grief into writing is a clearly rebellious strategy on the part of authors who are, at the same time, aware of their own internal mechanisms that seek to prohibit the circulation of such painful issues. 'To suppress' is all about making someone inarticulate: 'to restrain from utterance or manifestation; not to express' (*OED*). The modern authors of this study react to the threat of suppression by uttering, manifesting, and expressing. Writers and readers of suppressed grief function like Perseus figures who hold up the mirror of fiction to what Derrida imagines as a Medusa-like society that threatens to turn our feelings to stone. I hope that reading this study of childhood and grief in modern British fiction, using what Derrida calls the 'mobile strategy' of deconstruction, will move you.[39]

1   Translating the Foreign Language of Childhood Grief: Joseph Conrad's *Under Western Eyes*

> I 'worked' this morning, but you now know what I understand by that: mourning – mourning me, the us in me.
>
> Derrida, *The Post Card*

Sounding like Derrida, but in a letter rather than a postcard, Joseph Conrad imagines his writing as the work of mourning: 'It is thus, with poignant grief in my heart, that I write novels to amuse the English!' (*Letters* II.55). While Conrad grieves, he also acknowledges his British readers for whom he writes; one might call this the 'us in me.' Conrad's writing process, which is undertaken in a foreign language for foreigners, has the force to make his 'grief' seem merely an amusement. He must imagine 'the English,' for he has not been born or raised in their culture; yet he writes for them, to them, and about them. Likewise, the Russian characters of *Under Western Eyes* must imagine the English individual and they find him to be a withdrawn figure, 'cool as a cucumber' (21–2). Conrad employs this perspective in order to chart the ebb and flow of ostensibly Russian but, in fact, childhood grief, which is foreign to his British readers.

Positioning the narrator as an English teacher, Conrad explores both the shedding and the suppression of tears. The English teacher discovers that what democracies take for granted, namely, 'liberalism of outlook,' is certainly for autocratic Russia 'a matter of tears' (*UWE* 318). In this novel, Conrad connects the grieving self with the childhood self and, as Keith Carabine has shown, the link is personal: the author himself is 'haunted' by 'shadows' and these 'shades' are none other than the spectres of his parents, lost when he was a child (16).

For Conrad, mourning requires articulation: one must hear and one must speak. In telling the story of Razumov, who betrays fellow student Haldin, knowing he will be tortured and killed, *Under Western Eyes* portrays Razumov as one who has suppressed his childhood grief. Razumov's yearning for his father's love and approval, which he does not articulate to himself, is the driving force behind his betrayal of Haldin. Not only does Razumov communicate in a foreign language, but he is also, often, inarticulate. Throughout the novel, Razumov seems incapable of speech: he 'could only make a sort of gurgling grumpy sound' (254). He is closed off from communion with others, and thus his voice is 'muffled'; he forces himself 'to produce it with visible repugnance, as if speech were something disgusting or deadly' (346). He is 'full of unexpressed suffering' (342).[1] The English narrator usually draws our attention to the fact that he is translating and paraphrasing Razumov's diary as well as his behaviour.[2] However, in the final section of the novel, he quotes directly from his documentary source, Razumov's journal. Here, Conrad has us read Razumov according to his narrative 'I,' and we may thus assume that the British teacher of languages is merely translating.

Having direct access to the journal is significant, for there is a radical difference between Razumov's claim to Haldin, 'it's done,' when he betrays him and his confession to Haldin's sister, Natalia, in which he writes: 'I have done it; and as I write here, I am in the depths of anguish' (*UWE* 55, 361). No longer does Razumov feel that he is a victim; instead, his act of writing functions as an acceptance of individual responsibility. Paradoxically, Razumov's assertion of the 'I' in fact allows for his addressing, through his grief, what Derrida calls the 'us in me'; hence the belated anguish for the man he has betrayed. This is an instance of writing's being '*inaugural*,' carrying the trace of reading omens, initiating something sacred which 'is dangerous and anguishing' (*WD* 11). Derrida never underestimates the strain and risk of opening up to otherness, and *Under Western Eyes* details the suffering involved.

Drawing on Derrida's terms, it appears that Razumov has failed to acknowledge what must 'be rendered to the singularity of the other, to his or her absolute *pre*cedence or to his or her absolute *pre*viousness, to the heterogeneity of a *pre-*, which, to be sure, means what comes before me, before any present, thus before any past present, but also what, for that very reason, comes from the future or as future: as the very coming of the event' (*S* 28). Razumov betrays Haldin in the moment: he does not consider his past, his present, or the future he is erasing. Razumov believes that he and his victim are at opposite ends of the spectrum; everything about them is different. However, over the course of grieving, he comes face to face with Victor Haldin's full otherness by means of meeting his mother and sister. No longer can Haldin be categorized as a lawbreaker, wrongdoer, or revolutionary; suddenly, the young man has a previous life with previous bonds and commitments; thus, he begins to become much more solid to Razumov after he has been the instrument of his death. Razumov feels a debt to the past (the mother and the sister), which is like saying he recognizes his debt to the future (the mother and the sister). Paradoxically, by experiencing his victim's *pre-*, the future of Haldin's ghost is seen by his betrayer as wholly un*pre*dictable.[3] In other words, Razumov has a responsibility to Victor Haldin as a child loved by a mother and sister, to Victor Haldin as a revolutionary student, to Victor Haldin as perhaps a father of a child, but certainly he has a responsibility to him as a ghost and as a young man mourned.

How does one accommodate and encounter otherness? Conrad associates the shattering of the narcissistic mirror, the opening up of the 'me' to the 'us,' with the act of writing. In *Under Western Eyes*, the English narrator initially describes the journal as an image Razumov seeks to project: he 'looked at it, I suppose, as a man looks at himself in a mirror, with wonder, perhaps with anguish, with anger or despair' (214). These feelings allow him to remain whole. However, when he gazes into this mirror with grief, expressed in his confession to Natalia and then the revolutionaries, Razumov expects to be 'torn to pieces' (366). The narrator more aptly describes him as 'smashing himself' (370). He falls apart, owing to his opening up to grief.

Razumov confesses to the revolutionaries that he was the one who betrayed Haldin to the authorities. The revolutionaries drag him outside to brutally punish him. When the revolutionaries beat Razumov until he's deaf, they believe that they have encapsulated him, fixed him in stone, stopped him from communicating. They render him 'stone deaf' with the expectation that he 'won't talk' ever again (*UWE* 371–3). However, just the reverse occurs. As one of the characters explains, the revolutionaries continue to visit Razumov because, despite his deafness and in sharp contrast to his previous inarticulate self, 'he talks well' (379). Until his engagement with grief, Razumov is defined by his unwillingness to speak. He is solitary and taciturn. Yet across the gap or loss of death, through his deafness, Razumov begins to address others and thus to break apart the narcissistic mirror. Comparably, at the end of the novel, Haldin's sister, Natalia, devotes her life to grieving and she also defines it as breaking up; she attends 'the heartrending misery of bereaved homes' (378).

Derrida imagines writing as an activity that depends on an opening up or breaking up of one's self-as-presence in order to experience or know otherness; thus, he wonders if it is 'the writer [who] absents himself better, that is, expresses himself better as other, addresses himself to the other more effectively than the man of speech?' The next question he poses in this context is crucial for Conrad's novel and for all of the novels under discussion: 'And that, in depriving himself of the *enjoyments* and effects of his signs, the writer more effectively renounces violence?' (*WD* 102). Before he betrays Haldin, Razumov is dominated by the enjoyments and effects of his signs. Thus, when Razumov speaks to Haldin, he appears to be talking to himself, and a good portion of the time Haldin is confused about what he is saying. Initially for Razumov, Haldin is merely a mirror that reflects a variety of powerful feelings of, or about, Razumov's own childhood abandonment, his precarious position, his father's lack of love and respect. The enjoyment of and the signs of these feelings fuel his decision to be the catalyst for Haldin's violent death.

Razumov seeks for the signs of a blood relation; he looks for a family to love. When he discovers these signs, he adheres to them with an intense passion. He transfers the signs of his love onto his country. The death of his mother and the rejection by his father when he was a child lead Razumov to create a sense of belonging out of his bond to Russia. Yet throughout the story Razumov is unaware that what motivates his choices and actions are the absent parents for whom he grieves.[4] Razumov silences the voices that try to speak to him across the gap and instead listens only to his own narcissistic rhetoric. He 'felt the hard ground of Russia, inanimate, cold, inert, like a sullen and tragic mother,' and he concludes that what this maternal nation needs is 'a will strong and one: it wanted not the babble of many voices, but a man – strong and one!' (*UWE* 32–3) Razumov's gazing into the mirror of the strong man with his single voice leads directly to the betrayal of Haldin. If he turned to his journal and wrote about his decision, allowing for the babble of many voices, he would have better imagined Haldin as an other, with an extensive previous life and a future stretching before him. While writing, moving beyond the enjoyment of his own signs, he may have renounced violence. Certainly, writing has this role later in the novel as Razumov's grieving process unfolds.

With the word *brother* echoing in the background, Razumov bonds with autocratic Russia and silences the revolutionary Haldin. Refusing to hear the echoes of Haldin within himself, in outright denial of their similarity, Razumov nearly falls headlong into a pool of suppressed mourning.

What saves him is Haldin's haunting that reveals that the dead youth is, in fact, more solid than his betrayer, who is merely a projection of his own suppressed childhood grief. Razumov realizes: 'It was the other who had attained to repose and yet continued to exist in the affection of that mourning old woman, in the thoughts of all these people posing for lovers of humanity. It was impossible to get rid of him.' In this moment, Razumov is aware that it is actually himself whom he has 'given up to destruction' (*UWE* 341).

In *Specters of Marx*, Derrida suggests that one must open up the self to the 'babble of voices' that Razumov strives to silence. He considers the grieving, haunted Hamlet: 'One must lend an ear and read closely, reckon with every word of the language; we are still in the cemetery, the gravediggers are working hard, digging up skulls, trying to identify them, one by one, and Hamlet recalls that this one "had a tongue" and it used to sing' (*S* 114). In Shakespeare's play and Conrad's novel, the protagonist is pursued by a spectre. The ghost of Hamlet's father wants revenge. In contrast, the ghost of Haldin appears in a grieving pose: 'he saw Haldin, solid, distinct, real, with his inverted hands over his eyes' (*UWE* 36). This is the pose he strikes in Razumov's room after having 'burst into tears' and after having 'wept for a long time' (22).

Conrad evokes various forms of mourning from *Hamlet*; he draws on Shakespeare's play as a way of expressing his own writing process.[5] In *A Personal Record*, Conrad explains how he came to write *Under Western Eyes*, where he was determined to remain 'the figure behind the veil; a suspected rather than a seen presence – a movement and a voice behind the draperies of fiction' (9). Conrad depicts the suppression of mourning as immobility and deafness, then imagines his own writing process as its opposite, namely, movement and voice. Drawing on the structure of *Hamlet*, Conrad seems to position himself as a grieving son behind a veil of mourning. Just as Hamlet opens the stage curtains on a scene he himself inserts and directs, Conrad imagines himself as the moving force behind the 'draperies of fiction.' Moreover, the veil that covers his movement and his voice compares to the mourning veil worn by Haldin's sister, Natalia, as a signifier of her grief for her dead brother. Razumov wraps his journal in Natalia's 'black veil' and thereby suggests that his writing is a work of mourning (*UWE* 362). Conrad conflates this black veil of grief with a natural veil that offers self-knowledge: 'The steep incline of the street ran with water, the thick fall of rain enveloped him like a luminous veil' (363). Razumov is thus enlightened not by reason, but by grief.

When he tries to express his grief, the British narrator notes that the young man speaks 'with difficulty' and with 'strangled' phrases (*UWE* 338). Especially when grieving, Razumov sounds like an individual speaking a foreign language. Comparably, Derrida sees mourning as the breakdown of language. In grieving for a friend, he anticipates that his address will 'traverse speech at the very point where words fail us.' Those who open up to grief speak with 'tears in their voices' (*WM* 200). Derrida's phrase foregrounds the punning potential in Razumov's fear that tears will 'tear him apart,' which becomes his own knowledge that grief, his tears, will be what tears him. Thus, in his journal he wonders: 'What could I have known of what was tearing me to pieces' (*UWE* 358). In *Under Western Eyes*, breaking apart – eyes tearing – is the work of grieving.

Grief dismantles the adult, controlled self; thus, Conrad's English narrator praises taciturnity and silence. The narrator exclaims, in reference to Haldin's sister, who has just learned of her brother's betrayal and murder: 'I was grateful to Miss Haldin for not embarrassing me by an outward display of deep feeling.' He is impressed with her 'wonderful command over herself' (*UWE* 112). Such control is not only an English characteristic; a Russian character also advises: 'You've got to trample down every particle of your own feelings' (245). Thus, it becomes apparent that it is the uncontrolled, full of feelings child-self who is foreign, much more so than the Russians are to the British or the British are to the Russians.

Bernard Meyer identifies a comparable narrative construction in Conrad's *Nigger of the Narcissus*. When the 'Nigger,' James Wait, becomes ill with tuberculosis and his crew does not know what is wrong with him, Meyer sees their reaction as 'suggestive of a child's disbelief and inner turmoil when faced with the bewildering image of death.' He notes that the men of the crew 'despise him, yet they cannot refrain from mothering him tenderly.' Meyer discusses this behaviour in terms of Conrad's personal history and his psychological working out of personal grief; however, for the purposes of this study, it is interesting to imagine James Wait, whom Meyer identifies as part of Conrad's fascination with the outsider, 'the disruptive alien,' as almost an allegorical figure for a grieving child. The men of the story 'despise' him, yet feel compelled to 'mother' him. The character's role in the narrative is as an 'alien' because, when one becomes severed from the child-self, it becomes foreign, alien, and disruptive. Meyer concludes his portrait of James Wait by seeing him as a 'child-like helpless creature,' one whose tale needs telling despite the alienating effect of his grief.[6]

In *Under Western Eyes,* unlike his narrator, Conrad again emphasizes the need to tell the tale of grief. He celebrates emotive communication. In this narrative, he reveals how writing that denies the emotional self may turn one to stone, whereas fragmented writing may well have fertile, life-giving qualities. Thus, he writes that the 'broken sentences' of Razumov's grieving journal contain a 'dormant seed' (*UWE* 358); in contrast, he calls Razumov's polished, intellectual writing 'dead matter' (68). Natalia's desk is described as 'a mere piece of dead furniture,' but because it holds Razumov's grieving journal, for Conrad it also contains 'something living' (375).

Before feeling grief, Razumov has 'stony eyes' and immobile limbs (*UWE* 301, 355). The narrator says he looks 'as if his heart were lying as heavy as a stone' (344). Ironically, Conrad makes this quality attractive to Haldin, who seeks out Razumov because of his 'frigid English manner' (16). In response to her brother's execution and Razumov's confession, like Ovid's Niobe and in a transformation Hamlet wishes for his mother, Natalia is 'turned to stone': 'Her face went stony in a moment – her eyes – her limbs' (353, 111). In a strange reversal of what is native and what is foreign, the English narrator praises the woman's stoic response: 'It was a great victory, a characteristically Russian exploit in self-suppression' (375).[7] What attracts the Russians to the British is their rendering the emotive child foreign and thus appearing 'frigid'; what impresses the British about the Russians is their perception of the grief of the child as foreign behaviour and the domination of the suppressed adult self.

Haldin's and Natalia's mother also behaves with a 'frigid English manner,' which at the same time is a 'characteristically Russian exploit in self-suppression.' She suppresses her grief: she 'has not shed a tear' and thus her face appears 'as calm as a stone' (*UWE* 343, 322). In describing the mother, Conrad stresses the paralysing and alienating effects of suppressed grief, for she actually turns on her daughter with an accusatory silence; she becomes 'the motionless dumb figure of the mother' (324). She conveys 'mute distrust of her daughter' (372). These figures, expressive of both eastern and western heritage, bonded by believing the child-self to be the true foreigner, become silent statues as they refuse to grieve.

Natalia looks 'forward to the day when all discord shall be silenced' (*UWE* 376). While at first this seems to be a noble sentiment, the novel works to expose the dangers inherent in silencing the babble of voices that reside within and without. The English teacher participates, for he positions himself as 'the mute witness of things,' and, while he registers 'the stifled cry of our great distress,' he believes that it is 'hopeless to raise [his] voice' (*UWE* 381, 386, 374). Conrad links the babbling voice, the cry within *Under Western Eyes*, to the stifled child-self who haunts the work of mourning.

When Natalia first meets Razumov, she is disturbed by her show of grief and she connects it with being childish and foreign: 'She had behaved unworthily, like an emotional French girl' (*UWE* 171). Ironically for the novel, she further condemns herself: 'An emotional, tearful girl is not a person to confide in' (176). Haldin confides in Razumov, a young man who, like an Englishman, seems to have his emotions firmly in check and yet he betrays Haldin. Conrad ensures that his narrative makes us wonder whether, had Razumov appeared less stoic and more prone to grieving, he would have handed Haldin over to the police.

In *Under Western Eyes*, being an adult seems to require severing ties with one's emotional childhood self. Thus, scolded like a child, Tekla, one of the characters who serves the revolutionaries, weeps when she does not cook the eggs properly; yet she finds the almost-beaten-to-death Razumov without shedding a tear (*UWE* 166, 371). Conrad designs a split between her childhood and mature self. Derrida believes that the work of mourning is exactly what bridges this gap; thus, he reconnects with his childhood self in feeling grief. Faced with the loss of a dear friend, he seeks 'words as childlike and as disarmed as [his] sorrow' (*WM* 200). Both childhood and sorrow are basically inarticulate and both inform Razumov's journal in the section the British narrator chooses not to record because it is incoherent; it reads like a language too foreign to translate (*UWE* 357). The narrator can translate Russian, but he cannot translate sorrow or childhood.

Conrad contrasts immobile, stone-like writing with the movement and voice conveyed in the 'broken sentences' of the grieving section of Razumov's journal. Thus, stone-like writing describes the revolutionary work of Peter Ivanovitch, who requires Tekla to take his words from dictation and she must 'sit perfectly motionless' (*UWE* 147).[8] Ivanovitch requires Tekla's silence and immobility so that he can use her as a textual mirror to reflect his own ideology. He speaks; she records. He thereby strips her of her otherness, her independence, her capacity to move. Ironically, Ivanovitch believes that he is saved by a woman's 'redeeming tears' (124). However, he does not want Natalia to shed any 'tears'; he wants her to fight for the revolution (131).

Foregrounding a different kind of rebellion, Conrad has the characters repeatedly 'break the silence' to the point where the phrase carries a force beyond its idiomatic meaning.[9] Prior to writing *Under Western Eyes*, Conrad imagines his own writing process as the breaking up of stone.[10] In a letter to Stephen Crane, Conrad describes his distrust of himself as a kind of 'taint' and his remedy is to be a 'stone breaker': 'There's no doubt about breaking a stone,' although there is 'doubt, fear – a black horror, in every page one writes' (*Letters* I.410). Crane, the author of *The Red Badge of Courage*, is the sort of writer who understands Conrad's desire to break stone with his writing. Crane's novel not only details the living face to face with the dead and turning to stone (46), but it repeatedly depicts the men at war as children, often as grieving children. Thus, the commander speaks to his men 'in schoolmistress fashion, as to a congregation of boys with primers' and in that moment the soldier is likened to a 'weeping urchin' (32). One gains a sense of the significance of the babbling voices in *Under Western Eyes*, for in *The Red Badge of Courage* Crane has the young soldier note a man at his side who, mid-war, is 'babbling,' and he explains: 'In it there was something soft and tender like the monologue of a babe' (34). One has here a clear sense of the overlap between a soldier of the infantry and a baby in an infantry.

In *Under Western Eyes*, Razumov strives to break stone by grieving. In his journal, he expresses himself 'in broken sentences,' but the narrator does not quote from the 'page and a half of incoherent writing' (*UWE* 357). Conrad has us anticipate the idea of writing on stone or breaking up stone in the discussion with one of the characters, who speaks of the tragedy of 'broken lives.' Before he himself has opened up to grief, Razumov dismisses this woman's claim that the revolutionaries 'carve' their message on the 'hard rock,' for he believes they write 'in water' (263). Before grieving, broken writing and broken lives do not leave a trace in the stone-like Razumov.

In 'Tympan' (*T*), which is Derrida's introduction to his collection of essays *Margins of Philosophy*, there are two columns: on the left, Derrida exposes and resists philosophy's closures and, on the right, he quotes autobiographical material from Michel Leiris's memoirs. The columns appear side by side, and within the tension created by the two there is a discussion of breaking stone evocative of Conrad's description, in the letter to Crane, of his writing as a method of breaking stone.

While in the left column Derrida considers philosophy's resistance to deconstruction, with its dependence on hierarchy and envelopment (of otherness and margins), Leiris plays on the French for a type of 'low and deep' voice (*basse taille*) that carries the trace of the verb *tailler*, meaning to hew, to cut, to chisel. Thus, Derrida writes of philosophy's rigidity and refusal to move from certain positions, while the autobiographical memoir describes a type of voice that is like stone, immobile: 'this *basse taille*, with the idea attached to it, like a stone around its neck' (*T* xx, xxii). Leiris imagines the ear and the throat – the capacity to hear otherness and to articulate self / other – so full of fear of injury (piercing, or what Derrida imagines as puncturing) that they are 'soldered together by a cement of relationships hardened in broad daylight' (xviii–ix). Faced with a philosophical tradition that compares to a statue or stone archive, Derrida wants 'to philosophize with a hammer,' which compares to Conrad as the 'stone-breaker' and parallels Leiris's 'axe' for breaking stones (xii, xx). Providing a note for both marginal texts, Derrida writes a recall or reminder that the hammer 'belongs to the chain of small bones' in the ear and that it 'always has the role of mediation and communication.' He highlights the paradox: 'This small bone protects the tympanum while acting upon it' (xx).

Leiris calls the chapter of his memoirs quoted by Derrida 'Persephone,' and he imagines how the name of the goddess of the underworld, since she is queen of a sonorous cavern, forms a poetic parallel with the spiral inner realm of the ear. This earthly and bodily cavern, which he calls the 'deep country of hearing,' are protected and threatened by a '*perce-oreille*' (literally ear-piercer, in English an earwig; this creature also has an important role in *Finnegans Wake*). Leiris observes that both *Perse-phone* and *perce-oreille* are names that end with appeals to the sense of hearing: phone and ear. Thereby, Persephone becomes less the goddess of our demise and more comically what Leiris sees in the breakdown of her name as a 'telephone' for us to communicate or mediate through and / or with a 'gramophone' with its echo of *gram* (writing) [xiii–vii]. A voiceless void of emotions, a kind of death, becomes instead a call or a letter that opens up the self to otherness.

It is possible that it is the child-self who has the capacity to make the call, to write the letter, to philosophize with a hammer. Leiris writes about being a child told by his mother, as a strategy to make him quiet, to be seen and not heard, that if he is not careful, he might break his voice. He compares the danger of a loud sound to the ear's tympanum to the threat to the voice of being 'broken.' Haunted by his childhood ghost, Leiris recalls that one may break the voice with 'anger' or 'grief' or even in a childhood game of 'shrieking' (*T* xvii). If we layer this memorial trace of the 'broken' child-voice onto the adult-like, deep bass voice whose authority, like the mastery of philosophy, seems to silence others, make them still as listeners, and break the tympanum of their ear, then writing as stone-breaking makes sense. For it is the tiny hammer of the ear, wielded by the child-self with his capacity to listen and bring other-ness in, to loudly express grief, anger, and play, who will allow us to write and thus mobilize selves who seem turned to stone.

Derrida writes in this unusual way in order to pose the question: 'can one puncture the tympanum of a philosopher and still be heard and un-derstood by him?' (*T* xii). Derrida imagines philosophy as 'if it has always intended to hear itself speak, in the same language.' The ear of philoso-phy compares to the voice of Leiris's mother or the dictation of Conrad's character Peter Ivanovitch: they tune out and speak over others. Hence, Derrida strives to locate 'a place of exteriority or alterity' (xii). In *Under Western Eyes*, Conrad poses comparable questions and responds in paral-lel ways with the literal puncturing of Razumov's ears. The revolutionary thugs seek to seal off his ability to hear and thus to speak; however, the breaking open of his ears allows him to finally articulate his grief. The stony self breaks; the child's voice is let loose; the hammered ear begins to hear not only its own voice, but otherness.

Initially in *Under Western Eyes*, Razumov defines himself by being solid, like a statue. When he is first haunted by Haldin, whom he is about to betray, he appears coherent and consistent, a man without a breaking point: 'After passing he turned his head for a glance, and saw only the unbroken track of his footsteps over the place where the breast of the phantom had been lying' (*UWE* 28). His steps do not falter; the track is unbroken. At first, Razumov finds this a reassuring confirmation of his identity. Later, after having betrayed Haldin, Razumov returns to this haunting moment, but his discourse is breaking up: 'Razumov felt his voice growing thick in his throat.' He is choked up as he addresses Councillor Mikulin about his role in handing over the revolutionary Haldin: 'what is his death to me? If he were lying here on the floor I could walk over his breast ... The fellow is a mere phantom ...' Notably, the broken sentences, with gaps marked by ellipsis points, end with an image of Razumov's unravelling: 'Razumov's voice died out very much against his will.' In contrast, the Councillor's response is complete immobility: he does 'not allow himself the slightest movement' (96). The Councillor is as still as a statue and the General, who is also in the room, has a 'stony stare' (47). These are the men who torture and execute Haldin. Initially, Razumov strives to model himself on such suppressed, powerful figures; however, something within him, against his will, breaks up this plan. He becomes heartbroken, like his victim. When the two students exchange thoughts on the revolution, it is in broken phrases marked by ellipses and Conrad describes Haldin in this scene as 'heartbroken'; he speaks 'mournfully' and 'sadly' (62). While Haldin can speak his grief, Razumov experiences only an inarticulate emptiness: 'He felt sad, as if his heart had become empty suddenly' (200).

The sons of *Under Western Eyes* echo the haunted son Hamlet, who exclaims: 'But break, my heart, for I must hold my tongue' (I.ii.158). All three youths suffer from overwhelming grief that cannot be expressed and all three commit terrible crimes. As noted, Hamlet distinguishes, in an impassioned speech to his mother, the difference between mourning, 'actions that a man might play,' and grief, 'that within that passes show' (I.ii.82–3). Conrad seems to echo this line in the English narrator's unusual archaic phrasing to describe the foreign nature of Razumov's journal: it 'passeth [his] understanding' (*UWE* 5). According to Hamlet, mourning is the theatrical manifestation of what one feels, whereas actual grief seems beyond communication. Conrad's character, Sophia Antonovna, stresses this distinction when she confronts Razumov: 'What are you flinging your very heart against? Or, perhaps, you are only playing a part' (251). Hamlet is amazed at the power of an actor 'playing the part' of grief: 'A broken voice, and his whole function suiting / With forms to his conceit? And all for nothing! / What's Hecuba to him, or he to her, / That he should weep for her?' (II.ii.549–54). Conrad quotes the final line of this passage in a letter, and thus Razumov's 'broken sentences' may well be read as an attempt to vocalize what Hamlet calls a 'broken voice' (*Letters* I.247). This recalls the 'broken voice' of Michel Leiris's child, whose mother strives to make him silent when he too expresses 'grief' (*T* xvii). Conrad is the movement and voice behind the mourning veil of *Under Western Eyes*, in which he dramatizes the impact on self and community when one is deaf to haunting voices.[11] The editors of Derrida's collection of essays on mourning present him as laying out 'not so much a middle ground as a series of aporias, aporias that, curiously, do not paralyze speech but inhabit and mobilize it' (*WM* 9). Conrad translates into disturbing images the way in which the suppression of grief immobilizes and paralyses speech and thus the self. In *Under Western Eyes*, Conrad strives to mobilize grief and he suggests that storytelling is a way to translate the unspeakable.

Conrad makes the unspeakable a fundamental component of Razumov and Natalia's relationship; when she finally meets him, she stands before him 'speechless, swallowing her sobs' (*UWE* 172). Later on in the novel, her response to his confession of betraying her brother is silence: she never speaks to him again.[12] *Under Western Eyes* revolves around being unable to speak, refusing to speak, and being forced to speak. Seeking refuge in Razumov's rooms, Haldin explains that he came to him because he had 'confidence,' which serves to silence Razumov: 'This word sealed Razumov's lips as if a hand had been clapped on his mouth' (19). When Haldin realizes he has made a mistake, Razumov watches him leave 'with parted, voiceless lips' (63). The drama of whether to speak or not to speak becomes more intense as we see Razumov betray Haldin to the authorities: he must not be 'drawn into saying too much.' He then hallucinates about being on the rack, tortured for information (87–8). His 'dream-like experience of anguish' anticipates Haldin's fate. Ultimately, the record of Haldin's torture is quoted ruthlessly by Councillor Mikulin as 'Refuses to answer – refuses to answer.' Razumov defines Mikulin's 'art' as 'getting people to talk' (92). When Razumov meets the English narrator, his throat is paralysed by being so parched (184). This imagery of the desiccated self, as dry as a stone, transforms into the stormy tears of nature that rain down like a 'luminous veil' on the night Razumov wraps his journal in the grieving veil.

Haldin's terrible error is to believe that despite Razumov's 'frigid English manner,' he nonetheless could hear 'the sound of weeping' (*UWE* 16). Again highly suggestive of Hamlet, Conrad has Razumov deafened before he can hear of grief. King Hamlet is poisoned through his ear, and when his murderer, brother Claudius, sees Ophelia in her state of madness, he blames 'the poison of deep grief' (IV.v.75). The narrator imagines the grieving Natalia as being trapped in 'poisoned air' (*UWE* 356). Comparably, Natalia worries that her mother's 'mind had given way from grief' (360). Conrad provides a different way of assessing these figures, since in *Under Western Eyes*, it is the suppression of grief that brings on madness. Society silences grief, turns a deaf ear, fears that grief will infect and destabilize the coherent, and thus powerful, adult self. Hence, unlike Hamlet and the other men, Claudius is unable to hear the ghost of his brother and his victim.

In *Under Western Eyes*, Conrad defines his protagonist by his haunting: 'Every word uttered by Haldin lived in Razumov's memory. They were like haunting shapes' (167). Throughout the novel, the 'ghost of that night pursued him' (272). In 1907 Conrad planned to write *Under Western Eyes* quickly; however, as critics have discussed, the novel's composition took years, because the author was addressing a subject that had 'long haunted him' (*Letters* IV.14). In *Specters of Marx*, Derrida examines some of the ways in which we are haunted: 'If death weighs on the living brain of the living, and still more on the brains of revolutionaries, it must then have some spectral density.' Derrida stresses the weight of ghosts rather than their transparency: 'And the more life there is, the graver the specter of the other becomes, the heavier its imposition. And the more the living have to answer for it. To answer for the dead, to respond to the dead' (*S* 109). In *Under Western Eyes*, Conrad contends with revolutionaries and autocrats whose minds are weighted with death. He locates them in a 'land of spectral ideas' and defines them by the ways in which they acknowledge the weight of haunting (*UWE* 34). To Razumov, Haldin's living body has less 'substance than its own phantom' (55). Likewise, Haldin does not care what is done to his body, for his goal is to be 'the destroyers of souls' who 'shall be haunted' (58). This dismissal of the individual, bodily self in favour of a political position is what removes the weight, the density from these young men and allows them to commit destructive acts. It should weigh heavy on one's heart to bomb people, as Haldin does, or to betray someone to those who will torture and execute him, as Razumov does. It is when one can lightly dismiss others that violence becomes the chosen vehicle for political acts.

Derrida's concerns in the *Specters of Marx* deal with revolution, activated by the failure to integrate one's haunting double, which leads to a never-ending cycle of war. He writes: 'It is as if Marx and Marxism had run away, fled from themselves, and had scared themselves. In the course of the same chase, the same persecution, the same infernal pursuit.' Conrad conveys a comparable idea with the bronze figure 'Flight of Youth,' associated with both Razumov and Haldin, displayed in the Prince's home, eternally fleeing (*UWE* 43). Derrida sees this cycle as 'revolution against the revolution as the figure of *Les Misérables* suggests. More precisely, given the number and the frequency, it is as if they had been frightened by someone within themselves' (*S* 105). In *Under Western Eyes*, the British narrator describes the cycle as one 'where virtues themselves fester into crimes in the cynicism of oppression and revolt' (356). He notes that for Russians, the shadow of autocracy 'haunt[s] the secret of their silences' (107). Both Derrida and Conrad explore ways in which the political spectre relates to the ghostly child who haunts. Both Tekla and Sophia Antonovna, revolutionaries, stress the defining role of the child in their respective political identities. Tekla sees a 'ragged little girl' begging, and Sophia – 'almost a child' – watches her father die according to the dictates of an oppressive system (149, 262).

Conrad constructs both Haldin and Razumov as victims who carry death's load: not only does Haldin kill a targeted, political figure, but his bomb also kills his fellow revolutionary and a number of innocents.

Razumov knows that, when he hands Haldin over to the police, he will be tortured and executed. While both are caught in the cruel cycle of revolution, what distinguishes these murderous men is that Haldin grieves the death he causes, whereas Razumov must learn how to grieve throughout the course of the novel.

Speaking in broken sentences, Haldin tells Razumov of 'scattering death' among 'innocent people' and then he breaks down sobbing (*UWE* 22). In contrast, Razumov hides his emotions – 'Inwardly he wept' – and then he crushes them altogether: 'A strange softening emotion came over Razumov – made his knees shake a little. He repressed it with a new-born austerity. All that sentiment was pernicious nonsense' (40). Razumov is able to imagine saving Haldin, 'to pour out a full confession in passionate words that would stir the whole being of that man to its innermost depths; that would end in embraces and tears; in an incredible fellowship of souls – such as the world had never seen' (40). Instead of fulfilling the vision with Haldin, Razumov takes this passion and directs it towards his father, who has never cared for him because he is an illegitimate child. In the big political play, Haldin is the phantom; however, in the play within the play, it is the child-self of Razumov who truly haunts. This ghostly child is the driving force behind Razumov's betrayal of Haldin to the father who has rejected him.

Derrida asks: 'Is it not derisory, naïve, and downright childish to come before the dead to ask their forgiveness? Is there any meaning in this? Unless it is the origin of meaning itself?' (*WM* 44) It is exactly this childish act that Razumov needs to undertake; he needs to come before the child, dead within him and haunting him, and ask this child's forgiveness. This childish act could be described as the origin of Razumov's meaning within the novel. Yet just as he exhibits his power to himself by walking over the ghost of Haldin, rather than listen to it, he stamps his foot – like an angry child – upon Mother Earth: 'and under the soft carpet of snow [he] felt the hard ground of Russia, inanimate, cold, inert, like a sullen and tragic mother hiding her face under a winding-sheet' (*UWE* 32–3). This description of the mother seems full of contradictions. Razumov's mother literally died when he was a child; here, he projects her spectre onto Mother Russia, who appears like a corpse yet still conveys rejection, being 'sullen' and 'tragic' and hiding her face from her son. Until Razumov undertakes the work of mourning and grieves for the time when they were 'us,' he will be caught as a youth running, fleeing from his true work, and thus working for the cycle of powerful, manly, stone-cold leaders.[13]

As a university student, Razumov is called in to meet his father, who has financially supported him without ever seeing him: 'the most amazing thing of all was to feel suddenly a distinct pressure of the white shapely hand just before it was withdrawn: a light pressure like a secret sign. The emotion of it was terrible. Razumov's heart seemed to leap into his throat' (*UWE* 12). Conrad's description here of the son's emotion echoes the phrase commonly used to convey the effect of grief, a lump in the throat. A child, emotionally abandoned and yearning for affection, must surely have a double-edged reaction of joy and grief when the parent shows any kind of affection.

The abandoned son recalls Prince K— as 'the man who once had pressed his hand as no other man had pressed it – a faint but lingering pressure like a secret sign, like a half-unwilling caress' (*UWE* 40). It is heartbreaking that the only affection Razumov has ever received from this man is a slight, unwilling pressure, yet in response to the 'secret sign' he brings the terrible secret of the hidden Haldin to Prince K—, desperate for more contact. Almost reverting to a child's view of the world, a son sitting on his father's lap, Razumov imagines Prince K— according to his beard; he exclaims to Haldin, in an oblique attempt to justify to himself *and* to his victim why he must betray him: 'the most unlikely things have a secret power over one's thoughts – the grey whiskers of a particular person' (59). One might translate Razumov's confusing statement here in clearer terms as: the yearning of the lonely, abandoned ghost-child haunts my thoughts and directs my actions; for, as Conrad has Sophia Antonovna state, 'a man is a child always' (241). Razumov learns this too late, and thus he does not recognize the significance of feeling, as though his betrayal of Haldin and his subsequent dependence on corrupt authorities is like a child's 'game of make-believe' (314).

Razumov tries to explain himself to Haldin by telling him that he does not know family, he knows only teachers; Conrad ironically emphasizes this truth by having an English teacher tell his story. Razumov's reason has been well trained, but his emotional self has been starved: 'I have been brought up in an educational institute where they did not give us enough to eat. To talk of affection in such a connexion – you perceive yourself ... As to ties, the only ties I have in the world are social' (*UWE* 60). Razumov does not seem aware of how he seeks nourishment from a system that simply devours him. In discussion with Peter Ivanovitch, Razumov refuses to participate in the paternal rhetoric and call the Russian people 'children.' Instead, he wants them called 'brutes' and he forcefully argues: 'You just try to give these children the power and the stature of men and see what they will be like' (227). Conrad's irony seeps into this speech, for, of course, Razumov *has* conducted himself like a child seeking a father in his recent political acts, which have been nothing short of brutal.

Councillor Mikulin manipulates Razumov's hunger; thus, when he wants to use him as a spy against the revolutionaries abroad, he asks his father, Prince K—, to display some other form of paternal care so as to nourish the affection-starved child. Notably, what Razumov discovers from the 'sudden embrace of that man' is 'something within his own breast'; however, rather than feel a tie to Prince K—, surprisingly enough the illegitimate son recognizes the common humanity shared by this well-fed, powerful figure of the Russian ruling class and the revolutionary student who is 'famine-stricken.' Razumov's ability to articulate his hungry yearning for 'suppressed paternal affection' acts as a catalyst for the grieving work he needs to do after his betrayal of Haldin and the ruin of both of their lives (*UWE* 308). As opposed to seeing the distinction between the ruling power and the revolutionary power, Razumov suddenly identifies common humanity, and his treatment of Haldin and the destruction it brings into his own life thus requires grieving.

Derrida would identify Razumov's behaviour as a sign of what he calls 'spectrology': 'it is always to the father, the secret of a father that a frightened child calls for help against the specter' (*S* 106). Even more striking, it is almost as if Derrida is analysing Conrad's Razumov, with his illegitimate birth and parental abandonment. As Derrida explains in *Positions*, 'Plato said of writing that it was an orphan or bastard, as opposed to speech, the legitimate and high-born son of the "father of logos"' (12), and he contends that this distressed, abandoned act of writing rolls 'this way and that like someone who has lost his way, who doesn't know where he is going, having strayed from the correct path, the right direction, the rule of rectitude, the norm; but also like someone who has lost his rights, an outlaw [...] Wandering in the streets, he doesn't even know who he is, what his identity – if he has one – might be, what his name is, what his father's name is' (*D* 143). At the outset of the novel, Conrad stresses that Razumov is a man without a name: 'The word Razumov was the mere label of a solitary individuality. There were no Razumovs belonging to him anywhere' (*UWE* 10). One way to map the movements of Razumov, as he strays from the correct path in search of a father or for a name, is by comparing his two writing acts: one is correct, right, the rule of rectitude, the norm, namely, 'the prize essay.' And this prize essay compares to Plato's notion of speech. The other is more in the style of someone whom Derrida sees as wandering outside society with writing's capacity to gather all kinds of meanings indiscriminately to its words. In *Under Western Eyes*, the British narrator makes an effort to differentiate Razumov's two writing styles: 'In this queer pedantism of a man who had read, thought, lived, pen in hand, there is the sincerity of the attempt to grapple by the same means with another profounder knowledge' (357).[14] Although he suppresses Razumov's journal as simply too foreign, the English teacher does acknowledge that the grieving journal reveals Razumov grappling with something profound.

Conrad encourages his readers to identify the contrast in Razumov's two kinds of writing, for when the narrator is discussing his journal, he notes the abrupt shift from Razumov the author who seeks the 'silver medal,' to Razumov the author who writes incoherently of his grief (*UWE* 357).[15] Notably, the former's 'neat minute handwriting' becomes the latter's 'long scrawly letters,' as Razumov returns to an 'unsteady, almost childish' self (66). In the act of writing that allows grief to surface, Conrad reveals the orphan-bastard who haunts and unravels the words of the philosophy student who betrays Victor Haldin. Whether writing for the silver medal, an act of suppression, or writing his journal, an act of expressing grief, Razumov lives and dies by the pen. If Prince K— is defined by his whiskers, then the significant attribute by which we can identify Razumov is his pen. The father is physical, but the son is literary. The father is a character, but the son is a character and an author.

Razumov's thoughts on his prize essay are revealing: 'The winner's name would be published in the papers on New Year's Day. And at the thought that "He" would most probably read it there, Razumov stopped short on the stairs for an instant, then went on smiling faintly at his own emotion. "This is but a shadow," he said to himself, "but the medal is a solid beginning"' (*UWE* 14). The shadow of the father haunts Razumov's initial style: he writes for an almost divine figure, 'He,' despite the obvious truth that this man feels nothing but a financial obligation to his illegitimate son. Razumov seems to recognize that in striving to have his name published, so that he might place it beneath his father's eyes, he is betraying himself.

When he confronts Natalia, Razumov makes it clear that he 'had never known a home'; he must choose and create one (*UWE* 299). He explains: 'Do you know why I came to you? It is simply because there is no one anywhere in the whole great world I could go to. Do you understand what I say? No one to go to. Do you conceive of the desolation of the thought – no one–to–go–to?' (354) This is a striking comment on his attempts to please his father. Razumov expresses powerful emotion, but he calls it 'thought.' The silent dashes, used to dramatize his desperation and pain, construct a broken sentence. Conrad thus connects this sentence with the writer of the journal, the one who discovers too late that his true name is not the father's, but instead is Victor Haldin.

Debra Romanick's etymological research reveals that the name as it hovers between the German and Slavic roots – 'Haldin' – conveys both heroism and wretchedness. Since Razumov too is referred to in the novel as a 'wretch,' she concludes: 'Haldin's name – literally – reflects not Haldin's moral being, but Razumov's. The name is not an external referent, but an internal mirror' (49). Clearly, this is the reverse of the narcissistic mirror. This is the mirror that shows otherness into which one can gaze while investigating the way in which words cannot hold their identity. Razumov's tragedy is in believing that what he says and does refers only to himself. In naming his character Haldin, Conrad blends the betrayer with his victim, who is always there, but not seen, like spectral density.[16] In this alternative style of writing, the one that breaks the rules and strays from the correct way and that thereby allows him to see the overlap in names and sides, gains and losses, Razumov discovers his true identity: 'In giving Victor Haldin up, it was myself, after all, whom I have betrayed most basely. You must believe what I say now, you can't refuse to believe this. Most basely' (*UWE* 361).[17] While grieving, one looks into the mirror and sees reflected the image of one's loss. Razumov can only hope that the reader of his journal, Natalia Haldin, will grieve and will understand his foreign writing. However, she may remain a student of the old English teacher and not recognize that Razumov and her brother are doubles. While Conrad leaves it ambiguous, Natalia's act of handing the journal to the English narrator suggests that she hopes that the narrator may learn about the translation of feelings. Yet her decision to avoid Razumov as he dies complicates her response.

Razumov and Victor are traumatized by personal and political events. They are initially doubles because they commit brutal acts of violence in response to trauma and they are ultimately doubles because they grieve. Derrida argues that 'mourning always follows a trauma' and that 'the work of mourning is not one kind of work among others. It is work itself, work in general, the trait by means of which one ought perhaps to reconsider the very concept of production – in what links it to trauma, to mourning' (*S* 97). One way of understanding Razumov's act of betrayal is by recognizing his failure to respond to trauma. He does not grieve for his lack of home, family, and parents; instead, he turns to his secret father, in the name of his motherland, in order to stamp out the spectre Haldin, who seeks his help to escape. What exactly is the work of mourning that requires us to reconsider our concept of production?

In *Under Western Eyes*, the work of mourning is unproductive: it will not produce like the essay that may win the silver medal. Grieving will not advance Razumov's studies or career. It will not earn him a living. Nevertheless, the tragic force of the novel lies in revealing that without this kind of grief work, all other work becomes meaningless. Grieving is done within and for oneself; yet viewed from the outside, it looks unproductive. Razumov's work of mourning is in his diary.[18] The journal underlies the story of *Under Western Eyes* and thus Conrad undertakes the work of mourning in composing the novel.

When Conrad stopped work on *Under Western Eyes* in order to write his famous short story 'The Secret Sharer' (*SS*) he developed a connection and a contrast between the Sea Captain of the short story and Razumov of the novel in terms of their productivity. Both the Captain and Razumov realize that the man they hide in their room, the man who has committed murder, threatens their future. Conrad places a sympathetic killer, seeking protection, into the hands of each man: the Captain assists his secret sharer to escape; Razumov betrays his secret sharer to the police. The contrast between these two relationships highlights the Captain's sympathy and compassion; thus, Conrad implies that the work of mourning requires imagination. Despite his crew's sense that he is dangerously unproductive, the Captain performs his work within; in contrast, Razumov strives to be outwardly productive in order to earn the recognition of those in power.

In 'The Secret Sharer,' the Captain accepts Leggatt as part of himself, as a shadow that he casts, a ghost who haunts him. The Captain is able to imagine himself in a comparable plight. His command is marked by his imaginative integration of a murderous figure. In contrast, Razumov refuses identification with Haldin; he describes himself in disturbing terms to the man he has betrayed: 'I have no domestic tradition. I have nothing to think against. My tradition is historical' (*UWE* 61). Razumov strives to blot out the haunting figure of Haldin (341), but he fails. For although Razumov argues that his tradition is historical, in fact, it is domestic; it is the tradition of an abandoned child. Confronted with the revolutionary Haldin and the drunken driver whom Razumov is sent to find, he thinks that these two men are acting like children and his response to such a thought is revealing: 'It was a sort of terrible childishness. But children had their masters. "Ah! the stick, the stick, the stern hand," thought Razumov, longing for power to hurt and destroy' (31). In a raging fantasy about being the master of a child and beating this child into submission, Razumov repeatedly strikes the drunken man with a pitchfork. Thus, paradoxically, it is the ghost-child who is in fact master of Razumov's actions; he is the autocrat and the revolutionary who tear the adult apart. Therefore, until he grieves for the suffering of this haunting child, Razumov will not be able to respond to Haldin with sympathy and compassion. Although unaware of the import of what he says, the English narrator states that 'all ideas of political plots and conspiracies seem childish, crude inventions for the theatre or a novel' (109).

It is important to note that Razumov not only resembles the Captain in Conrad's short story, but he also compares in compelling ways to the secret sharer himself. The secret sharer originates in the sea and returns to the sea. In *Under Western Eyes*, Conrad describes Razumov in parallel terms; framing his story with the absent family, the narrator informs us of the betrayer's lack of domestic tradition, the loss of which he refuses to mourn: 'Officially and in fact without a family [...] no home influences had shaped his opinions or his feelings. He was as lonely in the world as a man swimming in the deep sea' (10). What distinguishes Leggatt, another swimmer in a deep sea, from Razumov is that the former tells his story with great force to a listener. If writing the diary that becomes *Under Western Eyes* is an act of mourning, then Leggatt's confession to the Captain may be read in a comparable way. However, Conrad renders both attempts at grieving irresolute, because neither traumatized man commands his own tale. Both Razumov and Leggatt must trust that the narrators of their stories will convey the grief.

When the Captain believes that Leggatt has been discovered and thus will be betrayed, his 'voice die[s] in his throat' and he goes 'stony all over' (*SS* 112). Both the Captain and his Secret Sharer know that his story will not be accepted; the judge and jury will not listen and understand. The grief is too foreign, and this thought turns the Captain to stone. In contrast, the kind of short story Conrad tells has the dynamic function of moving the reader beyond judgment to communion. Gail Fraser contends that what leads to the fulfilment of the Captain of 'The Secret Sharer,' in contrast to the destruction of Razumov, is the former's emotional engagement. The Captain, right from the start, allows for 'the preeminence of feeling over the sober consideration of fact.' Throughout, she analyses the 'conflict between reason and feeling' that shapes both the short story and the novel (117–18). Like Le Boulicaut, Fraser believes the writing process of the story was 'therapeutic' (129).

Leggatt shares his secret with the unknown Captain, and thus he is like an author who tells a story to an unknown reader. In contrast, Razumov tells the story of Haldin to the father who abandoned him – thus to the domestic tradition that betrayed him as a child. He does not recognize the haunting of this tradition and believes he acts according to the dictates of history. He was betrayed and he betrays. He sees himself as reasonable, without recognizing that his actions are fuelled by suppressed emotions.

Razumov attains relief from his suffering only when he writes in his diary. In this record, he writes to Natalia: 'I was afraid of your mother. I never knew mine. I've never known any kind of love. There is something in the mere word' (*UWE* 360). Exploring Derrida's experience of mourning, David Krell comments, with great relevance to *Under Western Eyes*: 'Mourning does not slice into an already constituted time; rather, in some unthought and undiscerned way, mourning opens time, whether in the desire to have a conscience, if memory is conscience, or the desire to confess – and confess in writing – the (m)other' (198). Derrida uses the figure of the spectre to develop this idea, this alternative way of living in time. We tend to rely 'on the simple (ideal, mechanical, or dialectical) opposition of the real presence of the real present or the living present to its ghostly simulacrum.' We cannot ever see ourselves or the world differently while we continue to rely 'on a general temporality or an historical temporality made up of the successive linking of presences identical to themselves and contemporary with themselves' (*S* 70). Razumov sees himself as part of his personal present and he responds to situations as if they are contemporary. He has no sense of precedents, previous lives, future lives. If time opened up for Razumov, he would not suppress the ghosts of his childhood self, his (m)other, his father and transfer these erased signs, full of emotion, full of violence (betraying and beating with a pitchfork), onto his contemporaries. This recalls Derrida's speculation noted earlier: the writer may well be the one who renounces violence because he 'absents himself better, that is, expresses himself better as other.' During his violent acts, Razumov is consumed with his own internal speech; he is full of his own rhetoric and does not imagine or hear otherness.

When Razumov seeks to express his grief, it is as though another speaks within him saying, 'I confess,' and this other voice emerges from what feels like torture. He experiences this interrupting voice as time, which seems to 'explode in his head' (*UWE* 66). Conrad collapses both self and time in this scene. Razumov shares in Haldin's torture, and the ticking clock that demarcates the distance between his childhood self and adult self explodes, so that in the shattering there is a reconnection. His articulation, his sharing, his recognition that the foreign child is actually native, all are part of the activity of mourning. In this act, he grieves for and thereby hears the voice of the lost (m)other.

Conrad's Tekla functions as a maternal figure in the novel. Rather than take one side or another, she breaks from her family's participation in an oppressive regime and then breaks from the revolutionaries who fight such oppression. She becomes the one who hears another's suffering and responds in the pose of a (m)other. The man she previously loved and supported was a lithographer, one who writes on stone or prints from stone (*UWE* 151). Derrida explains that when one analyses dreams, the path should lead 'back into a landscape of writing,' and he clarifies: 'Not a writing which simply transcribes, a stony echo of muted words, but a lithography before words' (*WD* 207). Trying to evade our tendency to organize and categorize the world into structures based on oppositional relations, Derrida imagines a dream interpretation that bypasses the structures and instead works like a lithographer, who writes on (leaves a trace, opens up traces) and prints from stone (recognizes other traces, produces other traces). For Derrida, the rock on which one writes is layered by sedimentation and thus, while one is reading, structures are 'undone, decomposed, desedimented' (*L* 272).

Tekla, who loves and mourns a lithographer, comes full circle at the end of *Under Western Eyes*, for she tends the dying Razumov, whose writing breaks stone. The novel thus ends with a new kind of phantom, for Tekla 'haunt[s] his bedside at the hospital' (377). Conrad duplicates the loss of Haldin and the loss of Razumov by an actual mother on the one hand and a symbolic maternal figure on the other. Haldin's mother becomes paralysed with 'the secret obstinacy' of her sorrow (340). She appears in a striking pose: 'Miss Haldin stopped, and pointed mournfully at the tragic immobility of her mother, who seemed to watch a beloved head lying in her lap' (355). Razumov distinguishes himself from the haunting Haldin by locating himself as 'on this earth where I had no place to lay my head' (359). Tekla claims to be a relative, so that the hospital where the near-dead Razumov has been taken will allow her access. Note the pose she takes with him: 'She sat down calmly, and took his head on her lap; her scared faded eyes avoided looking at his deathlike face.' In contrast to the parents who abandon him, Tekla does not want to leave his side. However, echoing the phrase used to describe Mrs Haldin, Tekla never 'shed[s] a tear' (371). At the end of the novel, both Haldin and Razumov are sons who are mourned; yet the mother cannot weep. The sons form ghostly doubles, and what Razumov discovers is that one cannot simply walk over a phantom to make it disappear. The whole force of haunting is in its imaginary, transparent gravity. It is significant that Conrad has Tekla transform in the novel from one who writes from dictation to one who cares for the particular human being who learns to express his grief in writing.[19]

Despite Natalia's resonant claim that 'victim and executioner, betrayer and betrayed' all shall be pitied together, when Razumov actually confesses, she turns 'into stone' (*UWE* 353). She cannot hear the ghost of her brother speaking through the mourning confession of Razumov. The failure to identify with, let alone recognize as a haunting double, is what generates the tragic events of Conrad's novel. Haldin's innocent victims form a backdrop of secrets unknown, losses unrecognized, grief inexpressible. Conrad opens his novel with a description of the mute figures left dead by Haldin's bomb: 'Through the falling snow people looked from afar at the small heap of dead bodies lying upon each other near the carcasses of the two horses' (10). Although not acknowledged, let alone mourned by Natalia and her mother, the innocents, blown up by Haldin's bomb, also generate the phantom lying in the snow that startles Razumov. Significantly, he sees this spectre.

Conrad stresses in his 'Author's Note' to *Under Western Eyes* his aim to reveal the inextricable bond between self and other: 'These people are unable to see that all they can effect is merely a change of names. The oppressors and the oppressed are all Russians together.' Conrad applies this belief directly to Razumov: 'Being nobody's child he feels rather more keenly than another would that he is a Russian – or he is nothing' (ix–x). Yet instead of keening for the fact that he is nobody's child, Razumov believes that he will reconnect with his father, and be something, and feel keenly, by constructing a bond built on the destruction of Haldin. Rather than his usual attribute of the pen, Razumov uses his 'penknife' to stab his credo of binary opposites into the wall: 'History not Theory. / Patriotism not Internationalism. / Evolution not Revolution. / Direction not destruction. / Unity not disruption' (66). If one erases the 'nots,' with which Razumov separates self and other, and replaces them with 'ins,' then the credo becomes one whereby the binary opposites are destroyed, revealed to be simply name changes: History in Theory. Patriotism in Internationalism. Evolution in Revolution, and so on. The words would no longer be 'foes of reality,' to quote the English teacher of languages (3); instead, they would become sharers of reality.

When Razumov confesses to the revolutionaries, a group of men take him outside, so that the terrorist Nikita can hit him, with the express purpose of rendering him deaf. Yet listen to Conrad's description of Razumov's deafness: 'In this unearthly stillness his footsteps fell silent on the pavement, while a dumb wind drove him on and on, like a lost mortal in a phantom world ravaged by a soundless thunderstorm' (*UWE* 369–70). Razumov strives to walk over and crush and then ultimately escape the phantoms that haunt him. Yet at the novel's end he enters a phantom world whose silence is deafening. His tragedy is that he learns too late the haunting gravity of secret selves: the suppression of grief makes one as heavy as a stone, striving to hear, although stone deaf. Haunting stories must be told, even with broken sentences. Derrida expresses this concisely: 'Ego = ghost. Therefore "I am" would mean "I am haunted"' (*S* 133). In deconstruction, ontology becomes hauntology. In *Under Western Eyes* Conrad reveals that the ghost who haunts is a hurt and grieving child.

2 Childhood Grief as Resident Alien in Jean Rhys's Five Novellas

In Joseph Conrad's *Under Western Eyes*, Razumov's journal, which details the suppression of childhood grief and the way in which it leads to his betrayal of Haldin, needs to be translated by the English teacher. Childhood grief is literally a foreign language in Joseph Conrad's novel. Ultimately, Razumov's grief cannot be translated into English because there do not seem to be words for it; thus, the teacher-translator omits it.

In Jean Rhys's five novellas, childhood grief is slightly more resonant. It is no longer treated as a foreign language; yet other than in *Wide Sargasso Sea*, the child speaker belongs to the past or dies before becoming articulate. In these novellas, childhood grief enters into British society, but does not have citizenship; instead, the grieving child in Rhys's fiction compares to a resident alien: present but foreign, part of society yet unable to fully belong. The child in her novellas is forced away 'suddenly' by 'others.' Thus, Rhys's narratives have an uncanny sense of moving backwards, so that writer and reader can discover the sudden moment as well as identify exactly who the others are that force the child away.

* * *

> When you are a child you are yourself and you know and see everything prophetically. And then suddenly something happens and you stop being yourself; you become what others force you to be.
>
> Rhys, *After Leaving Mr. Mackenzie* (1930)

In *Circumfession*, Derrida struggles with what he remembers and what is forgotten but haunts him nonetheless. He imagines (because he cannot recall) his infant circumcision as a 'knife above,' which is used to mark the child with 'the beginning the logos'; thus, he describes his approach as 'writing backward' to 'the moment when things turn around' (300). Layered upon this inarticulate trauma is the death of his cousin and his two-year-old brother and 'then expulsion from school and from Frenchness' (248). When he was thirteen years old, Jacques Derrida, the top student, was expelled from his school in Algeria because of French racial laws that affected France's colonies as well. Derrida was expelled because he was Jewish. He has never been able to, or wanted to, recover a seamless, correct mode of writing French. What inspires Derrida's theories is this initial childhood encounter with culture: 'circumcision remains the threat of what is making me write here' (202). These childhood traumas form a catalyst for his system of writing back to what Jean Rhys's character Julia calls 'being yourself,' the time in childhood before you were brought under the control of the logos, the religion, the government, the nation, the random acts of car accidents and illnesses. In Rhys's novellas, the traumatized child continues to reside within the self; however, it remains an unknown, an alien.

Derrida strives to reach a point where he can turn around – not back, but around – so that he might once again see and know the wounding of this child. Thus, as he contemplates inarticulate suffering, he speaks to his child: 'the cousin, one year older than *you*' (248; italics mine).

Jean Rhys wrote five novellas between 1928 and 1966, which can be read as five acts in a tragic play that stage the suppression of childhood grief. As in Derrida's writing, one is aware of this child, yet it cannot be assimilated. Both theorist and novelist strive to examine the impact of this haunting child, at the same time as they explore ways in which the child, as resident alien, may be offered status as a citizen within the self.[1] The child is paradoxically dead, gone, absent, yet fully alive and present in the adult self. This divergence occupies Rhys along with the other novelists of this study. The opening within each individual to the difference within, the otherness of the child-self, allows a reader to hear the haunting grief in the text.

In the first book, *Quartet*, Rhys writes a command to the reader: 'you must understand' (14). In her final novella, *Wide Sargasso Sea*, Rhys has her female protagonist exclaim: 'I have tried to make you understand' (111). Rhys's novellas seem geared towards having the reader understand the inarticulate realm of grief and of childhood, the two inextricably entwined.

In the second novella, *After Leaving Mr. Mackenzie*, Julia Martin indulges in memorial and imaginative recollection; both of the places she fantasizes about are images for suppressed grief. She dreams of 'a dark-purple sea, the sea of a chromo or of some tropical country that she had never seen' (9). As noted, in *Under Western Eyes* Joseph Conrad uses the figure of the lithographer, who writes in stone, and in the next chapter we will see Rebecca West's narrator imagine grief as located in a tropical zone. In the late nineteenth century, 'chromo' was the colloquial term for a chromolithograph, a picture printed from stone in colours. Like other modernists, Rhys explores the way in which suppressed grief turns one to stone. In a letter describing her brief stay at Holloway Prison, Rhys uses the image of turning to stone to represent the opposite of feeling compassion, for 'some of the prison officers aren't quite stone yet' (*Letters* 56). Moreover, she suggests that her expression of grief is what condemns her: 'I began to cry in the witness box and the magistrate sent me to Holloway to find out if I was crazy' (76). Notably, Rhys is not mourning the death of someone. She is crying because she is afraid or regretful or angry; regardless, she believes this emotion is enough to get her institutionalized. At the outset of *After Leaving Mr. Mackenzie,* her protagonist, Julia, is beginning to harden; by the end of the novel, she has become 'indifferent and cold, like a stone' (136).

For the modernists of this study, on the one hand, grief chills the body and soul until one becomes cold stone; on the other hand, childhood grief is suppressed to the point of appearing to the adult self as belonging to a tropical land, an alien zone far from the British climate, as far away as Conrad's Russia. Thus, the mother of Rhys's character Julia is born in the heat of Brazil, but she dies a paralysed woman who does not know her daughters, causing a 'cold weight' to descend on Julia's 'heart, crushing it' (*ALMM* 52). Although she is rigid like a statue, this dying mother cries 'loudly and disconsolately, like a child' (71). Near the end of the novel, a Mr Horsefield is on the verge of journeying into a life full of feelings: he wants to 'get something out of life before [he's] too old to feel. Get a bit of sun.' He imagines this tropical realm as the world that Julia inhabits, as he explains to her: 'You hate hotly like a child because you've been hurt. But I hate coldly, and that's worse' (121).[2] However, he chooses to remain in his world, which is 'a world of lowered voices, and of passions, like Japanese dwarf trees, suppressed for many generations. A familiar world' (127).

For Rhys, grief is powerful enough to paralyse the self, and the only way to get the blood moving is by sharing the grief with another and having it be heard. Thus, her characters struggle repeatedly to tell of their suffering. However, over and over again they are not heard or believed, and another limb becomes chilled into the rigidity of stone. Rhys has a sense of endowing silenced characters with speech and she believes this process is vital for herself as a writer.[3] One of the ways she bypasses silenced figures is by using disruptive children's voices.

Grief, childhood voices, tropics are layered over one another by Rhys as with each novella she moves closer and closer to her own childhood home in the West Indies.[4] She associates a tropical sense of power through fire imagery, which shoots up in various ways throughout her five novellas. Ford Madox Ford, in his preface to her short story collection, *The Left Bank*, remarks on Rhys's skill at expressing 'the emotions and passions of a child' (26).[5] Comparably, Derrida disrupts the adult world of philosophy by speaking as a child: 'survival or life by provision of Georgette Sultana Esther, or Mummy if you prefer' (*C* 73). The 'you' he addresses directly, the one who prefers the term 'Mummy,' is his spectral child, and the 'synchrony' created allows the child and adult to exist at the same time. While working on *Wide Sargasso Sea*, in a letter to her publisher, Rhys identifies herself as an inarticulate child: '*Continuez mon enfant.* (That is *me* – l'enfant)' (*Letters* 271). At the same time, in a letter to her editor, she presents herself as 'the crying child' (270).

In her first novella, *Quartet*, Rhys brings together the crying child, the inarticulate child, and the emotions and passions of the child. *Quartet* is told almost exclusively from an orphan's point of view. Marya is 'used to a lack of solidity and of fixed backgrounds' (14). Moreover, ever 'since she was a child,' she has been 'hunted' by fear: 'It was a vague and shadowy fear of something cruel and stupid that had caught her and would never let her go' (28).[6] It seems she has been without a solid family home ever since she was little. In a letter to Francis Wyndham, Rhys calls herself 'a hunted haunted creature' (*Letters* 284). In *Wide Sargasso Sea*, a book haunted by *Jane Eyre*, Antoinette (Rhys's creation of the youthful Mrs Rochester from Brönte's novel) worries that someone is following her: 'I did not want to see that ghost of a woman who they say haunts the place' (153). Of course, she herself is the ghost everyone fears. Moreover, the writing that Rhys calls '*The first Mrs. Rochester*' is ghostlike, for as early as 1949, she records in a letter: 'It really haunts me that I can't finish it' (*Letters* 50). In David Krell's book on Derrida and mourning, he remarks on Freud's insight into doubling, ghosts, and 'zombie effects' that occur when the 'labors of mourning are unsuccessful.' While Antoinette appears as a zombie-like creature, a double for her mad mother, she accuses Rochester of effecting this magic transformation within her. Both figures have not worked at mourning; thus, they are invaded by the 'bereaved object,' which for Derrida and for the modernists in this study are grieving childhood selves (Krell 15).

Rhys's original title for the novella was 'Le revenant' (The Ghost), which one may imagine as the haunting of Charlotte Brontë or her mad woman in the attic or the grieving child (*Letters* 213). Derrida uses this term to discuss the return of the father of another grieving child, Hamlet, while he considers Marx's opening to the *Manifesto*: 'A specter is haunting Europe – the specter of communism.' He writes: 'As in Hamlet, the Prince of a rotten State, everything begins by the apparition of a specter' and he stresses the anxious waiting with the knowledge that the '*revenant* is going to come' (*S* 4). The important act for Derrida is not witnessing the spectre, but speaking to it and thereby 're-membering' the absent and present selves (*S* 11; *C* 59). When one reads Rhys's letters about *Wide Sargasso Sea*, one realizes that she is haunted by, and needs to speak to, the ghost of Rochester as much as to the ghost of Antoinette: 'So now I have two "I"s, Mr Rochester and his first wife' (*Letters* 172). Before *Wide Sargasso Sea* writes the childhood of Antoinette, Rochester's mad West Indian wife, one might forget her. The madwoman in the attic of *Jane Eyre* might have been the end. However, *Wide Sargasso Sea* collapses the ending by offering a beginning. Rhys's novel argues that one cannot possibly know Brontë's Bertha without knowing her childhood; hence, she writes the story of Antoinette. In *Wide Sargasso Sea*, 'Bertha' is the name Rochester forces on his wife. Her real name is Antoinette. In Rhys's novella, then, the attempt of Brontë's Rochester to silence his wife fails. Both Brontë and Rhys bring this ghostly woman to the fore, but Rhys offers a double haunting with the former lovers Edward Rochester and Antoinette Cosway. Their passion occurs in a tropical landscape signifying suppressed grief.

Many of the characters in Rhys's novels are haunted by the return of childhood ghosts. Niall Lucy explains the way in which deconstruction 'is opposed to anything that claims to gather up, to unite, to bring together as one' because this 'would be to close us off from the others who are no longer living and the others who are not yet living' (*Dictionary* 78). In Rhys's *Quartet*, Marya, pursued by haunting fear, hunts fear and captures it. She thereby recreates, first with her thief husband and then as the lover of a married man, the cruel past of her childhood, even though she yearns to flee and oppose this doubling and repetition. At the outset of the story, she is married to Stephan Zelli, a man who does criminal deals in the art world. Two stolen articles detailed by Rhys juxtapose childhood and imperialism: 'a rocking horse played with by one of Millet's many children' and 'Napoleon's sabre' whose blade is engraved with 'In token of submission, respect and esteem to Napoleon Bonaparte, the hero of Aboukir-Mouhrad Bey' (*Q* 19). The stolen objects are significant, for the novella is about literal and figurative robbery: children being robbed of emotive childhoods is not only entwined with the stealing of sexual favours, it is also likened to the plundering of nations. Vulnerable children, women, and countries must offer tokens of submission to their masters. On the verge of being conquered by the Heidlers, a powerful British couple, the orphan Marya, whose husband has suddenly been thrown into jail, watches a child at a merry-go-round, reminding us of the stolen rocking horse. Marya stares at a 'little frail, blond girl' who makes her feel less like a 'grey ghost walking in a vague, shadowy world' (46).

The little girl haunts the adult woman, for her child-self has been suppressed, no longer speaks the same language, but is there nonetheless. It inhabits her like a resident alien. Rhys describes Marya's sensation as one of being a ghost, not seeing one. Derrida describes this phenomenon: 'The subject that haunts is not identifiable, one cannot see, localize, fix any form, one cannot decide between hallucination and perception, there are only displacements; one feels looked at by what one cannot see' (*S* 136). Marya cannot see this ghostly inner child; yet she feels looked at. In *Wide Sargasso Sea*, Ellen Friedman sees 'lunatic Bertha with her haunting twin, Antoinette' as one of modernity's defining gestures in its rejection of master narratives and its desire to stress duplicity (122–3). What Friedman sees as a 'twin' is not only a doubled self; when we factor in Rhys's narration of Antoinette as a child, the twin becomes a tripled self. Both of the adult twins, Bertha / Antoinette, are haunted by the child Antoinette. The emphasis then shifts from duplicity to grief, which, I believe, is one of modernity's defining gestures.

In *Quartet*, Marya is haunted by her missing family. Death steals Marya's parents, and then her robber husband becomes both father and son to her: she is 'the petted, cherished child' and he reaches his hands out to her 'like a little boy' (20). This loving familial relationship ends suddenly when Stephan is caught and must spend a year in jail. No longer able to care for her like a father, Stephan becomes an abandoned child: '"I'm not going to be able to stand it," he said in a small voice – a little boy's voice.' Forgoing the adult's grief, Rhys simply cuts to the voice of a little boy: '"I can't. I can't"' (36). She will use this same narrative technique when she constructs the character of Edward Rochester in *Wide Sargasso Sea*.

In *Quartet*, Marya's identity depends first on her family and then on her marriage. She is 'British by birth. Polish by marriage' and both nations exile her accidentally (29). She is without nation and thus vulnerable to conquering figures like the Heidlers. When Stephan speaks through the bars in his little boy's voice, Marya has already sold her dresses, composed a letter to her impoverished relatives begging for money, and thus must jump when she hears the 'masterful voice' of Lois Heidler (36). This woman acts as an evil stepmother to Marya; '"you're wet through, poor child!"' she exclaims (32) and uses this seeming parental concern to insist that the child come and live with her and her husband, a new mother and father, an abusive mother and father, for both Heidlers know that the plan involves the husband sexually conquering the 'poor child' within the symbolic family home. The wife resents Marya's, and thus the child's, expression of feelings: her motto is 'I grin and bear it, and I think that other women ought to grin and bear it, too' (76). While Lois Heidler appears with eyes 'swollen as if she had been crying,' she willingly exits the house so that her husband can seduce their symbolic child (62). For Mr Heidler, the husband of this suppressed woman, sex is 'Terrible as an army set in array,' and this is exactly the army he uses to master the nation, Marya (101).

Like a vulnerable country, she is without weapons or resources to resist a powerful invader and thus she submits to the married pair. Initially, Marya fights 'wildly, with tears, with futile rages, with extravagant abandon – all bad weapons' (Q 91). The weakness of Marya's strategy is that her attempt to defend herself depends on feelings, and Heidler is, like a well-trained child or soldier, one who – like his wife – suppresses emotion; as he explains: 'I've trained myself not to show things' (78). Marya herself recognizes the military advantage she lacks: 'That's what's the matter with me. No training' (92).[7]

On the night after the initial seduction, orchestrated by both husband and wife, the three dine together. Mrs Heidler stresses the fact that Marya is now like a child to them, vulnerable, without resources, and in emotional, possibly physical, danger. She announces, and Rhys alludes once again to the rocking horse and the merry-go-round: '"Let's go to Luna-park after dinner," she said. "We'll put Mado on the joy wheel, and watch her being banged about a bit. Well she ought to amuse us sometimes; she ought to sing for her supper; that's what she's here for, isn't it?"' The husband's face is 'expressionless' in response to his wife's threat to their 'child' (Q 67). Rhys ensures that her readers recognize the parallels between the woman's body and the national body, for nearing the end of the ugly affair, Mr Heidler, without any sense of irony drops to his knees and prays to God in the church St Julien le Pauvre, while at the same time looking down at his poverty-stricken lover as if she is a 'Kalmuck,' a member of a Buddhist Mongol people: 'Her head dropped backwards over the edge of the bed and from that angle her face seemed strange to him: the cheek-bones looked higher and more prominent, the nostrils wider, the lips thicker. A strange little Kalmuck face. He whispered: "Open your eyes, savage. Open your eyes, savage"' (102). Marya opens her eyes and says that she loves this man; yet she is 'quivering and abject in his arms, like some unfortunate dog abashing itself before its master' (102). Rhys describes this phenomenon as the structure behind an abusive affair and indicative of a warring society. Gayatri Spivak presents this kind of bond as the dominant structure Derrida's theories seek to identify: 'Humankind's common desire is for a stable center, and for the assurance of mastery – through knowing or possessing' (pref. xi). Disenfranchised like the poverty-stricken Russians of Conrad's novel, Marya finds a lover who can be compared to a powerful, imperialist nation. While Marya tries to destroy oppression with violence, she imagines it staggering on, 'bleeding and muddy' like Rasputin (96).

When Marya first hears of Mr Heidler, she is told that he has had a 'kind of nervous breakdown' (*Q* 10), but when she first meets him, she thinks he looks as if 'nothing could break him down,' for 'the wooden expression of his face was carefully striven for.' He and his wife, whose eyes have a 'suspicious, almost a deadened look in them' (11–12), frequent a restaurant that attracts all the British ex-pats in Paris, because its 'decent restraint gave them confidence' (32). As the husband explains, like a captain training his soldiers, appearances must be maintained: 'It was everybody's duty, it was in fact what they were there for' (89). The Heidlers suppress the break in their marriage; they suppress their own nervous breakdowns; they thus lure Marya into a 'love affair' that is in fact a 'fight' and a brutal break-up (91).

When Marya lashes out at the Heidlers for the twisted love triangle in which they all participate, the husband makes it seem that she is asking for money. This insult makes Marya furious; she hits him and calls him 'Horrible German!' Despite his usual 'expressionless' response to emotions, this time he mutters: 'You're quite right. Oh God! Oh God!' and begins 'to sob' (*Q* 81). When Heidler expresses grief in this climactic scene in the novel, his response is to say that he is drunk and he will not remember it. His wife says that he 'always does that.' Thus, while Marya attacks Heidler verbally with the post–First World War insult of being 'German,' she nonetheless recognizes that ultimately he resembles the icon of British imperialism and controlled mourning:

'Queen Victoria' (89–90). Although he appears to Marya as a feminine symbol of British society, she relates this suppression of feeling to becoming the masculine force behind the conquering of land and women: Marya knows that Heidler's wife and she are merely 'two members of a harem' (79).

When Heidler ends the affair, Marya meets a man who alludes to yet another conquered country. Rhys stresses what is revealed by language, for this character reinforces the terms of the affair, in which sex is like an army and marriage resembles an imperialist manoeuvre: 'The young man by her side began to talk. He told her all sorts of things. That he had been born in Tonkin, that his nurse had had a name which meant spouse. That most of the Annamite women seemed to have a name which meant spouse. That his family had returned to France when he was nine years of age. To Toulon. That was ten years ago. That he, also, was sad as his mistress had betrayed him' (Q 118).

Rhys has Marya, British by birth and married to a Pole, break up with her lover of German background, who nonetheless acts as a signifier for imperialist Britain. She salves her wounds in a one-night stand with a Parisian youth, whose family is part of the conquering of Vietnam and who as a child was cared for by a woman whose name, translated into English, means spouse, thus alluding to the partnership of marriage. What does Rhys imagine that these characters feel? The young man says he feels 'betrayed' and 'sad.'

Rhys entwines the desire to conquer countries and women with a kind of fear and hatred of children. Not once in her five novellas is there a loving moment depicted between a parent and child. Instead, she offers multiple split images of needy children and inadequate parenting. Thus, Marya gazes at advertisements depicting children and is disgusted: 'a horrible little boy in a sailor suit' and a 'horrible little girl with a pigtail' (Q 87). While Marya fantasizes about smashing a wine-bottle in Lois's face and watching the blood stream down, Heidler calls her his 'darling child' (97). Her husband just out of prison, looking emaciated and ill, Marya sighs 'deeply like a child when a fit of crying is over' (104). There is a woman in a bar who lavishes 'maternal' affection on her dog (108). The first time that Heidler approaches Marya to have sex, she receives him with the 'fright of a child shut up in a dark room' (71). In her novels, Rhys ensures that readers make the connection between destructive sexual relations and suffering children. The army marshalled in the bedroom, the war between lovers, the sexual conquering often originate in grieving children who yearn for understanding and love, but who, as resident aliens, are at risk in a society where they do not have citizenship. They do not have rights. No one speaks their language.

The man who tries to save Marya, a man who defines the world by its sadness (Q 73), imagines her as a lost child. His name is Cairn. A cairn is both a memorial marker and a landmark.[8] In a series of novels in which characters try to survive by forgetting trauma, where they associate being overwhelmed by grief with becoming stone cold, the name Cairn is resonant. He tries to save Marya from the immobilizing force of inexpressible grief, but he fails: 'her mouth was so hard and her eyes were so sad.' He wants to act as a guide, a marker for her child-self: 'Lost she looked. L'Enfant Perdu or The Babe in the Wood' (72). Rhys may appeal to the child-reader who hears names literally and thus understands another layer to a name being 'Cairn.' The child-self may hear or read language differently, as Derrida explains about himself: 'I slip the alliance,' spoken of by Geoffrey Bennington in reference to Derrida, 'to make it fall into the depths of my childhood, at the very surface of my tongue' in order to remind the other philosopher that 'alliance' for Derrida 'will always be a Jewish building on the rue Bab Azoun' in his childhood home Algeria (C 176).

In her second novella, *After Leaving Mr. Mackenzie*, the story seems to continue. The main character, Julia, has 'the hands of an oriental' and her eyes are 'childish in expression' (11). Like Marya, Rhys renders her doubly vulnerable: she is a child awaiting abuse; she is a foreign nation about to be attacked. Her plan is to 'fight,' but at the same time she would like to succumb to her feelings of grief and 'sob' (14–15). Like Marya, she is a ghost. Her memories are of the First World War as she watches a film with a Belgian who weeps at the bombardment of a town while she thinks, 'that was a funny time!' The disconnect between a childish and a mature reaction is painfully evident as she feels 'exultant and youthful' recalling the war: 'A funny time. A mad reckless time' (49). Julia weeps constantly through the novel because of being rejected by men and desperate for money and lacking in self-esteem. In contrast, she does not feel such waves of grief for the events of the First World War. Nor does she seem aware that the world has not changed for ten years: remembering the zany years of war, she walks into a café where a 'band filled the vast room with military music, played at the top of its voice. Grandiose.' In this café there are 'two rather battered-looking women with the naïve eyes of children' (49–50). Directly after the armistice, Julia's baby dies because of her poverty: 'He's so little. And he dies and is put under the earth.' And what is the mother's reaction? 'Not sentimental – oh, no.

Just a funny feeling, like hunger' (80–1). No tears are ever shed for the war, 'a funny time,' nor for the death of the child, 'a funny feeling.'

All of Rhys's novellas are haunted by the dead child. Notably, in *Quartet*, Rhys associates the recollection of grief with the potential animation and joy of this child. Thus, while Marya 'remembered her tears,' she feels 'a longing for joy' which she envisions as 'an unborn child jumping, leaping, kicking at her side' (59). The possibility of joy in these novels, a lively liberating joy, hinges on the ability to grieve and thereby speak with what Derrida calls a 'private language' used to talk to and articulate the child, the 'untranslatable one' (*C* 41).

In *Circumfession*, Derrida presents his grieving child-self: 'I wonder if those reading me from up there see my tears, today, those of the child about whom people used to say "he cries for nothing," and indeed, if they guess that my life was but a long history of prayers, and the incessant return of the "I want to kill myself" speaks less the desire to put an end to my life than a sort of compulsion to overtake each second, like one car overtaking another' (38–9). The first photograph included in *Circumfession* is of Derrida at about age two or three in a toy car. Acceleration is one way to leave behind the tearful child: the toy is replaced by a real car, like the one that kills his four-year-old cousin. Near the end of *Circumfession*, Derrida includes a photograph of a car and sitting in it are his mother holding him on her lap and his aunt holding his cousin (249). One child dies, literally; the other dies figuratively until he talks to it in his 'private language.'

As we saw with Conrad's characters, Rhys's characters cannot understand one another because they often speak in the foreign, untranslatable language of inarticulate children and / or grief. In *After Leaving Mr. Mackenzie*, there is an opportunity for Julia Martin to actually commune with a man. However, although the characters talk and talk, they do not hear one another. Likewise, Julia grieves without being able to make it meaningful. One discussion had by the two sad figures is about suffering trauma. Yet they merely state their own experiences as if they are parallel, without recognizing the correspondence; this is why they cannot build a relationship: 'She said: "D'you know what I think? I think people do what they have to do, and then the time comes when they can't anymore, and they crack up. And that's that."' Notably, the man replies by saying that he had a breakdown too, owing to 'the war.' Instead of responding to the trauma of what the man must have gone through, Rhys's character replies: 'I was twenty when the war started.' Then she adds: 'I rather liked the air raids.' This utterly silences the man, who begins 'to stroke her hair mechanically' (111). Directly after this disconnected exchange, Julia's arm hangs down the side of the bed 'like a child's arm' and Rhys reminds us that suppressing emotion takes place when one is very young (112). She wonders how early in childhood one forgets the feeling of being happy about nothing: 'How old were you? Ten? Eleven? Younger ... yes, probably younger' (115). In *Wide Sargasso Sea*, Edward Rochester asks the same question, but it is about hiding feelings, grief in particular: 'How old was I when I learned to hide what I felt? A very small boy. Six, five, even earlier' (85). Significantly, in her madness, Antoinette asserts the necessity of hiding everything important from her jailer, Grace Poole (149). The need to hide one's feelings begins in early childhood and translates into Rochester's hate and Antoinette's madness.[9]

In modern society, the separation from 'true feeling' leads Rhys to define herself as different, as foreign: 'You see I like emotion, I approve of it – in fact am capable of *wallowing* in it. Adore negro music for instance' (*Letters* 45). Like the music she adores, Rhys transforms emotion into expression, into art. In each novella, Rhys explores the failure of her characters to make their grief productive; in each case, the failure is due to an inability to speak or write the emotion in such a way that others listen and believe. Hence, they constantly write letters that they never send. Julia tells a woman painter about her failed marriage and the death of her baby and the woman does not believe her (41). She feels 'sweet sadness like a hovering ghost' (28). Rhys makes it clear that this inability to articulate is the defining feature of infants and of sadness; thus, Julia appears to the world 'like a baby. Her eyes were very sad' (31). Another way to read Julia's gaze on the world is that she has 'the look in her eyes of someone who is longing to explain herself, to say: "This is how I am. This is how I feel."' (37). Derrida writes that 'to haunt all places at the same time, to be *atopic* (mad and non-localizable), not only is it necessary to see from behind the visor, to see without being seen by whoever makes himself or herself seen (me, us), it is also necessary to speak. And to hear voices' (*S* 135). It is impossible to localize Rhys's characters, because they regard the world from behind the visor of the adult, yet the eyes looking out are those of the sad infant. As a result, they appear mad; they speak and hear voices, but the dialogue is mostly internal. Rhys records it. To these child-haunted, grieving adults, the novellas repeatedly offer memorable words, convincing sentences, moving statements. The internal monologues of Rhys's characters mean that her readers hear what society cannot.

Julia's representation of childhood is instructive in *After Leaving Mr. Mackenzie*. When arguing with her uncle, she exclaims: 'It's childish to imagine that anybody cares what happens to anybody else' (61). The male figures in the novel appear to have been trained out of childhood feelings such as caring for others: Mr Mackenzie smiles in a way that he has 'trained not to be bashful' (17), and Julia realizes that Mr Horsefield has 'been taught never to give himself away' (63). While Mr Mackenzie wrote a book of poems when he was a youth and wrote a letter to Julia when he was in love with her that began 'I would like to put my throat under your feet,' he ultimately hires a lawyer to bully his ex-lover into silence, for the code he lives by requires the suppression of feelings (18–21). Like Rebecca West, Jean Rhys imagines the throat as the site of childhood training and wounding.

In his chapter 'Mourning the Voice,' David Krell identifies Derrida's move away from philosophical tradition, for he avoids reduction of the 'the throat that our tradition has been able to suppress and ignore' (92). The throat has become the site of 'deconstruction': 'a site that by now is no stranger to mourning – to ululation and the keen' (101). Likewise for Rhys, the throat is the site of grief. In *After Leaving Mr. Mackenzie*, Julia wants to cry, but instead she simply has 'a lump in her throat' (84). In this novella, the characters constantly clear their throats as they are about to speak (22, 25, 58). Rhys uses the part of the body where one articulates oneself as the place to reveal Julia Martin in the midst of turning to stone: 'She felt an answering indifference, and at the same time pain and a tightness of the throat' (52).

Rhys details the loss of warmth from the tropical mother during Julia's childhood. The mother spurs the child initially to weave 'innumerable romances about her mother's childhood in South America'; however, the mother cannot respond to her child's questions and wondering because 'she was an inarticulate woman.' Rhys links her inability to speak to her daughter with the fact that she has been removed from the tropics: 'sometimes you could tell that she was sickening for the sun' (*ALMM* 76). This mother is the 'warm centre' of the child's world until a new sibling and worries lead her to insist her child suppress her grief: 'Don't be a cry-baby. You're too old to go on like that. You're a great big girl of six.' The initial caresses then become slaps (71). Julia can no longer express her grief and she approaches the world still as a childish woman who expects to be hit. At the age of nineteen, rejected by her first lover, she becomes as immobile as her mother: 'You felt as if your back was broken, as if you would never move again. But you did not make a scene' (78). In contrast, Rhys uses fiction to make a scene of immobilizing grief in her novellas.

Tears are so often wasted in Rhys's novellas that we wonder what allows a character to meaningfully express grief? Rhys suggests it is literature. The child invents stories about the maternal tropics, where feelings exist. When grown up, Julia cannot 'put her emotion into words'; at the same time, she constructs in her mind a literary scene: 'At that moment her sister seemed to her like a character in a tremendous tragedy moving, dark, tranquil, and beautiful, across a background of yellowish snow' (*ALMM* 73). Julia does not tell her sister, Norah, about this imagined understanding of how she feels. Moreover, Julia does not share her loving memory of carrying Norah across sharp pebbles when they were children (52). Instead, Julia verbally attacks Norah, yet watches in horror as her sister becomes like a statue 'white, with bluish lips' (99). Norah refuses to cry in front of her older sister; rather, she indulges 'a fierce desire to hurt her or to see her hurt and humiliated.' Norah picks up a Conrad novel, *Almayer's Folly*, and reads about the lack of hope for the slave. She turns from the novel to the mirror and studies her naked self. Then she begins to cry and cannot stop (75). While literature may act as a release for feelings, Rhys's women characters are never portrayed as writers. Perhaps this is because Rhys claimed the emotions of her characters, 'the feelings are always mine,' and *she* was the writer (Cantwell 24).

In *After Leaving Mr. McKenzie*, Julia Martin can only scribble the inarticulate realm of grief and childhood: 'when she took up the pen she made meaningless strokes on the paper. And then she began to draw faces – the sort of faces a child would draw' (134). In *Voyage in the Dark*, Anna Morgan addresses herself in the second person about her failure to write her grief: 'You make up letters that you never send or even write' (64). In *Good Morning, Midnight*, Sasha Jensen becomes a ghost writer of children's 'fairy stories' (139). And in *Wide Sargasso Sea*, Rochester draws in a 'child's scribble' the English home he will make for himself and his mad wife (134). Rhys has Antoinette claim that 'words are no use' (111); she, of course, learned this as a child, where she 'prayed, but the words fell to the ground meaning nothing' (51). Yet Rhys writes novels full of meaning.[10] As she writes her novels, she moves back in time, increasing her readers' understanding of how her characters came to their sad, suppressed lives. Thus, in *Voyage in the Dark*, Rhys circles back towards her childhood. She concentrates on the back-breaking first love affair of Julia Martin, when she was nineteen, which is merely mentioned in *After Leaving Mr. Mackenzie*. The most striking shift that occurs between the second and third novel is Rhys's decision to write in the first person as she approaches childhood.

The original ending to *Voyage in the Dark* was rejected by Rhys's publisher. In this version, Anna Morgan dies of the abortion. While she is dying, she has flashbacks of defining moments in her past. A mother insists her daughter 'smile please' for a photographer; she then becomes 'ashamed' when her child begins 'to cry.'[11] The photography flashback switches to another one, in which a girl is hurt, a nurse is weeping, and an English aunt is saying she cannot understand the 'nigger' tune of 'melancholy.' The song is about a daughter reaching out to a mother who cannot hear her. This glimpse then fades into a scene of leaving the islands: 'I began to cry and it rolled down my face and splashed into the sea,' where the mountains are named with the echo of mourning, 'Morne Anglais over there and that's Morne Piton.' The scene of the lover watching the death by abortion reinforces these childhood memories of being required to suppress grief, for the man insists: 'my darling mustn't be sad' (Howells 382–4). Ironically, this ending was suppressed.

Rhys's novellas start in Europe and then return to the West Indies. They start with middle-aged women, then shift to late teenagers, and then return to the ten-year-old narrator of *Wide Sargasso Sea*. They start in the third person and return to the first. Anna becomes Antoinette and shares her first-person narration with another suppressed, grieving child, Edward Rochester. Antoinette and Edward are meant to recall Brontë's literary child, Jane Eyre. Michael Thorpe reveals the conscious strategy to layer Antoinette's childhood suffering on Jane Eyre's: 'The real life of both, as children, is driven inward by maltreatment or indifference' (181). In a letter to Evelyn Scott, Rhys describes the 'big idea' of *Voyage in the Dark* as being 'that the past exists – side by side with the present, not behind it; that what was – is' (*Letters* 24). Once again we experience Derrida's idea of synchrony. In another part of *Circumfession*, while writing as Jacques Derrida the French philosopher, he still forces syntax to convey a sense of something being incredible to 'Jackie' whom he describes as 'the child I remain this evening' (12). The trace, a sign of the absence of presence, is of the child. The child remains.

In *Voyage in the Dark*, Rhys strives to show that the past (child) and present (adult) exist simultaneously. Rhys makes Anna Morgan aware of her self-division: 'I was thinking it was funny I could giggle like that because in my heart I was always sad' (14). Men find her sadness unattractive, and thus she trains herself to suppress it and replace it with gaiety (21, 30, 33, 44). She learns to dress herself richly and beautifully, but the split is still apparent: she tells the shopkeepers that yes, she will purchase the dress and keep it on, but her 'face in the glass looked small and frightened' (25). The child is not yet fully silenced and erased. The two selves, now and then, woman and child, English and West Indian, throughout the novel are disassociated or, as Anna describes it, 'two things that [she] couldn't fit together' (67). Rhys reveals through Anna's experience the anxiety and disruption that occurs when one does not erase the childhood self.[12] Anna falls in love with Walter Jeffries, a man who has successfully 'killed' his inner child that haunts him and that he projects onto others. Jeffries is drawn to and yet needs to conquer this childish self when it appears in others.

As in the other novellas, Rhys depicts Anna's grief as immobilizing; Jeffries tells her not to be a 'stone,' while at the same time realizing, as he watches her face go 'stiff,' that she freezes like a child believing: 'It won't hurt until I move' (V 44). Like Rhys's other protagonists, Anna uses alcohol to make the 'paralysed feeling' go away. Initially, with Jeffries, not just the whiskey returns her mobility, but also telling stories about her childhood (45). Of course, she does not realize that this man does not care about what she felt as a child. In this context, Rhys associates Anna with the black community to stress the connection: children, blacks, and poor women are resident aliens and slaves to men like Jeffries. They labour in their master's economy. They lack legitimate status. Therefore, recalling what it was to see the world through her childhood eyes, Anna tells Jeffries about the 'slave-list' she saw in the West Indies that she can never forget (45). While recalling this list, Anna's childhood self hears her stepmother remarking that the sins of the fathers 'are visited upon the children unto the third and fourth generation' (46). The stepmother's words apply to the sexual arrangement between Anna and the paternal Jeffries, for while she serves him, he abuses her; while she loves him, he uses her. The slave list returns to haunt Anna after she has sex with Jeffries (48).

Rhys offers merely one line in the novella to suggest that Jeffries is a wounded child who has suppressed his grief. Jeffries of *Voyage in the Dark* is a precursor of Rochester of *Wide Sargasso Sea*, and while we only have one minor allusion to his own sad childhood, which has rendered him cruel, it is nonetheless telling: '"I disliked my father," Jeffries said. "I thought most people did"' (47). Rhys allows us to imagine why it is that certain figures seek to colonize and abuse others – foreigners and women. Significantly, Jeffries's one line becomes far more fully developed by Rhys when she constructs Rochester in *Wide Sargasso Sea*.

Jeffries strives to create a father-child relationship with his teenaged mistress in order to exorcise the sins of his father upon a child of the next generation. He renders her dependent and then rejects her. Her attraction for him is being and appearing childlike. Not only is she called 'kid' by everyone she encounters through the novel, but Anna's affair with Jeffries is also framed by childhood allusions: when he first plans to have sex with her, he takes her out to a dining room that has an attached bedroom. A virgin, Anna imagines this room as having 'a secret feeling – quiet, like a place where you crouch down when you are playing hide-and-seek' (*V* 21). At the end of the novel, Jeffries has tired of her and is now absent, but he has given her money for an abortion. Anna is haemorrhaging and hallucinating; she returns to the Masquerade of her West Indian childhood where she dreams of 'an exaggerated swaying lilting motion like a rocking horse' (158). The rocking horse of *Quartet* returns.[13]

In *Voyage in the Dark*, Rhys implies that the attraction Anna holds is not her sexuality; not once is her body eroticized by Rhys. Instead, she appeals to Jeffries as a child might to an abusive parent, exactly as Marya appeals to the Heidlers as a child they can abuse. Jeffries's affair with Anna is referred to by his cousin Vincent as 'baby-snatching' (73). He calls Anna 'the child' and 'infantile Anna' (69). Vincent writes Jeffries's rejection letter to Anna with the opening line: 'My Dear Infant.' This address, which couples affection with a reminder of her inarticulate status, sinks into her like 'fangs' (79–80). Jeffries himself tells Anna: 'you're only a baby' (44). Making the figurative literal, Rhys has a baby aborted at the end of the novel.

Like Rebecca West, Rhys uses the literal death of babies and children to convey the emotional death of the child-selves of her characters. Required by her publisher to change the ending in which Anna dies, Rhys altered Anna's death by offering instead an even worse redemption, for the grieving child is silenced. Anna's girlfriend and the doctor laugh because now Anna can start 'all over again,' which one may reasonably assume means being sexual prey for men with money. The death of the child, who has caused so much irrepressible grief, has one final flash as 'the ray of light' that comes in under the door and seems 'like the last thrust of remembering before everything is blotted out' (*V* 159).

Rhys takes the title of her next novella, *Good Morning, Midnight*, from an Emily Dickinson poem, which she uses as an epigraph: 'Good morning, Midnight! / I'm coming home'; the short paradoxical poem ends: 'But Morn didn't want me – now – / So good night, Day!' If one reads the poem as punning on morning / mourning, it expands the meaning beyond the narrative of the jilted lover. Rhys is coming home in her fiction, as we noted about *Voyage in the Dark*; however, she flees this darkness rather than greeting it with a grim 'Good Morning / Mourning.' In this fourth novel, Rhys suppresses almost all references to the West Indies. She turns away from childhood and re-focuses her attention on an aging European woman. The only intimacy she retains is the first-person narrator who cannot stop crying (*GMM* 14, 24–5, 37, 44, passim). The only event that does not cause Sasha Jensen to weep is past or prospective war (34). In an echo of Julia Martin's belief that the war was a fun time, Rhys stresses the disassociation that has a generation so suppressed that they no longer can hold themselves or their relationships together. Moreover, they cannot fathom the vicious cycle that whirls like a merry-go-round: suppressing grief and enabling war. A minor character thus exclaims: 'Ah, what will happen to this after-war generation?' (75) In contrast, the question Rhys asks is: ah, why won't this after-war generation look back to discover how they became so warlike?

Sasha finds the war an entertaining topic while feeling vulnerable because she has 'left [her] armour at home' (*GMM* 42). This is a telling comment, for Sasha constructs her armour to protect her at the home front and thus takes that battlefield self out into the world. She hears others as though she is at war: 'Those voices like uniforms – tinny, meaningless ... Those voices that they brandish like weapons' (44). Of course, if one experiences the world as a war zone, violence is the required response; as a woman, Sasha cannot release her suppressed feelings at a world war and so she merely fantasizes about wounding others: 'crack your little skull,' 'rip your abominable guts out' (45). Associating this behaviour not solely with women, but rather with being British, Rhys has Sasha resort to the emotional realm in order to wound others. Her plan: 'get this man to talk to me and tell me all about it, and then be so devastatingly English that perhaps I should manage to hurt him a little in return for all the many times I've been hurt' (62). When wounded, when the resultant grief is suppressed, one seeks to wound.[14]

The unnamed woman who runs the house for poor women in labour speaks to Sasha like a soldier, telling her to have 'courage.' Without any sign of the father, family, or friends, Sasha comes from a hotel room to this house, where she gives birth to a son who dies a week later 'in hospital' (*GMM* 49–52). This baby is a signifier for suppressed grief and thus symbolizes the death of the inner child for Sasha and for a whole society. A nurse questions the new mother: '"Well, why can't you sleep?" she says. "Does he cry, this young man?" "No, he hardly cries at all. Is it a bad sign, that he doesn't cry?" "Why no, not at all. A beautiful,

beautiful baby … But why can't you sleep?"' (51) The nurse assumes that the crying of a baby or a 'young man' will keep a woman up in the night, when, in fact, the mother yearns to hear and respond to her child's grief.

Rhys does not merely depict the haunting darkness of one woman's loss; she does not merely describe the dark haunting of the First World War. She writes of the dark shadow of the Second World War, which looms over the war to end all wars. Sasha buys a painting from a 'Jew.' He is an artist who serves drinks in Japanese cups, makes West African masks 'straight from the Congo,' and plays 'Martinique music.' Amid all of the allusions to a colonial and racist world scene swirling around in a novel published during the first year of the Second World War, Rhys has Julia unable to stop crying and the painter exclaim: '"I often want to cry. That is the only advantage women have over men – at least they can cry"' (*GMM* 76–8). Suppression is often configured as a supremely British trait by Rhys, but in this scene she gathers up a world into a man, an everyman who yearns to cry, but is prohibited. The story alludes to the world war that has passed and clearly anticipates the world war in process, and in between there is a child who cannot stop crying.

Yet the child who dominates *Good Morning, Midnight* is a cruel one. At a very early age it has learned the lessons of colonialism and racism and lives in the world as if it is a war zone. The Jewish man who is everyman, tells a story in response to the 'subject of weeping.' He tells about a woman from Martinique who is a 'half-negro – a mulatto.' He finds her in the hallway of the boarding house in which he stays. She weeps endlessly and begs for a drink. When he lifts her up, she is 'like something that has turned into stone' (78–80). He hears how the West Indian woman said to a little girl: '"Good afternoon"' and the child replied: '"I hate you and I wish you were dead"' (81). Rhys concludes this exchange within the story by a framing device in her own novella: Sasha and the Russian man, who have heard the story told by Everyman, kiss and he comments that he felt 'so sad' when she cried. Note Sasha's description: 'I kiss him. Two loud, meaningless kisses, like a French general when he gives a decoration. Nice boy' (82). The good soldier is a good boy. Rhys ensures that her readers make the connection, even if her characters do not, that the war begins on the home front. The domestic training in suppression anticipates the world war; tears held in check may become violence unleashed. The hurt child is the one who seeks war.

Sasha imagines the gigolo in the novel 'like a little boy [who] whistles when he is trying to keep his courage up – loud, clear, and pure';

however, he informs her that in fact this is the 'march of the Legion' (*GMM* 138). The good brave boy becomes the good brave soldier of the Foreign Legion. Rhys not only superimposes soldiers on boys; she also reveals the little girls behind the depressed women who wear 'protective armour' (84). Hence, Sasha's friend Lise yearns for another war so that she might be lucky and get killed. This admission leads to her account of an abusive home: 'She is afraid of her mother. When she was a little girl her mother beat her. "For anything, for nothing. You don't know. And all the time she says bad things to me. She likes to make me cry."'[15] Her friends respond with the advice to 'Cheer up' and they all collapse in laughter (111–12). This scene fades into the next, which is of Sasha, very pregnant and terrified to have the baby, giving an English lesson to a Russian man who reads out loud from *Lady Windermere's Fan*: 'The laughter, the horrible laughter of the world – a thing more tragic than all the tears the world has ever shed' (115). Then Rhys has this scene fade into the next, which is of the new mother with her dead baby: 'But my heart, heavy as lead, heavy as a stone' (116). The juxtaposition of these scenes stresses the correlation between an expectation that one suppress grief from childhood to parenthood and an expectation that one must simply laugh, despite knowing that it is horrible and tragic. Why must we laugh? Because then it is possible to maintain a position of power; grief is associated with weakness, vulnerability, being a child again. Hence, in *Wide Sargasso Sea* the child, Antoinette, while watching her home burn to the ground, realizes that of all her gathered attackers, 'the ones who laughed would be the worst' (36).

In *Good Morning, Midnight*, as in the other novels, there is a young man with whom the female protagonist might establish a meaningful relationship. When he walks with Sasha, he almost brings her to tears, for he says it feels like walking 'with a child' (62–7). He is desperate to articulate himself: 'Have you ever felt like this – as if you can't bear any more, as if you must speak to someone, as if you must tell someone everything or otherwise you'll die?' (61). However, as in the other novellas, the possibility of articulation becomes a near rape scene, a sneering comment about money, and a throwing of the self at the enemy. Making love becomes making hate. Rather than exchange terms of endearment, Sasha and the gigolo use their words to hurt one another. Significantly, both are wounded in the throat and, as noted in Rhys's other novellas, this is the site where grief can be suppressed or expressed. Sasha and the gigolo do not have a chance, for she is so hurt that she is inarticulate: 'Something in his voice has hurt me. I can't say anything. My throat hurts and I can't say anything.' Likewise, the gigolo has a 'long scar, going across his throat' (144–5). So he laughs about gang rapes in Morocco and she says: 'You and your wounds – don't you see how funny you are? You did make me laugh' (154). The gigolo runs away and she curls up in the foetal position weeping: 'Who is this crying? The same one who laughed on the landing, kissed him and was happy. This is me, this is myself, who is crying. The other – how do I know who the other is? She isn't me' (154). Rhys establishes here the split that in *Wide Sargasso Sea* will tear apart Antoinette Cosway long before she encounters Edward Rochester.

In *Wide Sargasso Sea*, Rochester notes that the silence and blankness his new wife uses to protect herself are 'poor weapons,' which are the exact terms Rhys applies to the fervent emotions of the orphaned Marya in her first novel, published almost forty years earlier (76). In *Wide Sargasso Sea*, both narrators begin their parts of the novel with war terminology. In the opening sentence of Part One, Antoinette refers to the necessity to 'close ranks' when there is trouble (15), and in the opening sentence of Part Two, the unnamed narrator, who is Edward Rochester of *Jane Eyre*, speaks of their courtship in military terms: 'the advance and retreat' (55). The marriage becomes warlike: Christophine (Antoinette's nurse) advises the bride, 'do battle for yourself'; Rochester confesses to his new wife that he feels that the tropical island of her childhood 'is [his] enemy' (96, 107). Long before she meets her British suitor, Antoinette learns to battle to survive; as a little girl, she believes in her 'stick' and, echoing a patriotic song, thinks: 'I can fight with this, if the worst comes to the worst I can fight to the end though the best ones fall' (31). However, as we learn, the magical stick cannot save the child.

Rhys uses doubling in *Wide Sargasso Sea*: she has Antoinette haunted by the black child, Tia, who functions as both an independent character and a shadow of Antoinette. This works on a variety of levels, for it is representative of the way in which colonialists project onto others, onto foreigners, their own suppressed childish, vulnerable, dependent selves. The black community, recently emancipated, reverses the violence and sets the former slave-owner's estate on fire. During the chaos, Antoinette catches sight of her former friend and runs towards her; in response, Tia throws a 'jagged stone' and it hits Antoinette full in the face. The two children gaze at one another as if staring at a 'looking-glass': the attacker's face is covered in 'tears' while her victim's face is covered in 'blood' (*WSS* 38).[16] In this scene between the two girls Rhys creates an unforgettable image of the effects of suppressed grief and its relation to violence. In Antoinette's madness, Tia is the childhood friend to whom she leaps, imagining that the 'hard stones' are the childhood pool where she and Tia swam (155). When she leaps from the roof of Rochester's family home, there is no pool. She hits the stones.

One of Tia's few qualities that we learn about is that she never shows her tears and she walks with bare feet on 'sharp stones' (*WSS* 20). Tia is the *toi*, the 'you' in Antoinette's name that distinguishes her from her mother, Annette. The mother is cold and cruel to her daughter, coldness being one of Rhys's signifiers for suppressed grief (17, 19, 23). The mother's constant rejection of her daughter leads Antoinette to slowly harden: Antoinette feels that she 'never wanted to move again. Everything would be worse if [she] moved' (20). In the context of transforming into stone, Rhys makes clear the attraction of a little survivor like Tia, who no longer expresses grief, but instead appears all powerful; she just needs an enemy. When the two little girls fight, Antoinette sits on a 'stone,' with her back to Tia, 'cold' and 'hating her' (21). Their advance towards friendship becomes a hasty retreat to their own sides; they close ranks.

Rhys strives to reveal the suppression of grief, immobilization, and resultant cruelty of characters in both the white and the black communities. How can we assess who has suffered more: Tia or Antoinette? Rochester or Christophine?[17] The suffering makes Tia violent; it makes Antoinette's mother crazy; it makes Antoinette violent and crazy; it makes Rochester sadistic. Only Christophine escapes such grim distortion. Thus, Christophine's final lines, 'Read and write I don't know. Other things I know' (*WSS* 133), stress her Creole position as transplanted and now indigenous. Like the nurse in Ford Madox Ford's *Parade's End*, Christophine speaks the patois of loving parent to beloved child; this is not a read or written language. Notably, John Caputo describes Derrida's position as Creole in his study of *Circumfession*: 'Derrida is a graft or transplant, always being uprooted and planted somewhere else, made more welcome in a foreign land' (*Prayers* 305).[18]

When Antoinette is separated from the loving Creole of Christophine, her nightmares begin. Antoinette attends a Catholic boarding school in Jamaica. While in the walled convent, she dreams: 'He turns and looks at me, his face black with hatred, and when I see this I begin to cry. He smiles slyly. "Not here, not yet," he says, and I follow him weeping [...] We are no longer in the forest but in an enclosed garden surrounded by a stone wall and the trees are different trees' (*WSS* 50). The nightmare depicts the English garden of Rochester's childhood home, which traps him just as it will imprison Antoinette; thus, Rhys suggests that childhood trauma scripts the self for adult suffering. During their honeymoon, Rhys has Rochester echo the hateful words of the nightmare character: '"Not now [...] Not yet"' (70). In *Wide Sargasso Sea*, the cruel husband, whether in dream or actuality, is also a hurt child who has disassociated from his weeping childhood self and thus lives enclosed within an impenetrable stone wall. The garden, a kind of lost paradise, is where the wounded child was once whole.

Rhys establishes the terms of Rochester's childhood trauma as soon as he begins his narrative in Part Two. Thus, the journey to the honeymoon house where the marriage will become a war, the love will become hate, is haunted by references to little boys, unwritten letters from a wounded son to an uncaring father, stone, and a sense of being enclosed like the dream garden. He imagines the hills 'would close in on you' (*WSS* 59). There is a 'boy holding fresh horses' at the outset (55). Then three little boys come to look at the wedding party; the smile from Rochester causes the smallest one to 'cry' (56). Then the 'boy brought the horses to a large stone' (58). And seeing a stone road and ascending stone steps, all indicative of his stony heart, Rochester reaches the house and collides 'with a boy coming in the opposite direction' (60). The boyhood of Rochester haunts him, collides with him. The boy who yearns for his father's love shadows every move the adult self makes.

During the journey to the honeymoon house, Rochester notes his new wife's 'sad, dark alien eyes.' He does not realize that he is gazing into a mirror where the child within him, the resident alien, is reflected. Instead, he imagines writing a letter to his father. The men call Rochester 'master' (*WSS* 57), while Antoinette tells him that she wanted to die as a child. He asks why she did not tell anyone before about her desire to suicide. She replies: 'There was no one to tell, no one to listen' (76).[19] Antoinette's sharing of her desire to die has the power to save both herself and Rochester, for it reveals the contradiction at the centre of childhood grief: the desire to live, articulated by killing off the child-self or removing its rights. The present self turns around to see the past self's tears, but if there is no one for the child to tell, one may write it for readers when the child becomes an adult. Derrida believes that the writer 'absents himself better,' that is, 'expresses himself' more effectively and thus 'renounces violence' (*WD* 102). I hear in this statement that the adult, rational self becomes absent in writing, while the expressive child-self can speak up, and this process weakens one's wish to be in control, the master, the conqueror, the one who uses violence.

The innovation of *Wide Sargasso Sea* is that there are, in fact, four first-person narrators: Rochester's 'I' as a child and 'I' as an adult; Antoinette's 'I' as a child and 'I' as an adult. The traces of the suppressed, absent, grieving, childhood 'I's provide 'the clue' whereby Rhys sought to reveal the meaning of the 'childish.' In the section of her autobiography that she left unrevised before her death, Rhys writes: '*You are aware of course that what you are writing is childish, has been said before. Also is dangerous under the circumstances.*' And then the reply: 'Yes, most of it is childish. But I have not written for so long that all I can force myself to do is to write, to write. I must trust that out of that will come the pattern, the clue that can be followed' (*Smile Please* 133).

It is the inarticulate, silenced child Antoinette who accepts Rochester's proposal. Despite advice from her aunt, despite knowing the danger of her acceptance, Antoinette agrees silently, with a nod of the head, to marry Rochester. He refers to their marriage as a 'bargain' and she agrees (*WSS* 66). This is the term he imagines using with his father in reference to the family pressure to sell his soul: 'is it such a bad bargain?' (59) Rhys makes it clear that what motivates the marriage and its destruction are the familial scars that mark the daughter and the son. Thus, the adult selves carry traces of the childhood selves they know are there; yet they cannot truly know them because they are alien.[20] By reversing the terms and supplying the details of Rochester's destructive family, Rhys suggests that the men with money in the other novellas were similarly hurt children who cannot imagine relationships based on love because they did not experience love as children. They have relationships with women based on money because they are commodified children.

Rochester marries Antoinette for her dowry because he is an unloved child seen as an expense, a financial burden. With irony, Rhys has him think figures like Christophine are alien without ever realizing that they have deep similarities. Christophine might be bought and sold by foreigners such as the Cosways and Masons, but Rochester is objectified as a comparable financial transaction within his own home. His only value within his family is monetary. The son in Rebecca West's novel, discussed in the next chapter, also is a son whose parents treated him as a financial figure rather than as a child.

In *Wide Sargasso Sea*, with the characteristic repetition of negatives that reveal his sense of being worthless, a nothing, Rochester imagines writing to his father: 'I have a modest competence now. I will never be a disgrace to you or to my dear brother the son you love. No begging letters, no mean requests. None of the furtive shabby manoeuvres of a younger son' (59).

The letter Rochester imagines shows his twisted self-knowledge: 'I know now you planned this because you wanted to be rid of me. You had no love at all for me. Nor had my brother.' As he fantasizes about this letter, he guzzles rum 'mild as mother's milk or father's blessing' (133). Alcohol becomes the soothing drink that assists in keeping the grief at bay. His subsequent thoughts reveal the double-I speaking: 'I thought, I have been poisoned. But it was a dull thought, like a child spelling out the letters of a word he cannot read, and which if he could would have no meaning or context' (113). Rochester has drunk not poison, but rather a love potion. What makes the story tragic is that Antoinette loves him, but he cannot feel love; he can only feel childhood abandonment, a grief he suppresses while allowing hate to come forth. The childhood 'I' who needs to cry is suppressed by the adult 'I' who transfers the pain to another, in this case, Antoinette.

What makes Rochester such a disturbing character is that he cannot see that his present is utterly constructed by his past. He can articulate it with the words of an adult, but he cannot feel the inarticulate emotions. In a recall of *Hamlet*, Rochester is acting in a play that was written by an abusive parent and, instead of exiting, he performs his own trauma over and over again. Hence, he calls his own courtship 'a faultless performance' (*WSS* 64). The disassociated self of Rochester views the drama in a split way, so that Antoinette is both the villain and the victim of the piece. He sees her as the one holding the strings and the one who is the puppet pulled this way and that by others. The theme of the marionettes can be found throughout Rhys's novellas. In *Quartet*, during a violent scene of grief, Marya explains: 'She had felt like a marionette, as though something outside her were jerking strings that forced her to scream and strike. Heidler, weeping, was a marionette, too' (82). In *After Leaving Mr Mackenzie*, the name of Julia is surprisingly transformed by another abusive man into the rhyme for 'Antoinetta' that Rochester uses for his wife: 'Look here Julietta' (83). In *Wide Sargasso Sea*, after rejecting his wife and her feelings, which allows him to suppress his own childhood grief, Rochester sees Antoinette as 'a doll' who has 'a marionette quality' (123). He has fully internalized the paternal and colonial position that objectifies individuals. Rhys's characters never discover the strings that render them little more than puppets in a tragic show scripted when they were children.

In the present, Rochester promises 'peace' to Antoinette, but the past has already promised them war (*WSS* 66). During the same evening, he shows the potential to be a loving husband and realizes that these are the acts of someone 'young.' He takes Antoinette in his arms as he sees her turning to stone, her 'mouth was set in a fixed smile,' and he rocks her 'like a child' (70). This is a brief childhood exchange between the two to reveal what has been hidden and lost, for they cannot sustain such intimacy. As Rochester puts it: 'I was young then. A short youth was mine' (70). The child Rochester rocks the child Antoinette, but then they both grow up. Rhys has her readers look through Rochester's eyes as he sees his wife as the woman scripted by the past and the woman she could become if allowed to return to a time before she was hurt as a child: 'The cold light was on her and I looked at the sad droop of her lips, the frown between her thick eyebrows, deep as if it had been cut with a knife [...] As I watched, hating, her face grew smooth and very young again, she even seemed to smile' (114). Antoinette develops the disassociating scar down the centre of her forehead, just like her mother's. Rochester becomes a rejecting, paternal figure, just like his father.

Rochester returns to childhood in destructive ways. He thus becomes susceptible to Daniel and Amélie; both are figures who want revenge along with some of his money. He is vulnerable to their attack. Rhys makes Daniel Cosway the West Indian parallel to Rochester: he too has lost his mother; he too is a rejected son; he too is a younger brother resentful of the adored older sibling; he too is viciously in search of money. What makes his predicament worse is the label of bastard and the interracial blend of his parents, which was considered unacceptable at this time. However, Rochester, as a split self, finds this figure horrifying and utterly seductive at the same time, because, of course, Daniel's story echoes the voices that babble incessantly in Rochester's wounded mind (WSS 139–40).[21]

Like Rochester, Daniel's 'heart is like a stone for the grief.' The effect of his letter is to render Rochester even more stone-like: 'I walked stiffly nor could I force myself to think.' He finds relief in violence: he associates orchids with Antoinette and his gesture is to trample them (WSS 82). Thus, Antoinette laughs crazily and says: 'You see. That's how you are. A stone' (122). After Daniel's words contaminate Rochester's already contaminated mind and Antoinette tries to cure him with her love potion, he turns to Amélie as an antidote to the poison of real feelings. She provides strategies for suppressing grief. Not only does she offer him laughter, meaningless sex, and the chance to destroy Antoinette's love for him, but she also plays the lost mother and treats him like a baby: 'She cut some of the food up and sat beside me and fed me as if I were a child' (115). Both Daniel and Amélie are able to manipulate Rochester because they activate his sense of self in the childhood home, which is well known and thus feels more safe and secure than the frightening possibility of love and grief with Antoinette.

When mad and imprisoned in Rochester's British attic, Antoinette yearns to return to the defining moment when the suffering of childhood became so intense that she turned to stone, became a soldier. It is poignant that she imagines that, if only she could love Tia again as a flesh-and-blood child, a grieving child, and thus a joyful one, she could return to herself. For when she and Tia become enemies, Rhys stresses that Antoinette does not lose a friend, she loses herself. She has her first prophetic nightmare of Rochester and realizes 'nothing would be the same' (*WSS* 23). The word *nothing* offers the key to the childhood suffering that fuels the adult cruelty in the novella.[22] It is the most dominant word in Rochester's narrative; thus, he states: 'There was nothing I knew, nothing to comfort me' (96). One might argue that he feels this way because he is in the West Indies and his Creole wife has gone mad,' but, in fact, these are the defining terms of his whole life. In describing his feelings or lack thereof, Rochester uses negation: 'Tears – nothing! Words – less than nothing. As for the happiness I gave her, that was worse than nothing' (78). After negating grief, negating articulation, and negating happiness, Rochester describes his feelings for Antoinette as 'savage,' a word he applies to all that is alien, which makes it the perfect term for love. He believes the feeling to be lust, so that he can degrade it and himself. But at the end of the novella, he calls the little boy who is crying for love of him a 'half-savage boy' (140). Thus, Rhys reveals it is a term for the child within the man, the child who can care and cry. It is this child who must be civilized. Rochester wants to suppress savage feelings such as love and grief.

Rochester yearns to tell Antoinette about England, his home, but his hurt wife has become rigid and stony, and she negates the possible communion between them: 'her ideas were fixed [...] I could not change them and probably nothing would.' Using 'nothing' once more, Rochester expresses again his sense of rejection: 'Nothing that I told her influenced her at all.' He imagines her as an 'obstinate child.' This is a dangerous place for Rochester – not being heard, not being made to feel like someone worthwhile. It causes him to shift into the parental role as if he is dealing with a wilful child who must be stopped and silenced. The feeling of nothingness is too well known and too painful for him. Rhys expresses it as an almost incoherent pile-up of negatives, all of which lead to a yearning for violence: 'Desire, Hatred, Life, Death came very close in the darkness. Better not know how close. Better not think, never for a moment. Not close. The same.' He repeatedly offers her safety, while dreaming of murder. Yet the final negative is the truth for both of them: 'not close,' not intimate, not knowing each others' stories (*WSS* 78–9). Earlier, Rochester writes a letter to his father and tucks it into a drawer; he thinks about what he cannot write, namely, that the alien island means 'nothing' to him and neither does 'she, the girl' he plans to marry (64). He does not realize that the alien is, in fact, the suppressed, grieving child within him.

Yet Rhys offers some hope, as is true in the other novellas. In *Wide Sargasso Sea*, Rochester has an epiphany about the alien island. He understands that it is an internal landscape he has not yet lost; it is merely hidden within him as a paradise where feelings are natural and reciprocated. Rochester looks out at the tropical landscape, Rhys's location for grief, and imagines: 'It was a beautiful place – wild, untouched, above all untouched, with an alien, disturbing, secret loveliness. And it kept its secret. I'd find myself thinking, "What I see is nothing – I want what it *hides* – that is not nothing"' (*WSS* 73). Rochester sounds like a disbelieving child who must stamp his foot and demand with a double negative that a parent hear him: 'not nothing.' The child wants his parents to know that this beautiful landscape is within their child; it is something; it is worth knowing. However, years of hearing and experiencing his worthlessness according to his parents has rendered only the word *nothing* resonant to Rochester. This tropical space has become 'alien.'

As a child, Rochester was forced to suppress his feelings: 'How old was I when I learned to hide what I felt? A very small boy. Six, five, even earlier. It was necessary, I was told, and that view I have always accepted' (*WSS* 85). He admits that the people and the landscape of this island are thus 'unreal' to him, for his reality is constructed on suppressed feelings. Rochester gazes out at this garden, which like the little child hides something; he gazes into an interior landscape, one that is full of hidden feelings; yet the tragedy is he cannot see what it holds, because he has been taught that his feelings are nothing. Antoinette's hidden child is also imprisoned in this beautiful garden. As Daniel tells Rochester, when she was a little girl, 'she hide herself' (80). Regardless, Rochester tells her: 'You have never learned to hide' (109). He does not understand that she comes out of hiding for him, for love. He cannot bear that she reflects back to him the hurt, alien child within him.

What makes *Wide Sargasso Sea* particularly terrifying is that Rochester cannot allow himself the danger of feelings; yet he wants to cling to

Antoinette because he knows that she is the key to opening up that locked garden within. His two selves are so disassociated that he can no longer bring them into conjunction; the childhood self of feelings wants her to cry, so that he can be her protector; she can be a child with him: 'Antoinetta – I can be gentle too. Hide your face. Hide yourself but in my arms' (136). For him she is the access point into that hidden place, but the split self, the domineering parent self, cannot afford to have that key anywhere other than locked away. Thus, she must be imprisoned in the attic of his childhood home, and the other self thinks: '(*But it is lost, that secret, and those who know it cannot tell it.*) Not lost. I had found it in a hidden place and I'd keep it, hold it fast. As I'd hold her' (138). As enclosed in parentheses, the secret cannot be told because it belongs to grieving children, and they are doubly inarticulate with their lumps in their throats and their childish modes of expression. So he will trap her, hide her away. She has married him and he believes, because he is nothing, that she 'will have nothing' (140).

At the end of Rochester's narrative, the boy who haunts the beginning, who is clearly there as he and Antoinette journey to the honeymoon house, this inner child becomes powerful with desperation as the psyche recognizes that he will be left behind. Rochester can fully become Antoinette's heartless jailer only by abandoning this child, just as his father abandoned him. Antoinette is now considered mad by her husband, yet she manages to tell him an incredibly powerful and important story in response to his angry question about the 'nameless boy.' The child is as nameless as Rochester in this story; he leaned 'his head against the clove tree and sobbed.' Rochester hears this weeping as 'heartbreaking sobs,' but it creates within him a desire to strangle the child 'with pleasure' (*WSS* 140). Antoinette tells this child's story, which is the story of the child within Rochester before he recognized that he was nothing, before he encountered the world not as a person, but as a thing, to be bought and sold: '"He asked me when we first came if we – if you – would take him with you when we left. He doesn't want any money. Just to be with you. Because –' she stopped and ran her tongue over her lips, "he loves you very much. So I said you would. Take him. Baptiste has told him that you will not. So he is crying"' (140). Rochester's response is full of rejection and rage. He cannot love this child; he cannot hear his wife. He does not remember far back enough to a time when the world was about love, not money. Rhys has this child dominate the end of Rochester's narrative and she uses the key word, *nothing*, for his sense of self: 'That stupid boy followed us, the basket balanced on his head. He used the back of his hand to wipe away his tears. Who would have thought that any boy would cry like that. For nothing. Nothing' (142). The boy is crying for Rochester, who believes himself to be nothing. Yet as Arnold Davidson puts it: 'the child weeps for everything, everything' (38).

How does Rhys translate childhood grief into terms beyond articulation, so that, paradoxically, we can understand? She uses the loving patois of Christophine, the maternal figure who can hear and accept grief.[23] Antoinette reverts to the simple terms of childhood to introduce Christophine as her 'da' (*WSS* 61). The nurse can speak English and French and the language of the other Jamaican servants, but when she talks to the child Antoinette, she uses a loving Creole. Creole is an encompassing word that overrides distinctions: adjective, noun, black, white, all of the flora and fauna that flourish in the West Indies and elsewhere. Creole is the language Rhys uses for the terms of endearment constantly uttered by Christophine to her Creole daughter Antoinette: '*Doudou, ché cocotte. Ti moun. Doudou ché. Do do l'enfant do*' (61, 93, 123). This is the only novella of the five that depicts a loving parent / child relationship; Antoinette hugs and kisses the woman who she knows loves her like a daughter (76). She finds her smell 'so warm and comforting' (89). She goes to her when her world falls further apart: '*I came to you. Oh Christophine. O Pheena, Pheena, help me*' (120). And Christophine describes for Rochester the way she cares for this hurt child / woman: 'You want to know what I do? I say *doudou*, if you have trouble you are right to come to me. And I kiss her. It's when I kiss her she cry – not before. It's long time she hold it back, I think. So I let her cry' (124). In her madness, as Antoinette sets Thornfield on fire, she calls to Christophine for help (154). In this sensual, verbal, way, Rhys moves beyond English – both society and language – in order to take what has been labelled nothing and show its value. Instead of insisting that she dry her tears and be a good soldier, the nurse speaks Creole terms of affection that are like the kisses one gives to a crying child.

In *Wide Sargasso Sea*, Rhys tries to teach us not to say mountain – it is 'an ugly word' – instead, we must say in Creole: '*Morne*' (137).

3 Grieving the Child of the Shell-Shocked Soldier: Rebecca West's *The Return of the Soldier*

In *The Return of the Soldier*, we see a significant shift in the portrayal of the grieving child. While Conrad and Rhys position the sadness of childhood as foreign, West places it in the very centre of a British estate. In Conrad's *Under Western Eyes*, not only is the child as foreign to British readers as Russia, but the child is recalled only by adults; it is not a character in its own right. In Rhys's novellas, the child-self becomes more separate from the adult in that her protagonists are pregnant and sometimes even give birth. Yet the child is aborted or dies very soon after being born. In her final novel, using the narrative voice of the child Antoinette, Rhys breaks this pattern and brings childhood to life. Antoinette, however, maintains the position of alien within her own home, where she is rejected by her mother, and within Rochester's home, where she is seen as an alien because she is from the West Indies and because she is mentally ill. The child-self thus takes up residence in Rhys's final novel, yet she never is given proper rights, owing to her alien status. In West's novel, the child dies at the age of two, but a cousin of the father narrates the story, a cousin who is able to tell the story not only of the dead two-year-old, but also of the father's childhood, because they grew up together.

At the beginning of the novel, the father, Chris Baldry, has suffered shell shock in trench warfare, and he manifests his trauma by mentally retreating fifteen years to the time of his first romance. His cousin, Jenny Baldry, reflects throughout the novel on the death of the son; Chris's own childhood; the soldier's memory loss, which erases fifteen years of his life, including his marriage; and his return to his first love. This overlapping exploration of the stages of a man's life foreground the role of the child in the making of the adult. No longer is the child foreign: rather, he is right at home. The grief enters not only because of the death of the child in the home of a British estate, but also because of the emotional death of the soldier on the home front of the First World War. West has us look through the eyes of shell shock: 'The face that looked out of the dimness to him was very white; her upper lip was lifted over her teeth in a distressed grimace. And it was immediately plain as though he had shouted it that this sad mask meant nothing to him. He knew, not because memory had given him any insight into her heart but because there is an instinctive kindliness in him which makes him wise about all suffering, that it would hurt her if he asked if this was his wife, but his body involuntarily began a gesture of inquiry before he realized that that too would hurt her and he checked it half-way. So, through a silence, he stood before her slightly bent, as though he had been maimed' (*RS* 24).

In *The Return of the Soldier*, published in 1918, Rebecca West's good soldier is this man: perfectly fit, strong, young, powerful; yet he is maimed.[1] A smile appears as a grimace; silence is a shout; the body moves before the mind can stop it; thus, the disjunction between past and present reveals the soldier's internal wound. Derrida describes this way of reading as a kind of wound: 'The incision of deconstruction, which is not a voluntary decision or an absolute beginning, does not take place just anywhere, or in an absolute elsewhere. An incision, precisely, it can be made only according to lines of force and forces of rupture' already present in the 'discourse to be deconstructed' (*P* 82). This way of reading, by means of a wound that is sewn up and undone, that has scarred over, but still causes a 'phantom burning,' and that is positioned on the margin, the background, the offstage, is highly applicable to West's novella, because she ensures that the force of rupture within the self, caused by the war, is already present in the victim, Chris Baldry, owing to childhood wounding aggravated as he grows into the good soldier his father wants him to be. The incision into *The Return of the Soldier* can occur at a variety of moments in the narrative, yet they all open up to the same inner trauma linking childhood and war.

While shell-shocked, Chris returns to a symbolic boyhood. He loses his memory of the present and returns to an idealized past before he became a man. He forgets that society, represented by his oppressive family estate, Baldry Court, and Kitty, the wife that now adorns it, require him to forget childhood in order to be a good soldier. Being a good soldier means he must remember not only the war, but also the death of his two-year-old son.[2] The two are profoundly related in the book: the literal death of the child suggests the symbolic death that Chris endured during his own childhood. At the end of the novella, when he has undergone a simultaneous poison and cure, Chris no longer walks 'loose-limbed like a boy'; he now moves with the 'hard-tread' of a soldier (*RS* 90). The cure for the sickness of returning to boyhood requires Chris to fully confront, do battle with, his loss. The cure that returns his manhood also returns him to no-man's-land. A psychiatrist is called in to cure Chris's memory loss and his shell shock, and, surprisingly, he assists the soldier in grieving the death of his young son, a trauma that occurred before the war. Chris's memory returns as he suffers through the unbearable loss of his child; now he is well enough to return to the front lines.

Rebecca West was not only a novelist, but also a prolific journalist. Her critical work supports a reading of her novella as concerned with a lack of language to express grief, beginning in childhood and reinforced through societal training.[3] West presents R.C. Sherriff and Siegfried Sassoon as upper-class writers trained by their society to have 'no words to express their agony but the insipid vocabulary of their education' (Hynes 443). *The Return of the Soldier* details the suffering of characters taught to feel only superficially and given a paucity of language to convey the depths of suffering brought about by suppressed childhoods and world war. In another review, West ironically employs high-society terms while evoking the war: 'Both Mr Waugh and Mr Byron are under twenty-six. It is sobering to reflect that had they committed the indiscretion of being born ten years earlier, they would probably be lying dead in the mud somewhere in France, and these books would not be' (Orel 47). There is quite a gap between the euphemistic terms 'sobering' and 'indiscretion' and the more historically accurate ones 'lying dead' and 'mud.' These gaps are explored relentlessly in *Return of the Soldier*.

Derrida writes of his attempt to express wounding only to discover that his 'language' is 'circumcised' (*C* 71).[4] Thus, he returns to the baby, the nursling, the inarticulate, infant-self by means of following the tracks, the traces seen in the 'outside' happening to others, so that, paradoxically, he can see himself. He describes this process of 'the wound of circumcision in which I return to myself, gather myself,' but he hints, too, at the potential dark side of this infant pain, for it also leads him to 'cultivate and colonize hell' (103–4). Derrida and all the modernists in this study investigate how childhood wounding often leads to a need to oppress others, creating and cultivating the hells of colonies and wars.

In West's autobiographical novel of childhood, *The Fountain Overflows*, the family relocates to the house the father lived in as a child as if they are re-enacting the drama that led to his failure as a parent. West has the child, Rose, describe the children's feelings about their mother in striking terms: 'we felt about her as a soldier in a besieged citadel might feel about a comrade who is meditating desertion' (*FO* 66). These allusions to the military are common in the book. In a scene where Rose is at the piano, West establishes the sickly bond between the treatment of children at home and of adults abroad: 'Cousin Jock took my wrist and put my arm down by my side. It was a gentle movement yet extremely brutal. It told me that I had no rights, that I was a child' (103). In *1900*, West's memoir of the turn of the century, she speaks of parenting in condemnatory terms. She discusses the abuse that takes place in upper-class schools, well known by the fathers, who nonetheless send their sons to the same institutions, knowing they too will suffer, but making 'no effort to change the pattern' (124). An inarticulate acceptance of abuse is part of the legacy passed on to children.

In *Return of the Soldier*, West reverses this trend: she gives the shell shock victim, the 'frightened boy,' a narrative voice with which to speak. In contrast, the British government silenced shell-shocked men, seen as traitors, by killing them: 'During the period from the first day of the war until the end of March 1920 the British shot 345 men' (Hynes 214). Chris Baldry, a victim of shell shock, becomes a literary figure for Rebecca West, but in her novella a soldier is not only a boy or a man; he must be both and remember both. Carl Rollyson, commenting on West's pre–First World War newspaper articles, reveals that for West: 'Art and criticism were absolutely essential to the survival of civilization' because a 'humanity that forgets its art also forgets its collective memory of what holds humanity together and is amnesiac' (18). In *The Return of the Soldier*, West depicts an amnesiac soldier whose memory loss exposes the way in which his loved ones have forgotten what holds humanity together.

Derrida draws on the idea of amnesia to express his fears of what criticism or philosophy may become if it overwrites the child-self. His colleague, Geoffrey Bennington plans to write a book on deconstruction, a database that can anticipate and generate anything that Derrida may have written or may write. Derrida responds that he will produce an internal margin within this summarizing text that cannot possibly be assimilated by the other philosopher. Bennington takes up the challenge and writes *Derridabase*, but after reading the marginal *Circumfession*, he admits a gracious defeat. Early on in his margin, Derrida writes that his philosopher friend is 'forgetting me on the pretext of understanding me, and it is as if I were trying to oblige him to recognize me and come out of this amnesia of me' (*C* 33).

The initial scene of *The Return of the Soldier* immediately foregrounds memory, examining where we locate our recollections and how we hide them from ourselves and from others. The story opens up mid-conversation; while the topic of the dialogue is a missing soldier, the setting is the nursery of a missing child. The two absences, seemingly unrelated through most of the novella, become fundamentally connected as the story reaches its climactic ending.[5] The absent soldier's wife, Kitty, is refusing to be worried about the lack of a letter from her husband at war. Her response is jarring, for she boldly states that he has not written because he does not have any exciting war stories to tell: 'Besides, if he'd been anywhere interesting, anywhere where the fighting was really hot, he'd have found some way of telling me' (*RS* 3). There is a third absence signalled at the opening of the novel: a missing letter. The wife believes a letter has not been sent because there is no exciting news to share, as though her husband's experience at war is a thrilling adventure with lulls of peaceful drudgery. As the story unfolds, we learn that the letter is not written because Chris is shell-shocked. He has lost his memory of the past fifteen years and has been temporarily discharged. The soldier's unwritten letter implies that he cannot write his trauma – and certainly not to a society, represented by Kitty, that expects a story, a newsflash, a titillating account of masculinity in action, history being made.

Communication is at risk right from the start: the wife does not know how to read the censored statement from a two-week-old letter written 'Somewhere in France,' nor can she complete her sentences when they contain emotional material. While Kitty refuses to worry about the missing letter (which implies a missing solider), West complicates her statement by ending it with an extended dash: 'if a woman began to worry in these days because her husband hadn't written to her for a fortnight—!' (*RS* 3). Similarly, when Kitty contemplates the death of her child, West once again ends her statement with the extended dash: 'I wish Chris wouldn't have it kept as a nursery when there's no chance—' (4). The reader is left to consider the completion of Kitty's sentences and the underlying feelings she cannot articulate.

Kitty must confront Margaret, who is her husband's first love and the only one he remembers in his shell-shocked state. At first, Margaret initially appears to the high-society wife Kitty as a conniving woman from the lower classes. In this moment, Kitty uses language to wound; she speaks with 'the hardness of a woman who sees before her the curse of women's lives' (*RS* 11). She 'brutally' permits 'a silence to fall' (12). What motivates Kitty to speak is 'disgust' (13). The narrator, Chris's cousin Jenny, who also lives at Baldry Court, hopes that Kitty will let Margaret go 'without scaring her too much with words' (13). In Kitty's gloved hands, language is violent. She is hard, brutal, disgusted, and scary. Her use of language is so malicious that at one point Jenny shakes Kitty violently in order to silence her (31). Kitty is the woman Chris marries; Margaret is the first woman Chris loves and loses. Margaret speaks in a different way; her language resonates with grief. When she tells the women about Chris's condition, she seems to 'swallow something' and she speaks 'gently' (11). West uses Margaret to detail the conflict one has when articulating grief; hence the lump in her throat she must swallow in order to speak. She is an effective narrative device for demonstrating the complexities and contradictions of the modernist project when telling the story of grief's suppression.

David Krell notes that the throat, 'this sleeved site, so susceptible, so vulnerable,' is suppressed by philosophers from Plato to Hegel. However, as part of Derrida's philosophy of mourning, the throat corresponds with one's most intimate self, and exposure of this site causes feelings of 'rage and shame that would be appropriate to the full frontal exposure' (101). In *The Return of the Soldier*, West has Kitty imagine adulterous relations between Margaret and Chris, when, in fact, the infidelity occurs in the grieving, intimate throat.

In 'Tympan' his project being to 'write otherwise,' Derrida writes one column and puts it beside another column of material taken from Michel Leiris's autobiography (164). Leiris's column has the mother telling the child to keep quiet; he relates this to the danger of the inner ear being pierced. Leiris superimposes these two sites: 'a durable suture is thus formed between the throat and the tympanum,' since both 'are subject to a fear of being injured, besides both belonging to the same cavernous domain' (157–8). In the column beside this one, Derrida writes: 'It is the organ whose structure (and the suture that holds it to the throat) produces the pacifying lure of organic indifference. To forget it – and in so doing to take shelter in the most familial of dwellings – is to cry out for the end of organs, of others' (156). These are key concerns of Rebecca West: the danger of forgetting; the threat of indifference; the babyish retreat (pacifying) into the social, domestic tradition; all by means of listening to the status quo to the point where it becomes a kind of subtle violence, crying out for the end of self-articulation and the end of the recognition of otherness. Derrida undoes the suture; he opens it, opens up the lips of the wound that are the tympanum and throat.

Kitty cannot understand Margaret's apparent grief or her words. Margaret says that Chris is 'hurt' and his wife quickly tries to suppress this term and supply another: '"Wounded, you mean?"' (*RS* 11). It is a crucial distinction, because we discover that Chris is actually hurt. What hurts him is the fact that his parents would have sacrificed him in order to save their business interests; what hurts him is the death of his child. He hurts; he does not have a war wound. Not only a portion is damaged, the whole of the man is shocked and shattered. Putting Chris back together requires 're-membering' the whole, not only one part. Rebecca West's contrast of Margaret's and Kitty's terms encourages a rethinking of Chris's shell-shocked condition, which we ultimately learn involves an inability to grieve not only for his suffering at war, but for his suffering at home. To whom do we address letters about lost children and about suppressed grief? Chris cannot remember.

In *The Work of Mourning* Derrida muses on a double figure for loss: 'death and the immobilized monument,' which are 'two faces or two silences of the same forgetting' (96). With the loss of the childhood self and the child, one immobilized and the other dead, the soldier will appear as a double self throughout the novel, seen through the eyes of his first love, Margaret, and seen through the eyes of his wife, Kitty. The narrator, Jenny, is a vital character, for she can see both. Margaret perceives Chris's anguish; Kitty thinks he is 'pretending' (*RS* 31). And Jenny acts as a third, whose love for Chris renders her implicated and unreliable.

In *The Return of the Soldier*, our first introduction to the symbolic setting of the house is the nursery, which is described doubly: according to its present state, on the first day of spring, and according to its past, when the child was still alive: the sunlight is so bright 'that in the old days a fat fist would certainly have been raised to point out the new translucent glories of the rosebuds; it was lying in great pools on the blue cork floor and the soft rugs, patterned with strange beasts; and it threw dancing beams, that should have been gravely watched for hours' (3). The narrator, Jenny, evokes the spectral perspective of the child, so that she sees the room through his eyes, which can no longer see. On one level, the nursery functions as a mode of expressing what Chris cannot feel. Because Baldry Court is Chris's childhood home, this nursery contains the double absence of his own childhood and then his own child. An early indication that Chris's grief is building rather than being relieved appears in the nursery, for the room is 'kept in all respects as though there were still a child in the house' (3). The narrator is also in denial about the missing child, for she confesses: 'I had not meant to enter [the nursery] again after the child's death, but I had come suddenly on Kitty as she slipped the key into the lock and had lingered to look in' (3). The door to this room is locked; the women of the house, one who denies any fears for her husband at war and the other who wants to avoid the empty room of a dead child whom she does not name, do not want to experience feelings other than superficial or fashionable ones.

The family estate is where West begins to undermine the fearful, superficial value system of Kitty and Jenny. Baldry Court has appeared in the illustrated papers; cousin Jenny addresses the reader directly: 'You probably know the beauty of that view; for when Chris rebuilt Baldry Court after his marriage, he handed it over to architects who had not so much the wild eye of the artist as the knowing wink of the manicurist' (*RS* 4). Rebecca West's first description of Baldry Court hints at its dismantling: as the artist with the wild eye, she reclaims the estate for a reader who bypasses the illustrated papers in favour of the modernist novella. Through Chris Baldry's memory loss, West returns the house to its wild state before his marriage, before the architects, before the death of his son, before the war.

Cousin Jenny knows Chris before and after his marriage. Her story of him is constantly changing shape: she dismantles words as she speaks them, opinions as she voices them, values as she espouses them. Her narrative shuttles back and forth between then and now, the boy and the man (complicated because the man remembers and lives only as a boy). West poses a question about the relationship between infantry and infantry and the requirement to suppress grief during both stages. Cousin Jenny's struggle with language and syntax results from the essentially inarticulate force of both childhood and grief, which she strives to tell. West highlights her struggle by having another cousin narrate his version of Chris's situation in a letter.

The other cousin's epistolary writing represents a fixed, stable, judgmental point of view. In a letter, Cousin Frank sends Jenny a description of Chris's shell-shocked condition. Jenny's description of Chris's 'boyish' voice finds a resonant echo in this letter, which notes with distress his 'oddly boisterous' greeting that is reinforced in its strangeness by his 'boyish manner' (*RS* 19–20). While Jenny loves Chris's voice, which reminds her of his wonderful nature as a child, the other cousin uses this boyish voice to diagnose his confusion and memory loss.

. Jenny listens and approves of the childish voice (the other within Chris) and her story moves back and forth between the child and adult Chris, whereas Frank's approach to Chris's illness recalls Kitty's violent use of language, for he uses 'sharp common-sense' and confronts the unacceptable boyishness of Chris with the reality of dates. The shell-shocked soldier faints, losing consciousness. Not recognizing the irony, Frank prides himself on the necessity of this 'rude awakening' (*RS* 20–1). The fainting is not enough for Frank; thus, he is pleased to see Chris gazing at himself in a 'hand mirror,' which reflects his thirty-six-year-old face and thereby renders inappropriate his boisterous feelings and boyish voice. According to Frank's rigid system, Chris must be either a boy or a man, not both or one with a trace of the other. The soldier's feelings of being 'lonely and afraid' do not move the cousin, who then announces as a kind of shock therapy that Chris's father is dead. Chris breaks down and cousin Frank comments: 'I have never before seen a strong man weep and it is indeed a terrible sight' (21). Chris's tears put his strength in question. Strength and grief do not go together; one cancels out the other in this society. How then do these people conceive of grief?

West has Jenny describe the feeling of grief in significant terms: 'It is like a siege in a tropical city. The skin dries and the throat parches as though one were living in the heat of the desert; water and wine taste warm in the mouth and food is of the substance of sand; one snarls at one's company; thoughts prick one through sleep like mosquitoes' (*RS* 62). Not only does grief attack and bombard the self like an army, but it is utterly foreign or tropical, as we have seen in Rhys's fiction. Both cousins share a response to grief that depicts it as terrible, unacceptable, and alien.

In his letter to Jenny, Frank continues to document his assessment of Chris's shell shock: he notes that, while yearning for Margaret, Chris wants to know about Kitty, whom he cannot remember. Notably, Frank tells him about her voice: 'she had a charming and cultivated soprano voice' (*RS* 21). Kitty's voice matches her appearance, which is also charming and cultivated. However, Chris does not express pleasure at her socially celebrated voice with all of its training; instead, he is 'consumed with desire' for Margaret. Frank's comment is telling: 'I had no suspicion that Chris had this side to his nature and it was almost a relief when he fainted again' (21). Frank finds Chris's desire disturbing, which is reasonable because it is for a woman other than his wife. What is interesting is that the cousin has no sense that Chris's desire is part of being shell-shocked, being unable to remember beyond his pre-adult life. Frank is relieved when Chris faints, because then he does not need to hear the soldier as grieving, shocked, lonely, afraid, and desirous of being with the young woman who loved him in the days before he became a man. When Chris is unconscious, he is pleasing, for then he can appear as a strong and silent man, a good soldier. Ironically, West has Frank much more concerned for the 'shock' that Kitty will suffer (22).

Kitty's mode of expressing grief is beautiful. She resembles a 'rose in moonlight'; however, her suppressed grief seems, to use Derrida's phrase, to 'colonize and cultivate hell' as she lashes out at the gardener and maids, making all the latter 'cry' (*RS* 22–3). Mirroring her cultivated voice, she lives on a cultivated estate, which makes her relationships with others comparable to a colonized world where a staff of others serve her needs. And she can make their lives hell. Kitty cannot cry; hence, she hurts others to see their tears.

Into this estate ruled by 'a day-before-the funeral feeling' comes Chris's voice: 'Through the thudding of the engines came the sound of Chris's great male voice, that always had in it a note like the baying of a big dog.' Initially, Jenny experiences 'his absence as a kind of death,' and thus she now believes he will emerge 'ghostlike, impalpable' (*RS* 23). However, rather than a spectral appearance, Chris comes in as a young, animalistic self, the one who remembers the equally animalistic Margaret.

Jenny recalls that on the day that Chris left for the war, he sought out the horses and the dogs to say good-bye. Ultimately, horses and dogs are associated with Margaret's grief (*RS* 7). Thus, prior to his shell shock, Chris seems to have yearned for Margaret on some instinctual level, as I will examine later. West suggests that Chris's life at Baldry Court requires that he forget his own childhood self who grew into the young man who loved Margaret fifteen years before. One night he tells his cousin Jenny about their affair. In the middle of a jealous crisis in his romance with Margaret, Chris's father sent him to Mexico, where a revolution was underway. His job was to save the family fortune: 'I've sent for Chris. If the boy's worth his salt' (52). As Jenny recalls, when he was sent to the Mexican revolution, Chris's 'white face had a drowned look,' but it does not matter to his father, for the son succeeded in keeping 'the firm's head above water and Baldry Court sleek and hospitable' (53). Seeing Chris as a suffering child, rather than a spoilt one, makes us rethink critical assessments such as Ann Norton's, which argue that he has had 'a privileged youth and education' and then 'takes over his father's business' (9).[6] As stressed by Jenny, Chris's parents do not hesitate to drown their own child in order to keep their estate afloat. Hence, Chris loathes Baldry Court long before the war shocks him.

In her war novel, West symbolically constructs childhood as dead and gone. It cannot be retrieved; hence it cannot be articulated. She connects this loss to the shell-shocked soldier: he has lost his warrior mentality; he does not recognize the wife that married him as a good soldier. Instead, his traumatized mind returns him to a time between childhood and being a soldier. He lives, as a mentally ill man, in a liminal state of first love after childhood, but before his duty to family business, revolution, and world war. Derrida would define this in-between state as indicative of the man's grief: 'This clandestine war of denial would thus be waged in the shadows, in that twilight space of what is called mourning.' Here Derrida stresses the link between grief and love: on the one hand, when we mourn, it is for loss, but it is also for the anticipated 'death of those we love' (*WM* 146).

Notably, neither Chris's childhood nor his war experiences are ever recounted except in the briefest of details. His loss remains in the shadows. When he speaks of his romance with Margaret, the story takes place in 'darkness' and it has its most intense moment in 'darkness' (*RS* 31, 42). It seems that, while he can feel debilitating grief for these times, he struggles to articulate them. West's narrator, Jenny, has insight into the relationships between childhood loss, suppressed grief, and becoming a good soldier, without trying to tell them as stories. She brings us into contact with the grief, rather than distances it with articulation. As Jenny realizes, Chris's 'very loss of memory was a triumph over the limitations of language' (65). West plays seriously with the idea of return: to beginnings, to being before language and culture, to being whole. Thus, she uses the lost child and lost soldier as telling parallels. She explores their relationship in paradoxical ways: the child has died literally and the good soldier has died figuratively. While the infant can never return, the return of the good soldier means the death of Chris, figuratively and literally, as his 'recovery' returns him to trench warfare. This paradox is also expressed a number of times by Derrida as he writes of / to the wounded child in phrases that highlight limitations: '*you have to drag on in the old syntax, train oneself with you, dear reader, toward an idiom which in the end would be untranslatable in return into the language of the beginnings*' (*C* 115–16).

Cousin Jenny contrasts Chris in his childhood to the adult he is forced to become: 'When we had played together as children in that wood he had always shown great faith in the imminence of the improbable.' He expects enchantment 'with a stronger motion of the imagination than the ordinary child's make-believe' (*RS* 7–8). While he seeks a kind of alchemical 'revelation' that will allow him to feel 'inextinguishable joy,' there is no chance for him to attain it: 'Literally there wasn't room to swing a revelation in his crowded life' (8). The narrator lists the responsibilities that extinguish Chris's joy: having to care for 'useless' female relatives, having to cover his wife's immense spending, and having to learn 'to live after the death of his little son' (8). The loss of the child forms a seemingly straightforward part of a list of responsibilities that weigh on the man's life. Jenny quickly shifts the focus onto herself and Kitty as compensations for his 'lack of free adventure' with a 'performance' on the stage of beautiful Baldry Court (8). Yet in the novella, Chris struggles to be heard on this stage: the part the women have assigned him is that of the silent good soldier, certainly not the boisterous-voiced, shell-shocked soldier.[7] West's narrative moves the child and soldier from centre stage to the margins, so as to bring out the exclusion of grief. The novella includes two interrelated exclusions: the soldier is at war; the empty nursery is locked. Jenny and Kitty control centre stage; Chris, returned in grief, must remain in the theatre's shadowy wing.

Jenny and Kitty cannot understand, let alone recognize the implications of, Chris's condition. British doctors in the first year of the war saw many cases of what they called shell shock and one of the common symptoms was amnesia (Shephard 1). However, West has her two upper-class female characters oblivious to what may have brought about Chris's condition. While Jenny believes that Margaret broods over the term 'without arriving at comprehension' and thus hopes that she and Kitty's 'superior intelligences' will somehow decipher it, she does not know that Margaret has the transcripts of shell shock in her purse (*RS* 12). Margaret has Chris's telegram and letters and has great insight into what it means; she therefore has come to Baldry Court because 'it isn't in flesh and blood to keep it from his wife' (15). What Margaret does not understand is that Kitty is made up of what money can buy; she is a magazine cover girl, not flesh and blood. West chooses to name this woman 'Kitty,' knowing full well, as recorded two years previously during her 1916 journalist experience covering a munitions factory, that it is the term used for the substance inserted into shells (*Young* 388). Kitty carries as much explosive and wounding impact at home as a shell does on the battlefield. She, like trench warfare, shell shocks Chris.

Throughout the novella, West challenges our belief in clear communication; thus, the moment when Jenny believes Margaret's story, although

Kitty still does not, is when she takes Chris's telegram from her purse. Before the telegram is produced, Margaret's purse is vilified by Jenny as a sign of emptiness: 'I felt sure that had it not been for the tyrannous emptiness of that evil, shiny, pigskin purse that jerked about on her trembling knees, the poor driven creature would have chosen ways of candour and gentleness' (*RS* 12). Jenny imagines that the purse's 'emptiness' brings Margaret to 'this humiliation' and she hopes the scene will end quietly with the poor woman shedding a 'few quiet tears' (13). She misreads the inarticulate gesturing with the purse, for instead of being a sign of lack, it is a sign of fullness: it holds Chris's desperate, shell-shocked attempt at communication, an occasion certainly for tears, but not ones of shame.

Derrida explains that the '*letter*, inscribed or propounded speech, is always stolen. Always stolen because it is always *open*. It never belongs to its author or its addressee, and by nature, it never follows the trajectory that leads from subject to subject' (*WD* 178). West employs exactly this postal effect: owing to Chris's letters, Kitty thinks Margaret wants to steal from her, and then she feels that the letters represent how Margaret has, in fact, stolen her husband. The letters are addressed to Margaret, but they reach Kitty. Regardless, the Margaret they are addressed to is no longer present, but the older, married Margaret who brings them in her purse carries a trace of that young, absent girl. Chris has forgotten his present life at Baldry Court, but his letters arrive there.[8] West has the correspondence, as much as the spoken words, of *The Return of the Soldier* appear within this postal effect; yet she makes it a result of absent and present selves, previous love and present marriage, remembered feelings and forgotten duty.

The purse opens up the force that allows Chris to return as a ghost of his former self, a supplemented man: he is haunted by the loss of his childhood self, the loss of Margaret, the loss of his child, the loss of self at war.[9] What the purse contains is the very heart of lack, beyond perception of full or empty, positive or negative, because it is a site for grief. Margaret opens up the purse and inside is the telegram, a document that paradoxically records Chris's memory loss, as she points out, for it is addressed to the girl he loved fifteen years before. However, just as Kitty misreads the fragment from the letter at the outset of the novel, 'Somewhere in France,' she misreads the telegram. She reads it as a statement about Chris as an unfaithful husband (*RS* 15). She attempts to consider his wounded mind and then avoids it: 'Either it means that he's mad, our Chris, our splendid sane Chris, all broken and queer, not knowing us ... I can't bear to think of that. It can't be true. But if he isn't ... Jenny, there was nothing in that telegram to show he'd lost his memory' (17). Margaret makes it very clear that the telegram is addressed to the house she moved away from fifteen years ago; she has been married all this time. She has never heard from Chris, and hence Kitty's fear that the telegram does *not* indicate memory loss is simply a refusal. Kitty prefers to believe he is simply having an affair, rather than have to contend with his shell-shocked condition. Likewise, she chooses to believe that he does not have any entertaining war stories, rather than consider that he may be dismembered, a prisoner of war, dying, or dead. She fixates on how 'queer' it is that Chris ever loved a woman like Margaret, who is not beautiful or rich (17). Jenny finds Kitty's reaction unacceptable and notes the 'sick delight the unhappy sometimes find in ungraciousness.' Ironically, Kitty manifests sickness, 'sick delight,' at the same time as she refuses to believe in her husband's illness (17). Her response to his shell-shocked condition is to finally complete a sentence. First, dashes convey her inability to express feelings, and then ellipses characterize her speech. Finally, the ellipses are replaced by her wish to abandon Chris: 'If he could send that telegram, he ...' brought to completion by 'If he could send that telegram he isn't ours any longer' (17).

Kitty rejects Chris when he articulates his essential self. The psychiatrist, Dr Anderson, whose name suggests a kind of wholeness for the 'son' is present. Moreover, the name reminds us of how Kitty has locked away her grief for her son in the nursery that never changes 'And(her)son.' This psychiatrist defines for Kitty what constitutes selfhood: 'There's a deep self in one, the essential self, that has its wishes. And if those wishes are suppressed by the superficial self – the self that makes, as you say, efforts and usually makes them with the sole idea of putting up a good show before the neighbours – it takes its revenge' (*RS* 79). Chris's life has been marked by the loss of sons: first, himself as son to parents who risk his death to save their estate; second, his two-year-old son, who dies before speaking. Nonetheless, Chris soldiers on. He maintains a good show and plays the part written for him by Kitty specifically and society generally. However, when Chris goes to war and the two first losses collide with the death of sons on a massive scale, the suppressed essential self takes it revenge, not on Chris, but on society. He forgets the show for the neighbours and the essential self surfaces suddenly and wildly.

The architectural manicuring of the wildness of Baldry Court parallels the manicured hands of Chris's beautiful wife, whom he cannot remember. While the narrator gazes at the view, the author gazes beyond this view, drawing along with her readers, who are willing to have their knowledge rendered wild once again. The appearance of Baldry Court is specifically geared towards suppressing grief; hence, a flower border 'proclaims that here we estimate only controlled beauty, that the wild will not have its way within our gates, that it must be made delicate and decorated into felicity' (*RS* 55). What makes Margaret so out of place at Baldry Court is that she does not suppress her grief and display felicity. Disgusted, Jenny describes her as 'winking her tear-red eyes'; she contrasts this living woman with a piece of pottery and concludes: 'beside that white nymph, eternally innocent of all but the contemplation of beauty, her opaque skin and her suffering were offensive' (56). Margaret lacks delicacy and felicity while she is grieving.

If we return to the beginning of the novel and its incomplete dialogue, we note that Jenny makes a sudden shift: no longer captivated by Kitty's value and the stunning view, she instead provides the background to the conversation in order to show the feelings that contributed to her initial superficial and suppressed comments. The backdrop is formed by Jenny's nightmares of Chris 'running across the brown rottenness of No Man's Land, starting back here because he trod upon a hand, not even looking there because of the awfulness of an unburied head.' Through the horror of her dream, Chris successfully launches himself into a trench; however, the narrator comments that 'none but the grimmer philosophers would say that [he] had reached safety' (*RS* 5). West presents the safety as a double-edged sword, for like the empty purse, 'No Man's Land' in the novella is a signifier for grief.

Jenny reveals contradictory sides as she narrates: on the one hand, she is caught up in Baldry Court and its mistress's skin-deep beauty; on the other hand, she is well informed about the war and full of dread for her beloved cousin. Jenny positions herself as 'most Englishwomen' during the war, who do not care about 'the national interest'; their whole focus is 'wishing for the return of a soldier.' The narrator describes the feeling acutely as 'the keen prehensile gesture of our hearts towards him.' A gap is opening between the estate 'gardens that lay, well-kept as a woman's hand,' and the zoological term, 'prehensile,' that conjures up the image of a primitive grasp, a monkey's hand (*RS* 5–6). The place that Chris remembers in his shell-shocked state is not Baldry Court, but rather Monkey Island, fifteen years ago.

In his early twenties Chris fell in love with Margaret, who lived on Monkey Island. In his shell-shocked state, the woman that he loves is not his wife of ten years, whose increased spending the narrator likens to the image of a woman stretching 'a new glove on her hand,' but rather his

first love, who, according to the narrator, is 'repulsively furred with neglect and poverty' and thus has a 'seamed red hand' (*RS* 8). The narrator
thinks that Margaret may once have been like a 'good glove,' but one that
'has dropped down behind a bed in a hotel' and has thus become 're-
pulsive' with dust (10). The raw hand of Margaret becomes the most eloquent sign in the novel; it both wounds and heals by opening up depths
in a world constructed of 'surfaces' (6). As Margaret realizes and immediately pities Chris for it, Baldry Court is 'not built with hands' (56).

The gloves are dropped in *The Return of the Soldier*: characters fight
to remember grief they can never forget. Thus, at the beginning of the
novella, when Jenny looks into the nursery, she recalls how the 'fat fist'
of a curious child would be blissfully raised at the beauty and wonder
of the world. At the end of the novella, she works in conjunction with a
psychiatrist whose 'dissecting hand' has been hired to divide and separate Chris so that he can return to Kitty's magnificent black and white
bedroom, which corresponds on the home front to his return to trench
warfare (*RS* 80). If he returns to the status of healthy man, then he is
once again fit for battle.

When Chris initially goes to war, his final good-bye is to the dogs and
horses in his life. West associates grief with instinctual feelings that one
must suppress at Baldry Estate. As noted, Kitty and Jenny see Margaret
as a kind of animal. Jenny explains: 'there was something about her of
the wholesome endearing heaviness of the draught-ox or the big trusted
dog' (*RS* 10). Margaret responds to Kitty's cruelty with grief, and again
the narrator likens this emotional display to animalistic behaviour; she
recounts that Margaret fixes her 'with a certain wet, clear, patient gaze,'
and she concludes that it 'is the gift of animals and those of peasant
stock.' This low-brow expression of grief causes the narrator to feel a
powerful surge of pity, such as she would feel for 'an old horse nosing
over a gate or a drab in a workhouse ward' (14). Jenny regards animals
and working people on the same plane, and she responds to their feelings with a condescending sense that in their mute and pitiful state they
need her protection. Among the series of reversals and deferrals that
open *Return of the Soldier*, nearing the end of the novel it is Kitty, not
Margaret, who appears reduced to the pitiful position of an animal: 'She
swallowed her tears and passed on, to drift like her dog about the corridors' (87). Grief is imagined as instinctual, primitive, the ancestral monkey, the inarticulate part of the self.

When Chris seeks out the animals of his estate as he leaves Baldry Court
as a soldier, he doesn't touch them with his hands, since 'he felt himself

already infected with the squalor of war and did not want to contaminate their bright physical well-being' (*RS* 7). Initially, Margaret is imagined as being from a place that has the same capacity to poison and contaminate. As announced on her calling card, she comes from Wealdstone and Jenny informs us: 'That is the name of the red suburban stain which fouls the fields three miles nearer London than Harrowweald' (9). So the war and the working class seem to possess the parallel threat of poisoning those who have constructed a world out of leisure and beauty. Yet it is the war and working-class Margaret who cause Chris to grieve and thereby cure him so that he can return to being a man married to Kitty and ready for battle. Derrida uses the idea of poisoning during his 'mournful reading': 'it is such a regaining of presence, such a recrudescence or resurgence of presence or the mourning that had hollowed out in advance the so-called primitive or originary presence' (*WM* 148–9). Once again we have an echo of Claudius's idea in *Hamlet* that deep grief has the force to poison; it reappears in Derrida's notion of the force of 'recrudescence' in grief, with its implication of becoming raw and of its breaking out afresh in the form of disease or epidemic.

West uses place names to question the distinction between Wealdstone and Harrowweald. She reveals the ways in which they are, in fact, intimately related: one works to support and sustain the other and this other has a name suggestive of acute distress or pain. West uses 'harrow' several pages later with exactly this connotation when the women struggle to discuss Chris's suffering from 'shell-shock.' But Margaret does not allow the cousin and wife to believe he is dying: 'She was too kind to harrow us' (*RS* 12). Ironically, she will not *harrow* the women of Harrowweald, not let them suffer agonizing feelings of distress and pain. When Kitty refers to the *Harrow Observer*, to accuse Margaret of looking for money from the anxious wife of a soldier at war, the title of the paper speaks to us on a deeper level of the way in which Kitty harrows Margaret (14). West's use of the term makes us realize that we are the observers of acute feelings of distress and pain. Yet West depends on the double-sided meaning of harrow, for it is also the word for a cultivating implement; one harrows a field in order to cultivate a crop. Terribly afraid of the indignity of grief, the inhabitants of Harrowweald cannot know of the fertile opportunities for growth and nourishment in the process of suffering loss. Thus, Kitty cultivates a soprano voice and closes off the tympanum of her ear to the sounds of others.

If, like Jenny and Kitty, one constructs an identity based on a black and white distinction between Wealdstone and Harrowweald, rather than realizing that the places merely reflect one another, one may well transform into stone rather than weald / wield stone. One wields a tool or instrument; the etymology of wield is directed towards having control. West suggests with her place names that we turn to stone as we control our feelings.[10] Kitty turns to stone: she has become the sculpture of the 'white nymph' who droops over the 'black waters' (*RS* 56, 74). Considering that Chris comes from a home in which he drowns, it takes little imagination to see that Kitty gazes at him in the black waters, but sees only her own narcissistic face. Kitty's world depends on separating white from black, upper class from lower, leisure from work, Harrowweald from Wealdstone, felicity from grief. In contrast, Chris and Margaret exist in a silvery, grey zone, where the presence and absence of grief can be felt and the system of either/or is unravelled. The most significant collapse of the system of oppositions in the novel is the return of the soldier.

Literally, Chris returns from trench warfare; figuratively, he is gone, for he does not remember his present life. Literally, his return to mental health corresponds with mental illness, since it means his return to the madness of the front. In his shell-shocked state, Chris reverses memory itself so that, instead of forgetting his past, he forgets his present. Being a soldier requires that he forget everything but his purpose in killing his enemy and protecting his allies, but, for society, this kind of forgetting is considered sanity. It is Chris's shell-shocked belief that 'he would get well at once if only he could get home' (*RS* 19); yet the new meaning of 'home' is being with Margaret; thus, when he gets 'home' to Baldry Court, he is terribly distressed. The words of *Return of the Soldier* have layered, contradictory, reversing meanings that shock the reader into recognition beyond societal training.

One of the techniques West uses to destabilize the usual way of reading the world is to construct characters in conflict according to their visible and audible selves, as we saw in the description of Chris first greeting Kitty while shell-shocked, where his silent reaction to her grimacing smile is like a shout. Thus, one of the ways that West dismantles the socially acceptable mode of recording the beauty or squalor of surfaces is Jenny's attention to voices. The visible and the audible tell different, contradictory stories.

While cousin Jenny deplores the poverty of Margaret's appearance, she remembers and quotes the rich truthfulness of her speech. In the initial conflict with Kitty, Margaret stops herself from being catty like her aptly named hostess. Using a metaphor that appeals to our auditory senses, Jenny remarks that Margaret desists from the verbal fight 'because she realized that there were no harsh notes on her lyre and that she could not strike these chords that others found so easy' (*RS* 14). What complicates Jenny's assessment of Margaret, mostly built up of visible markers, is how she sounds. Jenny, who feels grand in initially allowing Margaret the privilege of telling her story, ultimately quotes the woman she originally believed to be as inarticulate as a dewy-eyed cow or trusted family pet.

When Jenny cries out, '"But Chris is ill,"' Kitty accuses her of 'saying what [Margaret] said.' Jenny concludes: 'Indeed there seemed no better words than those Mrs. Grey had used.' Then she repeats them again '"But he is ill"' (*RS* 17). When Margaret communicates effectively, it strikes Jenny as a combination of the auditory and the visual: 'Again her grey eyes brimmed. People are rude to one, she visibly said, but surely not nice people like this' (15). When she doubly communicates, the feeling she expresses is grief.

West has Mrs Margaret Grey's grey eyes, often brimming with tears, act as the windows through which Jenny learns to look beyond the surface into depths: 'her grey eyes, though they were remote, as if anything worth looking at in her life had kept a long way off, were full of tenderness' (*RS* 10). What stops Jenny initially from entering into grief is that she has been trained to believe it is undignified; thus, in the opening scene, when she condemns Margaret, it is because she feels threatened by the woman's sorrow: 'her dignity swam uncertainly in a sea of half-shed tears' (15). Grief, as captured in Margaret's name and eye colour, is a liminal state, not black and white: one experiences in the present a yearning for something lost; presence is experienced through mourning absence. In contrast, as noted, Kitty has established her identity on binary opposites of black and white. Not only is her correlative in art the white nymph bending over the black water, but also her most private space is a black and white bedroom (25). In contrast, Chris has grey eyes (32) and he believes that as the young Margaret of his memory mounts 'the grey steps' and 'assume[s] their greyness' it is symbolic of his love defined by twilight, which 'obscured all the physical details that he adored' and thus meant their love was 'changeless' (38).

Jenny offers a grey portrait of Margaret, for the hearing part of herself compassionately records the woman's 'sob,' while the seeing part of herself registers disgust at the poisonous grief: 'a spreading stain on the fabric of our lives' (*RS* 16). The detailed description of poverty is a learned art: the papers that photograph and celebrate Baldry Court also 'meticulously record squalor' (11). When Jenny believes that Margaret has come to manipulate Kitty into giving her money, she imagines the newspaper heading, 'Heartless Fraud on Soldier's Wife,' and then she imagines the story that Margaret will tell: 'at the first generous look on our faces there would come some tale of trouble that would disgust the imagination by pictures of yellow wood furniture that a landlord oddly desired to seize and a pallid child with bandages round its throat' (12). The utter lack of sympathy, the capacity to be as appalled by unfashionable furniture as one is by a suffering child, is disturbing.

Ironically, the bandaged throat of the child is emblematic of Chris, who is wounded in the site that used to connect his body and his mind; the sutured space of his throat (self-articulation) and tympanum (capacity to hear others, even other selves within, by means of memory). Chris has a middle-aged body, but his voice sounds forth from his newly youthful mind. The wound is in the throat, for it is the site of inexpressible grief. When Margaret holds him in his shell-shocked state, Jenny anticipates that this woman, 'not so much a person as an implication of dreary poverty,' will disgust Chris as she disgusts Jenny, since she exudes 'an open door in a mean house that lets out the smell of cooking cabbage and the screams of children' (RS 68). While Jenny condemns Margaret for her lack of monetary funds, overlaid upon her fullness of maternal funds, these qualities are exactly what make Chris desire her and heal through her. Thus, instead of Chris rejecting Margaret, Jenny discovers the two reunited and the focus is on Chris's throat: 'He lay there in the confiding relaxation of a sleeping child, his hands unclenched and his head thrown back so that the bare throat showed defenselessly' (69). Chris responds to Margaret's maternal impulse, which is clearly depicted as the opposite of the war. In her arms, this man can return to a healing childhood state and feel secure like a child. Defences down. The pose is 'confiding,' with its echoes of confidence and confession.

When Jenny considers or encounters Chris, it is often his voice that rings true. Lying awake and 'stiff' after her war nightmares, she recalls 'stories [she] had heard in the boyish voice, that rings indomitable yet has most of its gay notes flattened, of the modern subaltern' (RS 5). The narrator has the ideal position from which to fully tell this story, for she has known Chris through childhood; she has not forgotten his 'boyish voice' that once had 'gay notes'; yet she knows him simultaneously as an adult 'subaltern' – a word that on the surface conveys a junior soldier in the army, but also retains the etymological trace of 'vassal.' Jenny's description of Chris as a modern subaltern is particularly surprising, since we learn, in the first conversation with Margaret, that he in fact holds the superior rank of captain (11). What upsets Kitty most of all is not that her husband may be wounded, but that he is behaving in a 'common' way (17). Yet, midway through the novel, Kitty appears like a servant to the narrator; no longer is she the powerful mistress of the house: 'I could not talk about Kitty. She appeared to me at that moment a faceless figure with flounces, just as most of the servants at Baldry Court appear to me as faceless figures with caps and aprons' (46). Throughout the novella, West has her characters transform into their own opposites, thereby breaking down the fiction they cherish of an either/or society.

In the initial greeting between Jenny and Chris, West draws our attention repeatedly to how words have become unanchored from their safe, societal meanings. Thus, Jenny realizes that when he says he has 'dropped Frank in town,' he actually means that he has rejected Frank as a figure who 'has grown old.' Jenny says she's so glad that he is 'safe' and Chris repeats the word while sighing 'deeply' (*RS* 24). It takes the whole of Chris's 'cure' for Jenny to recognize that there is no shelter or safety in Baldry Court. The true disconnect is seen only when one compares the opening and closing of the novella: what we learn is that not only must Chris painfully bring his past and present selves into conjunction so as to return to war, but Jenny also must adjust one way of reading the world with another. Thus, at the opening of the story she believes that Baldry Court is for Chris an 'amulet' that he fingers through his shirt (7); at the end of the narrative, she states that he returns to the house 'as though it were a hated place to which, against all his hopes, business had forced him to return' (90). This recalls 'business' putting his young life at risk in Mexico.

When Chris and Kitty must first address one another through the shell shock, it is their voices that reveal the breakdown of their marriage. West has Kitty cry out 'as though she were speaking with someone behind a shut door,' and when Chris starts to see that the house is no longer the one he knew while courting Margaret, he sounds trapped: 'If the soul has to stay in his coffin till the lead is struck asunder, in its captivity it speaks with such a voice' (*RS* 25). In her most shocking reversal, West does not fully explore the harrowing implications of the marital discord until she reveals that it is Kitty who is truly ill, whereas it is Chris who is reaching towards some kind of health.

Kitty tries to seduce her shell-shocked husband by dressing herself as a 'bride.' She does not 'listen' to Chris's confusion because she is profoundly engaged in 'controlling her face into harmony with the appearance of serene virginity' (*RS* 26). While Kitty is furious that her husband's war trauma has caused him to return to a time of safety and happiness in his life, she simultaneously demands that he return to her as a newly wed husband when their lives were safe and happy. She does not want him to return to her as the husband with whom she lost her son. West has us wonder if, in fact, it is Kitty who suffers a more profound bout of shell shock, one that is without a cure. Enacting the reverse side of grief, Kitty is the feminine equivalent of No Man's Land, for she condemns Chris for his retreat from suffering at the same time as she requires him to retreat from suffering. How can he exist for this woman?

Kitty refuses to acknowledge trauma; it does not occur to her that the way she responds to her child's death forms a parallel with her husband's way of coping with war and thus reinforces his need to retreat. She wants to return to a time when she was a virgin, not a mother. Kitty blames the war for her marital crisis, but then treats her husband like a common adulterer (*RS* 29). Just as she does not seem to have registered the fact that her child has died, Kitty refuses to respond to Chris's war trauma. She treats his behaviour as if it results from his desire to have an affair: 'It means that Chris is a man like other men. But I did think that bad women were pretty. I suppose he's had so much to do with pretty ones that a plain one's a change' (31). West's exposure of Chris's 'captivity' is relentless: on the one hand, he must appear like a well-wrought urn in order to fit into the perfectly artistic world of Baldry Court; on the other hand, he is treated like an animal with basic sexual impulses that shape his actions. While Jenny has 'felt his agony all the evening like a wound in [her] own body,' Kitty does not see her husband as a man with feelings (31). She cannot fathom that he is hurt.

In contrast, Jenny speaks to Chris as if they are children; she asks him to tell his story – 'what seems real' – and begs him to 'be a pal,' for she'll never tell (*RS* 32). The term 'pal' in the novella is not only from childhood; it is also the word soldiers used for one another (5). West has Jenny frame Chris's own narrative by drawing our attention to the dual level of storytelling, for she hears his words and thus she 'visualized his meeting with love on his secret island' and somehow the combination of the two conveys Chris's 'truth.' The telling of this story makes Chris's eyes 'wet and bright,' and West reminds us that those who feel grief are also those who experience joy. While Jenny acts as the narrator of Chris's story, she interjects parenthetical comments reminding the reader that there are certain things not to be said in front of mentally ill people or children (36). His story, of journeying with Margaret to the 'wild part of the island' and then carrying her across the threshold of a circle of columns in the garden when they were young, dissolves like a film frame into the war: 'The columns that had stood so hard and black against the quivering tide of moonlight and starlight tottered and dissolved. He was lying in a hateful world where barbed-wire entanglements showed impish knots against a livid sky full of booming noise and splashes of fire and wails for water, and the stretcher bearers were hurting his back intolerably' (42).

Paradoxically, the war wound is what brings this early self back to life, and rather than damaging a part of him, it returns Chris to a kind of wholeness that has been lacking painfully in his life. He recognizes that society requires him to say, '"Yes, Kitty's my wife, and Margaret's somehow just nothing at all,"' but he cannot say it (*RS* 42). Jenny, who listens to his trauma, understands Chris's refusal to return to a state where he is dismembered. The next day, Chris can bear only to go boating, a 'boy's sport.' Jenny, despite her acknowledgment the night before of his yearning for wholeness, finds his return to childhood 'dreadful.' She reverts to the world of surfaces and tells him that Margaret is not beautiful: 'you can't love her when you see her' (43). Chris sets out on the pond to escape her.

Because Margaret expresses 'suffering,' Jenny imagines her as a 'cancerous blot' at Baldry Court (*RS* 56). When Jenny visits Margaret at her home, her revulsion mounts and she has to turn her 'eyes away from her,' for she becomes aware of her knees and her damp face and the dusting of flour on her hands from cooking. However, when Jenny describes Chris's shell shock and returns her eyes to Margaret, she sees the tears rolling 'down her cheeks' and is thereby moved (45). The force that Margaret has is through tears and Jenny is starting to wonder if that is what is lacking at Baldry Court. Again, West adds layers to the visible with the auditory, for as Jenny reassesses Margaret, she hears her as 'this woman whose personality was sounding through her squalor like a beautiful voice singing in a darkened room' (47). Nonetheless, Jenny anticipates that Chris will respond to Margaret's 'squalid mask' with a blank look, the same look that he offered to Kitty's 'sad mask' (57). Yet Jenny cannot know that Chris will reach out to Margaret in a radically different way.

West has us return to the empty nursery described at the beginning of the novella. Jenny is surprised that Kitty has entered the locked room (*RS* 58). She learns that Kitty is in the nursery because it affords her the best view of Chris and Margaret's first encounter. The room of a dead child provides the perspective from which West has them watch Chris run towards Margaret, not as a man full of lust, but as a man full of pain: 'How her near presence had been known by Chris I do not understand, but there he was running across the lawn as night after night I had seen him in my dreams running across No Man's Land. I knew that so he would close his eyes as he ran; I knew that so he would pitch on his knees when he reached safety. I assumed that at Margaret's feet lay safety, even before I saw her arms brace him under the armpits with a gesture that was not passionate, but rather the movement of one carrying a wounded man from under fire' (59). West dismantles the boundaries between sleep and waking, unconscious and conscious, male and female, domestic war and world war. Jenny's nightmare of trench warfare becomes a fulfilling dream in Chris and Margaret's love affair; the threat of death to the body at war parallels the threat to Chris's heart and soul at home; the seeking of safety is at Margaret's feet, not at the bottom of a trench as in Jenny's nightmare. With the bravery and strength of a soldierly comrade, Margaret carries the wounded Chris away from the battle that may destroy him both on the home front and at home.

Notably, Chris is horrified by his own reflection of age in the mirror offered him by his cousin Frank in the hospital; however, he does not register the passage of time or the harshness of life in his view of Margaret. As he explains to Jenny, what he feels for Margaret is beyond change (*RS* 41). Chris does not recoil when he sees the aged Margaret, and Jenny's shock at the former lovers' encounter causes her to undergo a kind of psychic break. She expresses herself with 'a conjunction of calamitous images.' Like a shell-shocked soldier, Jenny has a kind of war hallucination 'happening somewhere behind the front.' The landscape is war-torn: 'a church lacks its tower,' 'patches of bare brick show like sores,' and rafters stick out of roofs 'like broken bones.' She imagines Chris's spirit face to face with the 'soul of the universe' and having to choose between two spheres: one contains Margaret's eternal soul and the other contains the material existence of Jenny and Kitty. Chris chooses Margaret and inadvertently knocks the other sphere to the floor, where it smashes. Jenny admits that this is not an occasion for grief: 'No one weeps for this shattering of our world.' Nonetheless, the reader may want to weep for the slaughtering of Chris in this self-pitying war hallucination. Jenny casually slips in, West even notes parenthetically, that Chris is dead: '(This is his spirit; his body lies out there in the drizzle at the other end of the road.)' (67) Even in the afterlife, Chris's body and feelings are treated as irrelevant. Relegated to a line in parentheses, Chris joins the millions of other young men whose bodies lie rotting in the drizzle. One wonders if Jenny's vision is a premonition of Chris's fate once she and Kitty send him back to the war.

Like the characters in Rhys's novellas, Jenny initially compares grief to 'a siege in a tropical city,' a warlike, foreign emotion with the power to destroy. Moreover, Margaret's grief has been categorized as poisonous. Both of these images reappear in her sense of Chris and Margaret's reunion: 'There had been a hardening of the light during the afternoon that made the dear familiar woods rich and sinister, and to the eye, tropical.' The description of paradise threatened continues: 'There was a tropical sense of danger too, for I walked as apprehensively as though a snake coiled under every leaf' (*RS* 68). Jenny believes that Edenic Baldry Court is about to be poisoned by the snake of grief; however, what she discovers is that grief makes the garden a paradise regained: 'You know when one goes into the damp odorous coolness of a church in a Catholic country and sees the kneeling worshippers, their bodies bent stiffly and reluctantly and yet with abandonment as though to represent the inevitable bending of the will to a purpose outside the individual, or when under any sky one sees a mother with her child in her arms, something turns in one's heart like a sword and one says to oneself, "If humanity forgets these attitudes there is an end to the world"' (69–70). In a novella about losing one's memory through trauma, Jenny's insight about the importance of not forgetting grief is vital. The lovers in the garden are best conveyed by the image of praying or of a mother holding a child.[11]

When Jenny first sees Chris and Margaret return to one another, her war nightmare transforms into a dreamlike setting. Jenny alludes to this recurring nightmare three times in the novella. At the outset, the nightmare leaves her lying 'stiff,' in an image of death. West juxtaposes the narrator's dream with a brutal nursery rhyme from the war: 'My pal sang out, "*Help me, old man, I've got no legs!*" and I had to answer, "*I can't, old man, I've got no hands!*"' (*RS* 5) As noted, Jenny calls Chris 'a pal' when she wants him to tell his story. When Chris is returned shell-shocked to Baldry Court, the tension between the child-self and the adult-self, the one that speaks in patterned rhymes and the one that cannot speak about war, becomes intense. Jenny yearns for a pre-modern time when life and art were 'empty of everything except laughter,' for she is well aware that the modern era, inaugurated fully by the First World War, is a time of grief (29).

Since retreating from grief has made Chris unable to exist in the present, the psychiatrist, Dr Anderson, is summoned. Chris's home life surfaces slightly in the discussion. Notably, West connects the mention of Chris's sexual needs to his upbringing: Margaret responds to Dr Anderson's question about his turning to sex: 'he was always very dependent' (RS 81). The legal definition of a child is a 'dependant.' When the women discuss his condition with the psychiatrist, Jenny stresses Chris's unhappy relationship with his parents, and Margaret confirms that he turned to sex 'with a peculiar need.' Regardless of this discussion, Margaret believes and states that the way to bring Chris back to his fully conscious self is to make him face the death of his son (81). This is the only time sex is mentioned in the novella; throughout, the emphasis on Margaret is on her soul and her mothering qualities. Critics have suggested that she is a very sexual creature, in contrast to Kitty's frigid demeanour; yet there is no textual support for this observation. Making Jenny's nightmare a reality, when Chris runs to Margaret's open arms, the encounter is witnessed through the window of a dead child's nursery. Rather than meeting in the pastoral setting of traditional love narratives, Jenny sees that the modern lovers embrace in the midst of a battlefield. The man does not sweep the woman into his arms; she grabs him and props him up as a soldier would a falling comrade.

The third time West has Jenny reference the nightmare, she again quotes the childlike nursery rhyme about soldiers who are so dismembered they cannot help one another. However, the nightmare is reversed, for Jenny believes, in this moment, that Chris needs to remain shell-shocked, that in fact this is a finer state than the one that would lead him back into the 'hell of war.' The concept of safety is modified again: 'This wonderful kind woman held his body as safely as she held his soul' (RS 71). Yet it is exactly this woman, Margaret, who decides, along with Jenny, that they must do as the psychiatrist bids and return the shell-shocked soldier to full consciousness of the modern world and the war it wages. Out of love, the women decide that Chris cannot drink the sweet 'milk' of childhood passion and innocence any longer; he must drink an adult's wine, a 'draught of truth.' He must face the death of his son and the death of millions of sons at war. They need to get Chris out of the nursery and back to the battlefield; they want him to be a 'man' (87–8).[12]

Before the cure, West chronicles Chris's ironic discovery of the war in history books: 'Only that morning as I went through the library he had raised an appalled face from the pages of a history of the war' (RS 71). Chris becomes for a moment a strange figure for the reader, since he has forgotten his own experience at the front and, like most readers, can know the war only through books. Moreover, although the war is still on, it has become 'history.' Jenny realizes 'his soldierly knowledge' is 'deeply buried' and she is pleased because it ensures his safety: Chris, who has dismantled his soldierly self through forgetting, is now safe from being at the front (71). However, in the novella Chris's estate is constructed as a dangerous site: Baldry Court is the product of a maimed man: it is 'not built by hands' (56). What does it mean, in an echo of the war nursery rhyme, that Chris parallels the soldier without 'hands' who cannot help his friend without legs? He has returned to the home of his childhood and his marriage, a home 'not built by hands.'

While he is shell-shocked, Chris's hands are 'as warm as toast' and he and Margaret communicate with their hands: 'he stirred, groped for her hand and lay with his cheek against its rough palm.' West focuses on hands as communicators when one is without words: 'He caught her hand again. It was evident that for some reason the moment was charged with ecstasy for them both' (*RS* 72). West turns directly from this exchange to focus on Kitty's hands, which contribute to her beauty, a beauty that specifically depends on suppressing grief and seducing men. Kitty descends the stairs 'in a white serge dress against which her hands were rosy.' The narrator then comments that Kitty 'had reduced her grief to no more than a slight darkening under the eyes, and for this moment she was glowing.' The wife's concern is not for her husband's suffering; she is interested in attracting the doctor. Her grief is rendered delicate and felicitous, for, as the narrator explains: 'I knew it was because she was going to meet a new man and anticipated the kindling of admiration in his eyes' (74). Again, as a way to tame the wild, Kitty imagines her conduct as part of a 'civilizing mission,' so that all men will desire to work hard in order to secure her kind of beauty (75). Yet, as seen previously, hands in this novella also belong to the underside of the beautiful, civilized self: hands are wild; they convey the prehensile yearning of the heart; they build homes that shelter the self; they become raw and red with work; they hold.

Margaret's ability to grieve freely and use her hands to hold may stem from her own experience of loss. She, too, has lost her child. When she hears that Chris's son also died, she lays 'her hand across the child's photograph' (*RS* 78), and Jenny recognizes in this moment that she and Margaret will not be victorious in saving Chris from manhood and war. He must take his civilizing cure and return to the home front, where men battle in the name of beauty. He is not only a son, but also a father.

Dr Anderson argues for the significance of feelings and the articulation of the unspeakable. He does not act as if Chris's shell shock is a sign of weakness or cowardice, and he immediately connects trauma at home with trauma at war. Rather than being seduced by Kitty's beauty, he lashes out at her when she remarks that Chris just needs to make more of an effort. Dr Anderson retorts: '"Effort!" He jerked his head about. "The mental life that can be controlled by effort isn't the mental life that matters. You've been stuffed up when you were young with talk about a thing called self-control – a sort of barmaid of the soul that says, 'Time's up gentlemen,' and 'Here, you've had enough.' There's no such thing. There's a deep self in one, the essential self, that has its wishes"' (RS 79). While Kitty's childhood is never discussed in the novella, we do have a sense here of what happened to her when she was 'young.' She was taught to control herself, control her grief. Chris may not be the only one in this novel who is shocked into forgetting. Dr Anderson strives to discover what is the suppressed wish of Chris's deep self that is manifested by the shell shock.[13] Kitty responds that her husband, what with his fondness for her and Jenny and his vast wealth, wishes for nothing. The doctor turns then to Jenny, for she has known Chris all his life. Jenny states that his childhood was full of suppressed wishes because of a father who was 'jealous' and a mother who wanted a 'stupid son, who would have been satisfied with shooting' (81). In the novella's setting of the First World War, one feels the weight of a mother who wants a son to be satisfied with a life of 'shooting.' It reminds us that she is the mother who sends her son to possible death, during a revolution in Mexico, in order to attend to family business and thereby protect her extravagant lifestyle.

In discussion with Dr Anderson, it is only Margaret who speaks about the dead child, and West writes in such a way that we understand her statement on two levels: 'Remind him about the boy' (RS 81). Chris failed to save his boyhood; he failed to save his son at home; he also failed to save the 'sons' at war.[14] His shell shock is all about parents and sons. Chris has forgotten the loss of his son, his boy, while he has returned to his own boyish self. The cure requires that this boy, his boyish self, is forgotten by means of being reminded that his boy died. The doctor demands to know why Kitty did not tell him about the death of her son and her answer is unnerving: 'I didn't think it mattered' (82). Both the boy-self of Chris and the boy they lost and the boys dying on the battlefield do not matter to this wife/mother. Thus, West creates a disturbing female character who seems to contribute as much to the slaughter of the First World War as any male military leader.

Is Kitty the heartless villain of the book? West makes the situation more complicated. As a narrative device, it seems as if Margaret functions as the child that Kitty has suppressed. Margaret carries the trace of Kitty's child: she appears with the 'untidiness of a child' (*RS* 64) and walks the corridors of Kitty's house 'like a child paddling in a summer sea' (75). West ultimately superimposes the three women, so that it is Kitty who, near the end of the novella, surfaces with all of her beauty turned to the 'expression of grief' (87). Her grief is what makes the other two decide that Chris cannot remain in a kind of false childhood. In this moment, Jenny and Margaret kiss 'not as women, but as lovers do.' This is the only erotic moment in the novel. It seems as if the suppression reverses into expression when the very tissues themselves, which recollect the wounding, transform into vehicles for pleasure and creativity. The narrator defines the kiss as 'we each embraced that part of Chris the other had absorbed by her love' (88–9). West has two women, one a lover and one a family member, link the two types of love, suggesting that they are not different; one is simply a deferral of the other. In this moment, Chris becomes whole, for the women no longer expect him to be present to them in a single capacity: instead, he can be the boy he once was, a cousin, Margaret's young lover, Margaret's tragic lover, a soldier, Kitty's husband, the son of limited parents, the father haunted by his son's ghost, the officer suffering the death of his soldier sons, and so on. West's final, harrowing irony is that as soon as Chris attains wholeness – a man as defined by absence as by presence, a man with a memory – he is considered fit to return to dismembering at war.

In the moving scene of Chris's return to what the doctor would call 'normal,' Margaret must wield the toys and clothing of the dead son as weapons needed to terminate the boy and return the soldier: 'This is one of the blue jerseys he used to wear. This is the red ball he and his father used to play with on the lawn.' Margaret holds these spurs to memory in her arms and up to her face and exclaims: 'I think I know the kind of boy he was. A man from the first' (*RS* 85). Margaret is supposed to be the heroine to Kitty's villain; now, West has the heroine reject the possibility of boyhood and she has just shown us the villain, Kitty, awash with grief. How are we to understand West's blurring of boundaries? What does it mean that Margaret is mourning the loss of her son who died at the same time as Chris's boy and of the same unlikely cause – a cold or, perhaps, coldness. As Margaret explains: '"It's – it's as if," she stammered, "they each had a half life"' (77).

It is Jenny, who is without lover, husband, or child, who describes the bonds that assist us in understanding why West renders her villain and heroine inseparable: 'the childless have the greatest joy in children, for to us they are just slips of immaturity lovelier than the flowers and with a power over the heart, but to mothers they are fleshy cables binding one down to such profundities of feeling as the awful agony that now possessed her.' Jenny articulates this insight while watching Margaret hold the photograph of Kitty and Chris's dead son. She is surprised that Margaret does not 'look at' the photograph; instead, she presses it 'to her bosom as though to staunch a wound' (*RS* 78). When Margaret shocks Chris back into being a man, therefore being ready again for war, Jenny dimly sees 'a figure mothering something in her arms' (90). This maternal gesture occurs after the weapon-like jersey and toy have been produced: 'My spirit was asleep in horror. Out there Margaret was breaking his heart and hers, using words like a hammer, looking wise, doing it so well' (89). West's 'using words like a hammer,' so that Chris can feel his grief, recalls Conrad's idea of writing through fear and grief as working like a stone-breaker.

In West's passage, all the overlapping images of maternal holding, warlike wounds, being connected yet bound by one's very flesh to intense emotion, and the hammering of words with the power to break one's heart combine to leave the reader with an uncomfortable ambiguity. Like Jenny, confronted by such contradictions one is tempted to simply sidestep love, love's manifestation in children, and the attendant loss, whether literal or figurative. Yet she is also the one to reject the 'trivial toy of happiness' in favour of the 'wine of truth,' knowing all the while that 'it is not sweet like milk but draws the mouth with its strength' and it brings us to 'celebrate communion with reality' rather than 'walk for ever queer and small like a dwarf' (*RS* 88). Likewise, Rhys imagines the self without grief as a dwarfed self: 'a world of lowered voices, and of passions, like Japanese dwarf trees, suppressed for many generations' (*ALMM* 127). However, the reality cannot be held up in its glass like a fine aged wine to assessment by the senses; reality is not so clear a choice and neither is rejecting the sweet milk representative of communion with the childhood self. Must the childhood self be suppressed?[15]

Chris has been hammered and mothered by Margaret and he is now returning to Baldry Court and to Kitty as the picture of duty: he is being a good boy and a good soldier, but his experience can be expressed only through contradictions: 'He was looking up under his brows at the overarching house as though it were a hated place to which, against all his hopes, business had forced him to return. He stepped aside to avoid a patch of brightness cast by a lighted window on the grass; lights in our house were worse than darkness, affection worse than hate elsewhere.

He wore a dreadful decent smile' (*RS* 90). Because it cannot shelter the child, or the child's grief, his home is a hated place cancelling out the meaning of home; the light is avoided; the affection is hate. Chris does not smile; he wears a smile as a woman might wear a glove. And all of this is in the name of decency, 'dreadful' decency. Jenny's horror coupled with Kitty's delight disrupts a satisfying conclusion: Kitty excitedly asks: 'Jenny, aren't they there?' and she responds, 'They're both there' (90). Again West employs resonant ambiguity. Perhaps Jenny means that both Chris and Margaret are there; hence, she is not yet ready to say that Kitty is his wife and Margaret is somehow nothing. Or perhaps Jenny means that both of Chris's selves are there: the spiritual and the physical, the child and the adult, the boy and the soldier.[16] But we know that this is not possible, for Kitty makes Jenny be clearer as she creeps around to look for herself and Jenny is forced to admit he looks 'every inch a soldier'; so we know that he will return to 'that flooded trench in Flanders under that sky more full of flying death than clouds, to that No Man's Land where bullets fall like rain on the rotting faces of the dead' (90).

Kitty has the first and last word of the novella. She wins the war. She begins by stating that women must not fuss if their husbands haven't sent home thrilling war tales, and she concludes by whispering with the kind of satisfaction that almost takes her breath away: 'He's cured!' (*RS* 90). Chris returns to Kitty and then returns to trench warfare. This is a novella written to save the reader, since the characters, like the sons they have lost, are lost.

4   Childhood Grief on the Home Front:
Ford Madox Ford's *The Good Soldier* and *Parade's End*

Rebecca West brings the child home in *The Return of the Soldier.* In her novella, the child's nursery is part of the British home; yet the death of the child, before it is articulate, links her treatment of childhood grief with that of Rhys in her novellas. Although grief is still seen as 'tropical,' there is a shift from Conrad's and Rhys's sense of the child as foreign. The grieving son in West's fiction is native, part of society, albeit suppressed. This child, however, does not become articulate. He dies before speaking. Hence, Ford Madox Ford's narration of childhood grief reveals further development, since the boy in the four novels of *Parade's End* passes through the phase of being an infant or non-speaker and becomes a youth. In the novels of Rebecca West and Ford Madox Ford, while the fictional child comes home, he simultaneously must leave to fight a war. Thus, both West and Ford superimpose a child's grief and a soldier's grief, as they set their novels in the trenches of the First World War. Moreover, both West and Ford set a wound at the centre of their narration.

Ross Chambers believes that 'when it is not possible to fight disease, save lives, or escape pain, it is still important to bear witness to that impossibility, for as Sterne, in his wry way, noticed in *Tristram Shandy*, with reference to Uncle Toby's war wound, "the history of a soldier's wound beguiles the pain of it"' (vii). Ford has written an elaborate history of the soldier's wound in *The Good Soldier* (1917) and in the four novels of *Parade's End* (1924–8). As we saw in West's novel, surprisingly, the wounding occurs in the home, not on the battlefield. The war is waged by husbands and wives, fathers and brothers, not by enemies in an international struggle.[1]

Parade's End was published as four novels over the course of four years: *Some Do Not ...* (1924); *No More Parades* (1925); *A Man Could Stand Up*

(1926); *The Last Post* (1928). For the sake of economy, I will refer to the work as a whole under Ford's title, *Parade's End*.[2] The recounting of the soldier's wound, beginning in childhood, offers the reader a vital exploration of suppressed grief and the way in which it contributes to warrior-like adults. Levenson discusses Ford's childhood, where he was compared as a child with illustrious Victorian figures and made to feel as if he were 'a very small, a very sinful, a very stupid child.' Levenson sees this attitude as a unifying force in Ford's work: 'a refusal of 'adult' morality and an embrace of childhood insignificance and irresponsibility' (*Genealogy* 56–7). I am not sure about Levenson's terms. I believe Ford maintains the tension between the adult and the child-self; he does not privilege one over the other. Instead, Ford's goal is to have these two in dialogue, one that may occur through reading and writing.

Vincent Cheng sees Ford contending with 'a society engaged in trying to repress its passions' (*A Call* 105). What society pushes down or away Ford exhumes. As discussed in the introduction, Derrida imagines the work of mourning as bringing up, by means of articulation, that which is inhumanely buried, and in this way he connects grieving with being compassionate. In response to a repressive society, Ford's stories function as a way of facing pain, witnessing its work without hoping for release from such suffering. One way to interpret this gesture is to compare it to Derrida's concept of the work of mourning, which he sees as an activity that does not vanquish literature, but rather prevents 'it from neatly and cleverly sealing up the singular and flawless wound' (*WM* 44). In his novels, Ford critiques the kind of literature that seals up the realms of childhood and grief beyond access. Furthermore, he uses a grieving narration to open them. Before focusing on *Parade's End*, we will first examine the suppression of childhood grief in Ford's earlier novel, *The Good Soldier.*

In *The Good Soldier*, Ford creates characters who float from place to place like beautiful sailboats; at the same time, they seek some kind of anchorage that apparently is missing (8, 7, 23). The narrator calls himself 'a wanderer upon the face of public resorts' and ponders the way in which he drifted into his marriage (24, 17). He believes this is a quality of English soldiers, who drift 'about the world' (150). Paradoxically, it is the wandering that renders these individuals imprisoned and invalid (6). They digress literally and figuratively. In a clever equivocation, the narrator demands: 'Is all this digression or isn't it digression?' How can he ask us, when he is the one telling the story? The narrator then accuses the reader of being a participant in the whole act of denial by reading, wandering, or escaping: 'You, the listener, sit opposite me. But you are so silent. You don't tell me anything' (17). Ford writes in this equivocating, duplicitous way in order to crack open or fissure the structure of his story. Derrida believes that this type of writing would even benefit philosophy, which 'must accommodate duplicity and difference within speculation' (*WD* 113). Ford dismantles the landscape of the present so that a childhood past can appear. He admires this in other texts.

In a 1913 review of *Sinister Street*, Ford calls it a 'work of real genius' because it paints for him 'the landscape of [his] own boyhood' (*Essays* 113). As a reader, Ford responds to the promise of a return. Moreover, this technique allows for alternative ways of expressing emotion in a society requiring its suppression. Thus, in 1914 what Ford finds exciting about the Imagist movement is that it offers a new form 'for the narrative of emotion' (153). And in 1924, when he desires and addresses a 're-valuation of English,' Ford concentrates on the reader as 'a young boy,' because he believes 'there is no reading like that of a boy in the long dusks: it is the deepest abandonment of the soul that we know on this earth' (262–3). For Ford, the focus on the child is not about his being a good soldier, or even a good boy; furthermore, the child does not appear as insignificant or irresponsible; here the boy is regarded as the most vital reader of literature. The boy represents a state or time to which Ford wants to be returned. In a 1919 book review, he defines Virginia Woolf's fiction as articulating the 'unmistakable voice of one's childhood' (188). Clearly, Ford imagined a key relationship between the voice of childhood and literature.

In a discussion of Edmond Jabès and Jewish literature, Derrida writes: 'for what Jabès teaches us is that roots speak, that words want to grow, and that poetic discourse takes root in a wound' (*WD* 64). On one level, the root of the adult self is the child and for Ford, like Derrida as he expresses it in *Circumfession*, this figure is wounded. His narrative techniques expose and witness the roots where the wounding occurs, and they allow the words to grow by writing from a shifting, conflicted narrative point of view in order to articulate the inexpressible.[3] Both childhood and grief are unspeakable for his narrators; Ford records the stories of these silenced aspects of the self in the tormented narration of John Dowell in *The Good Soldier* and in the story of Christopher Tietjens in *Parade's End*. Yet there is a promise of a return to the root of the problem by means of reading.

John Dowell, the narrator of *The Good Soldier*, feels compelled to tell or write his story with contradictory motives that destabilize the either/or paradigm; he wants to act as a witness and to cover up the story (7).

Even more problematic, the story is full of self-reflective 'witnessing,' in which the narrator is brought along in order to watch the characters present 'to the world the spectacle of being the best of good people' (267). Why? The narrator responds: because they 'wanted, I suppose, to have a witness' (269). Yet his witnessing collapses, leaving him alone: 'No hearthstone will ever again witness, for me, friendly intercourse' (10). Admitting a similar contradictory desire in *Circumfession*, Derrida confesses: 'and for years I have been going round in circles, trying to take as a witness not to see myself being seen but to re-member myself around a single event' (59). Unlike Ford's narrator, by writing from and within his child-self, by trying to witness not by seeing but instead by feeling the inarticulate grief of this spectral child, Derrida seems to stop circling around and begins to remember. He acknowledges and accommodates his own disparate selves.

Derrida discusses the role of the witness while mourning in his tribute to Sarah Kofman: 'between the body and the book, between the open book and the closed one, there would be, here and there, the third, the witness, the *terstis*, testimony, attestation, and testament – but in the form of protest or protestation' (*WM* 168). In legal parlance, protestation in pleading contains the two contradictory possibilities of affirmation or denial. In the mourning texts under discussion, when a child is involved, protestation may be both affirmation and denial simultaneously, denying in order to affirm. Sarah, the child, had to hide from the Vichy police, who had her father killed; her books witness this denied child, act as a testament to the father, and protest the double disappearance. She must deny her existence in order to affirm it. Likewise, the narrator of Ford's novel strives to reach readers who share in the sadness of 'the poor child'd memory' (*GS* 134). In *Parade's End*, where children are taught to hide their true feelings from their parents, Christopher Tietjens believes that he 'would, literally, rather be dead than an open book' (342).

In *The Good Soldier*, trying to be a witness, Dowell struggles with the story's telling in a contradictory way expressive of both affirmation and denial. At one point he constructs a fantasy of recounting the sad tale to a sympathetic friend at the fire; at another point he crossly tries to organize the conflicting, complex actions and feelings into a diary format (242). This recalls Conrad's British teacher unable to quote Razumov's grief as recorded in his diary. Ford's narrator constantly reminds the reader that he has heard all of the confessions from self-interested players in the tragedy, which means one can never be sure of the accuracy, let alone the truth, of any portion of the drama. Ford highlights

Dowell's narrative confusion as a way to stress his avoidance of, and his encounter with, grieving.

In *The Good Soldier*, there are many attempts to get to the heart of the matter, in a story where various protagonists fake having damaged hearts. There are many attempts to construct some kind of origin or root for the cruel twists of social interaction in which each figure is denied what he or she wants (257–8). On the one hand, the excited narrator wants the reader to imagine that he tells a Gothic tale; on the other hand, he condemns the telling of the story at all (220, 210). When Edward Ashburnham, the most silent character, finally becomes 'vocal,' the narrator says he 'talked like a cheap novelist'; he then alters this assessment to say 'Or like a very good novelist for the matter of that, if it's the business of a novelist to make you see things clearly.' Returning to this anticipation of clarity, he adds that this story is told as clearly as something seen in 'a dream' (122).

The narration has a dream-like quality. The defining feature of John Dowell's effort to record the story is his use of ellipses and his repetition of the phrase 'I don't know.' The incompletion of his thoughts and the inability to articulate what he feels constantly strike the reader. At one point, he states that the flaws of his story result specifically from his fear of expressing grief. Yet he parenthesizes this admission: '(Forgive my writing of these monstrous things in this frivolous manner. If I did not I should break down and cry)' (*GS* 66). His desire to cry is remarkable, for when the story reaches its crisis point, he emphasizes his complete lack of emotional reaction: 'I don't suppose I felt anything'; 'No, I remember no emotion of any sort' (116). Earlier he notes: 'You ask how it feels to be a deceived husband. Just heavens, I do not know. It feels just nothing at all' (75). When we bring these statements into conjunction with his outburst about writing in a frivolous style so as to suppress his desire to cry, one is left wondering about the act of storytelling itself; for Ford denies the witnessing force of his novel and suggests it can function as its own reverse: a technique for avoiding one's feelings of grief. A narrator's use of 'nothing' to signify the fullness of grief and/or childhood is a technique we have seen both Rhys and West employ.

At the opening of *The Good Soldier*, the narrator states: 'This is the saddest story I have ever heard'; yet in the final pages of the novel, the narrator exclaims 'I don't want to sadden you' (5, 276). These opposing statements unravel the storyteller at the same time as express thwarted grief. Ford originally wanted to call the novel *The Saddest Story*, but his publisher requested a different title because of the unbearable sadness of the First World War, which dominated the minds of all in 1917, Thus, 'in hasty irony,' since he himself was overseas, a soldier on parade, he suggested *The Good Soldier* (xxiii). Ford leaves the reader with a sense of confusion, hearing the 'saddest story' told by a narrator who dreads sadness while admiring his friend and betrayer Edward Ashburnham, who is undone by grief at the same time as being 'a first-rate soldier,' able to put his feelings aside in the name of duty (13).[4]

Derrida admires the approach of Levinas that exposes philosophy's 'rigidity' that others believe to be 'solidity.' The approach progresses 'by negations, and by negation against negation. Its proper route is not that of an "either this … or that," but of a "neither this … nor that." The poetic force of metaphor is often the trace of this rejected alternative, this wounding of language. Through it, in its opening, experience itself is silently revealed' (*WD* 90). The narrative technique of *The Good Soldier* also employs a negating technique that wounds language in making it say and unsay itself. It is this wound that Ford wants us to witness. Because it is a root cause, a childhood wound, it is silent. Many philosophers and critics read words as if they are solidly present; in contrast, Derrida reads etymologically, to discover the root of the word. In Ford's novels, the traces of rejected alternatives reveal the roots of the good soldier's wound. Edward Ashburnham's character is simultaneously constructed and destroyed by grief, an emotion that revolves around rejected alternatives or losses.

Modernist tropes of grief surround the good soldier, who at the end of the novel the narrator likens to 'an immobile corpse,' with his wife and foster-daughter hovering over him 'like ghouls' (*GS* 260). The image of grief both as immobilized, and as haunting, appear in this condensed description and recur in other forms that I will discuss later. Edward's wife, Leonora, and his foster-daughter, Nancy, both from abusive homes, have become in these final scenes like native warriors who seek to torture the man they both supposedly love (260). The novel has given the reader enough information to reconstruct their respective childhoods, so that we realize they too have become good soldiers. Celia Kingsbury likens Nancy's 'mute madness' at the end of the novel to 'certain forms of shell shock' (16). However, like the protagonists of Rhys and West, Ford's Nancy has been traumatized at home, not on a battlefield. The vicious circle of brutal child-rearing appears in the narrator's explanation that the only thing that can 'unman' Nancy is the sound of her violent father's voice (142). What reduces Nancy to a feminine, emotional self, and therefore a self at risk, is her father. So she makes herself as manly as possible. Ford's novels brim with the suppressed tears of bullied children.[5]

The narrator, John Dowell, defines: 'all good soldiers' as 'sentimentalists – all good soldiers of that type. Their profession, for one thing, is full of the big words – "courage," "loyalty," "honor," "constancy"'; they speak of their time in India, their knowledge of horses and weapons (*GS* 29, 28). The possible victims or enemies are elided in conversation, but in Ashburnham's case, he fills such gaps by being well versed in literature and is a fine storyteller. The act of writing plays a seductive role in this novel of intrigues; it leads a good soldier like Ashburnham to create relationships out of fantasies and promises, a commitment to inspirational words rather than to flawed people and disruptive feelings; hence, he approaches each successive affair 'with his intense, optimistic belief that the woman he was making love to at the moment was the one he was destined, at last, to be eternally constant to' (30).

There is a clear link in the novel between appreciating literature and being a good soldier, as evidenced by the story of 'a most ferocious warrior' who fights with his heartless wife about 'the courtesy that is due to great poets' (*GS* 19). Furthermore, the good soldier himself selects a literary death. Although Ashburnham is a soldier and thus knows his weapons well, he chooses to kill himself with a literary implement. Our final vision of him is with a 'penknife,' which is more commonly used for making and mending quill pens (277). Moreover, as the narrator tells us several times, Edward's bookcases house 'guns' rather than books (231, 270). Ford explores the way in which escapist literature has a significant role in the suppression of feelings, beginning with the silencing of children. Ford criticizes the kind of literature that elides emotion, other than romantic love, and relates this kind of writing to the suppression expected of dutiful soldiers. Thus, when Leonora has a passionate conversation with her soldierly husband for the first time in many years, despite the fact that he is an avid reader, she discovers that he is utterly undeveloped: 'It was like opening a book after a decade to find the words the same' (69).

Keen on reading as an avoidance of unpleasant feelings, the narrator turns to literary works as a way to protect his wife, who suffers from a heart condition, from becoming overly excited: 'I had to keep her at it, you understand, or she might die. For I was solemnly informed that if she became excited over anything or if her emotions were really stirred her little heart might cease to beat.' Ford makes sure we read this description of the heart patient as indicative of a whole society, for he has the narrator add: 'I had to watch every word that any person uttered in any conversation and I had to head it off what the English call "things" – off love, poverty, crime, religion, and the rest of it' (*GS* 18). The fact that the English have the neutral, meaningless term 'things' for the types of topics that engage the heart, mind, and soul indicates that these topics are considered dangerous for the whole of the community. Yet the key themes explored in the drama of this novel may well be put onto the English list of taboo subjects: love (the various marriages and affairs of the novel), poverty (the near loss of Edward's fortune to prostitution and gambling), crime (infidelity and the buying and selling of individuals), and religion (Leonora's Catholicism and the crisis precipitated by Florence's presentation of the 'Protest' document). Notably, not only does the narrator, John Dowell, succeed at ensuring that Florence's emotions are never stirred, but he attains a similar position of neutrality for himself.

When Florence suicides, Dowell does not feel anything about her at all, for she has become the soothing literature he ensured that she read: 'I thought suddenly that she wasn't real; she was just a mass of talk out of guidebooks, of drawings out of fashion-plates.' If he had tried to save her life, 'it would have been like chasing a scrap of paper' (*GS* 134). Commenting on Ashburnham, another avid reader, just before he suicides, Dowell notes that he is the English gentleman right up to the end; however, he qualifies this assessment: 'but he was also, to the last, a sentimentalist, whose mind was compounded of indifferent poems and novels' (277). It is ironic that poems and novels fail to provide the good soldier with the capacity to put his own feelings into words. As he plots his own death, Ashburnham quotes a line of Swinburne's poetry to his wife: 'Thou hast conquered, O pale Galilean' (272). He imagines his wife as the mythological queen of death, Proserpina, and he will truly wed her forever in the underworld with his suicide. Ironically, it is the marriage of the Ashburnhams that kills the good soldier, not his military service. Of course, he wants his foster-daughter, whom he sends back to her abusive home, to continue loving him in a literary way, 'steadfastly as people do in sentimental novels' (264). This kind of novel is the antithesis of modernist literature that engages in grieving. It is the sentimental novel that 'neatly and cleverly' seals up the 'wound' and celebrates the romance.

The narrator's overall sense of marriage draws further on his analogy with literature, for he believes, along with Leonora, that sadly one's relationship becomes boring, like a book read too often (*GS* 128). Dowell exploits or dismisses literature, yet recognizes the potency of putting one's feelings into words: 'It was as if his passion for her hadn't existed; as if the very words that he spoke, without knowing that he spoke them, created the passion as they went along' (129). The passion described is the good soldier's final affair of the heart that the narrator considers true love and thus the catalyst for his suicide. However, while the soldier stirs amorous passion with his words, he is 'inarticulate' (61) especially in terms of his grief: 'Edward said nothing' (230); 'he never spoke' (231); 'whilst Edward sat absolutely silent' (232); 'the silent Edward' (261); 'he remained dumb' (262); '[he] whispered something I did not catch' (277). Hopelessly, Leonora tells Dowell that she talks 'in the endeavor to sting [her husband] into speech' (232). The good soldier not only maintains silence himself, he commands others to hold their tongue: '"Nancy, I forbid you to talk about these things. I am the master of this house"' (249). His inability to tell his wife about his feelings certainly acts as one of the key factors in the book's being the 'saddest story.' Ford defines silence as a form of 'cruelty,' because it 'is so apparently austere, restrained, non-communicative' (*Essays* 130). As I will examine in more detail, the words the good soldier cannot speak transform the women with whom he falls in love into signifiers for his suppressed emotional self at the root of all his suffering. With the exception of the Spanish dancer, every woman with whom he has an affair appeals to him because of her sadness.

Women act as mirror images of the good soldier's own grief that he cannot feel, articulate, or relieve. Thus, when he kisses the servant girl, his attraction is sparked by her 'mournful' appearance (*GS* 62). He kisses her in a 'half-fatherly' manner because she is 'quietly weeping' and he wants to 'pool their sorrows' (164). While Leonora believes the truth of his story, that he sought to 'administer fatherly comfort to a weeping child,' she does not realize that she herself will never attract him 'because she was never mournful' (154). Another mistress, Mrs Basil, has a 'soft mournful voice' (195). Ashburnham acts as the saviour to a waiter because he sees he has been crying; the man's grief stems from the loss of his 'girl baby,' whom the good soldier works tirelessly to have returned (103). Note the dream-like contradiction: the good soldier engages with another because of his or her tears and then he works to dry these tears; as soon as that happens, he must find another in tears.

Derrida describes this circular problematic of mourning: 'Words fail us, since all language that would return to the self, to us, would seem indecent, a reflexive discourse that would end up coming back to the stricken community, to its consolation of its mourning' (*WM* 200). The good soldier is always decent; yet words seem to fail him over and over again when he seeks others who grieve and tries to console them. Ashburnham cannot be faithful to a woman because he is faithful to his wound that he witnesses over and over again. Paradoxically, his repetitions make him stand still. The good soldier seeks out not only sad figures, but also childhood ones. His affairs reveal the repetition.

Ashburnham repeats his love affairs with child-mistresses, who seem to him to be sad children in need of comfort. Therefore, according to his wife, he sounds like the same book after ten years. According to Dowell, who, of course, uses Edward Ashburnham to reflect his own sadness, the good soldier is immobilized by grief. This paralyzing sorrow recalls Elizabeth Barrett Browning's sonnet 'Grief': 'if he could weep, he could arise and go.'[6] Yet Ashburnham does weep, and fairly often (*GS* 147, 177, 182–3). Weeping does not appear to bring any kind of relief or development beyond his vicious circle of love affairs. The good soldier needs to articulate his grief.

All the characters of *The Good Soldier* become immobilized. They turn to stone; most of them transform from mobile bodies into corpses marked by tombstones prior to their literal deaths. They avoid works of mourning that have the force to mobilize a corpus of feelings and of words and instead are immobilized by their grief. In a 1914 book review, Ford says that during his reading of *Time and Thomas Waring* he 'wept a handkerchief into a state of complete soppiness.' He explains that he was 'very much moved' by the novel (*Essays* 138–9). This movement, caused by a reading that opens up the wound and thus causes tears to flow, halts the tendency to become rigid and immobile, stone as opposed to flesh.

Ford continues the process of opening up the character of the good soldier by returning right to the beginning, to the root of his being. As noted, Ashburnham does not often speak; he is far more likely to 'gurgle.' This term recalls the sound of an infant, and it reminds us that he is more involved in the infantry as nursery than the infantry as foot soldier. Rather than saving comrades, he appears to be saving children; yet he also seeks to forgive seemingly violent parents. These activities are particularly inarticulate. The narrator tells us that the good soldier 'was a perfect maniac about children' (*GS* 63), and despite his own inability to communicate, he rouses all skills when confronted with a child's grief: 'he would do it quite inarticulately, set in motion by seeing a child crying in the street. He would wrestle with dictionaries, in that unfamiliar tongue ... Well, he could not bear to see a child cry' (103). In a recall of Conrad and Rhys configuring the grieving child as foreign, Ford's inarticulate soldier has to locate words in a foreign language, literally and figuratively, for the words for feelings, especially grief, are unknown. He marries a woman who suffers a similar initial wounding.

Not only have the Ashburnhams never learned the words to express grief, but no one teaches Edward or Leonora that the act of sex is fundamentally connected to the production of children. For several years into their marriage, they do not know of this connection and, as Dowell comments: 'it had a good deal of influence on their mentalities' (*GS* 161). They never seem to recognize that their sexual activities are inextricably tied to their yearning for children or their desire to act as witnesses to their own suppressed and damaged childhoods. Ford uses the tropes of blindness and insight in his depiction of the Ashburnhams' sense of childhood.

Dowell differentiates himself from his wife as 'she had the seeing eye,' which he 'unfortunately' does not (*GS* 16). He imagines his success at the resort as a 'blindfolded' man, which, of course, he figuratively is, since he does not see his wife's affair with Ashburnham (24). He fails to see, but, as noted, he also positions himself as an eyewitness, specifically a witness who puts on blinders and thereby transfers the image of the trauma he suffers: 'You may well ask why I write. And yet my reasons are quite many. For it is not unusual in human beings who have witnessed the sack of a city or the falling to pieces of a people to desire to set down what they have witnessed for the benefit of unknown heirs or of generations infinitely remote; or, if you please, just to get the sight out of their heads' (7). On the one hand, his motive for writing concerns acting as witness for the future reader; on the other hand, his motive revolves around taking the sight of the tragedy out of his head.

Ashburnham and the narrator's wife, Florence, use a more radical method of removing tragedy from their heads: they suicide. Ford is at pains to connect Ashburnham's suicide to a final gesture towards silencing the clamouring child within. Despite a critical tradition that foregrounds failing sexuality as the cause, in fact, Ford does not portray Edward or his mistresses as sexually motivated.[7] The novel lacks any kind of sex scene or erotically charged moment. Ford seems more interested in the emotional motivations behind the affairs, and sex seems like a bodily way to express feelings that one has been forbidden, since childhood, to express.

The narrator notes that a 'hopeless parting' in a novel causes tears to start in the good soldier's eyes (while he is reading), and the hopeless parting from the 'child,' Nancy Rufford, seems to be the impulse behind his suicide. Nancy functions in the novel as one of the representative child-mistresses. The narrator informs us that the good soldier loved 'all children' and he parallels children here with 'puppies' and 'the feeble generally' (*GS* 30), which is striking, because many of the adults in this book create parent/child relationships with one another and the attraction originates in a response to the other's feebleness or weakness. Dowell plays nursemaid to his invalid wife (10); Edward sees his job as 'nursing' his tenants (157); Leonora looks upon John as a mother might upon a son or a nurse upon an invalid (36–7); Florence sees her job as the educator, in a kind of fussy, maternal way, of Ashburnham (42). The Ashburnhams take on the role of destructive parents to Maisie Maiden (68–9) and to Nancy Rufford. Even Nancy at one point regards Leonora as if she were 'a tiny child' (235). In the minds of the adults, children parallel the ill and damaged, those who have 'hearts' (6). Leonora realizes that this neurotic acting out of child/parent roles is horrifying and 'unspeakable' (80). It returns as a repetition in her present life and it returns her to a past life.

One of the final gestures of the good soldier before he commits suicide is to ensure that a mother accused of killing her baby is released (*GS* 273). He swings back and forth from protecting the child to protecting the parent. Ashburnham strives throughout his life to save children; yet children must be denied and, if they somehow enter into the game, they must be silenced. Adults cannot be held accountable in this world for silencing children, or even murdering children. As the narrator concludes, children are like animals, specifically those raised for consumption: 'Yes, society must go on; it must breed, like rabbits' (275).

Comparable to West's and Rhys's explorations of the commodification of children, the wealth of Ford's characters serves to highlight the poverty of the child/parent relationship throughout the novel. The extramarital affairs translate into business transactions because that is the language that the children, now adults, have been taught. The Ashburnhams treat the husband's mistresses like children and like business deals. While Ashburnham, with the complicity of Leonora, cares like a loving father for the child-mistress, Maisie Maiden, his wife treats her like an abusive mother: 'She was hitting a naughty child who had been stealing chocolates at an inopportune moment' (*GS* 69). This corresponds neatly with Rhys's treatment of the Heidlers in *Quartet*. When Leonora strikes the girl, Dowell praises Leonora's ability to act as though *nothing* has happened. He attributes this fine display of suppression to her family history or background, which he contrasts with that of the child-mistress (aptly named maiden): 'Mrs. Maiden, however, was not a Powys married to an Ashburnham; she was a poor little O'Flaherty whose husband was a boy of country-parsonage origin. So there was no mistaking the sob that she let go as she went desolately away long the corridor' (58). Like West's working-class Margaret, Maisie Maiden, as a lower-class figure, has not had lessons in suppression inflicted upon her as have the children of more established social position, such as the Ashburnhams.

While in India, the Ashburnhams essentially 'bought' this girl without her knowledge. Her husband agrees to the transaction because the wealthy couple promise to take her to a retreat for the maintenance of weak hearts, a condition from which she suffers: '[Leonora] handed over the money to the boy husband, for Maisie would never have allowed it; but the husband was in agonies of fear' (GS 68). When 'the poor child' finds out, she is heartbroken literally and figuratively, and she dies. Ford describes the impact of her death as a final silence indicative of the child-self struggling to be heard in modernist fiction. The sob is swallowed. This paradoxically articulate silence becomes almost tangible while the character Leonora is reading. The silence is strained, 'as if there were something in the room that drank up such sounds as there were. She had to fight against that feeling, whilst she read the postscript of the letter.' The postscript is the ideal place for the child-voice to occur, for it comes after the signature; it is something beyond the signing of the adult. The postscript begins: "I did not know you wanted me for an adulteress" and Dowell comments: 'The poor child was hardly literate' (79).

In the letter Maisie leaves for Leonora, she wonders: 'How could you buy me from my husband?' (GS 79) The answer to the question emerges indirectly in the novel, as Dowell informs us that Leonora herself was sold by poor parents to Ashburnham's wealth: 'She had come of a penniless branch of the Powys family, and they had forced her upon poor dear Edward without making the stipulation that the children should be brought up as Catholics. And that, of course, was spiritual death to Leonora' (64). Likewise, Edward's parents 'arranged' his loveless marriage to Leonora (63). These aristocratic children, just like Rhys's Edward Rochester and West's Chris Baldry, are treated by their parents like commodities or business ventures, and thus they do not have any difficulty in treating others as commodities. Ford stresses this point by placing the purchased child-mistress, Maisie, in colonized India. Moreover, Ford has Leonora imagine her husband having affairs with 'native women or Eurasians' (194–5). Likewise, we saw that Rhys explores in many of her novellas the way in which individuals colonize those with whom they have intimate relations.

Not merely a British phenomenon for Ford, Dowell, an American, also appears to lack any sense of parental love; he never mentions his own family except in connection with class issues and land titles (*GS* 7). After Florence's suicide, he returns to his home in Philadelphia with a plan for solidifying his position as a good soldier: 'fighting with real life' and doing something 'masculine' (135). In this spirit, he looks up his 'relations' (168). This is the closest the narrator comes to mentioning his family. He seeks out an heir in the form of a 'sort of second-nephew.' Not surprisingly, this man presents himself as an heir, for he assists in the narrator's real estate and he is a 'good cricketer' (169). The lost characters of this book constantly transfer their yearning for a familial home onto real estate. And although he fails, it seems that Dowell has a desire to create a home for the grieving child.

Home life for the Ashburnhams is comparable. They possess a vast estate that seems divorced from family ties or even history (*GS* 23). The defining quality of the British estate is its denial of relationships other than those of possessor and possessed, master and servant; hence, Leonora appears flanked, not by family, but by 'a butler and footman and a maid or so' (23). When Edward gazes out upon this home, he exclaims: '"All this is my land!"' (32). When Leonora lets the estate in order to pay off her husband's gambling debts and prostitute, it leaves the good soldier 'with a feeling of physical soiling – that it was almost as bad for him as if a woman belonging to him had become a prostitute' (183). Dowell's assessment is jarring, for Ashburnham has just been with a prostitute, and his obsessive affair with this woman, which incurs his significant debts, does not seem to make him feel soiled at all. He appears to esteem his estate, Branshaw Teleragh, much more than his marriage, his wife, the 'woman belonging to him,' or his own body.[8]

The children of this novel, all of whom are grown up, have been taught that their worth is based on their contribution to the family finances and the family estate. Therefore, it makes perfect sense that Ashburnham denies the value of his physical body while being deeply concerned about not tainting the purity of his estate. And he cannot witness the relationship between the two, or the lesson he has been taught, because he has been taught to be emotionally silent and literarily forthcoming. The narrator mistakes the repression of Branshaw Teleragh for a quality of peacefulness: 'it was unbelievable that anything essentially calamitous could happen to that place and those people. I tell you it was the very spirit of peace' (GS 23). The narrator thinks he can buy this 'English peace' (275) without realizing that Branshaw Teleragh offers peacefulness based on the suppressed children who haunt it and who as adults turn it into a war zone full of soldiers trained by poisonous pedagogues.

Before she marries Ashburnham and his estate, Leonora Powys came from 'a bare, untidy Irish manor house.' She was raised in a convent, where she 'had been drilled – in her tradition, in her upbringing – to keep her mouth shut.' She is trained to resist the greatest temptation, the 'temptation of speaking,' and thus she desires 'above all things to keep a shut mouth to the world' (GS 193). When she returns home, her parents treat her as an outdated commodity that needs to be sold. The father has a photograph of his daughters taken for the purpose of display to the Ashburnhams: 'to give them some idea of the goods that he was marketing' (151). In this way, the Powys family successfully sells off Leonora. In her marriage, Leonora, who has lost the capacity to speak without despising herself (193), tries to express herself through financial transactions. She expresses her love for her husband by trying to deny herself, by caring for his estate, and by dressing him lavishly like an adored child (183). Their marital conversation, for you 'cannot be absolutely dumb when you live with a person,' focuses on the accounts of Edward's estate (184). Not having heard any, and not having been encouraged to express any, Leonora cannot articulate 'one word of tenderness' (148). Her husband's response is 'unbroken silence' (190).

Ford says and unsays his characters: he constructs them with different languages that are contradictory. Hence Ashburnham, steeped in literature, does not understand Leonora's financial mode of expressing herself. When he has the affair with the dancer, she too talks to him 'as if she had been a solicitor with an estate to sell.' For this woman, their sexual encounter is 'a perfectly reasonable commercial transaction.' In contrast, Edward sees it according to romantic fiction; he thus believes that she 'had surrendered to him her virtue, that he regarded it as in any case his duty to provide for her, and to cherish her and even to love her – for life' (GS 175). When he tires of her, he takes on an 'attitude of Byronic gloom – as if his court had gone into half-mourning' (179). These characters are made up of languages by means of which they learn to (in)articulate and (mis)understand themselves.

The good soldier's family – a military family, the Ashburnhams – conduct themselves in a controlling and threatening manner in relation to their son: 'one evening, Mrs. Ashburnham had with her boy one of those conversations that English mothers have with English sons.

It seems to have been a criminal sort of proceeding [...] next morning Colonel Ashburnham asked on behalf of his son for the hand of Leonora' (*GS* 153). Even Dowell, not usually known for his insights, recognizes something terrible in the upbringing of Ashburnham: 'the quality of his youth, the nature of his mother's influence, his ignorances, the crammings that he received at the hands of army coaches – I dare say that all these excellent influences upon his adolescence were very bad for him. But we all have to put up with that sort of thing and no doubt it is very bad for all of us' (166). When the good soldier's parents die, the discussion is businesslike; no grief is expressed (155). In contrast, when Leonora sells off two family portraits, Edward 'cried for two days over the disappearance of his ancestors' (183). He has conflicted feelings about his wounded roots; since he cannot have feelings for his own parents, he transfers his thwarted love, anger, and grief onto much more easily dealt with portraits of ancestors. The artifice and distance of these family figures renders them bearable. Notably, Leonora's 'esteem' for her husband is 'lessened' when she witnesses him grieve (183).

Regardless of how they react to the pedagogical model under which they were brought up, Ford has these figures conducting adult relationships in various versions of suppressed childhood experiences. Moreover, he connects the brutal parenting, which teaches children to obey, to be silent, to function in economic rather than emotional terms, with laying the groundwork for the First World War (*GS* 154). Florence imagines 4 August as being a magically important date in her petty life; it is also the day that England entered the war. The novel is full of allusions to politics entwined with the marital and familial dramas.

The present, damaged generation does not have any children, except the foster-daughter, Nancy. Her foster-parents, Edward and Leonora, decide she must be 'exported to India' like some sort of product or defence risk for 'the greatest good of the body politic' (*GS* 258). Leonora's father comes to visit against a backdrop of 'troublesome times in Ireland' (157). One of the parents is heard discussing the Belgian Congo: 'They must have been talking about the proper treatment of natives' (141). And in discussing Edward's affairs with the law, the narrator clarifies that his legal mistreatment cannot compare to what happened to Dreyfus (171). There is mention of 'the South African War,' to which the good soldier may be sent; however, his wife holds him back, not in fear for his life, but because she has heard rumours of the troops' financial extravagance (186). Anticipating the deafening sounds of the First World War is the 'long, silent duel with invisible weapons' (136) of a society made up of 'silent adversaries' (143). With the phrase 'Annexation of Alsace and Lorraine' ringing in the ears of contemporary readers, Florence's affair with Edward Ashburnham is described as 'annexing' his affections; she is driven by a desire to annex his estate, which once belonged to her family (80, 72, 108). Even Florence wants to get back to her roots. In this context, Florence conducts her life like a real estate agent or an imperialist nation. She marries Dowell, who promises that he will buy her a British estate (88), and she pursues her affair with Edward Ashburnham in order to secure Branshaw Teleragh. Her motivation parallels that of a lost child seeking a home, just like Rhys's character, Marya, described as 'L'Enfant Perdu.'

As the narrator muses on love or war, he explains: 'With each new woman that a man is attracted to there appears to come a broadening of the outlook, or, if you like, an acquiring of new territory' (*GS* 126). The First World War comes under scrutiny in Ford's novel, not in terms of history, but rather in terms of hurt children who no longer have feelings that can be expressed other than with violence, colonization, and annexation. When there is a scene of intense grief, any witness must be violently eliminated.

In a state of crisis, Leonora communicates her grief to her foster-daughter 'crying, crying, crying, with her face hidden in her hands and the tears falling through her fingers' (*GS* 228). Thus, she must destroy her: 'She imagined the pleasure she would feel when the lash fell across those queer features; the pleasure she would feel at drawing the handle at the same moment towards her, so as to cut deep into the flesh and to leave a lasting wheal.' This fantasy of wounding the child does, in fact, hit Nancy most profoundly, for it renders her mad: 'Well, she left a lasting wheal, and her words cut deeply into the girl's mind' (229). The release of grief, the opening up of the wound, the return to the root is so unbearable that it must be erased and eliminated, fully denied and silenced, by violence. If not, one may become mad, as Nancy does.

In *The Good Soldier*, Dowell gazes onto the world through a child's eyes, and Ford exploits this childish viewpoint to allude once again to the world war that lurks on the horizon of this story. While travelling through Prussia by train, the narrator records the sights as though he were a schoolboy: 'In the sunlight, gleams come [...] from the helmets of the funny little soldiers moving their stiff little legs in white linen trousers' (47). Gearing up for an imminent war enters into the book – the fictional time of the narration is from 1904 to 1913 – with the narrator's vision of what would appear to be toy soldiers. Rather than in any historical sense, military thinking, plans, and strategies occur in the narration as a simile for the designs of an outraged wife: 'Leonora had had such lessons in the art of business from her attorney that she had her plan as clearly drawn up as was ever that of General Trochu for keeping the Prussians out of Paris in 1870' (61). Ford has the protagonists of his novel conduct their marital and sexual affairs in unwitting anticipation of a world of equally wounded and suppressed children who act out in a fury their distorted passions. While in this book it is lovers who strategize, annex, conquer, and suicide, a year after the fictional closure of the story it will be world leaders who will do so.

In *The Good Soldier*, haunted by the First World War as Ford, himself a soldier, was haunted at the front,[9] Dowell claims that the only people he has ever loved were Edward Ashburnham and Nancy Rufford, and at the end of the novel he depicts these two figures in highly romantic, literary terms (273). With a build-up of gothic moments as the story reaches its end, Edward and Nancy exit as though they are Catherine and Heathcliff haunting the moors as 'tragic shades' (274). However, what renders these figures ghost-like is their intense grief and their inability to articulate it in such a way that someone listens. The estate denies and affirms the suppressed children whose grief appears as the 'dark pillars' that resemble 'mourning presences' (243). The 'sentimental' description of home causes Nancy to begin crying 'with long convulsive sobs' (244). Yet by the end of the novel, she will appear completely suppressed, quiet, and well behaved, but nonetheless completely mad. Now nursemaid to the madwoman, the narrator compares the peaceful atmosphere of Branshaw Teleragh to his mother's love (221).[10]

In the final scenes of the novel, Ford further develops the relationship between literature – what we read and the ways in which we are constructed by our reading material – and the lack of love that produces well-behaved, mad children, who become utterly damaged adults. Nancy Rufford (note the echo of the author's name), very much the child, fully launched now into her madness, and supposedly loved by both John Dowell and Edward Ashburnham, appears 'silent, utterly well behaved as far as her knife and fork go' (*GS* 275). She has become this society's perfect child, seen and not heard yet recognized, even by the narrator, as being nightmarish. Nancy's childhood has trapped her between 'the terrors of her tempestuous father' and the 'bewailings of her cruel-tongued mother' (124). When the good soldier tries to engage Nancy in yet another child-mistress affair, she responds with childlike delight, for this symbolic father, who has raised her since she was thirteen, offers her the love and praise she has been denied by her own parents. The narrator describes Ashburnham's amorous approach to his foster-daughter as though it 'atoned' for her abusive childhood (124). He may imply that it makes amends for what she suffered or he may suggest the older meaning of atonement, which involves coming into 'unity or concord' (*OED*). The twisted, selfish, sexually motivated love of Ashburnham can hardly make amends for a brutal childhood; the attempt to somehow smooth over differences and make life harmonious seems equally problematic. Ford's novel splits apart any attempts at unity; it smashes any hopes for simple concord. Through the contradictions of his narrator, the author foregrounds the sad implications of the atonement offered by the good soldier, for it functions, in fact, as the final gesture that sets in motion his suicide and her madness.

Earlier, Dowell questions the Ashburnhams' ultimate decision to send Nancy to her father; on the one hand, he believes it is 'the right thing'; on the other hand, there is 'concern and horror at the thought of the poor girl's going back to a father whose voice made her shriek in the night' (*GS* 231). However, the father's violence, which knocked her unconscious for three days at one point, does not compare to the emotional violence of the mother: 'she had so cutting a tongue that even Nancy was afraid of her – she so made fun of any tenderness, she so sneered at all emotional displays.' He concludes weakly: 'Nancy must have been a very emotional child' (139). Nancy herself recreates this kind of 'cutting tongue,' according to the narrator, who says she has 'a sense of rectitude' that 'was a thing like a knife' (138). And as the book reaches its end, he homes in on Nancy's learned emotional violence: 'For there was about Nancy a touch of cruelty – a touch of definite actual cruelty that made her desire to see people suffer' (259). Nancy, whose conscience tells her 'that her first duty was to her parents' (247) has become the truly good soldier of the novel, for she has adapted and put into effect the abusive practices of her mother and father. These skills learned in the home render her well behaved, cruel, cutting, dutiful, and a victim of the emotional game played by her foster-parents.

Like Leonora, raised in a convent, the narrator describes Nancy's attempts to understand the marital battle between the Ashburnhams: 'With her little, pedagogic sectarianism she remembered that Catholics do not do this thing. But Edward was a Protestant. Then Edward loved somebody' (*GS* 244). Ford treats as hopeless the struggle to understand emotions, such as love and grief, in a society that insists on their suppression. A letter from Nancy's father appears in the novel and Dowell comments: 'His letter was pathetic because it was so brief, so inarticulate, and so business-like' (255).

Dowell's first encounter with the Ashburnhams hinges on his delight at no longer being alone, but being part of a group committed to the denial of feelings (*GS* 37). This is an insightful assessment, considering that Dowell married a woman who silences him: Florence speaks to him without looking at him and she '[holds] up one hand as if she wished to silence any objection – or any comment' (15–16). Verbally suppressed by his now dead wife, John Dowell provides a whole novel's worth of pent-up expression. Yet Ford reveals that Dowell's fantasy of storytelling revolves around a place where sadness can be erased, as it can in 'Provence where even the saddest stories are gay' (15). Despite his hopes of controlling the story, surely even our narrator cannot avoid the sadness of his tale; yet he does so. His final response to the sadness at the end of the novel is silence. Rather than respond to Edward's 'soft and almost affectionate' parting just before he kills himself, the narrator, concerned about the appropriate British rejoinder, simply chooses to remain silent: 'I trotted off with the telegram to Leonora' (278). The grief inherent in the story he tells surfaces only through Ford's layering of the narrative voice. Hence, after the narrator's writerly sigh in his storytelling fantasy of the fireside chat, he describes a landscape seemingly without purpose, yet one that underpins the story: 'And the immense mistral blew down that valley which was the way from France into Provence so that the silver-grey olive leaves appeared like hair flying in the wind, and the tufts of rosemary crept in to the iron rocks that they might not be torn up by the roots' (15). This personified landscape conveys the emotional pain that one experiences while escaping to the place where 'even the saddest stories are gay.' What does the traveller do with the immense wind that bears down, blasting the hair and causing one to creep into stone places so as not to be torn up by the very roots? This 'immense wind' recurs later in the novel coursing over the fields of the yearned-for home, Branshaw Teleragh – ironically the site of suffering (117).

In Ford's narrative, writing has a dual movement: on the one hand, it records the life of people who have turned to stone within; on the other hand, the writing carved in stone becomes the solid rock to which one can cling in sadness and not be brutally blown to pieces. This story reads like an epitaph, written upon the tombstones of those who died or lost their minds to inexpressible grief. Derrida describes this force of writing, which 'creates meaning by enregistering it, by entrusting it to an engraving' (*WD* 12). In *The Good Soldier*, Dowell imagines Ashburnham's tombstone, upon which his wife will record his particularly English virtues: 'he was very well built, carried himself well, was moderate at the table, and led a regular life' (*GS* 165). Forming a contrast with this emphasis on suppression, the narrator confronts the near suicidal good soldier and he stresses the man's unvoiced pain: 'And that poor devil beside me was in an agony. Absolute, hopeless, dumb agony such as passes the mind of man to imagine' (23). With an echo of Hamlet's grief that 'passes show,' this man is in a wholly inarticulate state of anguish. The two radically different epitaphs are, in fact, branches of the same tree, and the root cause of this division is the good soldier's socially sanctioned, cruel, dehumanizing upbringing. Ford depicts the Ashburnham family tree as one whose root, buried deeply, produces a suppressed, yet suffering self.

Beyond imagined tombstones, Ford uses stone imagery further in his investigation of suppressed grief and the role of writing. Trying to clarify his storytelling motives, Dowell describes in detail the landscape of Beaucaire 'with the grey walls on the top of the pinnacle surrounding an acre and a half of blue irises, beneath the tallness of the stone pines. What a beautiful thing the stone pine is!' For a third time, he uses the phrase *stone pines:* 'the stone pines against the blue of the sky' (*GS* 16). Ford encourages us to reread this repeated phrase as the stone itself pining. Not only do the tombstones of those who have died in this story pine for something, but also the man turned to stone, John Dowell, pines for something of a similar nature. As he puts it: 'I was the walking dead'; thus, he belongs among the tombstones (121).

In contemporary usage, *to pine* means *to yearn* for something, but it also carries the archaic meaning 'to mourn' (*OED*). My sense is that the narrator and the three others, forming what he calls in one breath a 'minuet' and in another a 'prison,' pine for access to and relief from intense feelings of grief: 'It wasn't a minuet that we stepped; it was a prison – a prison full of screaming hysterics, tied down so that they might not outsound the rolling of our carriage wheels as we went along the shaded avenues' (9). Their prison in this scene is constructed of mindless rolling from one place to another, while the self, hysterical with grief, remains silenced. Throughout the novel, the narrator unravels within these feelings of grief, yet what become stone markers along the path of the reader's journey remain as stone walls imprisoning those within the story.

The name 'Beaucaire' means beautiful stone marker if we trace *caire* back to its origins in the Irish word *cairn* (*OED*). This trope has a striking correspondence with Rhys's use of Cairn as a name for a character aware of childhood grief. In *The Good Soldier*, Beaucaire serves as a symbolic place for Leonora in particular, as her roots are Irish. The *Petit Robert* reminds us that a cairn is 'a stone triangle elevated by mountain climbers or explorers as a point of reference or a marker of their passage' (my translation). Therefore, in a passage where Dowell presents himself as a traveller, while struggling to convey his purpose in writing, the story appears as a beautiful marker, not of the dead and buried, but rather of the living dead. And this stone marker pines.

The visual metaphor of Beaucaire is important here, for the 'blue irises,' enclosed in stone, on the surface refer to flowers; however, on another level they leave us with an impression of the irises of eyes blocked by stone walls. In his first encounter with Leonora, the narrator highlights her blue eyes, where you might see into 'the whole round of the irises.' In this initial description, he also describes her resemblance to stone: 'She seemed to stand out of her corsage as a white marble bust might.' When he imagines touching her, he thinks she would be 'cold' (*GS* 36). In a crisis scene, Leonora's 'irises' blend disturbingly with the stone and thus generate an image of Beaucaire: 'I had the feeling that those two blue discs were immense, were overwhelming, were like a wall of blue that shut me off from the rest of the world' (49). Considering the blue of his wife's eyes, as well as Ashburnham's eyes, the communion that our narrator entertains with these intimates is, in fact, more like the prison that he feels enclosing him. He mentions Beaucaire again near the end of the story, and this stone marker thus encircles his own story and blocks its witnessing (254). On yet another level, we realize that for John Dowell the act itself of narrating is a way of positioning stone walls that will protect the irises of his eyes from witnessing. This circular denial of characters transforms through the literary act into an encounter for readers with grieving childhood selves. While the characters bury their feelings, Ford exhumes them. The story takes root in the wound of the good soldier.

Like the narrator of *The Good Soldier*, the protagonist of *Parade's End* is a conflicted character. On the one hand, he is without emotions; on the other, he has extreme passions. He is well trained in the British pedagogical system: 'Christopher Tietjens' emotional existence was a complete taciturnity – at any rate as to his emotions' (6). Yet, unlike the characters in *The Good Soldier* and unlike those in Conrad's, Rhys's, and West's grieving novels, Tietjens has a child for whom his 'clumsy tenderness' is 'so marked' (15). Marking a notable shift in fictional treatment of childhood grief, this child survives beyond infancy. Clearly, Tietjens's son is a pivotal character; yet critics rarely comment on him.[11]

Tietjens, the hero-protagonist of the four novels, cannot express his feelings to his parents, brother, or wife, although in a state of desperation he writes down, while at war, that he is 'passionately attached' to his little son (*PE* 346). During his experience at the front, prior to writing the four novels of *Parade's End*, Ford writes: 'these cataclysmic moments make one desire to record' (*Letters* 75). However, in the tetralogy, one is left wondering if the cataclysm arises from a home life without feelings or a life on the home front of a world war.

Tietjens's journal or document is never read by anyone and seems to disappear. Notably, he writes of his love for his son in his 'pocket-book' with 'large penciled characters' that evoke the handwriting of a child (*PE* 345). Which child does Tietjens feel passionate about – his son or his inner child? Like West, Ford allows for both in his portrayal of the two boys: the inner child is absent, belongs to the past, and has been replaced by an adult; the son is present now, but is also absent, owing to being home while his father is at war. Tietjens writes about his love for his son, but he writes as a child; thus, Ford highlights what Derrida would describe as a 'play of difference,' which operates by means of 'syntheses and referrals' (*P* 26). This play prevents a simple answer to the question of which child is addressed and which child is loved. Ford interweaves the present parent/child bond with the ghostly parent/child bond of the past. This conveys his idea of child/adult 'synchrony' that Derrida foregrounds in *Circumfession* as vital.

In two encounters with symbolic parental figures – Valentine Wannop's mother and General Campion, both close friends of his parents, who are dead – Tietjens responds with grief to their 'tenderness.' When Mrs Wannop strokes his temple: 'He was quite aware that he had tears in his eyes; this was almost too much tenderness to bear, and, at bottom his was a perfectly direct, simple, and sentimental soul' (*PE* 115). Sentimental is Ashburnham's epithet as well and we may therefore expect a comparable good soldier in Tietjens. However, while Ashburnham suicides in an inarticulate state of duty to social mores as well as romantic ideals, Tietjens rebels over the course of four novels against the emotional suppression that he was taught as a child.

While at war, in a painful discussion with General Campion in which Tietjens speaks of how his father betrayed him by believing slanderous gossip and never asking his son the truth, the general merely utters the broken line: 'But I …' and Tietjens replies that, unlike his father, the general never 'believed anything against' his godson. The reaction in Tietjens is telling: he is 'sentimentally at rest, still with wet eyes' (*PE* 497). The general tries to reach out to this hurt, grieving man. He stretches out 'a sudden, ineffectual hand' and Tietjens lurches 'as an old house lurches when it is hit by a H.E. shell' (499). The father-figure's attempt to reach him with tenderness jolts him, leaving him exploded, collapsed, shell-shocked.

With the First World War as a backdrop, the true battle of *Parade's End* is fought between the trained, reasoning side of Tietjens and his inarticulate, emotional side. The battle is between the suppressed adult and the expressive child. Hence, a trench in this war appears 'shaped like the house a child draws' (291) and the war passages of the novel constantly refer to children and schoolboys. Tietjens's wife Sylvia, the enemy of expressing feelings in the epic, condemns the men at war as if they are 'school-boys'; her loathing for these 'boys' is acute (398, 413–14, 424, 427, 431, 437). Ford foregrounds the layered meaning of infantry, for the war zone of *Parade's End* resembles a nursery or schoolyard. Captain Tietjens holds a man dying in his arms 'as if he'd been a baby' (433). As one soldier exclaims: 'he mothered the lot of us' (399). A sergeant-major specifically draws attention to the overlap in meaning between infantry, as infants and as soldiers, when he confronts the troops: 'You *look* like a squad of infants' companions from a Wesleyan Sunday school' (318). When General Campion inspects the military kitchen, it appears to Tietjens as 'a childish dream'; he insists that it 'was all childish' (500). Watching one soldier die, Tietjens sees a 'very blond boy's face, contorted in the strong light, shrieking' (557). Tietjens saves the life of a soldier whom he describes as a 'very gallant child' (558). The captain feels 'a premonition that that child was going to be hurt' and, indeed, this soldier is killed before him (636). When he is saving a soldier's life, he feels 'tender, like a mother' (639). A subaltern is 'a good nervous boy' (586). A sergeant announcing the onslaught of the Germans has the 'tone of a resigned schoolboy' (567). When a soldier is killed, 'he had a smile like a young baby's on his face' (569). The soldiers seem like children 'playing a game of "I spy!"' and like 'children in the corner of the schoolroom' (561, 563). The good boys of this war have done what was expected; they have become good soldiers. Ford stresses 'the syntheses and referrals,' thereby participating in what Derrida imagines as 'a new concept of writing,' which, as noted, he calls '*gram* or *différance*' (*P* 26). *Parade's End* plays on the differences and similarities between infantry in the nursery and infantry in the trenches.

Tietjens struggles to adhere to the either/or paradigm he has been taught as a child, in which 'emotion stands against reason' and 'intellect corrects passion' (*PE* 87); however, when he tries to organize himself and his love, Valentine Wannop, into binary opposites, the system fails: 'he must play stiff and cold, she warm and clinging ... yet she was obviously as cool a hand as himself; cooler no doubt, for at bottom he was certainly a sentimentalist' (129). This admission corrects his initial sense that he is 'Yorkshire and stolid' in contrast to Valentine, who is 'south country and soft, emotional.' While she speaks about feelings, the 'Yorkshire man only grunts' and he assumes that she acknowledges 'the superior wood-enness of the north' (125). The self turned to wood is the first step in the self turning to stone. And in this society, stone is used as a weapon to crush sentimentalists; as Tietjens realizes that in 'a world such as this' one who is 'a sentimentalist – must be stoned to death. He makes the others so uncomfortable' (237). In this society, a person who is soft and emotional, flesh and feelings, acts as the signifier for grief.

Unlike his first wife, Sylvia, who imagines marital relations as being 'on the warpath' (*PE* 300), his present love, Valentine, is able to move the immobilized Tietjens with her words; thus, 'Peace' is defined by him as having 'someone to talk to' (607). When Tietjens meditates on Valentine, he realizes that he must seduce her in order to speak with her and then he defines their 'intimate conversation' as 'love' (629). By talking with Valentine, the good soldier can express his grief; on their first visit together he decides to take a holiday 'from the suppression of emotions' and their encounter ends with his being shaken by 'clumsy sobs' (129, 143). He asks her to be his mistress beneath a 'weeping willow' (279, 285).

Initially, before his love affair with Valentine, both Christopher and his brother Mark Tietjens appear wooden to others and the symbolic feature of their childhood estate is the 'Groby Great Tree.' This family tree is rooted in a wound and it transforms the children raised in its shade into wooden adults. Thus, the estranged wife, Sylvia, wants to make her husband's 'wooden face wince' (*PE* 381). Valentine thinks of Tietjens's 'calculatedly wooden expression' and his 'wooden countenance' (518, 646). When Sylvia speaks with Tietjens's older brother, Mark, she is struck by his 'brown-wooden features' and notes that he 'expressed no emotion at all' (420). Even with his own brother, Mark uses a 'wooden gesture' (203) and his face is 'walnut-coloured' (677). We learn of the significance of the Groby Great Tree indirectly, since one of Tietjens's ways of communicating through his silenced self is by talking in his sleep

(457). Tietjens not only talks, but also *writes* while asleep: 'It was very queer,' he is informed, 'Almost ghostlike ... There you sat, your arms on the table. Talking away. You appeared to be writing a letter to her' (457). Tietjens has been yet again a victim of his wife's attempts to wound him, and he pours out his grief to Valentine in a broken form, a letter, written while he is asleep, when the reasoning, intellectual mind is shut off and the hurt, grieving self, hidden since childhood, has a chance to emote. Valentine notes that Tietjens begins to talk about the 'Groby Great Tree' in his sleep 'as for years, at times, he had talked, dreadfully, about the war' (813). The childhood tree haunts, just as war trauma haunts. Tietjens is devoted to the tree without realizing that it traps him in his suppressed childhood suffering, paralleling war trauma.

Like West, Ford evokes the overlap between home and the home front. The central war organization for Britain appears in Ford's epic as if turned to stone. Just after a confrontation with his brother about how 'unforgivable' he finds their father's refusal to speak to him during crisis, Tietjens fantasizes about a bomb going off in the War Office in London, which he depicts as 'the mean grey stoniness of that cold heart of an embattled world' (*PE* 222). The paternal cold heart could be read as either his father's or his society's heart. The fantasized explosion describes the double work of *Parade's End*, in which Ford shell shocks his characters, and readers into feeling their grief and hearing their child. This bomb detonates only during acts of reading and writing and it shakes the 'stoniness' of the parent and of the society to their foundations. Derrida argues that structure 'can be *methodically* threatened' and he refers to this activity as 'soliciting.' He explains his use of this term according to its Latin roots: '*shaking* in a way related to the whole (from *sollus*, in archaic Latin "the whole," and from *citare*, "to put in motion")' (*WD* 6). As noted, one of the linking features of the modernist novels under discussion is the tension between mobility and immobility, being moved and being petrified.

When Sylvia thinks about her former husband, whom she still pursues, she imagines him entering as a statue with a 'face of stone' (*PE* 793). Thus, comparable to the imagery used in an explosive modernist text, she *solicits* him by having Groby Great Tree cut down: 'Christopher's boyhood's bedroom had practically disappeared'; she prides herself on the 'nice shock' he will get (801). Because Sylvia has been equally well trained to adhere to the system of suppressed emotions – the silencing of the child-self, and the social advantages of presenting a stony face to the world – she does not realize that cutting down the tree will not wound him. It will open up the childhood wound. Hence, cutting down the tree acts as an antidote for the poisonous pedagogy administered to Tietjens's childhood self. She thinks Christopher will be shell-shocked, as he was during the war, without realizing that the 'nice shock' she gives him sends him back, just as his war shell shock does, to his childhood self and allows him to relearn the world. This dual meaning of shell shock can be compared to the trajectory West puts Chris Baldry on in *Return of the Soldier*. Ironically, Sylvia Tietjens's poisonous gesture cures her husband of his suppressed childhood grief. She shocks him back to emotional life.

Tietjens renounces the world that requires his emotional suppression. He works at failure, which Ford stresses most strikingly in the final novel, where nine different voices narrate and Tietjens appears only briefly while paradoxically being at the centre of the story. While in *The Good Soldier* John Dowell produces endless narrative strategies, buys up the estate, and marries a mad woman, Christopher Tietjens becomes narratively unproductive. He refuses the family estate and exits his marriage to a destructive wife. Drawing on a theatrical metaphor, employing a tension between the actor and the prompter (*souffleur*) so that the former draws on the 'the fecundity of the *other* breath [*souffle*],' Derrida imagines this withdrawal from an assertion of selfhood as a kind of 'unpower,' which is 'inspiration itself,' for it accommodates and recognizes others and otherness (*WD* 176). Further developing and focusing this idea, Tietjens's acting out failure according to his society's terms forms what Derrida sees as a mode of mourning. As he contends with sorrow over the death of a friend, Derrida writes: 'here comes a work without force, a work that would have to work at renouncing force, its own force, a work that would have to work at failure, and thus at mourning and getting over force, a work, working at its own unproductivity' (*WM* 144).

Derrida's idea of mourning returns us to Hamlet and offers a different way of thinking about him: he is criticized for being unproductive while he grieves; only when he becomes actively violent and is killed can he be praised by his society: 'Let four captains / Bear Hamlet like a soldier to the stage' (V.ii.400–1). Ford has Tietjens refer to Hamlet's inactivity when he self-critiques: 'Now what the Hell was he? A sort of Hamlet of the Trenches! No, by God he was not ... He was perfectly ready for action' (*PE* 630). This is the standard view. And then he qualifies it: 'Not even a picture postcard! For two years! A sort of Hamlet all right!' (630). Ford compares Tietjens to Hamlet, first as a seemingly unproductive man, one who doesn't act, and second, in terms of his failure to grieve or commune with the woman he loves through writing. Both strive to be good soldiers, but both fail as they withdraw from power on the one hand and grief on the other. They do not kill on command, nor do they express their sadness or love to Valentine / Ophelia.

While Shakespeare's female character dies of grief, Ford's spirited Valentine exclaims: 'Now why do I say that? What's Hecuba to me?' (*PE* 539). Hamlet's interrogation of his inability to grieve, contrasted with the player's elaborate acting of sorrow, returns in *Parade's End* when Valentine questions her own adherence to the social system of suppression to preserve the honour of the man she loves. She defends his wife to protect his reputation and laughs at the irony. Thus, ultimately, their love defies their childhood training; it rejects and mocks the social system. Ophelia drowns, but Valentine moves in with Tietjens and becomes pregnant with his child.

For Tietjens, grieving is productive *within* while it appears unproductive without. Likewise, the child-self is unproductive in the working and social world while being highly productive within if enabled to express itself. From the start of *Parade's End*, Tietjens appears to be floundering socially in a world that praises his emotional suppression while he develops in productive ways as a child-self. Valentine believes that in terms of his own affairs he is 'so simple as to be almost a baby' (*PE* 236). Hence, she says to him: 'You're as innocent as a child' (239). When they converse: 'It appeared to her as if a child were speaking' (236). Ford further develops this child productivity of Tietjens, linked to mourning, in his treatment of shell shock: 'Mett ... Metter ... His face illuminated itself like the face of a child listening at a shell' (166). Ford undermines the beauty of the child listening to a seashell, for the good soldier, Tietjens, has had a portion of his 'brain wiped white' from shell shock during trench warfare. Yet he heals by having his slate wiped clean of his childhood lessons; it becomes a space for a new kind of writing. But it also seems that he listens to an explosive 'shell' that shakes up his stony self. He re-enters the world with his wound 'as a new-born babe' (170). Valentine goes to meet him after the war and, knowing he has shell shock, believes that the experience will be 'like tending your baby!' (646).[12]

After shell shock has done its erasing, what might the new language that Tietjens writes on his childhood slate look like? We noted that Sylvia succeeds in having Groby Great Tree cut down and it pulls down with it Tietjens's childhood bedroom. Mark, Christopher's older brother, reminisces about the tree to which his sibling is so deeply attached: it 'overshadowed the house' and 'you could not look out of the schoolroom windows at all for its great, ragged trunk.' More ominous still, 'all the children's wing was darkened by its branches,' which he recalls as 'black ... funeral plumes' (*PE* 736). The fall of this family tree symbolically crumbles the deeply rooted pedagogy that raised the wooden brothers through wounding. Indicative of a life of suppression, the older brother has become literally paralysed, figuratively turned to stone, by the novel's end. Yet he too makes a valiant effort to rebel against his training and release his childhood voice and feelings. Paralysed, Mark Tietjens cannot speak, but after the tree has fallen, in a rare loving gesture towards his brother, he whispers for the pregnant Valentine the verses his nurse (not mother) sang to him as a child, 'Twas the mid o' the night and the barnies grat / And the mither beneath the mauld heard that,' and he continues, 'Never thou let thy barnie weep for thy sharp tongue to thy goodman ... A good man! ... Groby Great Tree is down' (827). Then he holds her hand and dies. The nurse's dialect is a foreign language of love and tenderness singing in the child, a language that is suppressed by the formal English of the adult self. We noted that Rhys also employs this nurse's language, the foreign terms of patois, in Christophine's comforting of Antoinette in *Wide Sargasso Sea*.

Only one other time is patois mentioned in Ford's epic work. One of the final narrating voices is the interior monologue of Mark's wife, Marie Léonie. As a foreigner, she can better articulate the emotional events, for she has not been trained, like her British lover, to turn to wood. While he is defined by 'immobility' and 'absolute taciturnity,' she is highly verbal and Mark regards her with the 'ironic indulgence that you accord to a child' (*PE* 687, 682). She is a chattering, foreign child. Marie Léonie notes that when the brothers articulate strong feelings, they speak in 'patois': 'Naturally they returned to the language they spoke in their childhoods – when they were excited, these unexcitable people' (772). We might characterize the languages now appearing on Tietjens's slate as belonging to foreigners, children, the speakers of patois. As seen in Conrad and Rhys novels, this is the language of non-power inspired by the breath of others and otherness.

The Tietjens brothers have rarely spoken to one another, but after the war they discuss the family home. Tietjens, despite his love for the family estate, Groby, will not accept it from Mark, his older sibling, to punish him for past emotional wounds. Ford presents the battle between the brothers with grief tropes: turning to stone and being wounded in the throat. However, no emotions are expressed by either. When Tietjens rejects his brother's offer of the family estate, Mark feels that the 'fact had gone into [him] as a knife goes into a stag's throat. It had hurt as much, but it hadn't killed!' (*PE* 763). Later, when Tietjens hears that Groby may be rented to others, he 'nearly jumped out of his skin – that is to say he had sat as still as a lump of white marble' (760). However, Tietjens battles with the suppression that threatens to turn him to stone, and he seeks throughout the epic to find a way to articulate his feelings. One method Tietjens uses to break out of the social mould is to visit his son conceived with Sylvia; he 'played with his boy' (186). This anticipates the dreams that Valentine has, while pregnant with their child, of the joy she will have in mothering (821). There is no mention of placing a nurse or nanny in the role of parent. Again, there is a double movement here, for the absent inner child haunts the father's play with the present child. The past child connects with the future child, while the adult acts as the medium or mediator between the two. Ironically, we witness Tietjens being a loving father while he is at war. He responds to soldiers openly and humanely, not at all with the wooden paralysis that was taught to him at home by his father. Thus, Ford encourages us to imagine Tietjens as a compassionate, non-oppressive father to his own silent son.

The foundational relationship of fathers and sons has already become shaken with Tietjens's fatherly treatment of his infantry at war. While his inner child is the spectre who haunts him, the young men he addresses are likely to literally become ghosts. Yet Tietjens does not suppress his grief. Instead of speaking woodenly, he calls out commands to his soldiers – 'cannon fodder' – with 'tears in his voice' (*PE* 362). Derrida uses the identical phrase to describe the way one talks to the dead, addresses the lost ones who haunt: 'With tears in their voices, they sometimes speak familiarly to the other who keeps silent' (*WM* 200). The silence one needs to hear grief is one of the reasons why Derrida claims: 'We must find a speech which maintains silence' (*WD* 262). Speech, which maintains silence, is another way to think about writing.

As noted, while at war Tietjens tries to write in order to sort out his feelings: 'Better put it into writing' he thinks. And more forcefully: 'He was determined to get it expressed. He wrote on again' (*PE* 345, 346). In his writing, he does not address the cannon fodder, the young men who become ghosts around him during battle. Instead, he writes about his own internal ghost, the self he might have been if he had not learned at an early age to hide his feelings. In writing, Tietjens notes that he and Valentine are not 'persons to talk about the state of our feelings'; thus, they have 'exchanged no confidences.' He realizes that he is 'damn good at not speaking.' Yet at the same time he declares that he is 'passionately attached' to his son (346). Who is this boy, loved by an expressionless father who writes about him?

The child of *Parade's End* haunts his father's every move. Throughout the four novels, this absent child hovers on the periphery of the action, appearing only in his family's thoughts and feelings. Since, as Peggy Kamuf reminds us, 'deconstruction always works at the margins, on the limits,' a Derridean reading foregrounds rather than avoids the marginal child of *Parade's End* (introd. xviii). At the opening of the first novel, the child is discussed in legal and financial terms because his mother, Sylvia, has run off with another man. He is not named, referred to by his father and grandfather only as 'the child' (*PE* 6). Despite being discussed in front of his grandfather as merely a business concern, this absent child functions as the catalyst for Tietjens's conduct throughout the four novels: he will not divorce his wife for infidelity or insist on his own innocence, because he does not want his son to be known to have a mother who is a 'whore' (77). When, near the end of the epic, the son actually appears as a character, he is inarticulate: 'The boy at the foot of the bed was making agonised motions with his throat' (727). The boy has become a chip off the old block, but the block is in the process throughout of shattering into articulation.

When Sylvia visits Tietjens unannounced while he is at the war front in France, she recalls how he saved their son's life by bathing him in an ice-cold bath, despite the child's pain, in order to reduce his fever. She notes that, as a soldier, he suffers in an equally silent way; during both crises, he appears 'rather as if he had a cold in the head – a little suffocating, with suppressing his emotions' (*PE* 437). The son at home forms a parallel with the sons of war: infantry in the nursery and infantry on the battlefield; the 'Tommie' at home and the Tommies at war. At the outset of *Parade's End*, the child is called 'Tommie' by his father and sent to stay with his aunt in Yorkshire (7). Tietjens explains to Sylvia that he has loved their son with all his 'heart' and 'soul' since the 'first minute,' but he seems incapable of naming the child, which forms a parallel with not being able to keep him. Likewise, Sylvia refers to her son only as 'child' in pronouncements such as 'I hate my child' and when detailing her plans for hurting her husband 'by corrupting the child' (38, 41). In the central war scenes of the novel, Ford, true to history, refers to the British soldiers as 'Tommies,' but the echo is strange, since this is the original name of the son (167, 350). Further unravelling the father-son bond, marked by the proper name, Sylvia refers to their son as 'Michael' (401). This son, no longer a child, appears at the end of the work before his paralysed Uncle Mark and refers to himself as 'Mark Junior' (728). Later, the name of the son, as Mark, surfaces in the mother's interior monologue, for it is the child who decides to switch from the name 'Michael,' representing his maternal heritage: 'he had said that he intended to call himself Mark from then on – By the name of his father's brother, of his father's father, grand-father, great-grandfather' (781). The name is obviously an assertion of the son's desire to honour his estranged father; for the reader, this name draws attention to the name Tietjens initially uses, Tommie. His son is the child-soldier 'Tommie' still missing in action, still voiceless, still grieving in *Parade's End*.[13]

No longer merely a legal, patriarchal, business concern, Tommie / Michael / Mark Tietjens is a boy. He becomes a boy that is like one of Tietjens's soldiers; he is loved by his father. His improper status, like the lowly, foreign dialect of tenderness, remembered by his dying uncle, whose name he seeks to use, offers him an emotional life denied his father and uncle by their legally rightful parents. Tietjens plays with his son Tommie and speaks to his Tommies with 'tears in his voice'; thus, he uses a language inspired by grief and supplemented with the childish, foreign echoes of patois. He does not give his son a proper name.

As *Parade's End* concludes, Tietjens's beloved Valentine is living with him as a mistress; she is pregnant with a son whom she will name Christopher, after his father Christopher Tietjens. However, Valentine still must save her unborn child (the symbolic child-self of Christopher) from Sylvia, who represents society and thus has turned to stone. The estranged wife arrives and speaks with 'the voice of a frozen marble statue' and she appears with a 'pallid face of stone' (*PE* 146, 177). Previously she has tried to ruin Christopher and Valentine's love for one another, and in this final scene she appears as immobilized stone at the top of a flight of stairs: 'a marble statue.' Faced with this figure, Valentine feels 'as if she held the child covered in her arms, as if she were looking upwards, bending down over the child' (820–1). In a fiction of sacrificed, suppressed, denied children, Valentine affirms and protects the child. Sylvia speaks 'marmoreally' and 'someone sobbed!' but Ford does not specify who (826–7). If the statue weeps – and we can feel those wet tears – then perhaps it can arise and go. If the mother sobs, then she will not turn to stone and her child will be able to express its grief. Perhaps the sobbing is that of the reader. Our desire to organize the novels into an interpretation and establish certain markers is displaced by a final question. In this book about haunted selves and the displacement of grief, one is left to question who 'someone' is and why he or she is 'sobbing.' Yet, in striving to respond, this is exactly what preserves the novels, the characters, society, and ourselves from become immobilized; instead, all is set in motion.

In *The Good Soldier*, the characters try to find a home for the grieving child; however, they return to the site of suppression, the childhood home, and simply repeat, in a paralysed way, their own pasts. In *Parade's End*, Ford Madox Ford has his protagonist break with tradition, refuse the childhood home, ignore legal rules, and thereby create a home where grief can be expressed, adults can utter tender words, and children can be heard, even when they have tears in their voices.

5 Creating a Space for Childhood's Sound Waves: Virginia Woolf's *A Haunted House* and *The Waves*

In Ford Madox Ford's fiction, he conflates the domestic home and the military home front. He locates within this superimposed space a good soldier and layers within him a grieving child. However, he renders the child not only inarticulate, but silent. Thus, when we shift focus from Ford and the novelists discussed before him to the fiction of Virginia Woolf, what is most notable is that she actually lets the child-self speak.[1] Although struggling throughout with the suppression of grief and its return as aggression, Woolf's fictional child has fully lost its alien status; furthermore, the child no longer has to communicate in a foreign language. In *A Haunted House* and *The Waves*, Virginia Woolf creates a home, a shelter within the fictional space, a place where children's voices, even if they are grieving, can express themselves directly.

In 1921 Virginia Woolf published eight short stories under the title *Monday or Tuesday*; this collection went out of print in her lifetime. In 1944, after her death, Leonard Woolf published six of these stories and other short fiction she had written throughout the years, under the title *A Haunted House*. Much of the haunting in the collection comes from suppressed childhood and grieving selves; thus, it forms a provocative parallel to some of the narrators in *The Waves* who develop a system of military values from being trained to hold back their tears in childhood. Scholars have noted that Woolf writes childhood in powerful ways; however, the child-voices have not been connected to suppression of grief or resultant aggression.[2]

As Mark Hussey states, 'all Woolf's work is deeply concerned with war,' and thus 'from her earliest to her final work she sought to explore and make clear the connections between private and public violence' (3). Rather than exploring gender and war, which have been treated richly in

Woolf scholarship, I want to shift the focus to child-selves and war in her fiction.[3] In the following chapter, I highlight childhood selves in Woolf's fiction according to my specific interest in suppressed grief. Rather than addressing the selected works as wholes, I will draw from them in an interwoven manner in order to explore Woolf's investigation of childhood, the suppression of grief, and the creating of good soldiers.

* * *

> Have I read you right? But the human face – the human face at the top of the fullest sheet of print holds more, withholds more. Now, eyes open, she looks out; and in the human eye – how d'you define it? – there's a break – a division – so that when you've grasped the stem the butterfly's off – the moth that hangs in the evening over the yellow flower – move, raise your hand, off, high, away.
>
> (*HH* 21)

In this story from the *Haunted House* collection, entitled 'An Unwritten Novel,' Woolf offers a contradictory portrait of a character / narrator / writer. When one looks at this portrait from a Derridean point of view, it makes sense that it refuses to comply with the 'metaphysical line of thought' or 'logocentrist' line of thought, because such a thing depends on the 'suppression-repression of contradiction' (*P* 73) and Woolf is interested in contradiction. Woolf's contradictory figure imagines a story for a woman sitting across from her in a train compartment, who she believes is a grieving woman. While the narrator reads the *Times*, she glances over the top of her sheet of print and realizes that the face across from her (with)holds surplus meanings beyond her reading and thereby transforms her provocative question, 'Have I read you right?' so that, addressed to both reader and character, it turns into a telling pun: 'Have I read you right / write?' Has my reading of you being accurate, fair, real? Have I read you while you write? Or has my reading silenced you, not recognized the you as writing? This silencing of the other is exactly Derrida's concern with traditional philosophy's insistence on 'thinking its other.' He asserts that the danger of this stance is that 'one reappropriates [the other] for oneself, one disposes of it, one misses it' (*T* 149–51). Hence, this layered self allows Woolf to dismantle the tendency to silence, with a focus on grief, in 'An Unwritten Novel.'

To return to the above quoted passage, there is a break, a division in the human eye / I, and one of the ways to obliquely express such an idea is to see the self as a butterfly and a moth, a diurnal and a nocturnal creature. The writer / narrator appear, reaching towards this complex creature, moving, raising the hand; yet the butterfly / moth is ultimately out of reach.[4] Within this story, the mobile moth acts as a force to defy the immobilizing of grief in childhood. Like much of Woolf's short fiction, this story develops a strategy of unwriting / unrighting: the novelist must unravel writing, undo society's weaving in order to discover her own sense of what requires articulation.[5] Vicki Mahaffey discusses 'unweaving' and quotes from Derrida's *Positions*, in which the theorist renders 'almost identical and entirely other' the acts of reading and writing; thus, the deconstructive ex-position reveals that in relation to reading: 'Writing is the complementary process of centralizing what was marginal' (192–3).[6]

Derrida studies Barthes's mourning for his mother as a model of conduct through loss. He highlights the 'relationship to the photogram,' where 'the return of the referent indeed takes the form of a haunting.' He imagines that the 'spectral arrival in the very space of the photogram indeed resembles that of an emission or emanation' (*WM* 54). A photogram provides an intriguing correlative to what Woolf seeks to reveal. A photogram is a shadow-like picture made by placing objects between light-sensitive paper and a light source and then developing the latent photographic image. How better to see the ghost or the moth? It functions as a technique to reveal who is lost and why one mourns. Woolf presents narrators and characters who grieve for lost childhood selves; yet they are haunted by them, without being able to address them.

In *Three Guineas*, Woolf describes photographs as a way to comment on fascism: 'those certainly are dead children, and that undoubtedly is the section of a house. A bomb has torn open the side' (164). She describes their impact: 'Those photographs are not an argument; they are simply a crude statement of fact addressed to the eye. But the eye is connected with the brain; the brain with the nervous system. That system sends its messages in a flash through every past memory and present feeling. When we look at those photographs, some fusion takes place within us; however different the education, the traditions behind us, our sensations are the same; and they are violent' (165). Here Woolf expresses powerfully the force of her own writing: she strives to flash through us, cause fusion between thought and feeling, the articulate and the inarticulate self, present moment and buried past.[7] Reading Woolf's articulation of grief, one remembers that the brain is inextricably fused with the nervous system; hence, the collapse of the binary oppositions between intellectual / emotional, child / adult, and self / other may well cause 'a violent sensation.' In order to maintain one's own presence in the face of the photographs of dead children and exploded homes, one must suppress 'every past memory and present feeling.'[8] Derrida, building on Freud, sees the modernist era as dismantling the 'epoch of presence,' where self-presence was constructed on the 'opposition of consciousness to unconsciousness' (*WD* 198). Woolf belongs to this epoch.

Throughout *A Haunted House*, Woolf demonstrates a keen interest in the suppression of feelings and memories. Thus, she uses recollections of childhood to unravel the adult belief in presence. In one of the stories, the protagonist is a prominent, wealthy jeweller, yet 'he dismantled himself often and became again a little boy in a dark alley' (101). The jeweller bets his mother he will succeed; yet the narrator asks: 'was he not still a sad man, a dissatisfied man, a man who seeks something that is hidden, though he had won his bet?' (102). The jeweller wears his grief on his tie in the form of a pearl, for he sees heart's blood in rubies and '"Tears!"' in pearls (102–3). At one point what causes him to transform into a simultaneous adult and child is the sight of 'the heads of the Roman emperors that were graved on his sleeve links.' This sight causes him to unravel: 'again he dismantled himself and became once more the little boy playing marbles in the alley where they sell stolen dogs on Sunday' (103–4). Can it be coincidence that what recalls the child-self for the jeweller is the sight of the Roman emperors, signs of stoicism captured in the 'be a good soldier' motto as well as signs of empire and its desire to parent other lands and peoples in an aggressive and oppressive way?

In *The Waves*, the schoolboy, Louis, considers himself a companion of Virgil (64); he presents himself as the most impervious, yet he imagines: 'I am the weakest, the youngest of them all. I am a child looking at his feet and the little runnels that the stream has made in the gravel' (65). Like the jeweller, Louis has created, through economic success, a sense of adult security; nonetheless, it can be dismantled quickly, for behind his presentation of power and prestige, he is haunted by a vulnerable child.

Perhaps not as insecure, but definitely as enamoured of Roman times, Neville of *The Waves*, at school with Louis, imagines his book as 'a block of marble' (59), and he thinks that the boy he adores, Percival, not only 'should have a birch and beat little boys for misdemeanours,' but also that he 'is allied with the Latin phrases on the memorial brasses' (24). Louis considers Percival as one who 'inspires poetry' (27). Not only an inspiration for Virgilian-style poetry, inscribed on marble tablets, Percival also inspires a mindless desire to follow him into war: 'Look at us trooping after him, his faithful servants, to be shot like sheep, for he will certainly attempt some forlorn enterprise and die in battle' (25). In *The Waves*, the boys, steeped in Roman history and poetry, honour the self turned to stone, and Percival, much more of a signifier than an individual character, thus appears in the novel like a statue 'monolithic, in giant repose' (55). Percival, who dies working for the British Empire and representing its ideals in India, functions as a contemporary figure for the Roman Empire, whose language is celebrated by Neville for its 'severity and virtue' (121). Imagining himself as part of a conquering army, blending the shells of the First World War with the large-game hunting of a colony like India, Bernard enters London with a plan to shatter motherhood: 'We are about to explode in the flanks of the city like a shell in the side of some ponderous, maternal, majestic animal' (74–5). All the boys who think in this way are bonded by being at boarding school from an early age. Woolf never depicts in *The Waves* a nurturing mother.[9]

It is important to note that the child narrators are recorded from their first days at boarding school; thus, their preschool lives are unknown except through allusions in their thoughts.[10] Percival's early childhood is fully erased; all we know is that he comes to represent everything that his society expects from him. Critics tend to see the children as scripted by school and by society (Phillips; Meisel). However, right from the start, each child has a radically different way of being in the world, owing to family relations, and Louis, whose father has abandoned him, thus can never be identical to Susan, who has a loving farmer father. Nonetheless, in all their work these critics point to the play or tension between Woolf's fictional children and the pedagogical, political, literary, and social forces that impact them. Her child characters are not simply independent individuals, symbolic containers, or carries of social forces; they are all these elements and more. They are more accurately defined by Derrida's concept of 'gram as *différance*,' which is 'a structure and a movement no longer conceivable on the basis of the opposition presence / absence.' Thus, these child figures are revealed by Woolf to constantly be pulled back and forth between presence and absence. Derrida further clarifies the applicability of this idea to Woolf's child characters when he writes: '*Différance* is the systematic play of differences, of the traces of differences, of the spacing by means of which elements are related to each other' (*P* 27).

The children of *The Waves* come to school carrying the traces of their early childhood; then they begin to experience the world through the spaces between one another. Early on, they pursue different educations in different rooms, according to whether they are boys or girls. The opening section of the book details movements towards and away from one another with the traces that are left. School shapes the children on all levels, from the pictures that hang on the walls to the baths they are given and the books they read. As one aspect of the self is erased, suppressed, vanishing, another aspect is scripted, recalled, emerging.

In Woolf's fictional world, childhood grief is overwhelming and society insists it be suppressed; yet she creates child and adult characters who are fissured and cracked, thereby revealing intense moments of sadness. Most of the time the adult self conspires in silencing grief. Thus, in the *Haunted House* collection, a narrator demands, while listening to a Mozart piece in 'A String Quartet': 'Why then grieve? Ask what? Remain unsatisfied?' While the adult self tries to suppress these questions – 'I say all's been settled; yes; laid to rest under a coverlet of rose leaves, falling' – some other self recognizes in the mindless chatter of the audience a link to childhood: 'The tongue is but a clapper. Simplicity itself. The feathers in the hat next me are bright and pleasing as a child's rattle' (*HH* 31). Earlier in this short story, the self pursues the grief welling up from the music: 'Sorrow, sorrow. Joy, joy. Woven together, like reeds in moonlight. Woven together, inextricably, commingled, bound in pain and strewn in sorrow – crash!' (30).

In 'A String Quartet,' the narrator's abrupt question, 'Why then grieve?' brings to a halt the exploration of music's power to express the interwoven joy and sorrow within the 'vulnerable' self. The self opened up by 'resonant communication' is brought back to the banal by someone's noting the technicality of the musicians: 'The second violin was late you say?' (*HH* 31). No longer moved and in touch with grief, Woolf's listener almost turns to stone: 'Eyeless old age, grey-headed Sphinx ... There she stands on the pavement, beckoning, so sternly, the red omnibus' (31). This nearly blind woman seems threatened by the music; thus, she exits the concert in order to silence her feelings with the mindless sounds of the omnibus. While the stony self marches out to the curb, the listening self enters a reverie of exotic locations with escaping lovers as the music plays on. The satisfaction comes from discovering a city 'bound in pain and strewn in sorrow.' It almost sounds like a city post war: 'Firm establishment. Fast foundations. March of myriads. Confusion and chaos trod to earth' (32). Although this urban landscape is so clearly a painful place – 'Leave then to perish your hope; droop in the desert my joy; naked advance' – it is nonetheless vital, since it is the site of the emotional self, the antithesis of being turned to stone: 'this city to which we travel has neither stone nor marble; hangs enduring; stands unshakable' (32).

In a variety of ways, Woolf returns again and again to this city where one can express naked emotion, where one moves freely, where one has the right to suffer. In *A Room of One's Own*, Woolf muses on Coleridge's idea that 'a great mind is androgynous' and imagines that one of its attributes would be that it 'transmits emotion without impediment' (128).

In his foreword to *A Haunted House*, Leonard Woolf describes how the ideas for these stories and sketches surfaced throughout Woolf's life and during her larger writing projects; they thus offer insights into her recurring concerns. The tension between tucking these sketches away in drawers and rewriting them 'sometimes a great many times' indicates how much significance these narrators and characters had for Woolf at the same time as how difficult they were to convey (*HH* 7). The stories themselves often revolve around what the self keeps hidden in drawers or in diaries and what the self displays on the mantelpiece or in the shop.

The first two stories in the collection are about seeking, questing after some treasure. In 'A Haunted House,' 'a ghostly couple seek their joy,' at the same time as the living couple unconsciously quest after the 'ghostly lovers' who used to live in the house (*HH* 10). After reading 'A String Quartet,' one cannot simply hear 'joy' without considering the idea that this emotion is 'woven together, inextricably, commingled' with sorrow (30). The living couple discovers the ghosts and their treasure while reading, or while setting after them only to forget why they came upstairs, or while sleeping. The emphasis on reading as an activity that allows us to get in touch with haunting past selves is continued into the next story, 'Monday or Tuesday.'

This story, once the title piece of the collection, describes the writer at work: 'Desiring truth, awaiting it, laboriously distilling a few words, for ever desiring' (*HH* 12). All kinds of day-to-day sounds, 'omnibuses' and 'children,' interrupt this intense labour of desiring truth and putting it into words (12).[11] As is apparent in 'A String Quartet,' where the omnibus and the child again form a tension, specifically in terms of listening one imagines the writer struggling to hear the one over the din of the other. In 'Kew Gardens,' Woolf poses the question of whether or not 'the voices of children, such freshness of surprise' have the force to break 'the silence'; then she responds that these child-voices do not have a chance, for 'all the time the motor-omnibuses were turning their wheels' (42).[12] The omnibus symbolizes the drowning out of childhood grief by society's demands. In Ford's work, the wheels that drown out the hysterics belong to carriages. In West's novella, the spinning wheels of revolution are what give Chris Baldry a drowned look.

In *The Waves*, Woolf looks at the way characters suppress their vulnerability by means of powerful signifiers like the omnibuses. Jinny, who has
conducted her life as a femme fatale, notes her age and is frightened by
her appearance in the mirror. She first brings 'the whip down' on her
own flanks as she thinks of herself as a 'whimpering little animal,' and she
regains her sense of self with the roar of the 'superb omnibuses.' Jinny
portrays this moment of overcoming a sense of vulnerability, first like a
Roman military triumph – 'this is the army of victory with banners and
brass eagles and heads crowned with laurel-leaves won in battle' – and
second, through imperialist rhetoric, as she compares London's streets
to 'sanded paths of victory driven through the jungle' (*W* 130–1). The
sound of omnibuses, the procession of the military, the language of
colonialism – all effectively silence one's vulnerability, one's relation to
time, one's inner child.

The writer who wants to hear the voices of vulnerability and of childhood must seek out silence, and one of the best ways to create silence is
to read or write.[13] In 'Monday or Tuesday,' during the struggle of voices
to overcome traffic, it seems the child voice wins out: 'Now to recollect
by the fireside on the white square of marble. From ivory depths words
rising shed their blackness, blossom and penetrate. Fallen the book; in
the flame, in the smoke, in the momentary sparks – or now voyaging.'
Gazing into the marble surround of the fire or onto the black marks
upon the white page, this recollection that becomes a reverie, almost beyond the time of literacy – 'fallen the book' – leads the author again to a
city: 'the marble square pendant, minarets beneath and the Indian seas'
(*HH* 13). Again, we have the flash of childhood as foreign, removed,
elsewhere; yet for Woolf this exotic city belongs to literature, as a story
heard as a child. As in 'A Haunted House,' Woolf has the self reading,
holding a book, in order to open up a silence where the ghostly self, in
this case a childhood self, can be recalled.

Woolf tells the story of one of the novels that she kept in the drawer. As
noted at the beginning of this chapter, in 'An Unwritten Novel' Woolf explores the process of a writer struck by the sight of a woman's sadness in a
train compartment. The story is woven, or unwoven, from the narrator's
probing confrontation with grief. The (non)writer appears to be reading
the news, but is distracted by grief: 'Such an expression of unhappiness
was enough by itself to make one's eyes slide above the paper's edge to
the poor woman's face' (*HH* 14). For the first time in the collection,
Woolf examines the act of reading as an escape from grief. We saw that
Ford explored the power of escapist literature to collude in childhood's

suppression in *The Good Soldier.* Woolf, as well, distinguishes this kind of literature from the modernist project that opens inner wounds rather than seals them off.

In a later story, 'The Mark on the Wall,' she posits reading as a way to escape the self, and thus the narrator imagines stretching out her 'hand at once for a book in self-protection' (*HH* 46). Reading has the capacity to open up the depths of the self or seal them off from any kind of access. In 'An Unwritten Novel,' Woolf outlines the various techniques the other train passengers employ to avoid the woman's sadness: 'Five faces opposite – five mature faces – and the knowledge in each face. Strange, though, how people want to conceal it!' Sounding very much like John Dowell in *The Good Soldier*, the writer begs the grieving woman to 'play the game' (14). Woolf later stresses the impact of this society in denial upon the self who grieves: 'The eyes of others our prisons; their thoughts our cages' (21). Rather than completely retreat, the narrator maintains a silent dialogue with this woman; she imagines her sighing and saying, '"If you only knew!"' to which she replies, '"I know the whole business."' In this silent, imagined exchange, the narrator quotes the newspaper opening with a statement about the war's end: 'Peace between Germany and the Allied Powers was yesterday officially ushered in at Paris.' After a few other newspaper quotes, she concludes: 'We all know – the *Times* knows – but we pretend we don't' (14, 15). This society, represented by the train passengers and by the newspaper, what the narrator calls the 'great reservoir of life,' at the end of a four-year world war of devastation unrivalled in history, knows about grief yet pretends it does not exist. Woolf exposes the cycle whereby the adult who cannot respond to the feelings suppressed in childhood on the one hand remains a child and hence conducts his or her mature life like a child who wants to play games and play pretend; at the same time, this adult becomes an efficient war administrator or soldier.

In 'An Unwritten Novel,' Woolf then has the passenger employ the terms of the child, trying her best to be a good soldier, to describe the confrontation with grief. The narrator folds up her newspaper to create an impervious 'shield,' but the grieving woman 'pierced through [this] shield' (*HH* 26). As in Ford's novels, grief functions like a healing wound, a pinprick that photographs, writes with / in light, the shadowy, interior self, the self that is not heard. In *Circumfession*, Derrida yearns for a pen like a 'syringe' that could directly translate the inner self into the realm of the outer self, the inside coming directly to the outside by writing with blood (12). He exclaims: 'I write with a sharpened blade, if it doesn't bleed the book will be a failure' (130). The syringe belongs to an early childhood memory; the bleeding of the book is in order to translate blood spilt in infancy (135–6).

The narrator of 'An Unwritten Novel' imagines the grieving woman, who has pierced her shield, as knitting up holes in her glove to renew 'the fortifications' (*HH* 26). Reversing the expectations of the good soldier, the woman 'gazed into' the narrator's eyes 'as if searching any sediment of courage' to acknowledge, rather than deny, her grief (15). Suddenly, the inside and outside blend with, or contaminate, one another; the narrator begins to exhibit the symptoms of the woman's grief, even though the woman does not share her story: 'A smile of infinite irony, infinite sorrow, flitted and faded from her face. But she had communicated, shared her secret, passed her poison' (17). Echoing Claudius's belief that Ophelia has been 'poisoned by deep grief,' the woman's grief infects the narrator with broken sentences: she says a few disconnected lines and manifests signs of unhappiness (16). Thus, the narrator imagines writing an unwritten novel about the woman's grief. However, the story-within-a-story technique falls apart at the end, since in the initial, now framing, tale of the train compartment, the supposedly grieving woman arrives at her station, joins her son, and walks off contentedly. The reader is left wondering whether or not the story, fabricated by the narrator to match the woman's grief, does not, in fact, tell us more about the narrator's grief. Woolf encourages this line of thinking in 'The Mark on the Wall,' when she writes: 'As we face each other in omnibuses and underground railways we are looking into the mirror' (47). In 'An Unwritten Novel' it seems that the novel one cannot write is one that speaks grief.

In 'An Unwritten Novel,' the narrator's story has the ostensibly grieving woman shop for ribbons instead of rushing home to care for an infant sibling: 'She runs, she rushes, home she reaches, but too late. Neighbours – the doctor – baby brother – the kettle – scalded – hospital – dead – or only the shock of it, the blame? Ah, but the detail matters nothing! It's what she carries with her; the spot, the crime, the thing to expiate, always there between her shoulders. "Yes," she seems to nod to me, "it's the thing I did"' (*HH* 19). The narrator recounts the death of the child with nearly inarticulate, broken phrases.[14] In the narrator's story of grief, it remains a novel 'unwritten' because the true tragedy, the actual event that causes the disturbing grief might be that the narrator's own child within has been neglected while she goes through life shopping for ribbons and this child has been buried, has died. And the blame? Can well-meaning pedagogues who strive to raise good citizens be blamed? Can loving parents be blamed? Can writers who deny grief be blamed?

If we return to the terms of the writer seeking truth in 'Monday or Tuesday,' the desire, suppressed in this story, is to 'laboriously' distil 'a few words' in order to articulate the cry: 'a cry starts to the left, another to the right' (*HH* 12). And this cry may well be that of the newborn – born through fiction – child. The narrator, deep into her story at the same time as she analyses her process, considers the woman full of grief, with a tale that will not be told, as an unborn child who clearly compares to 'An Unwritten Novel': 'But no; she's of the unborn children of the mind, illicit, none the less loved, like my rhododendrons' (23). However, as Woolf discovers, rather than this woman and her sadness, the pages of novels are filled with ridiculous characters. Woolf contains these safe, mundane fictional creatures under the name 'Moggridge' (23). She employs the same image of immobilization in stone for this man who drives around in a 'carriage.' Like the blind woman of 'String Quartet,' he 'sometimes sits so solemn staring like a sphinx, and always there's a look of the sepulchral' about him, for this man belongs to the race, exposed in Ford's *The Good Soldier*, of the living dead (24). In contrast, when the novelist, who cannot write this novel, turns to the grieving woman, important questions are posed: 'But when the self speaks to the self, who is speaking? – the entombed soul, the spirit driven in, in, in to the central catacomb; the self that took the veil and left the world – a coward perhaps, yet somehow beautiful as it flits with its lantern restlessly up and down the dark corridors' (25). This description, reminiscent of the Greek myth of Cupid and Psyche, sends us back to 'A Haunted House,' where the ghostly couple wander through the corridors of their old home holding a 'lantern' above the living couple who sleep (10–11).

The story of the mythological lovers operates on a variety of levels; however, relevant to my concerns is the wakeful Psyche, who does not know if her lover is a monster or a god and, in beholding him as he sleeps, she burns him with a drop of hot oil, just as Woolf's grieving woman is thought to have allowed the child to be scalded by the hot water of the kettle. The love is lost, just as the child is lost. More significant, however, is that Psyche must labour in order to earn her lover back; she must perform tasks that regain his trust and love. Likewise, the writer must laboriously distil words that will articulate what is lost or at least articulate the grief of the loss, and perhaps by such a process the writer brings back the child's voice. The myth of Cupid and Psyche is about being wakeful, disrupted, divided; one self jolts awake the slumbering self, who mindlessly buys ribbons or drives around in carriages or worries incessantly about the price of eggs (*HH* 21). Yet the myth is also about trusting the self who sleeps, dreams, and journeys in the much more telling realm of the suppressed.

In 'An Unwritten Novel,' when the question is asked, 'When the self speaks to the self who is speaking?' one may plausibly answer: it is the child. Woolf conveys this idea, as the unwritten woman of the train carriage emits 'her sob,' with the 'splendours and pageantries glimpsed in girlhood' (*HH* 25). The narrator considers banal, girlish dreams for her 'character,' the grieving woman; nonetheless, the self that speaks is the one who was 'entombed' and 'driven in' during childhood. Paradoxically, the narrator in 'An Unwritten Novel' discovers the fiction of her fiction when the supposedly grieving woman joins her son and they walk off 'side by side' (27); yet her fiction of grief gives her access to joy: 'If I fall on my knees, if I go through the ritual, the ancient antics, it's you, unknown figures, you I adore; if I open my arms, it's you I embrace, you I draw to me – adorable world!' (27). In contrast to the childhood self who 'took the veil and left the world – a coward perhaps,' the narrator, whom the woman implores to have the 'courage' to come face to face with grief, thereby achieves communion with the world. Rather than constructing impervious shields and fortifications, the narrator opens wide her arms for an embrace with suffering, grief, ghostly selves; Woolf suggests this communion in the fragment 'children swarm' (12).

More bleakly, Woolf sets up a relationship between the suppressed childhood self and the war in the story 'The Mark on the Wall.' The narrator contemplates this mark, which not only halts childhood reverie (*HH* 43), but also acts as a sign for culture's ideas of nature: 'I understand Nature's game – her prompting to take action as a way of ending any thought that threatens to excite or pain' (50). The narrator focuses on the mark as a way of 'putting a full stop to one's disagreeable thoughts' (50). Rendering the mark more complex, the narrator switches gears and insists that, in fact, the reality of this mark transforms the powerful figures of his society in the middle of a war into 'the shadows of shades.' He clings to the mark on the wall as a man will grasp 'a plank in the sea' (50). What is the mark – an escapist fantasy or a saving reality?

The narrator of 'The Mark on the Wall' maintains that what drowns out the voice of the suppressed childhood self so effectively is actually the language of the good soldier. In reference to 'generalizations,' the narrator exclaims: 'The military sound of the word is enough. It recalls leading articles, cabinet ministers – a whole class of things indeed which, as a child, one thought the thing itself, the standard thing, the real thing, from which one could not depart save at the risk of nameless damnation' (*HH* 47).[15] Woolf's narrator shows that the military-sounding 'generalizations' form a barrier between one's depths and the society that finds pain and excitement disagreeable. Not to name the world properly is to bring upon oneself a kind of damnation that leaves the rebelling child without a name, hence 'nameless.' Derrida expresses similar concerns about the inability of children to access names and thus to speak their own experience. He quotes from a notebook, in which he has written for many years about a childhood trauma: 'if I wanted to be moving, I would describe a child incapable of articulating what is going on, even if it sees and knows everything' (*C* 196). When readers are moved, they shake out of the paralysis originating in suppressed childhood grief.

In 'The Mark on the Wall,' Woolf concentrates on the child-self who lacks a vocabulary to articulate what the narrator insists is the vital source for novelists: the individuals we confront in our daily lives function as mirrors for our own 'depths.' In the modernist shift, 'novelists of the future' must pursue these 'phantoms' of the suppressed self and no longer bother with descriptions of so-called reality (*HH* 47). Woolf describes a fantasy for the child-self in this story who believes the 'rule for everything' until suddenly he discovers that what society presented as 'real' was in fact 'half phantoms'; hence, 'the damnation which visited the disbeliever of them was only a sense of illegitimate freedom' (47). The act of articulating the depths, writing the ghosts, accessing the child before the rules of suppression are in place is a rebellious act of naming the unnamable. However, as Woolf's title for the story suggests, this is a dream for the future; the writer must labour like Psyche, distilling words so that the 'mark' on the wall can become legible. For Woolf, as for the other novelists in this study, there is a sense that it is a matter of life and death that we learn to read the writing, the marks, on the wall.

The narrator of 'The Mark on the Wall' describes how dangerous it is to speak out against the power of generalizations, the military sounds of words spoken by those with authority. Woolf details a memory, when she was a child yet not a child, of being caught in such a situation with her father and not being able to risk 'nameless damnation.' In *Moments of Being*, Woolf describes this family drama, in which Leslie Stephen berates his daughter Vanessa about expenses: he flings words at her 'Have you no pity for me? There you stand like a block of stone'; then he appeals to Virginia, who is 'speechless' because her feelings are

unacceptable: 'For not a word of what I felt – that unbounded contempt for him and of pity for Nessa – could be expressed' (144). Woolf
articulates the family moment when the child has no voice, no words,
no right to speak. Both daughters turn and are turned to stone.

Immobilized, stone-like characters predominate in *Mrs. Dalloway.*
Woolf has the shell-shocked Septimus Smith being haunted by his friend,
the soldier Evans, who has been killed in the war. Notably, Evans haunts
him as a statue. Smith sees the ghost of Evans 'raising his hand like some
colossal figure who has lamented the fate of man for ages in the desert
alone with his hands pressed to his forehead, furrows of despair on his
cheeks' (63). This is not Shelley's Ozymandias, whose stony face registers
warrior-like pride. Instead of towering over others because of his power
and desire to conquer, what is colossal about this figure is his immobilizing grief that has turned him to stone.[16] Septimus's parodic dream
of Shelley's sonnet brings together both versions of the suppression of
human sentiment that turns the self to stone: whether immobilized in
the pose of the good soldier, or in the pose of despairing grief, both figures are 'colossal Wreck[s]' (Shelley 672).[17]

In *The Waves,* Woolf locates the immobilization of feelings and the
attendant inability to articulate them in childhood. Bernard describes
Louis as 'stone-carved, sculpturesque' (78). Louis turned to stone in
childhood. As a child he is a 'boy in grey flannels,' yet he sees through
the 'lidless eyes of a stone figure' (8). Poignantly, he yearns to move and
be moved: 'I have tried to draw from the living flesh the stone lodged
at the centre' (136). Louis's identity split depends on childhood vulnerability covered up by an adult who is 'marmoreal' (148). Also concerned
with having a stony self, another of the child narrators, Susan, believes
that what creates the 'hard thing' like a weight in her side is being sent
away to school then to finishing school, where one is taught to become
stone-like (66). Woolf portrays the head of both the boys' and the girls'
schools as resembling stone (21, 30). Hence, she presents the trope of
turning to stone specifically in terms of childhood suppression and how
it is taught by parents and pedagogues. Louis believes that if he could
write, at first 'one line of unwritten poetry' and then, more forcefully,
'one poem on a page,' he might make sense of the 'stone lodged at the
centre' of his being and at the centre of life itself (45, 137). Comparably,
Neville connects writing poetry with the need to 'sometimes weep' and
the removal of 'hard accretions of all sorts' (134).[18] It is painful in this
context to think of Woolf filling her coat pockets with stones so as to
drown herself.

In *Mrs. Dalloway*, when Septimus has a hallucination of the dead soldier Evans as a grieving statue, it is striking that he imagines himself as 'the giant mourner,' a responding figure of colossal grief (63). Septimus turns to face the crowd, who appear to be 'prostrate' with grief: 'The millions lamented; for ages they had sorrowed. He would turn round, he would tell them in a few moments, only a few moments more, of this relief, of this joy, of this astonishing revelation' (64). He yearns to tell them of the discovery Woolf reveals in 'The String Quartet,' that one's ability to feel sorrow is what allows one to feel joy. Septimus's paradoxical revelation is that the communication of grief is joyful. However, despite his wife, Lucrezia's, attempts to show him 'beauty [is] behind a pane of glass,' he feels he cannot reach it, except perhaps by going through it (79). Woolf makes his suicidal leap through glass a contradictory one: he jumps to his death to escape those who refuse to hear his grief, but he also leaps through the glass that seems to prevent him from sharing his discovery that the acceptance of sorrow opens the self to joy. Derrida writes of this dual effect of sorrow and joy, loss and recovery, without trying to diminish what one must suffer: 'Work: that which makes for a work, for an *oeuvre*, indeed that which works – and works to open: *opus* and *opening, oeuvre* and *overture:* the work or labor of the *oeuvre* insofar as it engenders, produces, and brings to light, but also labor or travail as suffering, as the enduring of force, as the pain of the one who gives' (*WM* 142).

In 'A Haunted House,' Woolf writes: 'Death was the glass; death was between us; coming to the woman first, hundreds of years ago, leaving the house, sealing all the windows; the rooms were darkened' (*HH* 10). The dark house is now haunted by the couple who seek the 'light in the heart,' which seems to involve unsealing the windows. In *Moments of Being*, Woolf asserts the need to 'break the pane of glass' which separates the self from other people (110). In *The Waves*, she has Neville note that Bernard, the writer who cannot write, marks passages in Byron with 'a moth-like impetuosity dashing itself against hard glass' (58). There seems to be a danger in reading and registering the passages of others. The moth, as the creature of the moonlight, is what one needs to attend to, the shadowy passages, the suppressed self, the ghosts that haunt. Perhaps these darker figures lead one through the glass. Light in the heart paradoxically remains dark to the daytime, rational mind; it can be revealed only through the shadowlike imagination, the part of the self that speaks to ghosts. Woolf expresses her grief when her mother died in such haunting terms: 'But now and again on more occasions than I can number, in bed at night, or in the street, or as I come into the room, there she is; beautiful, emphatic, with her familiar phrase and her laugh; closer than any of the living are, lighting our random lives as with a burning torch, infinitely noble and delightful to her children' (*MB* 40). The ghost of the mother, the haunting of the child, these figures have more tangible force and potency than the present. As Woolf writes in her memoir: 'Those moments – in the nursery, on the road to the beach – can still be more real than the present moment' (67). Likewise, Derrida connects writing to the nursery and to a mother who hears and supports his childhood grief, which allows him to experience joy: 'the immense, insolvent pain and also the supreme enjoyment for all, first of all for him, me, the nursling' (*C* 217). He notes: 'that's the origin of tears, I weep for myself, I feel sorry for myself from my mother feeling sorry for me, I complain of my other, I make myself unhappy, she weeps over me, who weeps over me, syntax to be invented' (128). For both Woolf and Derrida writing and allowing grief to surface are connected. In her fiction, Woolf strives to articulate these 'real' moments from 'the nursery,' instead of writing the 'reality' of adulthood. However, for Woolf, Derrida, and for the other novelists discussed, this childhood voice has been shocked into silence.

Like West and Ford, Woolf specifically explores the bonds separating specifically and binding shell shock and childhood trauma. In *The Waves*, Woolf silences society's omnibus in order to send forth the voice of children. Entering into the minds of six child narrators, often speaking to or within themselves, is an unforgettable experience. In *The Waves*, Woolf distinguishes the child voices with a verb for speech, 'said,' at the same time as it is clear that these are thoughts and feelings articulated to the self: '"I see a crimson tassel," said Jinny, "twisted with gold threads"' or '"I hear something stamping," said Louis. "A great beast's foot is chained. It stamps, and stamps, and stamps"' (6). Jane Marcus offers a different reading, whereby Woolf 'mercilessly parodies' the 'violent homosocial narrative of English national identity, in its simple-minded racism (and sexism) and nostalgia for class bias' using the 'infantilized fictional focalization of "he said" and "she said"' (137). In contrast, I believe Woolf uses the simple child's way of speaking to stress the way children learn to structure their identity according to the national narrative, especially when nurturing parental influences are almost wholly absent. I find a lack of textual support for Marcus's sense that Woolf's representation of these children is a merciless parody.[19]

I find equally problematic Marcus's argument that 'Bernard's production of culture is authorized by the politics of the elegy in the history of
poetry,' and Woolf thus exposes 'the cult of the hero and the complicity
of the poet in the making of culture as he exudes cultural glue' (142–3).
What makes such a comment problematic is that Woolf attributes specifically to Bernard the rejection of 'lily-sweet glue,' covering over loss
with 'phrases,' that culture requires in order to contain the fragmenting
force of a friend's death (*W* 179). Moreover, Woolf has Bernard voice a
strikingly modernist comment on language and literature: 'But for pain
words are lacking' (178). I am therefore not convinced by Marcus's belief that 'Bernard is a parody of authorship' or that *The Waves* writes 'the
swan song of the white Western male author' (145).[20] Although I concur
fully with Marcus that imperialism is critiqued in the text, I wish to approach it from a different angle, through the absence of a compassionate family supporting the child.

Thus, to reverse Marcus's terms that denigrate the 'infantilized fictional focalization,' I want to foreground it as the vital technique of
interior monologue, which allows Woolf to portray these children seemingly speaking – he said, she said – while simultaneously suppressing
their spoken-out-loud thoughts and emotions. As Geoffrey Hartman
expresses it: 'the reader sees that the extreme eloquence of *The Waves*
hides silence and incommunicability' (82). Initially, not only do the children express emotion, but more important, they accept intense feelings
in one another.[21] In *Moments of Being* and in *The Waves*, Woolf details the
experience of strong emotion as it occurs and as it leaves a trace on her
narrators. Later, these strong emotions resurface or remain suppressed;
regardless, the trace (their present absence) is as vitally important as
whatever else is happening in the moment.

What are the child-narrators' strong emotions? Jinny kisses Louis.
Susan reacts: 'Now I will wrap my agony inside my pocket-handkerchief.'
Bernard seeks to comfort her: 'I shall follow her, Neville. I shall go gently behind her, to be at hand, with my curiosity, to comfort her when she
bursts out in a rage and thinks, "I am alone."' (He finds her crumpled
up with 'sobs' (*W* 9, 10). Rather than denying her emotion, or finding
it unacceptable, the child Bernard comforts her and, as John Hulcoop
emphasizes, he responds to her grief with storytelling (476). Close to
death, Bernard still considers Susan's tears 'terrible, beautiful; both,
neither' (*W* 167). Woolf ends this initial dramatization of grief by having Susan make a statement about childhood with an awareness that
adults do not realize the intense emotions that characterize this early

time of life: '"Though my mother still knits white socks for me and hems pinafores and I am a child, I love and I hate"' (11). The mother lacks a sense of her daughter's emotional life. Hence, the child concentrates her love and her free expression of feelings on her father: 'Out the day will spring, as I open the carriage-door and see my father in his old hat and gaiters. I shall tremble. I shall burst into tears' (36).

While Bernard sympathizes and comforts Susan in her anguish, Woolf has him participate in a ceremony that revolves around suppressing his own grief: 'The horrible ceremony is over, the tips, and the good-byes in the hall. Now there is this gulping ceremony with my mother, this hand-shaking ceremony with my father; now I must go on waving, I must go on waving, till we turn the corner' (W 20). This child has learned the importance of crushing his feelings: 'I must not cry.' Notably, Bernard's strategy is to build up a wall of words in order to protect himself from expressing his grief: 'I must make phrases and phrases and so interpose something hard between myself and the stare of housemaids, the stare of clocks, staring faces, indifferent faces, or I shall cry' (20). This family ritual of suppression that teaches the child to gulp down tears, to shake hands rather than hug, to offer money in place of affection or gratitude reveals Bernard in the act of turning to stone. In a self-reflexive manner, Woolf renders the writer in the novel, Bernard, unable to write. He thus recalls the fragmented subject of the short piece 'Unwritten Novel.'

Neville notes that Bernard is disconnected; he describes him repeatedly as 'a dangling wire' (W 26). Highly self-conscious of himself as a writer, imagining his own biography, laying down phrases and notes in books, Bernard cannot even complete a letter (53–4). In an early story-telling scene at school: 'Bernard's power fails him and there is no longer any sequence and he sags and twiddles a bit of string and falls silent, gaping as if about to burst into tears' (26). Later in the novel, Bernard sees himself with disgust, since he appears to 'gape like a codfish,' which Woolf has earlier recorded as a facial expression that replaces the need to cry (124). The codfish is a sign for death and immobilization from the earliest childhood section of the novel. Neville sees a murdered man in childhood whose 'jowl was white as a dead codfish' and he defines the vision by its 'rigidity' (16–17). Likewise, instead of shedding tears, Bernard appears gaping. One realizes his efforts can no longer generate stories; instead, he uses his power to suppress his desire to cry. Hence, with a shocking realization that he has 'lost [his] youth,' he turns into a 'mechanical' creature (125). He can write about public ceremony; what he cannot do is 'follow people into their private rooms' (34). When school ends, he thinks: 'This is the last of all our ceremonies. We are overcome by strange feelings' (40). No longer having a sense of identity, he has lost his 'I'; Bernard assumes 'we' and imagines that the others find their feelings strange, foreign. Recognizing this dislocation in Bernard provides insight into why these figures project onto foreign landscapes, gardens, and peoples the unconscious selves they desperately want to control or discover.

In the short story 'The New Dress,' Woolf renders contradictory the societal meaning of the word *native*, so that her character's fantasy about an exotic life, triggered by the sight of a 'native,' is, in fact, about *her* native self. In *The Waves*, Jinny presents herself at a dance: 'There are girls of my own age, for whom I feel the drawn swords of an honourable antagonism. For these are my peers. I am a native of this world' (70). The coupling of the slippery term 'native' and war imagery resonates and intensifies the links between this short story and *The Waves*. Whereas Jinny articulates her sense of belonging – 'This is what I have dreamt; this is what I have foretold. I am native here' (69) – the narrator of 'A New Dress' dreams and foretells her fantasy of the other, the native 'in a turban,' the very figure who courses throughout *The Waves* in the italicized images of the waves themselves: '*The waves drummed on the shore, like turbaned warriors, like turbaned men with poisoned assegais*' (51).[22] Home fails to nourish and support an emotional life; thus, one creates a fantasy home, an exotic, foreign space of the imagination where one can be a conqueror. Previously, we have seen the alien landscape as a site where one can freely express grief; here Woolf generates this fictional home as grief's inverse: aggression. In *The Waves*, Woolf explores the effects of toughening up children. Focused on Rhoda, Jane Goldman highlights the 'images suggestive of education as submissive inscription into empire,' which lead the child to fantasize about being a fearless, conquering empress; she adroitly concludes: 'Rhoda's classroom sense of alienation is reversed' (12–13). Thus, what is inside, one's truth, becomes projected onto the world; one's sense of alienation is thereby projected onto 'natives' and Woolf plays on the contradiction inherent in this word.

Foreign land, populated by the native (self), this home away from home, must be dominated and exploited in the way that the British Empire ruled India. Thus, when he loses his youth and turns into a mechanical man, Bernard's first act is to buy a ticket to Rome, the ancient site of empire, whose language of 'severity and virtue' was taught to him as a schoolboy. When Bernard is in Rome, he recognizes his illness and he begins to speak like a child: 'I sit here like a convalescent, like a very simple man who knows only words of one syllable.' While dying, he stresses his need to return to these words: 'I need a little language such as lovers use, words of one syllable such as children speak' (*W* 199). Echoing Shakespeare seems an effective way to block out the risk of vulnerability inherent in an infantilized mode of speech. Yet, while in Rome, Bernard comes close, with a sense of 'foreboding,' to the 'queer territory' that renders him both in a state of recovery and in recovery of a childlike language; however, he veers away from his discovery (125). Woolf, in contrast, returns again and again to the site of his loss. Learning to suppress his emotions at home, Bernard remains inarticulate, like a sensitive child; while unable to experience his own feelings, he has become hypersensitive to those of others (51, 56). Considering his inability to write, he imagines the contrast between the articulate novelist and his own writer's block: 'He would not have this devastating sense of grey ashes in a burnt-out grate. Some blind flaps in my eyes. Everything becomes impervious. I cease to invent' (*W* 54). The wall between Bernard and his own feelings, his own private self, is impenetrable; yet the waves of the italicized sections seem to have, as the book reaches its conclusion, the power to break through what Bernard believes to be an 'impervious' block to his ability to invent. One cannot help but think of the paralysed prison imagery of Conrad, Rhys, Ford, and West.

Midway through Woolf's novel, the waves '*spattered the walls of a cave*' leaving '*pools inland.*' Then the waves seem to withdraw; they '*no longer visited the further pools or reached the dotted black line which lay irregularly upon the beach*' (*W* 112, 122). The writer, Bernard's, inability to sign his own name, his lack of an identity, renders the image of the dotted black line awaiting a signature, an act that may occur only by means of the crashing apart of the impervious wall built through childhood suppression. The sense that this wall might not always be so impervious resonates, for the waves '*fell in one long concussion, like a wall falling, a wall of grey stone, unpierced by any chink of light*' (140). The idea of being pricked or pierced by grief and this wound allowing one to access the buried self, the light in the heart, resonates in the image of the impervious, stony self above. One of Neville's insights is to see Percival's journey as a mode of escaping the wall sealing off the self: 'We are walled in here. But India lies outside' (91).

Pursuing Bernard's link with the waves, through his gesture of waving, the private inner space, once inaccessible to Bernard, appears once again as a hint or glimpse, a potential in the image of the waves sending '*white shadows into the recesses of sonorous caves*'; however, the waves come full circle, returning us to the beginning of the novel and the story of childhood suppression. Woolf echoes the opening description of the novel – '*The sea was indistinguishable from the sky*' – in this passage: '*Sky and sea were indistinguishable.*' And although the waves penetrated the stone wall surrounding the self, entering into the cave-like space with their sonorous possibilities, they '*then rolled back sighing over the shingle*' (*W* 159). Woolf has the waves rush back into the sea with a sigh, and one wonders if it is a sigh of regret. The final line of the novel leaves resolution ambiguous: '*The waves broke on the shore*' (200). Woolf leaves the reader with a process, the impact of the salt water, nature's analogy for tears, pounding against the dry land of the self.

Rhoda expresses emotional anguish in terms of a desiccated landscape: 'I doubt; I trembled; I see the wild thorn tree shake its shadow in the desert.' Likewise, Bernard imagines Jinny 'dancing like a flame, febrile, hot, over dry earth' (*W* 72, 78). Neville imagines studying literature as an act that supports the dried-out self, impervious to flow: 'That would be a glorious life, to addict oneself to perfection; to follow the curve of the sentence wherever it might lead, into deserts, under drifts of sand' (59). Intellectual activity seems to keep the wet, emotional self at bay. While reading may keep one emotionally dry, in Bernard's fantasy of writing, he makes contact with an authentic part of his inner self and evokes the power of the wet waves pounding upon the shore: 'My true self breaks off from my assumed' (53). Woolf draws on wave imagery when Neville confronts Bernard's lack of self coupled with his desire to imitate others: 'Like a long wave, like a roll of heavy waters, he sent over me, his devastating presence – dragging me open, laying bare the pebbles on the shore of my soul' (60). Woolf has Neville not only relate words and waves, but also relate them to an expression of emotion in the form of crying: 'Now begins to rise in me the familiar rhythm; words that have lain dormant now lift, now toss their crests, and fall and rise, and fall and rise again. I am a poet, yes.' This writing, like the waves, causes Neville's eyes to 'fill with tears' (56). Yet as soon as this intense writing moment occurs and the writer is moved, the scene shifts abruptly to a fear of inauthenticity. The poet's intense experience of emotion while writing leads into the sustained comparison of the waves to horses, which Woolf elaborates throughout the italicized interludes: 'Words and words and words, how they gallop – how they lash their long manes and tails, but for some fault in me I cannot give myself to their backs; I cannot fly with them scattering women and string bags. There is some flaw in me – some fatal hesitancy which, if I pass it over, turns to foam and falsity' (56). The connection between waves and words suggests that the force that breaks down the stone-like self, the self surrounded by an impervious barrier, is modernist literature, poems, and stories. At the same time, Bernard experiences Neville's heavy wave-like roll of waters over his soul; he leaves him a poem to read, in a violent way, as 'the stab, the rent in my defences that Neville made with his astonishing fine rapier' (60). Modernist fiction may well have the force to open up the shore of the soul, but Woolf implies the experience is painful and the poems and stories a kind of violence.

Keeping in mind the pain and the violence, I return once again to the scene where Bernard conducts the ceremony of suppression with his parents and consider its relevance to the title of Woolf's novel. It seems that if writers want to bring down the walls blocking the self from its feelings, then they may need to return to childhood and specifically to the damming up of childhood grief. According to Woolf, the return and the act of articulation – tearful, hesitant, seemingly false – is violent and painful.

Remember that Bernard's leaving-home ceremony requires him to crush his childhood desire to cry and instead he 'must go on waving' to his mother and father (*W* 20). Bernard's solemn act of suppressing his emotions, taught, encouraged, and sanctioned by the parents, offers one way of reading Woolf's title for this work. *The Waves* are not only the ones that beat upon the shore; they are also the gestures of children who are being trained not to cry. When narrating from beyond death, Bernard returns to this ceremony of suppression as a mode of expressing the end of his life: 'From me had dropped the old cloak, the old response; the hollowed hand that beats back sounds' (193). Aptly captured in the social dictum that children should be seen and not heard, the sounds of childhood, inextricably linked to the sounds of grief, are silenced by the hollow gesture of waving; only in death can Bernard shed this old response to life.

Instead of expressing his grief, Bernard must wave and wave and wave. Without knowing its source, Neville recognizes the damage done to Bernard that blocks him from writing and imagines him frantically waving: 'He tells our story with extraordinary understanding, except of what we most feel.' In this moment, Bernard appears 'waving his arms on the platform,' for he has missed the train literally and figuratively (*W* 47). As an older man, Bernard asks himself: 'Waves of hands, hesitations at street corners, someone dropping a cigarette into the gutter – all are stories. But which is the true story?' (147) Bernard's 'waves of hands,' as a mode of pleasing parents and suppressing childhood grief, functions as one of the paradoxically true stories of *The Waves*, and what makes it true is that Bernard cannot recognize or articulate it. It is a story one cannot tell straightforwardly, but it can appear in a modernist fragment as 'waves of hands.'

While dying, Bernard wants answers. Returning to a childhood moment, he imagines the 'old nurse who turns the pages of the picture-book' commanding him to 'Look. This is the truth' (*W* 194). He also imagines addressing his childhood friends: 'I went from one to the other holding my sorrow – no, not my sorrow but the incomprehensible nature of this our life – for their inspection' (180). Notice the immediate suppression of grief replaced by a philosophical problem. Musing on narrative itself, Bernard compares this possible end of the story to 'a last ripple of the wave'; he then wonders: 'if there are no stories, what end can there be, or what beginning?' (180) Woolf creates a beginning and ending through her unconventional use of the italicized interludes where the waves function as storytelling devices to indicate some kind of ambiguous development. A gesture expected by his parents and society, Bernard's childhood waving anticipates a striking aspect of the waves of the italicized sections, which Woolf initially describes with natural and feminine images, but as the children become adults and more readily resemble good soldiers, the waves appear in military guise.

The first descriptions of the waves conjure up images of the forest and of the sea. Notably, they open at dawn and are compared to a sleeper *'whose breath comes and goes unconsciously'* (*W* 5). The waves form an analogy to the awakening selves of the children, who are also at the dawn of their lives and whose physical growth and development parallels the passing of the day described in the interludes. Initially, the waves have a feminine quality, as Woolf describes them as *'a thin veil of white'* and then *'a quick fan,'* which fills with *'water-coloured jewels'* (5, 19, 49). The waves again appear as best expressed through analogies to a rich natural world: they sparkle like *'mackerel,'* their depths possibly *'traversed by shoals of wandering fish'* (49). Yet subtly and inexplicably, the waves take on masculine, warrior-like qualities: *'The waves drummed on the shore, like turbaned warriors, like turbaned men with poisoned assegais who, whirling their arms on high, advance upon the feeding flocks, the white sheep'* (51). At first, they resemble hunters: *'They fell with a regular thud. They fell with the concussion of horses' hooves on the turf. Their spray rose like the tossing of lances and assegais over the riders' heads'* (73). Then they become part of an army: *'the sea beat like a drum that raises a regiment of plumed and turbaned soldiers'* (*W* 74).[23]

In *The Waves*, Woolf associates the warrior-waves specifically with Louis, who hears from the start of the novel 'something stamping [...] A great beast's foot is chained. It stamps, and stamps, and stamps' (6); moreover, he sees 'men in turbans' in the ancient home about which he fantasizes as a replacement for a home in Australia where he is not wanted by his family. As a prelude to Percival's fall from a horse, linking the event to Louis and what he hears as a child: '*The waves were steeped deep-blue* [...] *which rippled as the backs of great horses ripple with muscles as they move. The waves fell; withdrew and fell again, like the thud of a great beast stamping.*' This description of the waves is followed by: '"He is dead," said Neville. "He fell. His horse tripped"' (101). Percival serves the warrior society of colonial Britain in India and, remarkably, although Woolf depicts him as a fantasy figure, akin more to his mythic namesake than to a child or man, Neville believes that this fantastical figure gives 'solidity' to the others, who are merely 'hollow phantoms' (82). What makes Percival this solidifying force for Woolf's narrators?

Bernard argues it is because Percival is 'a hero.' Moreover, his warrior-like self impacts the others at the dinner table, anxiously awaiting his arrival in striking terms: 'We who yelped like jackals biting at each other's heels now assume the sober and confident air of soldiers in the presence of their captain' (*W* 83). The narrators, gathered together to say goodbye to Percival, who is leaving for India, connect with one another by recalling their communal childhood spent at the boarding school, recounted at the opening of the novel. Woolf here repeats the key scenes for the narrators of this institution. The implication is that Percival also boarded; he also was bathed by Mrs Constable; he also knew the bootboy; he also knew of the apple tree and the leaf dancing in the hedge; however, he did not have a voice (83). If this novel strives to record the childhood depths of its narrators, while suppressing such a realm with the evasions each one activates to avoid self-discovery, why does it not give Percival a voice? In *The Waves*, the hero's defining feature is his silence.

After his death, Bernard recalls that 'as a boy' Percival had a 'curious air of detachment' (*W* 103). Percival seems to be a fantasy that renders the projections of others solid. The narrators appear in Bernard's thoughts as 'yelping like jackals,' an obviously derogatory description of articulation; in contrast, the silent, commanding presence of Percival resembles a military captain who has the power to transform 'yelping' individuals into soldiers, good soldiers, ones who are listening rather than talking; yet he does not speak.

Notably, Bernard's contribution to the childhood recollections is the traumatic event of suppressing his grief as he went away, further away, to school: 'the cab came to the door, and, pressing our new bowler hats tightly over our eyes to hide our unmanly tears, we drove through streets.' Bernard concludes his sense of this event: 'A second severance from the body of our mother' (*W* 84). Woolf reverses the Bildungsroman pattern, so that as Bernard is forced to sever himself again and again from his mother, while he presses down his hat just as he is expected to press down his grief, his identity progressively weakens. When Percival dies, Bernard's grief is completely self-conscious and in parentheses, '(my eyes fill with tears and are then dry),' and thus he plans '(An entry to be made in my pocket-book; contempt for those who inflict meaningless death)' (104). The once sure child of the garden who rushes to comfort Susan's grief transforms through suppression into a mature, 'mechanical' man.

Bernard, faced with the birth of his son and the death of Percival, has a moment of incredible insight into his own suppressed child, whom he imagines behind doors that are opening and shutting. Through these doors, he catches sight of a 'child playing' and this sight makes him 'weep.' The glimpses he has of this child, which fill him with grief, 'cannot be imparted'; hence, he is overwhelmed with 'loneliness' and 'desolation' and concludes: 'I turn to that spot in my mind and find it empty' (*W* 105). Woolf reveals in this scene the double bind of suppressed childhood: one cannot articulate these lost feelings; yet one's ability to communicate them is what creates communion with self and others. Bernard's grief comes to the fore at the sight of this child, but he has been trained to hide his 'unmanly tears.' Therefore, he does not enter that door into the mind, for he is terrified of its emptiness; instead, he strides manfully out the door into the world with plans to 'subjugate' what he finds (98). Conversely, Woolf enters that spot in the mind and uses her fiction to create voices, cries, yelps, anything to convey that glimpsed child. One of the ways she conveys this seemingly empty spot in the mind is by using the contradictory narrator, Percival, for he never actually speaks, but this is the paradoxical force of his inarticulate language, his silence. The recurring motif of the dinner party, after his death, is its silence (151–2). Coming together in the absent figure of Percival is the force of phantom grief and the ghost child. One can never remember this child; hence, one can never forget. Neville's remark that Percival gives 'solidity' to the others, who are merely 'hollow phantoms,' makes sense in this context. Grieving for Percival, as though he were a lost child, Bernard exclaims: 'No lullaby has ever occurred to me capable of singing him to rest' (164). Bernard, who suppresses his grief, cannot sing this childish, soothing song, whereas Woolf, through her fiction, can.[24] The lullaby forms a parallel with the soothing patois of Rhys's and Ford's nurses. Notably, these are maternal figures, but not mothers.

At the final meeting of the childhood friends, Louis thinks, 'it is difficult not to weep, calling ourselves little children,' as he recalls a moment from their shared past (W 154). He gazes out at Hampton Court and focuses on a bird flying 'homeward' at the same time as he wonders how to put together the 'confused and composite message' sent from the phantoms of the many dead; he specifies boys and girls along with adults. (155). The confused and composite message cannot be deciphered; it surfaces from the difficulty of suppressing the desire to weep when one thinks homeward about childhood and how it haunts. After this party, Bernard falls asleep clasping 'the return half' of his ticket, and when he is dying, he recalls that in brief moments of confidence, Louis would 'describe how the surf swept over the beaches of his home' (159,165).

At the end of the novel, with the phrase '*The waves broke on the shore*,' the turbaned warriors represent the enemy Death against whom Bernard, like Percival 'when he galloped in India,' confidently rides and falls: 'Against you I will fling myself, unvanquished and unyielding, O Death!' (W 200) The warrior waves blend Bernard's, Louis's, and Percival's sufferings, thus merging the childhood suppression of the first two with the latter's early death. On one level, Percival functions as the inarticulate sign of the others' childhoods; moreover, he represents inaccessible grief. Neville confronts the group of narrators after Percival's death and asks, 'what do we feel on meeting?' And he answers in such a way that Percival almost becomes an allegorical figure: 'Sorrow. The door will not open; he will not come' (142). Sorrow / Percival will not appear at the door. At this dinner party, what appears, instead of childhood sorrow, are the adults who have worked so faithfully to become good soldiers; these men and women emerge out of the darkness 'like the relics of an army, our representatives, going every night (here or in Greece) to battle, and coming back every night with their wounds, their ravaged faces' (156). These are Rhoda's last recorded thoughts before her suicide: the transformation of those she knew as children into good soldiers fighting what Bernard calls 'the perpetual warfare,' 'the daily battle' (182).

Anticipating the transformation, from sorrowing children into soldiers, is the send-off dinner party for Percival as he leaves to represent the British Empire in India. Bernard's final thoughts at this dinner party are revealing. The concluding moment involves fantasies of the 'globe.' Bernard's musings convey his belief that one must silence and subdue others in order to set forth on 'the illumined and everlasting road.' Thus, he exclaims: 'We are not slaves'; instead, he believes: 'We are creators' and his concept of creativity involves striding 'into a world that our own force can subjugate' (*W* 98). In Bernard's dream of the British Empire's colonization of India, Percival figures prominently. Most remarkably, he speaks. While the 'natives' appear 'chattering excitedly,' Percival applies 'the standards of the West, by using the violent language that is natural to him, the bullock-cart is righted in less than five minutes. The Oriental problem is solved.' Bernard's vision ends with the natives regarding Percival 'as if he were – what indeed he is – a God' (92). The grown-up children at the table 'sing like eager birds' (83); comparably, the natives chatter like birds. Only Percival, with his silent military presence and, when needed, his 'violent language,' earn the respect, awe, and worship more commonly offered to a god. Articulation is censured unless it is to solve the problem of otherness, to render the native self silent, and to transform the recollections of childhood grief into the silence and atten- tion of good soldiers.

In *The Waves*, Neville also condemns what is written with anything less than what Derrida calls the 'Sergeant-Major pen, parental writing'; at the send-off party, he deplores 'the wild, the weak and inconsequent cries that we utter when, trying to speak, we rise; when we reason and jerk out these false sayings, "I am this; I am that!" Speech is false' (93). Derrida describes this kind of writing as if it is put on paper by a pen, 'that very hard weapon with which one must inscribe, incise, choose, calculate, take ink before filtering the indescribable' (*C* 12). The violent language of Percival is clearly the language of a powerful western adult; whereas the wild, weak, inconsequent cries that Neville imagines, that are not even spoken but ring out like a gong, sound very much like the language of a vulnerable western child. Louis thinks that their lives as children were like 'gongs striking' (*W* 27). The children, the native selves, who have been suppressed at home, re-enact this suppression on native selves abroad.

While the reader does not have access to the imperial soldier's, Percival's, thoughts or suppressions, Woolf elaborates Louis's transfor- mation into a fine commercial soldier. Louis, in a seemingly unconscious attempt to become cold and powerful like his banking father, serves the commercial side of imperial Britain around the globe: 'I roll the dark before me, spreading commerce where there was chaos in the far parts of the world' (*W* 113). At the good-bye dinner party for Percival, Louis and Rhoda connect through a fantasy of India: 'There is a dancing and a drumming, like the dancing and the drumming of naked men with assegais' (94). As noted, these men with their spears surface in the italicized interludes as part of the wave imagery and ultimately they reveal Louis's profound depths. Louis considers himself a child, but in disturbing terms: 'I, Louis, I, who shall walk the earth these seventy years, am born entire, out of hatred, out of discord' (26). It appears that as a very young child he was in an institution, as opposed to a home; in a memory of Christmas that humiliates and haunts him, a woman noted his isolation and his lack of presents and handed him a 'shiny Union Jack' from the Christmas tree (23). Abandoned by his parents, he is offered a flag from his institutional home, a place where his colonial, Australian accent reveals and degrades him, a place where those hired to care for him forget, and then pity, him. His response is 'fury' not grief (23).

Louis's childhood at boarding schools appears structured by suffering: 'Jinny and Susan, Bernard and Neville bind themselves into a thong with which to lash me' (*W* 14). Hence, Louis becomes a good soldier of imperial 'commerce' in an attempt to cleanse himself of the 'defilements' of his childhood: 'the woman who gave me a flag from the top of the Christmas tree; my accent; beatings and other tortures; the boasting boys; my father, a banker at Brisbane' (113). Louis constantly expresses shame about his father, who is a banker; yet he himself becomes one, for he is the 'best scholar,' although he purposely fails school. Louis never mentions his mother (62). He is put into schools on the other side of the world, while he constantly thinks of himself 'down under,' on the other side of the globe. Like Ford's Edward Ashburnham, Louis dislocates family onto pre-parent origins. He superimposes his 'home' onto ancient societies such as those flourishing on the banks of the Nile. Louis recognizes his denial – 'if I now shut my eyes, if I fail to realize the meeting place of past and present' – and its implications: 'human history is defrauded of a moment's vision' (45).

Like Conrad's Razumov, Louis likes to believe that his memory is historical, depersonalized. He remembers 'rumours of wars; and the nightingale'; he has 'felt the hurrying of many troops of men flocking hither and thither in quest of civilization.' He remembers the 'confused cries and toppling pillars and shafts of red and black in some nocturnal conflagration' (64). His memories sound like scenes out of classical literature – Herodotus's wars, Ovid's Philomela, Virgil's destruction of Troy – and thus he imagines himself as 'the companion of Plato, of

Virgil' (64). Louis does not recall his father or mother with longing or affection; yet he believes that others interact like a family: a waitress serves her customers 'like a sister' and they are 'her brothers' (65). In contrast, rather than feel sibling relationships with others, Louis expresses himself in financial terms, as Bernard has been trained to do: 'I slip too large a tip, a shilling, under the edge of my plate, so that she may not find it till I am gone, and her scorn, as she picks it up with laughter, may not strike on me till I am past the swing-doors' (65). While he realizes there is something tragically comic in replacing family bonds with financial ones, he cannot help himself.

At first in a seeming parallel to Louis's suffering, the girls' school also requires the suppression of grief; Susan thinks: 'If I do not purse my lips, if I do not screw my handkerchief, I shall cry.' As a further strategy in suppressing her grief, Susan promises herself: 'I will find some dingle in a wood where I can display my assortment of curious treasures. I promise myself this. So I will not cry' (*W* 22, 23). In the couples' quest in 'A Haunted House,' in Mrs Dalloway's question about what Septimus Smith attains in suicide, and with a child's promise in *The Waves*, Woolf associates 'treasure' with one's suppressed emotional life. This recalls Rhys's island paradise, where one 'hides' the suppressed childhood self. However, far more harsh than Susan's experience of the girls' school, where one suppresses the desire to cry, in the boys' school Louis is conflicted by the desire to become a good soldier and thus be strong and protected, while at the same time being sickened by the behaviour of the school bullies: 'They are always forming, into fours and marching in troops with badges on their caps; they salute simultaneously passing the figure of their general. How majestic is their order, how beautiful is their obedience! If I could follow, if I could be with them, I would sacrifice all I know. But they also leave butterflies trembling with their wings pinched off; they throw dirty pocket-handkerchiefs clotted with blood screwed up into corners. They make little boys sob in dark passages' (32). Not only does Louis's lover, Rhoda, play a game with petals as ships, but she also is compared to a butterfly by Louis (12, 15). Unable to resist the seduction of the bullies' order and obedience, violence and power, the side of Louis that loves Rhoda ultimately joins the ranks of the warriors and becomes one who works for a shipping company, turning a child's petals into financial power, and one who leaves a butterfly trembling with its wings pinched off. Woolf seeks to articulate the butterfly self; thus, this image of warrior-like boys ripping off the wings is particularly striking. Susan also considers her time at school so painful that she describes the days as 'crippled days, like moths with shrivelled wings unable to fly' (36). Thus, the butterfly/moth self who figures in Woolf's fiction suffers torture and decline in the pedagogical institutions that supposedly teach these children meaningful material and necessary skills; consequently, Susan decides: 'I will not send my children to school' (42). In contrast, Louis, the self who abhors the cruelty of the boys, like Rhys's protagonists, turns into a 'ghost,' allowing Louis, the self who always hears the threat of the chained beast, to become more solid (45).

As Bernard dies, he strives to render more solid the ghostly voice of the child, even if that requires resorting to 'broken words, inarticulate words.' He recognizes the difficulty: 'like children we tell each other stories'; yet these stories are drowned out by 'ridiculous, flamboyant, beautiful phrases.' As a strategy to overcome the adult's fixed and articulate words, he divides the self into a child turning 'over the pages of a picture-book' and an adult providing a gloss: 'I will add, for your amusement, a comment in the margin' (*W* 161).

The Waves functions in a similar manner; the novel records a story broken into six different voices and one silent narrator; its details emerge in recollections and repetitions that are certainly not inarticulate, but that de-articulate expectations of character, plot, setting, and identity. Each child in *The Waves* is as much constituted by his or her job or lover or duty as he or she is by the remains of childhood. Thus, returning to one of his own hauntings from childhood, Bernard implores society, parents, nurses, and pedagogues, not to 'squeeze the sponge over that new body' (162). Reversing the teaching/parenting model, Woolf suggests that the child may well have a story to tell with that new body, the one that comes before a cold, societal soaking.

While dying, Bernard prides himself on developing his shell earlier than most, which allows him to bring his 'sentence to a close in a hush of complete silence.' Yet he quickly identifies such a skill as part of the mistake, the fallacy of precision, of 'orderly and military progress' (*W* 172). Underneath this lie, this making of phrases to create a hush in one's listeners, he discovers 'a rushing stream of broken dreams, nursery rhymes, street cries, half-finished sentences and sights.' The sights he notes are those from his childhood; sights that 'rise and sink' as one performs the ceremonies of adult life (173). Bernard's participation in hand-waving ceremonies all his life has silenced his grief – 'pain is absorbed in growth' – and this process turns his child-self into a phantom; thus, he 'must leap' in order to tell the story (174). Bernard describes the leap when he tries to escape the pain of Percival's death and realizes he cannot retreat into articulation: 'But for pain words are lacking. There should be cries, cracks, fissures, whiteness passing over chintz covers, interference with the sense of time, or space; the sense also of extreme fixity in passing objects; and sounds very remote and then very close; flesh being gashed and blood spurting, a joint suddenly twisted – beneath all of which appears something very important, yet remote, to be just held in solitude. So I went out. I saw the first morning he would never see – the sparrows were like toys dangled from a string by a child' (178). In this almost audible passage, Woolf fuses a violent battle scene like those dreamt of by West's narrator, Jenny, with a view of the world from a child's perspective.[25] Its powerful refusal to simply suppress grief and cover it over with words and its emphasis on cries, cracks, and fissures, ending with the child's experience in the world, together comprise a way to convey the new era, the first mourning. Bernard's passage works as a striking modernist manifesto and thus provides an insightful introduction to *Finnegans Wake*.

6   The 'Laughtears' of the Child Be Longing: James Joyce's *Finnegans Wake*

The grieving, joyful child-self belongs in *Finnegans Wake*. The child is longing for this sense of belonging and finds it finally in modernist fiction's most radical, innovative text – a text that is most indicative of a break with lessons learned in the past. Thus, the pedagogical directive to be a good soldier and dry one's tears is drowned out in the river of 'laughtears' that courses through the *Wake*.[1]

The tragedy of Woolf's narrators in *The Waves*, who express themselves simultaneously as children and as adults, revolves around their suppression of the native childhood self and the resultant need to suppress natives abroad. To create an alter*native* space for childhood grief, one that does not result in aggression, Woolf creates a home within fiction. In *The Waves*, and in the short stories and fragments of *A Haunted House*, Woolf reveals the role writing may play in allowing child voices to resonate, even when what they yearn to express is grief. Woolf seeks the words that one might use for 'pain.' The discovery of these childhood words, these grieving words, paradoxically results in an entrée to joy, for joy and sorrow commingle inextricably in her fiction.

In *Finnegans Wake*, Joyce develops further this idea of joy and sorrow or, as he puts it in the made-up language of Wakese, 'laughtears.' In the *Wake*, Joyce brings the child-self home to speak its pain-filled, inarticulate words, which allow for an access of comedic joy. Joyce writes of the longing of the child to belong, to speak, to grieve, and to laugh, even if the mode of expression is laborious, owing to its pain, which Woolf hears in *The Waves* as 'cries, cracks, fissures, whiteness passing over chintz covers, interference with the sense of time.'

As discussed earlier, Ford Madox Ford describes the power of some fictional works to take us back to the 'boy' we once were and thereby give us access to 'the deepest abandonment of the soul' (*Critical Essays* 262–3). Comparably, for Jacques Derrida, reading Joyce's final text makes him feel like a child: 'A coincidence nonetheless, for that seminar on translation I followed all the Babelian indications in *Finnegans Wake* and yesterday I wanted to take the plane to Zurich and read out loud sitting on his knees, starting with the beginning' (*The Post Card* 240).[2] Derrida imagines returning to the funerary statue of Joyce in Zurich to read while sitting on his literary father's lap. Yearning to be in a grave-yard, he writes of an overlap between mourning the dead and babbling like a baby.[3] Returning to the beginning of one's self, represented by the other writers as a root, wound, or blow, seems to be crucial in reading Joyce's final work.

As genetic criticism has shown, *Finnegans Wake* 'emerged through constant revision, rewriting, and textual accumulation and distortion' (Crispi, Slote, and Van Hulle 12). The text constantly opens up to greatly diverse and varied readings; yet one can find elements in it that fuse. Joyce describes this phenomenon in an early letter to his patron, Harriet Shaw Weaver, during the process of writing. He seeks to explain how the *Wake* works. He speaks of Vico's 'theory of history,' which becomes a key structuring element of the text in its finished form. He sees this histori-cal process as set forth 'by the four eminent annalists who are even now treading the typepress in sorrow.' The typing out of sorrow (within a comic text) is what I pursue in the following chapter, and, as expressed here, it is constructed of what Joyce says are 'not fragments but active elements,' which ultimately 'fuse themselves' even though they come to us in language full of accumulation and distortion (Crispi, Slote and Van Hulle 14).

In one section of the *Wake*, the children of the text play a game, and Joyce incorporates into this section of the text poetry he wrote when he was nine years old.[4] At the end, there is a new kind of prayer, one that transforms the formal words addressed traditionally to God into the sorts of terms that make kids laugh: '*merde*' (shit, in French) and '*mingere*' (urinate in Latin). Yet there is also an elegiac tone conveyed by press-ing requests such as 'O Loud, hear the wee beseech' and 'Loud, heap miseries upon us yet entwine our arts with laughters low!' It ends with 'Mummum' (259.3–10). The maternal ending combines the German word 'mumm' (courage) and the command 'mum' for silence. But there is clearly a sense that the wee ones beseech a Loud god as their Lord and perhaps turn to a more silent or listening mother to hear them. As will be discussed in the following chapter, throughout the *Wake* Joyce entwines his 'arts with laughte[a]rs low' as a way of hearing and recording the grieving child.

Like the other figures of the *Wake*, Joyce's baby would be comic if only he was not so tragic: 'The googoos of the suckabolly in the rockabeddy are become the copiosity of wiseableness of the friarylayman in the pulpitbarrel' (472.2–4). Joyce suggests that a baby has something to teach the adult reader about a layman's brotherhood (friarylayman), as opposed to constant news through the late 1930s of a pending war.[5] Joyce responds to suppression with (copiosity), a copyist who produces copious amounts of able wisdom (wiseableness) if allowed to preach his word (or his googoos) from the 'pulpitbarrel.'[6]

Joyce collapses our adult ways of thinking and interpreting the world, so that we can return to childhood before we became 'Toughtough, tootoological' (468.8). In the *Wake* it is 'the child which gives the sire away'; thus, if 'yur not freckened of frank comment,' then the text can let 'loose on his nursery' (375.20–1, 521.23, 520.2).[7] In a reversal of the Bildungsroman, some of Joyce's characters grow younger as the *Wake* proceeds. Andrew Treip discovers a 'rhythmic system that hesitates between ordered history and repetitive, infantile regression' ('Lost' 645). John Bishop discusses the 'infantile thinking of Vico's first men' in the *Wake* (185–93). Margot Norris reads 'The Mime of Mick, Nick, and the Maggies' as 'an infantile failure of knowledge' and thus, as a subversive reaction to Enlightenment, plans to educate and socialize the child. She calls the mime an 'anti-Bildungsroman' (*Web* 183). As Jed Rasula puts it: 'Joyce's "futurism" is properly that of babies, and his amalgamated language in the *Wake* is actually the linguistic magma of infants' (542).

Moving backward, the *Wake*'s Shaun becomes a baby – at least he babytalks with gurgling and cooing. Likewise, Derrida imagines his writing project in *Circumfession* as striving 'to track down the event by writing backward' (300). By the time the *Wake*'s Shaun appears to die and an inquest is launched, he has reached the fully inarticulate phase of infancy: 'a wail went forth' (474.1).[8] This wail makes you feel 'as were you suppose to go and push with your bluntblank pin in hand upinto his fleshasplush cushionettes of some chubby boybold love of an angel' (474.14–16). Yet there is no rest for this baby. On the one hand, an alarm clock; on the other, a call to arms. As we have seen in West's and Ford's fiction, the home front of war and the 'home fires' of childhood are superimposed: 'When, as the buzzer brings the light brigade, keeping the home fires burning' (474.16–17). In many ways, the *Wake* is a 'newseryreel' (489.35), which can be read by the adult self as a newsreel and by the child self, as a nursery real.[9]

In *Finnegans Wake*, while Joyce draws on epic and modern terms of warfare, he locates brutality first within the home.[10] He reverses the Latin phrase, *Amor regit Heva* (love rules Eve), in order to offer a domestic scene of violence, where 'Roman Tiger' is the motto the woman and child must learn in order to avoid being hit: 'For your own good, you understand, for the man who lifts his pud to a woman is saving the way for kindness. You'll rebmemer your mottob *Aveh Tiger Roma* mikely smarter the nickst time.' For if not, this husband and parent will: 'Give you one splitpuck in the crupper [...] till you yelp papapardon (445.11–14). This paternal figure causes 'a child's dread for a dragon vicefather' (480.25–6). And this is how one looks emerging from such a home: 'The black and blue marks athwart the weald, which now barely is so stripped, indicate the presence of sylvious beltings' (564.23–5).[11] The pedagogical idea of breaking the child's will, popular at this time, is presented by Joyce from the child's perspective and he/she feels 'dread.'

Joyce writes within a society that questions his concern with children and his exploration of unmanly emotions. Wyndham Lewis attacks Joyce as part of a modernist 'child-cult' and condemns him for using 'the language of childhood.' He wonders why 'a grown person should wish to be a child,' which is how he interprets the 'forms of infantile or immature life' appearing in modernist writing. Lewis simply dismisses this movement as 'irresponsible, Peterpannish' (52–3).[12] He yearns for a return to the characters in Russian novels, who are 'ardent, simple and in some cases truly heroical,' while he registers dismay at the 'dropping, simpering, leering, "bitter" and misunderstood, spoilt-child conscious' of Joyce's characters (99). Joyce responds to Lewis with the inarticulate language of childhood in *Finnegans Wake*.[13]

Joyce compares himself to Aeneas, who must tell the story of '*infandum doloren*' (unutterable sorrow). Joyce imagines being a 'voted disciple of Infantulus' (*FW* 166.22–3). The Latin word *infantulus* carries echoes of *infandum*, thus bringing together the unutterable force of childhood and grief in the *Wake*.[14] Parodied by Joyce, tough modernists like Wyndham Lewis see devotion to the infant as a feminine fault; thus, he has them lament the lack of masculine power, coupled as always with a need to deplore women: 'the femininny of that totamulier will always lack the musculink of a verumvirum' (166.25–6). Drawing on Latin, *tota mulier* (complete woman) and *verus vir* (real man), Joyce has his detractors continue the questioning of the child cult, which critiques women as feminine ninnies in the eyes of society, owing to their complete devotion to the 'tot.' Women will never be able to flex their real man's 'musculink' if they continue to care about children.

In contrast to the social climate, where children are to be seen and not heard, in the *Wake* the 'tot reigns' (129.28). The Letter of *Finnegans Wake*, which is lost and resurfaces throughout and acts as the symbolic figure for the text, is 'undone by a child' (94.9). Joyce thus provides a radically new way of considering, understanding, and even depending on children. Perhaps they can undo what has been done. The child-self speaks within; hence, one feels 'I have something inside of me talking to myself' (522.26). On one level, it is the child's voice within that takes articulate English and dismantles it into seemingly inarticulate Wakese. Discussed by critics like Lucia Boldrini, the language of the *Wake* is reminiscent of the mix of languages after the fall of the tower of Babel; blend this fallen language with a child's babble and you have the lullaby 'Rockaby, babel' (278 left margin). As discussed earlier, Woolf also imagined her novel *The Waves* as a lullaby. And Derrida imagines Babelic language as divine grief: 'it's God weeping in me, turning around me, appropriating my languages, dispersing their meaning in all directions' (*C* 224).[15] Notably, as discussed in the first chapter of this study, Conrad's Razumov put his belief in the power of autocratic Russia, which he claims wants 'a man,' an adult, not the 'babble of many voices,' the speech of infants.

As an Irish colonial subject, Joyce refuses to speak English dutifully; thus, he explodes and commands all languages. He cannot be a 'man' using the language of oppression, so he integrates the babble of those who cannot speak. Likewise, another exile and outsider, expelled from school as a Jew, Derrida puts his faith in 'letters.' Autocratic, imperialist Russia oppresses Conrad; he then suppresses Russian grief in his novel. Ford and Rhys use patois as a language that opens up English to suppressed selves within. Joyce speaks as though broadcasting from the Tower of Babel/babble. These authors rewrite the alphabet taught to them by those who excluded them. The Algerian Jews called the Bar Mitzvah 'communion' (*C* 72), and this contradictory ceremony for Derrida thus brings together, and at the same time collapses, the binary oppositions that political parties and religious sects use to condemn otherness. He refuses to be 'locked up' in Hebrew; he relinquishes the French they take from him; instead, he returns to an infantile state of 'ignorance,' where his Eucharist, his 'taste' for the 'word,' is all about grieving and celebrating his loss. Derrida explains: 'a child incapable of articulating what is going on' is moving, but he or she 'cannot be quoted, only incorporated' (*C* 196–7).[16]

Comparably, and in this moment using the idealistic terms of Esperanto, the *Wake* speaks childishly, using '*parolas infanetes*' (565.28). This hopeful cry in the night spurs the archetypal parents of the *Wake* to comfort the child; then they return to bed and make love. Joyce makes us wonder if an adult's response to a child's grief may result in love, as opposed to the controlling of emotion by means of what Woolf calls 'violent language' and then connects to our history of oppression.

Finnegans Wake gives voice to those who cannot express themselves. The writer-figure of the *Wake*, Shem the Penman, 'lifts the lifewand and the dumb speak' (195.5). The suppressed voices of children, entwined with grief, surface and are broadcast. For children, one of the sins, established by their society, is talking. Alternatively, Joyce celebrates their breaking of the rules, for 'childhood's age being aye the shameleast' (227.34). Because the child 'shames!' the family in using the 'gift of [his] gaft' to tell 'garbage abaht our Farvver!' revealing dirt or abuse in the home, we are advised to 'Shun the Punman!' (93.13–21). Therefore, although the text is frustrating and makes one feel like a child again because one cannot easily read nor understand, and although we have a tendency not to believe children, it is important to be like Issy, who is 'listening all she childishly could' (157.9–10). Not only must we listen with the ears of childhood, we can also strive to see with childish eyes. Joyce relates this to being able to grieve. During the *Wake*'s school lesson, it seems that if we stop voicing falsely cheery greetings like 'top of the morning to you,' then we can go beyond or 'past Morningtop's necessity,' to admit the mourning and see through to 'the clarience of the childlight' (266.12–13).[17]

The text strives to open up layers in the adult self, so that the childish or youthful self can be recalled and expressed, for, as the adult narrative voice tells his or her spectral child, 'the days of youyouth are evermixed mimine' (*FW* 194.3–4). While reading *Finnegans Wake*: 'We are once amore as babes awondering in a wold made fresh' (336.16–17). Even HCE, the father figure of all time, is just 'an overgrown babeling' (6.31) whose sleeping state, John Bishop reveals, has 'regressively return[ed] him to the condition of "first infancy" (22.1)'; thus, he advises, 'one must become a child again if one is to read the *Wake*' (149, 332).

The silenced selves of *Finnegans Wake* that I focus on are grieving children and soldiers, infants and infantry, whose voices generate Joyce's 'madh vaal of tares' (110.9). Beyond the 'soldier's scarlet,' I listen for 'his deepraised words' (536.23–5). Yet it is so difficult to hear grieving terms, for 'the jenny infanted the lass to be greeted raucously' (97.35). One cannot deny that we should greet the *Wake* as a raucous, humorous, comic text; yet we do not need to treat as a non-speaker, as an infant, the loss, which here is presented as a childish, feminine loss, a lass. Echoing loss, and blending lass and alas, Joyce reveals again the force of laughter to suppress the painful feeling of sorrow: 'Eve takes fall. La, la, laugh leaves alass!' (293.21–2). It is one thing to cry a river of tears; it is quite another to lose one: 'Hoangho, my sorrow, I've lost it!' (213.6–7) Joyce uses 'Hoangho,' an Asian river, also called 'China's Sorrow,' as he explores our inability to grieve and what this loss entails.

One of the aspects of paradise lost for Joyce is that it represents a place and time in which one could freely express sadness, whereas now, our time is dominated by a 'lack of lamentation' (*FW* 100.3). However, while reading we can volunteer to grieve: 'We can recall, with voluntears' (116.12). *Finnegans Wake* leads us through the gate of sorrow with Joyce's surrogate language: 'The speechform is a mere sorrogate' (149.29). Echoed in 'mere,' is the French term for mother (*la mère*), which creates the image of a maternal sorrowgate and suggests one of the roles women play within the text. It appears that women are allowed to grieve more freely.

The text investigates the 'form masculine' and the 'gender feminine' and after listening to science decides in a very indecisive way: 'It reminds of the weeping of the daughters?' (*FW* 505.25–30). More decisive proof comes in another gender contrast: while 'manmote, befier of him, womankind, pietad!' (128.19–20). While man might (archaic, *mote*) be proud (French *fier*), making masculine pride his goal, women, in contrast, appear as mourning their dead sons as Mary mourns Jesus in the Pietà. Women express their grief openly – that is, of course, when they are not suppressing their own and others' emotions.

In this contradictory text, mothers may block the expression of their children's feelings even though they have no right: 'No mum has the rod to pud a stub to the lurch of amotion' (*FW* 365.26–7). Joyce has turned into childlike, congested Wakese a line from a speech Parnell gave in Cork in 1885: 'No man has a right to fix the boundary of the march of a nation.'[18] Here, the *Wake* superimposes the suppression of children's emotions and the oppression of a nation of people; he thereby connects the familial self with the political one.[19] While Parnell in his speech addresses his adult followers, who live colonially oppressed and who strive to create an independent Ireland, Joyce uses a childish voice of rebellion to explore the origin of these suppressed adults. He locates their loss in childhood. Like the authors of all the other modernist texts examined, Joyce imagines feeling emotion, being moved, as mobile 'amotion,' whereas using the rod on children in an attempt to 'stub' or stop their lurching feelings may turn them to stone.[20] However, in the *Wake*, the self that is turned to stone through grief has found a writer. This shift recalls Conrad's 'lithographer' and Rhys's 'chromo-lithograph,' which also record grief. Deconstructive reading, which Derrida imagines as 'transformational' (*P* 63), works with writing that 'creates meaning by enregistering it, by entrusting it to an engraving, a groove, a relief, to a surface whose essential characteristic is to be infinitely transmissible' (*WD* 12). This kind of writing, Derrida calls 'extraction, graft, extension' (*P* 71). It takes what is immobile and mobilizes it: it makes stone malleable. In *Finnegans Wake*, '*muta*' (note the echo of mute) refers to the condition of turning to stone: tacking on a Latin dative and ablative plural, he speaks of 'Petrificationibus!' (610.3).

In the *Wake*, the paternal figure turns to stone, while the maternal figure flows like a river. Often in the text we find that woman is 'formed mobile,' while man is 'static' (309.21–2), and part of the fluidity of one and the stony quality of the other may result from the former's venting of grief and the latter's suppression of it. ALP, the mother and the river, has the last word of the *Wake* and she notes her own suffering and bereavement while brave others hide their feelings and become divided: 'Why I'm all these years within years in soffran, allbeleaved. To hide away the tear, the parted. It's thinking of all. The brave that gave their' (625.29–31). It is the non-grieving brave who so often march off to give their all in battle.

Like mother, like daughter: the girls of the *Wake* belong to the hydrologic cycle of the text, which at times expresses grief. When the girls of the text are 'mourning,' they let loose with 'a cry of genuine distress'; they are 'in tears'; they 'wail'; turning a French day, *aujourd'hui*, into an 'Oh jourd'woe' (470.6–26). In contrast, as noted, grieving is considered unacceptable for the men of the text. The advice is handed down: 'let ye not be getting grief out of it' (453.27). Moreover, as a mocking voice intones: 'Did a weep get past the gates of your pride?' (145.12–13). Even worse, one dreads to be thought of in lactating, maternal terms, as 'A Boob' who 'Was Weeping' (106.6). Because grief is considered self-indulgent and even sickening, Joyce transforms the jolly greeting, 'top of the morning to you,' into 'Up from the Pit of my Stomach I Swish you the White of the Mourning' (106.7–8). There is nothing worse than

being 'at the movies swallowing sobs' (166.13–14). And the most serious issue about grief, which is stressed in the epic tradition and will be
examined later, is that it stops a man from fighting 'while his countrary
raged in the weak of his wailing' (148.34–5). A country can be contrary
and rage only if its men do not wail.

In contrast, Joyce reverses the idea that if a man grieves he cannot
be a warrior. Joyce inverts a mother's critique of her son, specifically
Boabdil, the last Moorish king of Granada, who, when he went into
exile, heard from his mother: 'You do well to weep like a woman over
what you could not defend as a man.' Joyce transforms this critique so
that it reads: 'bewailing like a man that innocence which I could not
defend like a woman' (*FW* 194.1–2). In Joyce's version, the man is wailing and the woman is procreating; instead of war, there is sex; instead of
death, there is birth. In contrast to the mother of Boabdil, the maternal
figure of the *Wake*, with her procreative sexual powers and her love of
children, transforms the revenge cycle of the Old Testament: 'she who
had given his eye for her bed and a tooth for a child' (101.33–4). The
four annalists of the text, or Evangelists, also move beyond the revenge
cycle and become womanly as they grieve: 'truly they were four dear old
heladies' (386.14–15), all of whom appear 'sighing and sobbing, and
listening' (384.4–5).[21]

The writer figure of the *Wake*, Shem the Penman, is condemned
throughout the *Wake* for his expression of grief and is frankly told to stop:
'can that sobstuff, whingeywilly! Stop up, mavrone' (232.23). He is called
'willy,' which seems to be short form for the tree which throughout the
text signals sorrow: the 'fallen griefs of weeping willow' (207.3–4). He is
ordered to shut down his whining and whimpering and told to stop up
his expression of grief, referred to with the Anglo-Irish word, *mavrone*
(my grief). The mocking voice implies that, if Shem is going to shed so
many tears, he should simply leave life, or at least his mother: 'With tears
for his coronaichon, such as engines weep. Was liffe worth leaving? Nej!'
(230.24–5) Crowning Shem as king allows tears to fall, because this kind
of coronation echoes the Irish *corónach* (funeral dirge). If Satan weeps
like an angel in Milton's time, the satanic modern-day Shem weeps like a
big machine, an engine. Shem is a crier and the maternal figure of ALP
is a river of tears, among other things, and in the *Wake* he does not need
to leave either.

Shem defines the *anima* (his or another's or ours) as sorrowful even
if society finds it foolish: 'My animal his sorrafool!' (*FW* 301.15). The
soul then becomes part of a dialogue on war. Questioned about 'Wasting

war and?' (499.29), the text turns to the bible to respond with grief. Blending Latin, *anima mea* (my soul), and French, *triste* (sad), we hear nothing but sadness in answer to war's rallying cry: '*Tris tris a ni ma mea.*' Immediately, a mocking voice wonders outraged: 'what static babel is this, tell us?' (499.34).

In Shem's 'new Irish stew,' a culinary version of the text, one finds 'onions you cry over' (*FW* 190.5). In its textile version, the text is woven from tears: 'wapt from wept' (34.24). Shem the Penman is the 'tragic jester' who 'sobbed himself wheywhingingly sick of life' (171.15–16). The Shakespearean insult, 'whey-face,' conveys disgust at less than manly behaviour. Nonetheless, Shem continues to produce 'crazy elegies,' regardless of the fact that he appears to be 'Shemming amid everyone's repressed laughter' (190.33–4). While monkey-like versions of men have 'no sentiment secretions,' one knows to call on this writer to 'weep cataracts for all me, Pain the Shamman!' (192.22–3). Shem seems to align himself with the 'Girl Cloud Pensive' rather than the 'wartrophy' (82.20, 83.14). In fact, his open expression of grief puts him with the women and separates him from the men; thus, Shem 'clings to her, a wholedam's cloudhued pittycoat, as child,' while in the men's camp the 'wararrow went round' (43.19–21). Shem clings like a child to grief, which is sexualized and feminine like a petticoat, but it offers a cloak of pity that is grief hued. It is potentially procreative, in contrast to the masculine alternative in which the arrows of war zing around.

Shem is an anomaly, for it seems that society raises its boys to become soldiers: in the knapsack of the endlessly contradictory mother one finds diapers and keys, but also 'bloodstaned breeks' and 'howitzer' guns (*FW* 11.20–4). Caretakers of children realize that they are early on suited up for war: 'How a mans in his armor we nurses know' (361.13–14). The mother's bag contains both joy and sadness, 'loffs' and 'pleures' (11.25, Fr. tears); yet it seems that grief is associated with the maternal figure, Anna Livia Plurabelle, for here the name occurs as 'pleures of bells.' However, the child seems to become a warrior, since, when one looks in his knapsack as he attends 'Sunda schoon,' one discovers a war comrade: 'every warson wearrier kaddies a komnate in his schnapsack' (350.33–4). Despite being a son of war, this kiddie seems weary.

Pedagogy, masculine and feminine values, our yearning to weep, and our lusting for war, are entwined in the *Wake*.[22] Thus, the mother's bag is full of tears *and* guns. The father and mother try to stop their child from expressing his feelings; yet they come running when he cries out in the night.[23] Joyce leads us to question a rigid belief in 'spare the rod, spoil the child,' for in *Finnegans Wake* Joyce transforms the idea to read sadly of wounded children: 'speared the rod and spoiled the lightning' (131.14). The light-filled child is extinguished by the parent who spears with the rod. A page later, Joyce describes the abusive parental effect again: 'we go into him sleepy children, we come out of him strucklers for life' (132.8–9). These children go to their father, who strikes them, which leads them to struggle henceforth for life. Joyce associates night with an allowance to grieve, and thus 'tears of night began to fall' and 'the tired ones,' the washerwomen, 'weep now with them' (158.21–3). On this 'night sublime' the reader might even be 'tramsported with grief' (452.14). While the nighttime washerwomen weep with the children, the father figure of a few pages earlier is bottled up, at the same time he's drunk, and he hails from Cork, like Joyce's father: 'my corked father was bott a pseudowaiter, whose o'cloak you ware' (155.1–2). Whether the child wants to or not, (s)he wears the father's cloak, since his time, his o'clock, may well effect what the child becomes. Joyce recognizes that a child may well become 'a dismantled noondrunkard's son' (125.2), for the father is 'mildewstaned he's mouldystoned' (128.2). This father has the force to turn his children to stone like him, coming to life only by drinking and becoming 'mouldy' (drunk in Irish slang). Ah, the text implores, 'If Standing Stones Could Speak' (306.22–3), and it pities the immobilized paternal figure: we 'shall wail him rockbound' (6.36–7.1).

Shem, as Glugg, a drunkard in his own right, is a 'chip of old Flinn the Flinter, twig of the hider that tanned him' (*FW* 240.23–4). Joyce takes the threat to a child, 'I'll tan your hide,' and blends it with the idea of a child 'being a chip off the old block' to remind us that professions and characteristics are not all that is passed on from father to son. Shem may well learn the art of beating those who are small and weak; moreover, he may develop a serious drinking habit like the textual father, HCE. In contrast, the maternal figure of the text gazes at her husband and sees him as 'a boy in innocence, peeling a twig.' Alluding to the tarot card for the Sun, and punning on son, Joyce has the maternal figure exclaim: 'The child we all love to place our hope in for ever' (621.30–2). Perhaps the world would be more hopeful if one recognized the child within the adult and twigs were used as childish toys instead of objects to administer beatings with.[24]

Dating back to our earliest recorded literature, the child-self must be buried or suppressed for the sake of battle. Just before he alludes to this epic tradition, Joyce describes a beautiful, flourishing child-self: 'He, A.A., in peachskin' is putting on weight or 'gaining fish considerable';

he says 'grace' and has 'smily' blue eyes (*FW* 240.30–3). Shem is often aligned with Aeneas and here it is in terms of the stated father-son bond: 'He repeat of him as pious alios' (240.33). While the alias, Aeneas, is significant as a son who suppresses grief, Priam in the *Iliad* is resonant as a father who expresses grief: 'Not true what chronicles is bringing his portemanteau priamed full potatowards' (240.35–241.1). As will be discussed in more detail later, from the ground Priam gathers dung, which he rubs all over himself, as an inarticulate gesture to mourn the death of his son, Hector. Here the earth is being dug down to potato level in order to produce a new kind of grieving language that puts words together that seem to be nonsense like Lewis Carroll's portmanteau terms, but, in fact, that assessment is 'not true.' This chronicle is a fiction in a blended language that is a truth in letters deeply buried or suppressed, underground, nourishing, like potatoes.[25] The *Wake* is a book written in sober truth or 'in sobber sooth' (353.3). The act of grieving intensely, sobbing, leads us to *sooth*, an archaic term for truth. The notion of sober is complex in the text, for often Joyce suggests that the lure of alcohol is to drown one's grief; hence being a 'sadfellow,' with an echo of the French adjective for sad, *triste*. Drowning one's sorrows leads to an alcohol-soaked liver in Trieste, where Joyce and his family lived for many years: 'And trieste, ah trieste ate I my liver' (301.16). In the *Wake*, 'wine' assists in holding 'the heavyache off his heart' (362.19–21).[26] Therefore, do we access truth by being sober? According to the *Wake*, it seems we cannot return to the truths of grief in childhood while being sober and logical; instead, the return requires a kind of drunken abandon, which leads to a mo*u*rning after. What brings Finnegan back to life but whiskey? What brings the grieving self to the fore but laughing? Thus, he 'lauffed till the tear trickled drown' (319.31) and the girls are 'weeping like fun' (558.24). Joyce suggests that our logical, rational minds cannot help us to understand this kind of truth: 'One could naught critically'; however, he questions whether reading the epic tradition could return us to our buried feelings: 'could one classically?' (241.12–13).[27]

Joyce extracts from, grafts onto, and extends his text into the epic tradition in order to express his unique and shared history of grief and its relationship to war. The first key link with the epic tradition in terms of grief in the *Wake* appears early on. Joyce establishes with the Prankquean episode the recurring exploration of the role of grief, its expression and suppression.[28] The episode foregrounds children who are simultaneously comic, riddle-loving imps and vulnerable, easily manipulated creatures.[29] Joyce uses the Irish pirate, Grace O'Malley, and the Earl of Howth, whose heir she kidnaps, when he refuses her entry into the Castle, in order to detail three historical attempts to reshape the beliefs and institutions of Ireland. In the episode, there are three children and, after the first one is kidnapped, he describes how the other two in 'their first infancy were below on the tearsheet' (*FW* 22.1). This early stage allows for grief, for tears to be recorded, written on the sheet. Sheets of paper and bed linen: sheets in the *Wake* need constant cleaning, for they are records of sexual sins and sins of violence, such as the 'bloodied warsheet' (131.20). One must use a washing tool, a battledore; yet one must wash out the battle blood. Thus, the washerwomen of the text are commanded to 'wallop it well with your battle and clean it' (196.16–17). These same washer-women, in a poignant echo of Psalm 137 – 'By the rivers of Babylon, there we sat down, yea, we wept' – explain: 'For we, we have taken our sheet upon her stones where we have hanged our hearts in her trees; and we list, as she bibs us, by the waters of babalong' (103.9–11). As noted above, these women grieve with children, and thus we might de-scribe them as '*keening after the blank sheets in their faminy*' (340.14–15). Blended with the child who suffers infamy within the family, the blank sheet, most dreaded by writers, suggests a block. One cannot keen; one cannot write.[30]

The twin boys stolen by Grace O'Malley, Tristopher and Hilary, are figures for happiness and sadness taken from Giordano Bruno's motto: '*In tristitia hilaris; in hilaritate tristis*' (In Sadness Cheerful; in Gaiety Sad). The pirate first takes the sad twin and makes him jolly: 'he became a lu-derman' (*FW* 21.30). When the pirate takes the other twin, the descrip-tion of the kidnapping alludes to the First World War: 'So her madesty a forethought set down a jiminy and took up a jiminy and all the lilipath ways to Woeman's Land she rain, rain, rain' (22.7–9). Joyce's Wakese, which replaces 'majesty' with 'madesty' recalls how the royal family feud made the world a sty, a revolting pen unfit for humanity. Comparably, Joyce alludes to the central war of western tradition when he transforms the name of a commoner from the *Iliad* who rails against the kings: Thersites thus becomes 'our thorstyites' (137.24). Joyce correlates the Great War of the modernist era with the Trojan War, which still influ-ences and shapes our beliefs and behaviour.

So the majestic pirate Grace O'Malley puts down one emotion in this passage, one of the Gemini or twins, and picks up another. O'Malley, seeking ransom, pursues a variety of 'lilipath ways' as she runs away, rains away. As icons for the Resurrection, and thus representative of an end to grief and a time to rejoice, lilies function ideally in the Prankquean episode with its playful shifts from sadness to gaiety. Joyce notes our tendency to feel grief, becoming mellow once again after mourning, and what better way to do so than to reconfigure a death as a resurrection: '*toomellow aftermorn and your phumeral's a roselixion*' (*FW* 346.12–13). In the Prankquean episode, Joyce's shift from the death and destruction of the First World War's no-man's-land to the term 'Woeman's Land' suggests that, beneath the art and laughter of the episode, one of the riddles posed from a place of suffering is: how is one to be a man when there is no land for masculinity? Woeman's Land is the feminine equivalent of No Man's Land, and both locations exclude men. Men meet destruction and death in the one and, in the other, they cannot express their grief, for if they do, they become women.

We noted in the Prankquean episode that the children's first infancy allows for grief upon the 'tearsheet.' In contrast, their 'second infancy' has left tears behind and is dominated by sexual conquest: 'kissing and spitting' (*FW* 22.25–6). Joyce reminds us of another way in which society traditionally separates the men from the boys: sexual prowess. The Trojan War is fought over Helen, and myth and epic are ambiguous about whether she runs away with Paris or if he abducts her. In the *Iliad*, Homer begins his epic treatment with a microcosm of the Trojan War: just as Greece and Troy fight over who gets Helen, Achilles and Agamemnon battle over who gets the concubine, Briseis (1.119–422). Thus, Joyce echoes the Italian *tròia* (harlot) in calling the mythological city, 'the Troia of towns' (448.11–12). In the children's mime, a reenactment of courtship and marriage rituals, he emphasizes the city's allure as a site for the battle of the sexes or the battle of sexual identity: 'just with a shrug of their hips to go to troy' (225.3–4). As the *Wake* suggests: 'violence to life, limb and chattels, often as not, has been the expression, direct or through an agent male, of womanhid offended' (68.36–69.2). On the one hand, war rages over a woman's seduction or abduction; on the other hand, war seems to arise when men need to hide their womanly feelings, 'womanhid.' Thus, although the Letter 'pledged peace,' it has the potential to cause war, for it is 'uptied by a harlot,' but as noted previously, it is also 'undone by a child' and thus has the potential to unravel suppressed feelings creating a more peaceful self and community (94. 5–9).[31]

Paradoxically, women function as the cause and prize of war because they make a man look and feel powerful at the same time as they allow a man to share his feelings of vulnerability. Often depicted as seductive creatures, the girls of *Finnegans Wake* may connect the self with feelings of grief or they may spur on battle by suppressing grief.[32] Thus, at one juncture, when 'girl' is conveyed by the Italian *fanciulla*, we are warned about her association with the weeping willow and falling under the spell of grief: 'Bewise of Fanciulla's heart, the heart of Fanciulla! Even the recollection of willow fronds is a spellbinder that lets to hear' (278.7–9). At another juncture we learn that the girlish heart is full of fun: 'And how war yore maggies? 'They war loving, they love laughing, they laugh weeping, they weep smelling' (142.30–2). Here we discover a connection between loving war and loving laughter or generating war and not being able to grieve.

Joyce's oft-quoted term 'laughtears' (*FW* 15.9) suggests that laughter without tears is potentially destructive and may even become its reverse, conveyed in the deadly overlap between laughter and slaughter.[33] A passage from Edgar Quinet, resurfacing throughout the *Wake*, blithely imagines society as a jolly passage from slaughter to laughter and back again: '*les civilisations se sont choquées et brisées, leurs paisibles générations ont traversé les âges et sont arrivées jusqu'à nous, fraîches et riantes comme aux jours des batailles*' (civilisations have collided with one another & smashed, their peaceful generations have passed through the ages & have come up to us, fresh and laughing as on the days of battles; 281.9–13).[34] Are there alternatives to this cyclical pattern of laughter and slaughter?

Finnegans Wake presents and questions the danger of entering into a post-war lotus-land of forgetting in order to transform sadness into happiness: 'to forget in expiating manslaughter and, reberthing in re-marriment' (62.6–7). This quick fix for grief parallels Woolf's concern about patching up with 'lily-glue' in order to switch grief into celebration. Yet it also blends man's laughter and manslaughter. The pattern Joyce identifies is when 'first man's laughter' becomes 'wailful moither' (433.29–30). Our refusal to grieve is like wilful murder of one side of the self, while our (s)laughter keeps us from regaining paradise. Although on the surface rather amusing, the question is a serious one: who will one be? 'Mr Shallwesigh or Mr Shallwelaugh' (37.27–8). Can one be both when the *Wake* constantly makes us wonder 'whether to weep or laugh' (226.1–2)? According to Derrida, 'art and laughter, when they go together, do not run counter to suffering, they do not ransom or redeem it, but live off it' (*WM* 173). Hence, while not for a minute suggesting we lament rather than laugh, Joyce and Derrida reveal grief's natural role in life and thus the dangers inherent in suppressing it. The point for both writers is not choosing, privileging, or creating a 'violent hierarchy' of one emotion over the other. As Joyce puts it, we strive for a 'poignt of fun,' where we are 'crying to arrive' (*FW* 160.32–3). So the *Wake* commands: 'Cry not yet!' (20.19). At the same time, the text commands us to cry, for it is while shedding tears that we can think deeply at the same time as return to a time of feelings when we were wee ones: 'weepon, weeponder' (344.5–6).[35]

In the Prankquean episode, Grace O'Malley's 'rain, rain, rain' connects with the rest of the female figures in the text, for throughout the *Wake* Joyce overlaps the tears of humanity, most often shed by women (and Shem) with the feminine hydrologic cycle: thus, 'weep the clouds' (29.11). When the river ALP flows into the sea, Joyce calls it 'the night she signs her final tear' (28.28–9). For the feminine child, Issy, grief appears as natural and cyclical as the hydrologic cycle which flows through the text: '[Nuvoletta] climbed over the bannistars; she gave a childy cloudy cry: *Nuée! Nuée!* A lightdress fluttered. She was gone. And into the river that had been a stream (for a thousand of tears had gone eon her and come on her and she was stout and struck on dancing and her muddied name was Missisliffi) there fell a tear, a singult tear, the loveliest of all tears [...] for it was a leaptear. But the river tripped on her by and by, lapping as though her heart was brook: *Why, why, why! Weh, O weh! I'se so silly to be flowing but I no canna stay!*' (159.6)

The river flowing through *Finnegans Wake* and functioning as a central feminine symbol is a river of tears. Joyce has the 'childy' daughter cry out in French, directly expressing her grief as an analogy to a cloud filling with moisture and raining into streams and rivers. Usually referred to as a 'leap year' girl, here Issy is a 'leaptear' who seems to receive little response from the maternal river who courses by laughing, lapping, silly, and dismissive. Like the text of the *Wake*, Issy leaps through eras, languages, and cultures and thus her 'singult tear,' with echoes of sin and guilt, comes from the Latin *singultus* (sobbing). She grieves into an Irish river blended with an American one: Liffey and Mississippi. She cries out in German to express her inarticulate sadness: *Weh, O weh* (woe is me) and defines herself as a cloud in both Italian and French: *nuvoletta* and *nuée*.

By means of Derrida's paradoxically articulate grief, one discovers the full resonance of correspondence in the *Wake* between weeping a river of tears and the 'gorgeups' that is the site of release, yet also the lump in the throat. Mourning Max Loreau while reading his poetry, Derrida transposes in an impressionistic way, as expressive of his grief, the river as gorge, as a voice to which he is listening 'from the other side, the side of the body, deep down in the throat where it is engorged (and I even hear in this expression the name of the gorge cut into a mountainside, not far from some spring or source, but also the fall: the fall, and then the torrent, the dam, high tension, danger of death)' (*WM* 103). Most important for my purposes, Derrida emphasizes that one can feel this grief if one reads and/or listens intensely to the voice from beyond. And this act of hearing the voice returns us to a source or spring. Elsewhere, as noted, he has written of the Pacific and one wonders if this is the source to which he turns: an ocean brimming with salt tears and emblematic of peace. ALP as the river returns at the end of the *Wake* to the sea that Joyce superimposes on the gorge, wherein it seems language battles with bows and arrows: 'Jumpst shootst throbbst into me mouth like a bogue and arrohs!' And yet: 'Sea, sea! Here, weir, reach, island, bridge. Where you meet I. The day. Remember!' (626.5–8)

One of the major themes or principle structures of *Finnegans Wake* is the fall, whether it be from a ladder, the garden of Eden, the tower of Babel, Parnell's political collapse, or even from our emotions that make us vulnerable: 'First we feel. Then we fall' (627. 11). As quoted above, Derrida suggests, through imagery, the fall of a river as it overflows its bounds. The river is a maternal force in the *Wake* that is vitally connected to the gush of grief from the body, which may take the form of flow and blockage, tears in the eyes and lump in the throat, the battling site for words and the place where you meet I.

In contrast to the flow of wo(e)man, man in the *Wake*: 'Business bred to speak with a stiff upper lip to all men and most occasions the Man we wot of took little short of fighting chances but for all that he or his or his care were subjected to the horrors of the premier terror of Errorland' (62.21–5). What does the stiff upper lip lead to in the *Wake* but 'the fighting,' 'the horrors,' the 'terror.' This recalls the items honoured in the 'museyroom': the 'gunn' and 'bullets' that produce 'sheltershock' (8.10–12, 30). Joyce's Wakese transformation of shell shock once again recalls the overlap in Ford, West, and Woolf of the domestic and military home fronts. Moreover, like these other novelists, Joyce's neologism 'sheltershock' suggests that that shock occurs at home, one's so-called shelter.

Another reference to the term stresses that it affects one's masculinity and one's speech: 'Where he fought the shessock of his stimmstammer' (*FW* 272fn4). Shell shock reveals the weak feminine self, the *she*, who surfaces during trauma. Surrounding this footnote from the children's 'Night Lessons' are allusions to the epic warrior tradition: 'Hoploits and atthems' (272 left margin), as well as 'Foamous homely brew, bebattled by bottle, gageure de guegerre' (272.28–9). Hoplites, or heavily armed foot soldiers of Ancient Greece, with their war songs or – clear the throat, ahem, anthems – occupy the margin of a comical blend of war and drink. Wagers (Fr. *gageure*) and battles (Fr. *guerre*) mix with foamy, famous, Homer home brew, bottled and battled in one intoxicating blend. The wounded womanly self, full of grief, may well drown her sorrows with the guys at the bar.

The errors that dominate present-day Ireland are the mistakes that we continue to revere and study in the museums and great epic traditions; hence Joyce's description of his nation, 'Errorland,' as 'The wastobe land, a lottuse land, a luctuous land, Emerald-illium' (*FW* 62.11–12). This description begins with reference to Eliot's post-First World War poem *The Waste Land*; Joyce then suggests a modernist forgetting of what home means, as it becomes a roaring twenties lotus-land (with a nod to Homer's crew after the Trojan War); he then draws on the Latin term for sorrowful in 'luctuous land'; and concludes with an overlap between the great fallen city of Troy (Lat. *Ilium*) and the present-day site that is falling, Ireland. As noted, Joyce links Shem to 'pious' Aeneas, hero of the Trojan people. Just as Aeneas journeys through great peril to find a home for his people, Shem, as the 'pious author' (34.14), strives to regain Eden for us, but rather than the biblical version, it will be a 'teargarten' (75.1). Like the Trojans recovering from the ravages of war, the modern self can only dream of 'prefall paradise peace' (30.15). Yet *Finnegans Wake* may lead us to 'Moorning and the Dawn of Peace' (222.18–19). The dawn of a new era for Joyce will return us to paradise lost, a time and place when one could openly *mourn*; a safe harbour to *moor* our ship. Again echoing Aeneas's journey across the sea to seek a homeland, being able to moor one's craft in a port where emotion is not a threat to masculinity could bring peaceful times. In contrast, it seems that the stiff upper lip, the suppression of emotion, leads to an endless cycle of fighting.

Full of sorrow for the death of Louis Marin, Derrida feels his grief 'like the end of the world,' and then, 'there was another emotion that came to overwhelm this first mourning, this common mourning, coming to make it turn upon itself, I would almost want to say to reflect it to the point of vertigo, another emotion, another quality and intensity of emotion, at once too painful and strangely peaceful, which had to do, I believe, with a certain time of reading' (*WM* 158). One layer of the work of mourning, which involves suffering and pain, is clearly connected to reading. Derrida does not participate in mourning rituals or funeral games; he labours to open himself up, turn himself inside out, to the point of vertigo, in order to hear, through reading, the sound of the absent voice present in words. Moreover, he imagines himself as the kind of writer who produces texts from this suppressed place: '*I am, like, he who, returning, from a long voyage, out of everything, the earth, the world, men and their languages, tries to keep after the event a logbook, with the forgotten fragmentary rudimentary instruments of a prehistoric language and writing, tries to understand what happened, to explain it with pebbles, bits of wood, deaf and dumb gestures*' (*C* 169). Derrida's project recalls Shem, who 'lifts the lifewand and the dumb speak.' Derrida strives in writing to hear and record the language of infancy, before language and history. He uses infant's tools like pebbles and bits of wood. However, he writes for readers who find this forgotten, fragmentary approach unacceptable, for 'To speak of the child's hell you prefer "minimalist" decency' (311). Like Augustine, like all the voices in what he paradoxically calls '*Everybody's Autobiography*,' Derrida expresses grief, then anticipates being scorned for such feelings.

In *Finnegans Wake,* Joyce dreams of a future where men can express grief without shame; he puns on the word *morning* in order to suggest that a new dawn may unfold upon our renewed capacity for *mourning*. And like Derrida, Joyce bravely turns to the possibility of grief's becoming peaceful, rather than full of rage, by means of reading. Hence, in the final reference to the Letter, we learn that it will come by 'Morning Post' (*FW* 617.22). This kind of epistle is radically different from the 'war souvenir postcards' we usually read (27.32), the kind of postcard that Kitty wishes her husband would send in West's *Return of the Soldier.*

In the first reference to the Letter, Joyce imagines a tomorrow where there is an end to war and joy for all children: 'But it's the armitides toonigh, militopucos, and toomourn we wish for a muddy kissmans to the minutia workers and there's to be a gorgeups truce for happinest childher everwere' (*FW* 11.13–16). Tomorrow, when one can mourn, (toomourn) an armistice will be established that in the idealized, encompassing language of Esperanto brings peace 'paco' to war 'milito.' If only the child's holiday of Christmas could bring happiness for all little (minutia) workers, forever, everywhere. For Joyce, it is exactly the gorgeous gorge (gorgeups) that allows for the expression of emotion leading to more peaceful times; yet he acknowledges that one is more likely to have a lump in the throat as the self revolts and the gorge rises (ups).

At the same time as Joyce presents the childish dream of peace, he deconstructs it, for it signals the father, HCE (**h**appinest **c**hildher **e**verwere), upon whom depend the happiness of the nest (happinest) and the acceptance of feminine emoting in his children (childher). HCE's response to grief later in the *Wake* is to turn those who feel the flow of grief into stone: he 'is a gorgon of selfridgeousness; pours a laughsworth of his illformation over a larmsworth of salt' (137.33–5). The rigid self, already turned to stone within, laughs at the salty tears (Fr. *larmes*) of children. The allusion to the gorgon – the monster who turns any who see her to stone – also belongs to the classical world. This passage is where Joyce mentions the name of Thersites from Homer's *Iliad*; the name occurs ten lines earlier in this long definition of the paternal HCE, 'our thorstyites' (137.24). Later, as R.J. Schork notes and translates, HCE receives the epithet 'Anaks Andrum,' an echo from the *Iliad* (240.27), meaning a 'battle-king of warriors' (*Greek and Hellenic Culture* 73). And even more interesting, Joyce quotes from his brother Stanislaus's memoir, in which he exposes their father's cruelty by calling him 'Thersites-like' (77). Notably, Joyce refers to the great classical war directly after the passage discussed above, where he outlines the dream of a future where peace and happiness and the allowance to mourn make every day Christmas for children in the world. If a reader is moved, or affected emotionally, in reading the *Wake*, it is because Joyce has taught us, according to Jean-Michel Rabaté's understanding, that reading this work is the opposite of immobilization; thus, the reader must be aware of how the voices 'are inserted into a mobilization of the potential energies of language itself, in so far as it permits the accomplishment of acts and gestures' ('Lapsus' 82).

In a pattern of allusions to the Trojan War, Joyce stresses that the first recorded war of western culture involves a deadly suppression of grief, and he links the epic battle between the Greeks and Trojans with the battle of the First World War, so that we 'steal our historic presents from the past postpropheticals' (*FW* 11.30–1). Joyce awaits the 'Morning Post' which brings a post-prophecy from the *Iliad* about war and grief. Thus, in the *Wake*, the sirs of Troy and Greece rise and fall as the one army sacks the others' city, while at the same time, Wilfred Owen's poem 'Isaac' surfaces as the Abrahams of his generation sacrifice their sons. As conveyed in the *Wake*: 'if yous ask me and I saack you. Hou! Hou! Gricks may rise and Troysirs fall (there being two sights for ever a picture)' (11.35–6). Layering over the procreative event of pricks rising and trousers falling, Joyce addresses the parental/child relationship that is its result. In contrast to the divinely required sacrifice of the son, Joyce presents a seemingly feminized Abraham, who not only wears an apron, but is also pregnant with child's meaning: 'One would say him to hold whole a

litteringture of kidlings under his aproham' (570.18–19). What seems
like litter to some, the garbage of both kids and a group of kids, within
Finnegans Wake is read as literature.

Constantly referring to the 'Gricks' and 'Troysirs,' as well as exploring
the bond between fathers and sons, Joyce exhorts his readers to contend
with war past and present: 'I want you, witness of this epic struggle, as
yours so mine, to reconstruct for us, as briefly as you can, inexactly the
same as a mind's eye view, how these funeral games, which have been
poring over us through homer's kerryer pidgeons, massacreedoed as the
holiname rally round took place' (*FW* 515.21–5). We are not pouring
over Homer's epics: they are 'poring over us.' Hence, the *Wake* makes a
demand: we are to be witnesses, to be brief, and to reconstruct just how
it is that funerals become games. Grief is replaced by men with competi-
tive feats of strength, or one turns to the mass or the creed or even the
OED, as captured in the Wakese term 'massacreedoed.'[36] This is an attempt to massacre (conduct a massive war) and then destroy or massacre
the resultant grief. We cannot help but laugh through our tears when
Patroclus's funeral pyre has become an 'Ump pyre' refereeing the various
sporting events underway (516.15). Blending an allusion to Priam and
the tradition of funeral games – 'Dock, dock, agame! Primatially' – with
the German words *doch! doch!* (o yes!), Joyce more disturbingly sets the
scene in Nazi Germany with its swastika 'swaystick' (569.17, 19).[37] This
is our cultural home; thus, we can follow Homer's carrier pigeons, his
homing pigeons, back to this site of western culture, but what we discover is a chronicle of war and the inability of the warriors to articulate
grief. Known as the 'Pigeonhouse,' Dublin is more specifically for Joyce
'pigeonheim to this homer' (129.23).

An ideal image to convey the release of dammed emotions comes
from Irish legends that tell of rivers (of tears) bursting forth at the burial
of heroes: 'And rivers burst out like weeming racesround joydrinks
for the fewnrally, where every feaster's a foster's other, fiannians all'
(*FW* 277.3–6). The passage occurs during the children's lessons and the
section is footnoted. The two notes serve to link the Irish legend and the
epic tradition. In one note, the question is posed: 'Will ye nought would
wet your weapons, warriors bard?' (277fn3). In the other, Macaulay's
Lays of Ancient Rome is transformed into the 'lays of ancient homes'
(277fn4), which contain Virgil's Rome at the same time as echoing
Home(r).[38] Both the Latin and the Greek epic traditions ritualize grief
with funeral games; in the *Wake* these traditions are superimposed upon
the Irish legend of grieving rivers bursting their bounds, so that the

'sons of bursters won in the games' (621.10–11). In the above quoted passage, these games become the rallies of the 'fewnrally.' The 'races-round' is washed away by 'weeming.' This term describes tears that well up from below, from a 'weem,' which is an underground dwelling place. While the *Wake's* funeral games seem effective in tapping into a deep well of grief, in the *Iliad* Homer examines the failure of funeral games to release and heal grief. Instead of having a river of tears flood its shores, Homer leads his readers through painful scenes of grief's suppression in the Greek camp and shocking scenes of its inarticulate expression in the Trojan camp.

In the *Iliad*, Achilles participates in what Joyce calls the 'fiounaregal gaames' (*FW* 332.26); however, it does not relieve his grief for the death of his beloved, Patroclus. Achilles' inability to grieve causes him to drag the body of Hector, who killed Patroclus, around his dead friend's funeral pyre. The frustration of grief results in rage, hate, and degradation – emotions we associate with war. Homer positions Achilles alone as he continues to mourn Patroclus; the lack of community stresses the Greek hero's inability to articulate his crushing grief (24.11–21). Just before directly naming Achilles in the *Wake*, Joyce echoes a sentence in Greek that asks how one is doing, but he inserts the Anglo-Irish word *mavrone* (my grief) (247.14–15). It seems as if Joyce asks Homer in his own tongue about the grief of the *Iliad*. The setting for this question foregrounds the transition from boy to man – 'the use of reason' and 'brake of his voice' – to the tune of a First World War military song, 'Tarara boom decay' (247.5–6, 28). The child self feels 'invaded' by this new adult self (247.8). The response is barely covered-up crying: 'Boo' and 'Hoo' (247.12–13). Notably, this transition from boy to man emphasizes the suppressing of emotion in favour of 'reason' and the halting of expression, in that the voice does not break; rather, society puts a halt to speech: 'brake of his voice.' Likewise, Joyce's rendition of the well-known military song avoids rallying patriotism and instead concentrates on the death – 'boom decay' – awaiting the boys who have become reasonable, silenced men.

In the midst of allusions to grieving, military songs, and the frustrated attempt to identify and expose the mystery of womanhood, which may well have as much to do with grief as with sex, the *Wake* asserts: 'My top it was brought Achill's low' (248.11). On the plot level of the text, as Schork reveals, Issy tries to help Shem with the answer, 'heliotrope,' and thus the top of the word 'hel' is evoked by her allusion to Achilles' one vulnerable spot that brings him down, his 'heel' (Greek and Hellenic Culture 75–6).

John Gordon sees 'Helen's face' in the reference to the 'top' that brings him 'low,' since this face launched the war and brought about the hero's death (180). The riddle also recalls more broadly Aristotle's tragic plot, in which the proud hero reaches a pinnacle and falls into an endless stasis of grief. Achilles feels 'low' and behaves in a 'low' way with Hector's body. According to the *Wake*: 'So warred he from first to last, forebanned and betweenly, a smuggler for lifer. Lift the blank ve veered as heil! Split the hvide and aye seize heaven!' (247.29–31). Achilles' life is war from first to last. He 'smuggles' away the lives of many soldiers. By the hellish veering of his chariot he 'seize[s] heaven.' He horrifies Homer's gods by dragging Hector's corpse, which splits the Trojan warrior's 'hvide.'

Rather than concentrating on his feats as the Greeks' most powerful, semi-divine warrior, Joyce presents Achilles as a man consumed with grief: 'He wept indeiterum. With such a tooth he seemed to love his wee tart when abuy. Highly momourning he see the before him' (*FW* 247.17–18). When Achilles was a mere boy, 'abuy,' society purchased his power and his taste for life's sweetness becomes indefinite weeping for the brutal killing of his friend. Now that Achilles is at the height of mourning, 'past Morningtop's necessity' (266.11), he sees 'the before him'; he lives in the past. He is at the top of grief and immobilized by grief; there is no future, and being at this top brings him low. Richard Beckman, analysing another scene in the *Wake*, suggests a comparable reading of HCE's 'imperial sacking': he sees as a possible interpretation of the hump on his back 'that he carries the past, that which is behind him, in back of him, even while he moves into his probable future, prospecting' (85). Certainly a feature of acute grief, it thus connects with future sacking and imperial advancement.

Epic funeral games are a way to re-establish and advertise masculine power: 'Since alls war that end war lets sports be leisure and bring and buy fair' (*FW* 279.5–7). When the question is posed, 'Is the Pen Mightier than the Sword?', its answer is drowned out by modern-day funeral games: 'The Dublin Metropolitan Police Sports at Ballsbridge' (306.18–19, 24–5). With a place name suggestive of male prowess and the name 'Ajax' beside the passage in the margin, the reader cannot help but make the connection between funeral games and male conflict. In the *Iliad*, Ajax fights with Ulysses at the funeral games for Patroclus: 'clusters of raw welts broke out on ribs and shoulders / slippery, red with blood, and still they grappled, harder, / locking for victory' (23.97–9). If, as in *Ulysses*, Ireland is a 'pawnshop,' we are once again 'out of the paunschaup on to the pyre' (*FW* 209.31). While the funeral games are meant to re-establish male pride and strength after death has felled a comrade, the events in honour of the pyre seem to reflect the problematic issue of the warrior mentality itself. Even funeral sports are violent and inflammatory. Yet they are simultaneously symbolic of rebirth: 'our own sphoenix spark spirt spyre' (473.18). The phoenix dies and is reborn from its ashes. The funeral pyre may well herald, through recuperative grief, a new era for a community.

While reading about Achilles in *Finnegans Wake*, one's mind wanders incessantly to Aeneas, for 'one has thoughts of that eternal Rome' (298.32–2). Joyce conflates the Homeric and Virgilian epics in his 'explosition' of war, grief, and children (419.11). Thus, one might be 'as merry as the gricks still,' yet at the same time 'be sore should ledden sorrow,' with an echo of the Latin, lighten, and Greek, suffering (620.30–1). Shaun says that 'shemsletters' is 'Greek!' and demands to see it because he is as 'Roman as pope and water' could christen him (419.19–22). While reading this text, one must wear 'half a Roman hat, with an ancient Greek gloss on it' (390.17–18). While reading this text, one must sleep in 'a bed as hard as the thinkamuddles of the Greeks and a board as bare as a Roman altar' (409.18–19).

Joyce superimposes Achilles' frustrated sorrow upon the suppression of grief required of Aeneas in Virgil's *Aeneid*. Joyce's allusions to time, specifically in reference to sadness, anticipate the mourning post, 'tomourn' as tomorrow, Issy as the 'leaptear' girl, and Achilles as a mourner who looks to the 'before' because he cannot move into the future. All of these moments become enriched by association with Virgil's epic poem. His hero, Aeneas, is a master of stoicism except for his one disastrous affair with Dido, the queen of Carthage. Joyce alludes to the romance between pious Aeneas and the brazen queen in the *Wake*: 'At this time it fell out that a brazenlockt damsel grieved *(sobralasolas!)* because that Puppette her minion was ravisht of her by the ogre Puropeus Pious. Bloody wars in Ballyaughacleeaghbally' (14.7–10). Aeneas is called 'two-faced man' by Dido in the *Aeneid* (4.418) and in the *Wake* Aeneas is comparably constructed as a dual figure: on the one hand he is 'Puppette her minion' and on the other he is 'the ogre Puropeus Pious.' A puppet of the gods, Aeneas becomes her lover, and again ruled by the gods, he must leave her to fulfil his pious duty of founding a new home for the Trojan people. *Puppette,* doll in German, also recalls the doll-like Cupid who sits on the queen's lap, disguised as the child Ascanius, in order to infect her with poisonous love (1.973–85). The italicized term, containing 'sob' and 'alas' as indicative of Dido's grief, is Spanish for 'over the waves,' which recalls Aeneas setting sail and looking back over his shoulder to see the smoking pyre upon which Dido throws herself in a dramatic suicide (5.1–9).

Before stabbing herself and falling to the pyre, becoming what Joyce calls a 'fiery quean' (*FW* 328. 31), Dido curses Aeneas and the Trojans: 'Coast with coast, / In conflict, I implore, and sea with sea, / And arms with arms: may they contend in war, / Themselves and all the children of their children!' (4.863–75). Dido's curse results in the 'bloody wars' the Trojans must fight in order to establish their Roman homeland. Joyce imagines these bloody wars in Dublin, for the circular term 'Ballyaughacleeaghbally' echoes the Irish name for Joyce's home city: 'Baile Átha Cliath.' The bloody wars that establish the Roman Empire and ultimately the Rome of Catholicism are aptly echoed by the bloody wars of Catholicism and Protestantism that continue to tear apart Ireland; hence, the circular name is appropriate. As noted, in the *Specters of Marx* Derrida expresses concern about fighting activated by the failure to integrate one's haunting double, which thereby leads to a never-ending cycle of war: one flees from oneself, one persecutes and pursues oneself; one is frightened by someone within [himself] like the Irish against Irish (*S* 105). Dido's curse of never-ending war reaches into our time.

Thus, the *Wake* taunts provocatively, 'I'll light your pyre' (466.9), reminding us that political and religious empires are established upon pyres like Dido's. Not only do these pyres honour the dead; more important, they seem to be effective in marking the end to sadness and a recovery of the will to fight: 'Halt there sob story to your lambdad's tale! Are you roman cawthrick 432?' (486.1–2) Stories of grief must be halted, especially if they are associated with a lamb-like father telling tales. This gentle era ends with the arrival of St Patrick in 432 A.D., which paradoxically heralds a return to the Roman values of suppression in the name of power, both political and religious. In contrast to the lamb-like father, Ireland and the world are dominated by 'primapatriock,' a combination of *Priam* and *Patrick* and a whole *patriotic* history of fighting for one's country and turning to *rock* or stone rather than emoting in a fluid way (531.33).

A radio broadcast blends St Patrick's 'Cry of the Deer' with the 'swift deer' who is the catalyst for the war between the *Aeneid*'s Trojans and Latins (7.687): 'We'll gore them and gash them and gun them and gloat on them' (*FW* 500.7–8). Those in a position to grieve the loss of their loved ones, 'widows and orphans' are informed: 'the cry of the roedeer it is! The white hind.' The further explanation is 'Christ in our irish times!' (500.10, 12, 14). Joyce here spins the newsreel, relocating St Patrick's

'Christ with me, Christ before me' into contemporary newspapers: the *Irish Times, Irish Independent, Freeman's Journal,* and so on: 'Christ in our irish times! Christ on the airs independence! Christ hold the freedman's chareman!' (500.14–15). We do not learn from 'childsplay,' nor do we 'follow the baby spot' (501.11, 14); instead, if we want to instruct our children about becoming dedicated, warlike adults, we should teach them religion and the classics.

As presented keenly by Woolf in *The Waves,* in the education system, children are taught according to 'the rule of Rome' (*FW* 129. 25–6). While a child must learn Latin, 'and present and absent and past and present and perfect arma virumque romano' (389.18–19), it seems that the substance of the story – the war, duty, abandonment of love, suppression of emotion – is absent. So the opening to the *Aeneid,* 'Arma virumque cano' (I sing of arms and a man) has become an exercise in language, which changes the 'I sing' to 'by a Roman.' Potentially, this kind of instruction lays the groundwork for decking out in 'Roman Catholic arms' (389.26) in order to prepare for the ongoing battle. In *Finnegans Wake,* Roman stoicism is regarded as the reverse of love: 'Are you imitation Roma now or Amor now' (487. 22–3). In Roman imitation, a well-taught Irish boy can 'suck up, sure enough, like a Trojan,' for he is taught to 'read the road roman with false steps' (381.30–1, 467.34). Thus, the text hints at the explosive power of epic poetry: 'handle virgils like Armsworks Limited!' (618.2).

What is notable in Virgil's epic is that the gods intervene twice in order to suppress grief: Jove blocks Aeneas's desire to emote with Dido and then the fates, in response to 'God's will,' stop Aeneas's 'once kindly ears' from hearing and thus responding to Dido's 'tears' (4.455–7, 607–9). Joyce identifies the pious or dutiful behaviour of Aeneas as he blocks the tympanum of his ears, thereby suppressing his seemingly feminine feelings of grief. In the *Wake,* Aeneas obeys: 'irrepressible piety that readily turned his ladylike typmanzelles capsy curvy' (470.31–2). We have noted the significance of the ear, the tympanum, for Derrida in its capacity to open up and take in the words of otherness. More moving and compelling in this context are his 'tears of love,' which break the endless cycle of fighting and wounding that passes on to the next generation the wounds carried from childhood. Derrida confesses: 'I must have kept myself from these crimes by ruminating my life in them, turned around them to protect my sons from them, like gods, forewarn them even against circumcision.' Thus, he sheds 'tears of love,' which acknowledge 'life bleeding like the overflow of these murders I carry within myself' (*C* 297–8).

Derrida returns to the otherness of the child within who believes the death of a brother by illness and a cousin by a car accident are his fault. He carries these 'murders.' He knows the wounding of circumcision. Yet by 'ruminating,' by carrying and knowing this otherness, this suffering from long ago, he becomes the protector instead of the warrior for those children who follow. Derrida lets flow tears of love and, using ambiguous phrasing, seems to treat his sons as gods or to protect them from gods, whereas Aeneas's grief is immobilized by the gods while Trojan soldiers begin mobilizing for war.

In the *Aeneid*, even before his affair with Dido, Aeneas's wife Creusa, who has been killed in the Trojan war, appears to him as a shade to insist he suppress his grief. She asks him: 'What's to be gained by giving way to grief / So madly my sweet husband?' (2.1007–8). With the prophetic knowledge possessed by the dead, Creusa tells Aeneas of the duties he must fulfil and the great deeds he will accomplish. He must not mourn for her, which turns him to the past, making him comparable to Achilles, who sees only the before when Patroclus lived. Instead, the hero must suppress his grief and turn to the future. Men who have active, constructive futures do not have time to grieve. Thus, suppressing tears is emblematic of entering into new battles, founding nations, and carving out homelands. Both Achilles and Aeneas are threatened by grief, but they overcome it, and the lesson they learn is that if they suppress their grief, it will fuel their devotion to and energy for war. In this context, Derrida's work, to turn himself around, carries more weight. While those who look to the future arm for war, Derrida provides in *Circumfession* a photograph of himself as an adult visiting his nursery school. He turns around to the child, who gets 'caught up by school' when he wishes to be with his mother, and he shares with the mother he loves, whom he is losing, a capacity for 'silence and amnesia,' which stops the highly educated, the philosophers, from positioning his work as 'tenable or valid' with a 'thesis that could be refuted' (272–3). Derrida's turning to the past with grief and with ears open to the child within allows his work to be on the margin of the battle, not take sides but instead reveal their co-dependence, their interrelationship, essentially their inseparability. One needs to believe in absolute opposites to go to war.

Significantly for *Finnegans Wake*, not only are warriors debilitated by grief in the *Aeneid*, but artists are as well. Daedalus, a key mythological figure for Joyce's concept of himself as an artist, has carved a temple in Virgil's poem that marks the entry to the world of the dead. In the final passage detailing the panels of the temple, the poet presents Daedalus as unable to sculpt because of his grief for his son: 'In that high sculpture you, too, would have had / Your great part, Icarus, had grief allowed. / Twice your father had tried to shape your fall / In gold, but twice his hands dropped' (6.47–50). Grief halts the inventor; it blocks the artist, and therefore it may threaten the production of the grieving text of *Finnegans Wake*. Shem the Penman, the 'tragic jester' must circle back beyond the *Aeneid* to its 'before,' which is the *Iliad*. Joyce takes the tragic, high epic style of Homeric poetry and honours the grief by transforming it into the comic, bawdy epic poetics typical of his *Wake*.

In the *Iliad*, there is a scene of inarticulate grief in the Trojan camp that forms a telling twin with Achilles' destructive grief. Despite the fact that he is irreverently referred to by Joyce as 'the palsied old priamite' (*FW* 513.20), recall that the corpse of Hector, dragged by Achilles, was once the proud son of King Priam. Note the way in which Homer describes the dignified, elderly king and the way he grieves for his dead and desecrated son, Hector: 'Sons huddled round their father deep in the / courtyard, robes drenched with tears, and the / old man amidst them, buried, beaten down in the/ cloak that wrapped his body ... Smeared on the old / man's head and neck the dung lay thick [t]hat he / scraped up in his own hands, grovelling in the filth (24.194–8). Now that is what Joyce would call 'homereek' (*FW* 314.23). In Priam's expression of grief, what he feels is beyond words, grammar, or syntax. Joyce, recognizing that the king's former cultured self has symbolically died, tells us in the *Wake*: 'He's stiff but he's steady is Priam Olim!' (6.22–3). He is a stiff, a corpse, but he has also maintained his force throughout cultural time; he is steady. His inarticulate grief paradoxically still speaks powerfully to us today about masculine modes of mourning. Joyce keeps the two epic traditions in dialogue with the Latin word *olim* (once) and an earlier reference to 'romekeepers' (6.4). Death is one of the fundamental principles of Joyce's text, so that it is constructed as a ritual act of mourning, a wake: 'Sobs they sighdid at Fillagain's chrissormiss wake, all the hoolivans of the nation, prostrated in their consternation and their duodisimally profusive plethora of ululation' (6.14–17). Thus, whether the figure is Parnell or Christ or Finnegan or Julius Caesar or Patroclus or Hector, the *Wake* explores the resultant grief expressed through the inarticulate wailing of 'ululation' set beside a list of festive baking that echoes a military song of 'drums & guns, guns & drums' (McHugh 6.16).

Signalling the Greek and Latin epic tradition, Joyce tells the tale of Buckley and the Russian general.[39] The story references '*empyreal Raum and mordern Atems*' (*FW* 353.29). The scene of inarticulate grief from the *Iliad* is turned into a bawdy, patriotic tale of Ireland. The *Wake* positions itself in the role of a Homeric bard; it models itself on a 'homerole poet' (445.32); yet it acknowledges that the epic tradition 'outpriams al' his parisites' (131.8–9). The modern writer studies the classic stories and seeks to be the winner or at least the Priam or primary recipient of the wisdom of the ages. One hopes to be 'winner of the gamings, primed at the studience, propredicted from the storybouts, the choice of ages wise!' (427.30–2).

Joyce conducts a kind of comic funeral game with Homer as he parodies the Trojan king's scene of inarticulate grief for his son. Priam, bereaved, smears dung on himself; the Russian general likewise is seen 'beheaving up that sob of tunf' in order to wipe himself after defecating (*FW* 353.16). The double grief allusion, echo of bereave and 'sob' for sod, entwined with scatological humour, recalls the primal scene of writing, where Shem turns excrement into expression. The kind of analysis necessary to 'invent a writing' like Wakese requires being 'learned' by means of reading or 'raiding' the classics and ultimately performing 'eschatology' (with its echo of scatology and shat). All this in order to open the ears to the wail of grief suppressed: 'if an ear aye sieze what no eye ere grieved' (482.31–5).

The story of Buckley and the Russian general draws on boys' bathroom humour, a childish reaction to war, so that passages offer a mixture of totally disturbing, anticipatory references to the Nazis at the same time as giggles at pooh-pooh. In David Carradine's historical survey of First World War soldiers' reactions to trauma, he identifies rude humour as one coping strategy for the young men raised, through public school training, to march proudly into war: 'Irreverent, ghoulish, macabre badinage might be the sign of heartlessness, or merely a cover for inner feelings almost too sorrowful to be recognized' (208). Simon Carnell identifies this technique throughout the *Wake*. If we layer the bathroom humour over Priam's expression of grief, perhaps all of our discordant selves can be heard: 'the stormtrooping clouds and in the sheenflare of the battleaxes of the heroim and mid the shieldfails await of the bitter-accents of the sorafim and caught the pfierce tsmell of his aurals' (*FW* 344.23–6). When the shield fails, one is wounded, one's suppressed self breaks through, one hears wailing. The new warriors, storm troopers, just like the ancient 'heroim,' wielding their 'battleaxes,' endlessly fight. Thus, the beautiful celebration of love in the Song of Solomon becomes a 'song of sorrowmon' (344.5).

While Joyce draws on epic and modern terms of warfare, he locates brutality first within the home. As noted in the introduction, he reverses the Latin phrase, *Amor regit Heva* (love rules Eve), in order to offer a domestic scene of violence, where a Roman Tiger is the motto the woman and child must learn to avoid being hit: 'For your own good, you understand, for the man who lifts his pud to a woman is saving the way for kindness. You'll rebmemer your mottob *Aveh Tiger Roma* mikely smarter the nickst time.' For if not, this husband and parent will 'give you one splitpuck in the crupper, you understand, that will bring the poppy blush of shame to your peony hindmost till you yelp papapardon' (*FW* 445.11–17). Margot Norris notes the deconstruction in the *Wake* of the 'symbolical fiction of home as the locus of infantile security, nurturance, and comfort' by means of Joyce's opening up of 'the social reality of homes in which the child is at greatest risk from parental abuse and violence' (*Web* 208–9). She quotes the use in this context of 'infant' by Joyce's brother Stanislaus for a cousin who was 'six or seven' and begging not to be beaten by his father (209).

How does one look emerging from such a home: 'The black and blue marks athwart the weald, which now barely is so stripped, indicate the presence of sylvious beltings' (*FW* 564.23–5). The body that suffers violence echoes the landscape of Phoenix park, 'Finn his park,' where political violence occurs; lurking behind this mode of being in the world are the 'grekish and romanos' (564.8–9). How do children, the swaddled, cope with tumbles and troubles in the home? Not yet armed or suppressed Roman style, one tot responds with depression; he simply turns his face to the wall: 'Arms arome, side aside, face into the wall. To the tumble of the toss tot the trouble of the swaddled, O' (444. 9–10). Another child may respond to trauma with the obscene.[40] With his description of ALP, Joyce echoes the scene of Hera's beauty preparations in the *Iliad*, which are undertaken in order to seduce her divine husband, Zeus, away from the battlefield (14.161–86; *FW* 206.29–207.14). The adult self imagines the classical catalogue of beauty as a goddess at her toilette, whereas the troubled toddler who becomes the school-age self sees it as 'all improper, in a lovely mourning toilet' (*FW* 395.15–16). Toilet humour seems to be a child's antidote to and expression of mourning.

While Joyce deconstructs the warrior mentality and the silencing of grief with the paradoxically 'childishly gleeful' (*FW* 178.20) stories overlaid on grieving terms, Achilles and Priam behave in brutally inarticulate ways: they become barbaric as they fail to express their grief. Likewise, but transforming the sadness into hilarity, death into rebirth, Joyce has Shem the Penman recount in Latin, which he calls 'lingua romana mortuorum' (the Roman tongue of the dead; 287.21), how he made indelible ink from his own excrement and urine. Derrida, like Joyce, sees mourning as productive of both litter as waste and litter as babies. Derrida parallels the work of mourning and the work that brings a child into the world: 'the work or labor of the *oeuvre* insofar as it engenders, produces, and brings to light, but also labor or travail as suffering, as the enduring of force, as the pain of the one who gives. Of the one who gives birth, who brings to the light of day and gives something to be seen.' He transforms the suffering of grief into the labour involved in taking 'the pains to help us see, read, and think' (*WM* 142). In *Finnegans Wake*, as a work of mourning, Shem's own bodily waste becomes the ink to record what Joyce is taking pains to help us to see, read, and think. It is the work of mourning.

Called 'pious Eneas' in this scene, Shem takes the ink, produced from his 'wit's waste' and writes on the 'only foolscap available,' namely, 'his own body' (*FW* 185.27–36). Anticipating this self-reflective examination of the writing of *Finnegans Wake* is war imagery, a grieving response, the conflation of the two, and then a discussion of writing, Joyce's in particular. Thus, there is a concentration of war terms: 'smeared with generous erstborn gore,' 'bloods of heroes,' 'agush with tears of joy,' 'slashers and sliced alike,' and 'the slop after the war-to-end war' (178.9–25). Among a whole host of effects interfering with being a good student, the reaction to the battles is certainly grief: 'the drop in his eye, a lump in his throat,' not to mention 'the wail of his wind, the grief from his breath' (180.19–21). The writer's literary production in such a setting is provocative: 'an epical forged cheque on the public for his own private profit' (181.16–17). Perhaps Joyce's own private struggle with grief leads him to return to the great public epics and forge within the crucible of his own text something that profits us all, even though so many read his *Wake* as a madman's forgery, just as so many thought *A Portrait of the Artist as a Young Man* to be 'endlessly inartistic portraits of himself' (182.19), and *Ulysses* to be a 'usylessly unreadable Blue Book of Eccles' (179.26–7). Joyce winds up this investigation of his writing by invoking the term 'infanted' (non-speaking) to recall the way in which the publishing and printing world tried to suppress *Dubliners* (184.33–185.5). Derrida, likewise, imagines his writing as starting with 'the despair of the innocent child' forced into culture with a wound at a moment when he was inarticulate; hence, Derrida's overflow of words breaks the cycle of violence and makes authority fearful, 'terrorizing the others through the instability' it carries 'everywhere' (*C* 307–8).

In *Finnegans Wake*, the reaction to war, grief, and society's demand that such feelings be suppressed acts as the catalyst for Shem's literary journey: 'romeruled,' or schooled in the epic of Rome, 'he winged away on a wildgoup's chase across the kathartic ocean and made synthetic ink and sensitive paper for his own end out of his wit's waste' (184.33–185.8). Like the use of 'irises' in Ford's *The Good Soldier*, here the ocean journey is a metaphor for an 'irised sea in plight' (318.34). The eye is full of tears, which threatens the self with an internal shipwreck on the reef, 'Noeman's Woe' (321.14–15), which Joyce has echoing throughout the *Wake* from Longfellow's 'Wreck of the Hesperus.' The yearning to shirk one's feelings and to refuse to claim one's woe recalls the transformation of no-man's-land into 'woeman's land' in the Prankquean episode.

However, perhaps Shem will not shipwreck, because rather than negate his woe, he claims it, and seeks to address it. The epic tradition requires the suppression of grief so that one can turn forward and become active, a hero and a warrior; in contrast, Joyce and Derrida foreground the expression of grief so that one can turn back, turn around and become contemplative, a thinker and a tearful laugher. While Virgil's Aeneas obeys the gods in suppressing his grief and deafening his ears to Dido's sorrow, Joyce, a modern day 'pious Eneas' plans to be 'conformant to the fulminant firman' when 'the call comes' to produce from 'his unheavenly body a no uncertain quantity of obscene matter' (*FW* 185.27–30).

When contemplated by the maternal figure, the female and the male child come together as expressive of grief, present and past: 'So on Izzy, her shamemaid, love shone befond her tears as from Shem, her penmight, last past befoul his prime' (*FW* 212.17–19). The grammar blends the brother and sister together so that the tears seem shared between mother and children. At this moment, the world of women in the text, infused with sexuality and childbearing, forms a contrast to the warring world of men. The daughter is a shame maid, at the same time as being Shem-made; likewise, the son is a figure who hovers between possibilities. Shem is a writer and his power is expressed with the 'pen'; like Priam, who befouls himself with dung, Shem is the last one in a long line from the past who writes grieving, thereby befouling his prime, his kingly state.

Shem's sobs are recorded on his body: 'he bares sobsconcious inklings shadowed on soulskin' (*FW* 377.28). The body's skin shadows the soul's skin. The sobs well up from the unconscious, but they are mere inklings and shadows until illuminated by writing. Moreover, not only does Shem write on his body, but he reads it: 'And, reading off his fleshskin and writing with his quillbone,' he produces 'a most moraculous jeeremyhead sindbook for all the peoples' (229.29–32). Rather than rejecting the body, he reads it and writes a lament, a dolorous piece, a jeremiad, but for society it is a jeer-my-head, an opportunity to jeer at such expressions of sadness and complaint. With the slang terms quill and bone, Joyce makes the height of masculinity a sexual, literary conquest spilling semen and ink rather than blood. Creation is the result, not destruction. Derrida also uses his skin, his body's container, as the site for writing grief: 'one book open in the other, one scar deep within the other' (C 308). Otherness resides within; thus, Derrida dreams of replacing the pen, a 'very hard weapon' with a pen that writes like a 'syringe' drawing the otherness from within like a 'suction point' to the surface of writing (12). He collapses difference with his own blood, which is the same as all others and indistinguishable in the syringe regardless of whether or not one is Jewish or Arab or French or Irish or British. Joyce makes the same argument comically with excrement.

For Joyce, the obscene is the ideal place for the expression of grief because it is the *ob-skene* (Greek) or off-stage of culture; hence the desecration of Hector's body; hence rubbing dung on one's head. What is remarkable in *Finnegans Wake* is that Joyce does not degrade the body; he celebrates it. It becomes the 'fleshskin' that he reads and the 'sensitive paper' on which he writes. He does not smear dung as a gesture of self-destroying grief. Instead, written in Latin in the *Wake*, translated by Roland McHugh: 'weeping & groaning,' putting his 'own dung' into 'an urn once used as an honoured mark of mourning,' Shem produces ink. Joyce employs the language of the bible to describe how Shem writes the grieving waste, the weeping obscene of culture: 'Lingua mea calamus scribae velociter scribentis' (My tongue is the pen of a scribe writing swiftly) (185.15–22). In *Finnegans Wake*, as in Derrida's *Circumfession*, the body becomes the site of culture itself, the place where writing must occur if we are to avoid an endless cycle of war and mourning, which leads to more war and more mourning or, as Joyce states at the outset of the *Wake*, using the French word for tears, *larmes*, to reveal the inseparability of war and mourning: 'Arms apeal with larms, appalling' (4.7). For Joyce, tragedy is in fact 'tragoady,' as we goad one another to battle with pricks and wounds (5.13).

Shem seems to write what many would consider mere dung, turf, waste (of time). Likewise, Joyce writes: 'a (suppressed) book' in 'keener notcase,' which society tries to 'turf aside for pastureuration.' However, 'packen paper paineth whomto is sacred scriptured sign. Who straps it scraps it that might, if ashed, have healped' (*FW* 356.20–6). In this passage, Joyce alludes to the refusal of a publishing house to bring out *Dubliners*; instead of asking if they could heal/help the writer and his society by acknowledging his pain, Messrs John Long Ltd burnt 'the sacred scriptured sign.' They scrapped it, 'ashed' it. Feelings must be suppressed, bracketed in a society that likes to sterilize or pasteurize the production of 'fermented words' (184.26). However, the 'notcase' (nutcase) Joyce, responds with the irrepressible *Wake*: a real 'keener' that keens.

Feeling grief as if it is a wound, Derrida writes of 'the necessity of textual weaving of words and images, the imbrication of glosses sewn upon the iconic tissue' (*WM* 150). Imbrication is a word that suggests repair, whether it is the overlapping of shingles on the roof that shelters or the successive layers of tissue in the closure of a wound. The paradox that weaves through both Derrida's and Joyce's works of mourning is that the layers are representative of voices that open rather than close up the self. Hence, healing appears in the layers of discordant, inarticulate, fragmented, pointed, and piercing words and images. They overlap in a healing way, so that the blood may well be stemmed, but the tears continue to fall. The inarticulate feelings as one swallows the lump in one's throat must become, through the labour of writing grief, the glosses sewn upon the iconic tissue or the only 'foolscap' available. Then, one might be able to say while grieving with Derrida for Sarah Kofman, who has committed suicide, yet another child-victim of differences used to enact hate and violence: 'Transfigure me into a corpus' (*WM* 169). The philosopher and all the novelists of this study have transfigured the child into an eloquent, provoking, grieving body of work.

Conclusion: Creating Fictional Space for the Grief of the Child

A sustained reading of the requirement to suppress grief in the works of Conrad, Rhys, West, Ford, Woolf, and Joyce reveals that certain modernist novels deconstruct the model of grief inherited from their predecessors, and that they do so by inserting into their texts a form of grief-language associated first with childhood memories, then with children themselves, and ultimately with child-narrators. Employing literary experimentalism and sharing the metaphor of turning to stone by means of suppressing grief bring these novelists into dialogue. All strive to break out of the pedagogical mould they have inherited. They write about the damage that occurs when one tells a child to be a good soldier and dry his or her tears. They reveal the disturbing overlap in our gathering children in a nursery, an infantry, and our gathering foot soldiers for war, an infantry.

At the outset of this study, in Conrad's *Under Western Eyes*, the child is seen as foreign, expressing itself to British readers in language as remote as Russian. In Jean Rhys's novellas, the child is comparable to a resident alien, a colonial figure residing in England, who struggles to express herself in English, but who ultimately responds to the hybrid words of Creole. In Rebecca West and Ford Madox Ford's texts, the child has fully regained its place in the British home, but has been suppressed to the point of silently influencing its counterpart, who functions as a First World War soldier. Thus, both novelists layer infantry of children upon the infantry of war. The child's inarticulate expression thus forms a parallel with the shattered speech of a shell-shocked adult. In Virginia Woolf's selected texts, the voices of children narrate directly, but are not heard by their society. Nonetheless, their distinctive way of being, which often is expressed by the shedding of tears for losses of many different kinds, dominates. Finally, in *Finnegans Wake* the voices of children, as seemingly inarticulate as grieving voices, emerge to claim a kind of citizenship that encompasses the world rather than divides it. The grief then becomes connected to joy.

The significance of the six authors analysed in this study is a revelation of a common bond in terms of how grief is experienced and how its suppression affects the self and the community. Using Derrida's method, written from a childish perspective and writing from within childhood, as opposed to an adult viewpoint whereby children are interpreted and diagnosed, opens new avenues for assessing the relationship between modernist authors. It allows scholars and readers to recognize that one of the concerns of modernist fiction is to look at the relationship between immobilizing grief and mobilizing soldier-selves.

The first two chapters of the study reveal the way in which modernist authors connect suppressed childhoods with larger political institutions. The first chapter analyses Joseph Conrad's novel *Under Western Eyes*, which revolves around Russian oppression and revolutionary forces. Conrad distances the recollected grieving child of the protagonist Razumov by means of a British narrator who is clear about his nineteenth-century admiration for stoicism and 'self-suppression.' The British narrator functions as a storyteller of Russian tragedy driven by political ideology. He also is the translator of Razumov's journal, which he can only barely recognize as a text made up of 'broken sentences,' which 'grapple' with grief. In this chapter, we can see Conrad imagining a kind of writing whereby syntax and grammar break down. While in *Under Western Eyes* Conrad suppresses the grieving journal, at the same time he makes it a focus of his story. The journal is kept at bay by a safe, controlled, calm British narrator, who translates when appropriate and suppresses when excessive. Violence can be detailed, but grief is silenced. There are no children in this novel; a brutally sad childhood is merely recalled.

In the second chapter, an analysis of Jean Rhys's five novellas demonstrates a clear movement towards giving a voice to silenced children. The middle-aged European narrators transform over the five books into the narrative 'I' of a ten-year-old West Indian girl. Like Conrad, Rhys explores the suppression of grief, especially childhood grief and its relationship with larger political movements, specifically colonialism and gender politics. Comparable to Conrad's approach, Rhys has the figure of *Jane Eyre*'s Rochester behave in cruel ways while being clearly motivated by childhood suffering. The more Conrad's Razumov and Rhys's Rochester strive to suppress their vulnerable inner child, the more they

act in ways that significantly wound others. While Conrad has his protagonist attempt to access forgiveness by writing a journal in Russian;
Rhys has the opportunity for parent-child love expressed in the foreign,
yet indigenous, speech of Creole. Both authors – one Polish, one West
Indian – writing for a British public, express childhood grief in ways that
are consciously constructed to appear foreign to a literary tradition.

Jean Rhys's *Wide Sargasso Sea* anticipates the next two chapters, which
focus on West's and Ford's novels, since she actually opens her final novella with a narrating child. Rhys's child grows up into the tragic protagonist Antoinette and haunts her, as Razumov and Rochester are haunted
by their own suppressed childhoods. But at least the child articulates
independently at the outset. A distinction becomes apparent when the
protagonists of Rebecca West and Ford Madox Ford not only are figures
with suppressed childhoods, but also become parents. The child figure does not merely haunt, but also emerges as a separate being. Thus,
chapters 3 and 4 reveal modernist authors moving closer to articulating
childhood grief, in that the protagonists of both Ford's and West's novels
actually are parents of children who shape their decisions and who specifically bring them in touch with their own suppressed grief.

In the third chapter, focused on Rebecca West's *Return of the Soldier*,
a child is born, but dies before he becomes articulate; nonetheless,
this child impacts his father powerfully. Nothing the child says is ever
recorded; yet he is the cornerstone of the protagonist's identity. West
is clear in her connection between the actual child and the inner child
of the protagonist; moreover, she makes a link between the child as an
infant and the father as part of the infantry of the First World War. In
her novel the little boy dies at the age of two and his father's shell shock,
which is triggered by trench warfare, is cured by his grieving the death
of his little boy. The shell-shocked soldier's grief at the loss of his son
and grief at the horror of war are tightly wound together. West brings
in a psychiatrist to cure him and, when he is better, he can return to the
trenches. By highlighting the joy of the wife at the end, who knows her
husband must now return to battle, West's *Return of the Soldier* makes dramatic the social price one pays for grieving one's lost child.

The fourth chapter focuses on Ford Madox Ford's *The Good Soldier*
and his series of four novels, *Parade's End*. The narrator of the first novel
positions himself as a witness to tragedy and grief, but at the same time
he struggles to suppress the story of both. In *Parade's End*, an omniscient
narrator focuses on a soldier in the First World War who suffers shell
shock, but, much more difficult to recover from, he also suffers from

emotional suppression throughout childhood and in his marriage. The omniscient narrator gives way to a series of narrators in the final novel. Moving beyond the recalled children of Conrad and Rhys and the son who is born and dies at the age of two, Ford features a boy in this set of novels; while the child never speaks, he nonetheless impacts every decision his father makes. The father seems to fight through his stony, suppressed self in order to reach his son. At the end of the novel, there will be a new baby born who will carry the name of the father, Christopher; thus, the unborn baby serves as a figure for the father's inner child. There is an effort made at the end of Ford's war epic to save this baby from society's attempts to turn it to stone.

In the final two chapters, a notable shift occurs: both Virginia Woolf and James Joyce write from a child's point of view. What makes these two authors radically different in their approach to childhood grief and its required suppression, is that they write from this perspective and even use the potentially inarticulate language of children. At the outset of *The Waves*, Woolf employs a strategy of intense, seemingly random, reactions and responses to life in early childhood interspersed with italicized passages marking the movement from dawn until nightfall. Through the repeated indicator 'he said' and 'she said,' the reader realizes that the children are speaking to themselves and recording their feelings. However, the social world of family, school, and business never hears these early words. The child appears silent. Like the short stories and interwoven, echoing fragments collected in Woolf's *A Haunted House*, the bits and pieces of multiple narrators combine to reveal a passionate exploration of childhood experience and specifically the need to express grief. Thus, she creates fictional spaces in which these suppressed voices can resound. In both of these texts, Woolf clearly links the silencing of children's grief with the development of a soldier-self who crushes the native self by ruling natives.

In *Finnegans Wake*, Joyce goes one step further and writes with a new language altogether, one that can be read on one level as a grief-language. Like an infant who has not yet acquired the language of a particular culture, the multilingual approach of the *Wake* allows more freedom for the expression of childhood grief and thus for the access to joy. Using this eloquent, inarticulate language to express unutterable things, Joyce's final text brings us full circle by returning to the war epics of the classical era, which establishes a pattern of slaughtering, mourning, gaming, and laughing, until we start killing again. Into this pattern, Joyce carves out a home for the world of babies, infants, childishness, and children. He questions mourning and wonders about grieving. The text explores violence in the home and the wounding and silencing of wee people. *Finnegans Wake* thus lifts a kind of literary wand that gives voice to the dumb: the nursing infantry and the warring infantry find voices.

Reading these well-known modernist texts from the angle of grieving children has been made possible by looking at them in a new way, using Jacques Derrida's grieving approach, writing from a childish perspective, and writing from within childhood, as opposed to the traditional adult perspective whereby children are interpreted and their difference is integrated. When Derrida reads, he 'uncovers and remarks' the gaps in a text such as the one revolving around childhood and grief during the modernist era. As Peggy Kamuf further explains: the 'gap, in French *l'écart,* which can also mean a divergence, is that opening to difference, to an outside, to an other – to absence and to death – which, in any theory based on fully present meaning, will have been covered over' (introd. 5). This approach opens new avenues for assessing the relationship between modernist authors and their exploration in fiction of grief's suppression in children. It allows readers to reconsider modernist literature as being concerned with creating a fictional space, a home, to which not just the soldier but also the child can return. Once seen as foreign, in modernist fiction the child reclaims status as the native self, indigenous to the adult.

To date, scholars have not focused on child figures or child voices emerging in modernist novels. I believe this lack is due to the Freudian paradigm that has powerfully influenced our ways of reading children, and thus they have been read as part of an hierarchical system, which Virginia Woolf, as early as 1910, sees as changed. Derrida's non-hierarchical approach allows us to work with this changed relationship between parents and children, which Woolf sees as a fundamental tenet of modernism. Derrida asserts in *Circumfession* that the grieving child is the catalyst for deconstruction, and thus his collapse of the binaries foreign/native, child/adult, mobile/immobile provides an effective means to interpret the concerns of modernist authors. One of the ways we can examine the impact of modernist authors' treatments of childhood and grief is to look at those they influenced directly.

A significant inheritor of the modernist shift, in terms of the hierarchy of parents and children, is Samuel Beckett, whose play *Endgame* offers a striking example of the mobilization of childhood grief and the way in which it has found a home in fiction. By writing in French, Beckett sidesteps the suppression of grief in English. He constructs a dislocating drama in which a grown man, who like an infant cannot walk, recalls how he cried at night and his parents consciously, even with a kind of twisted delight, ignored his grief. In Beckett's *Endgame*, the audience is confronted with Hamm's parents sitting rather tragically and hilariously in dustbins. Hamm's father poses a series of cruel rhetorical questions: 'Whom did you call when you were a tiny boy, and were frightened, in the dark? Your mother? No. Me. We let you cry. Then we moved you out of earshot, so that we might sleep in peace' (56). These parents move the child out of earshot, whereas modernist fiction specifically brings the grief of the child within earshot.

The father's notion of 'tiny boy' becomes more precisely an infant in the drama, since the immobilized adult, Hamm, left to cry as a child, hears a disturbing sound in his mind that he cannot express: 'There'll be no more speech. / (*Pause.*) / Something dripping in my head, ever since the fontanelles. / (*Stifled hilarity of Nagg*)' (50). Hamm's father responds to his son's grief with laughter and his son becomes a man who thinks: 'You weep, and weep, for nothing, so as not to laugh, and little by little ... you begin to grieve [...] All those I might have helped' (68). Replacing tears with shallow laughter, despite a deep undertow of suppressed grief, constructs a self without compassion, a self unable to reach out to others, perhaps even a self who witnesses and participates in cruelty to others. Hamm's grief began in infancy, when the hollow in his head between the fontanelles, more commonly known as the baby's 'soft spot,' has not yet hardened. The 'hollow' remains for this man, and his grief constantly nags, in an echo of his father's name, Nagg. It resonates like a death knell, in echo of his mother's name, Nell. The child's inheritance from such parents is tragic. The parents laugh at their son's hollow existence marked by his tears.

In contrast, Beckett has the child figures of the play, all grown up, imagine that being whole results from being able to grieve. Clov observes: 'He's crying' and Hamm responds 'Then he's living' (62). *Endgame* critiques war by means of returning the infantry to the infantry. Bypassing the intellect, the silenced soldier is superimposed upon the inarticulate infant. Beckett depicts the collapse of language in trying to express the post-war figure of Hamm, whose tears were ignored, at the same time as he suggests that inarticulate grief acts as a catalyst for the play itself. As Hamm explains: 'Then babble, babble, words, like the solitary child who turns himself into children, two, three, so as to be together, and whisper together, in the dark' (70). The grieving child, abandoned to his sorrow and laughed at by his parents, imagines characters who babble and whisper. This may well be a direct referral back to the 'babble of many voices,' which Conrad's Razumov scorns in *Under Western Eyes*, and the tower of babel/babble in *Finnegans Wake*.

In the *Wake*, language is collapsed and/or enhanced in a reversed scene of parents rushing to their child's bedside to comfort his tears in the night. The language is a combination of childish patter and adult comfort, both echoing the affectionate terms parents use: 'While hovering dreamwings, folding around will hide from fears my wee mee manikin, keep my big wig long strong manomen, guard my bairn, mon beau' (576.14–16). The protective parents come hovering to the dreaming, distressed child, enfolding their kin, their bairn, their beauty (Fr. *beau*), and even a youthful version of the adult self, the inner child, the 'wee mee.' Joyce uses his own made-up language, his Wakese, in order to trick the interfering intellect, that may abort his attempt to access the inarticulate.

Comparably deconstructing theatre conventions, Beckett's ostensibly absurdist drama makes perfect sense in a world where 'modern history domesticates the fantastic and normalizes the unspeakable' (Fussell 74). According to Helen Carr, in a discussion of Jean Rhys, Samuel Beckett is 'also a kind of Creole – neither part of the Home Country nor wholly native to his native land. (When Beckett was asked in Paris if he was English, he famously replied, "*Au contraire*")' (41). Beckett's choice to write his play in French seems utterly expected, when his literary father, Yeats, reacts to war poet Wilfred Owen with 'hostility' and in his own elegies 'shuns "tears" and "pity"' (Ramazani 176).

Looking further beyond the modernist era, we learn that the suppression of grief in children, and thus adults, is still common practice in western societies today. Writing about the death of his wife, C.S. Lewis strives to teach his readers about grief: 'On the rebound one passes into tears and pathos. Maudlin tears. I almost prefer the moments of agony. These are at least clean and honest. But the bath of self-pity, the wallow, the loathsome sticky-sweet pleasure of indulging in it – that disgusts me. And even while I'm doing it I know it leads me to misrepresent H. herself. Give that mood its head and in a few minutes I shall have substituted for the real woman a mere doll to be blubbered over' (6). Like Joyce, Lewis resurrects Homer's *Iliad*, where Achilles' teasing terms for Patroclus condemn him as a little girl. Achilles demands, 'Why in tears, Patroclus? / Like a girl, a baby running after her mother, / begging to be picked up, and she tugs her skirts, / holding her back as she tries to hurry off – all tears, / fawning up at her, till she takes her in her arms .../ That's how you look, Patroclus, streaming live tears' (16.7–12). Lewis believes that shedding tears for his wife transforms him into a blubbering little girl with his doll. When he cries, he is no longer the soldier marching onward to heaven by refusing to indulge in human sentiment. Lewis is threatened with what Claudius calls the poison of deep grief, which, like Shakespeare's murderous character, he sees as unclean and dishonest. Like a child who wants candy, the bereaved man is tempted by the 'sticky-sweet pleasure' of grief. However, Lewis fights back and relishes a warrior's 'agony' in place of the 'loathsome,' disgusting desire to cry.

The only thing that makes Lewis forget to suppress his grief is his beloved wife's voice: 'her voice is still vivid. The remembered voice – that can turn me at any moment to a whimpering child' (15). When he hears this voice, not words, but the sound of her voice, then he finds a way to read and write his sorrow: 'Grief is like a bomber circling round and dropping its bombs each time the circle brings it overhead; physical pain is like the steady barrage on a trench in World War One, hours of it with no let-up for a moment. Thought is never static; pain often is' (36). The only way for Lewis to articulate his suffering is through the language of the *Iliad* and then the terms of the First World War. He tries to give words to grief, which he associates with childhood, and is disgusted. Then, he resorts to the tropes of battle in order to translate the blubbering of infantry into the machines dominating infantry. The child's tears become the sound of bombs and the barrage of trench warfare. Neither stage of infantry has any words.

Robert Ackerman, professor of sociology, writes in his study *Silent Sons*, published in 1993: 'suicide is the third leading cause of death among teenagers. It is often difficult to notice when the teenage boy can no longer handle emotions that are suppressed. As long as he is going through the motions every day, others may not notice the decline in his spirit' (89). In a study published in 1994, Jonathan Shay, a psychiatrist who works with war veterans, addresses the 'suppression of social griefwork' (39). He demonstrates that in contemporary military culture, mourning is 'dreaded, perfunctory, delayed, devalued, mocked, fragmented, minimized, deflected, disregarded, and sedated' (67). Although studying boys at home rather than at war, William Pollack, co-director of the Centre for Men at McLean Hospital / Harvard Medical School, concurs in his text *Real Boys*, published in 1998: 'Boys learn the Boy Code in sandboxes, playgrounds, schoolrooms, camps, churches, and hangouts, and are taught by peers, coaches, teachers, and just about everybody else. In the "Listening to Boys' Voices" study, even very young boys reported that they felt they must "keep a stiff upper lip," "not show their feelings," "act real tough," "not act too nice," "be cool," "just laugh and brush it off when someone punches you"' (23). In his study, geared towards addressing the rising numbers of men who under-achieve, suffer serious addiction, behave violently, and suicide, Pollack argues that today men are confused by 'society's mixed messages about what's expected of them as boys, and later as men, many feel a sadness and disconnection they cannot even name' (xxii).

My study of modernist literature, drawing on the elucidating terms of Derrida's way of reading, strives to offer a name for the sadness and disconnection; paradoxically, this name is uttered through plot, imagery, a dual child-adult narrator, seemingly inarticulate grief-language, tempo-ral shifts to reveal childhood, and the transposition of war trauma onto the home front, where it began.

The defining feature of the modernist fiction discussed here is that it strives to break apart a hierarchical system that oppresses the child-self. Joseph Conrad positions himself, in terms of his writing, as a 'stone breaker.' Notably, he experiences doubt, fear and 'black horror' in his attempts to break down the barriers established to keep childhood grief at bay. Jean Rhys focuses on the nervous breakdown that besets various characters. The affairs and marriages that dominate her novellas are focused on the break-up and thus her characters are torn by 'heart-breaking sobs.'

Rebecca West returns us to Conrad's idea of the 'stone breaker' when she imagines one character 'using words like a hammer' to break a sol-dier's heart. Again the focus is on marital breakdown as a way to ex-plore the suppression of childhood grief. Ford Madox Ford shifts the idea slightly, so that he concentrates on what happens not only when there is marital breakdown, but also when there is a break with tradition. Ford explores the reaction when one breaks society's rules specifically in terms of owning and expressing feelings of grief.

Virginia Woolf returns again and again in her fiction to the moment when one breaks the silence. She imagines the moment when there is a break, when one breaks down. She pushes her characters to break the pane/pain of glass that separates them from an emotional life. Thus, in Woolf's fiction 'the true self breaks off from the assumed.' And James Joyce foregrounds the pedagogical idea that the adult must break the child's will. He depicts this painful scene in all of his fiction; however, in *Finnegans Wake*, there is an influx of joy, owing to the 'brake' within the child's voice, which stresses a halt to the old system and a sense that on the horizon one will discover a new way of imagining childhood grief as a natural, local, native way of expressing one's deepest self and thus opening one's being to laughter.

Finally, if we return to Derrida's idea that, while grieving, he needs to sit by the Pacific, we find in contemporary fiction – which has inherited this modernist collapse of the adult / child binary – an understanding that grief is still foreign, as foreign as a hurt child. Yet it must be read about and heard for peace to be a possibility.

In Vancouver, a city on the edge of the Pacific Ocean, novelist Wayson Choy was born the year the Second World War began. In 1995 in his novel *The Jade Peony*, he writes of boys in Vancouver during this era and the way they are encouraged to be soldiers, which hinges on the way they suppress their grief. The six-year-old Jook-Liang notes that their grandma 'was proud of her warrior grandsons' (15). The four-year-old Jung-Sum hears the adults around him, who have taken him from an extremely brutal home, praise his suppression of grief: 'Jung strong boy. Never cry' (90). Choy deftly sidesteps our training to hold back our tears by writing with the voices of children whose native language is not English. The badly hurt four-year-old Jung-Sum has not yet learned his lesson well enough and in his childish poetry he translates back to us some of our silenced grief: 'Kiam told me *Hahm-sui-fauh* was the Chinese name for Vancouver because it was a city built beside the salt water of the Pacific Ocean. Until Kiam told me, I thought it was where all the salt tears came to make up the ocean, just as my mother told me in one of her stories about her own father's coming to Vancouver. And then I told myself, this is the way the world is. I felt I would never need to cry again. Never' (90). Choy translates with a child's Chinese phrase, so that I, an English speaker, can understand grief. Sometimes we become so alienated from our emotions we can recuperate them only through foreign terms.

Notes

Introduction to Children's Grief: The Return from Exile

1 For an excellent exploration of sexuality and Oedipal violence from child to father as seen through Freudian, Lacanian, and Kleinian approaches, see Elizabeth Abel's study of childhood in Woolf's *To the Lighthouse* (45–67). In this chapter, Abel also analyses the way in which children (James and Cam) articulate their thoughts in intriguing, gender-scripted ways. Abel does not examine grief, mourning, or the fragments of *A Haunted House* or *The Waves*. We can effectively add this dimension to her treatment of childhood in Woolf's writing in order to more fully investigate this focus in the novelist's work and the way in which she shared a concern about these issues with other modernists.

2 John Caputo, who has written a study of the fifty-nine periphrases of this text, calls it a book of 'formidable difficulty (even by Derridean standards)' because the 'text disseminates in so many directions – autobiographical, psychoanalytic, literary, political, pedagogical, theological, and philosophical – as to make nonsense of the idea of definitive commentary' (*Prayers* 285). Caputo's interest is in the theological strand; my interest is in the inarticulate (infant) self who grieves in the text.

3 See also Atle Dyregrov, John Holland, Margaret Pennells, and Nancy Boyd Webb.

4 As Carol Shloss puts this modernist paradox: a writer like Woolf 'could show both the horror of being incomprehensible and at the same time invent a language for rendering illness intelligible' (372).

5 I find Ramazani's questions about Wilfred Owen's possibly sadomasochistic psychology, based on Freud's essay, 'A Child Is Being Beaten,' indicative of the adult tendency to reject a child's testimony and move rapidly into

a need to protect the sanctity of the adult. Comparable to Freud's and Breuer's argument that young women's testimonies of sexual abuse within the home were girlish fantasies, we find a comparable belief, directly after the First World War, in Freud's analysis of 'childhood fantasies' of being beaten as being 'a distorted expression of being loved – being loved by the father in particular' (Ramazani 83). How much is fantasy? Being beaten as a child by a parent is unspeakable. In *Dubliners*, Joyce's fictional presentation of the beaten child responds powerfully to adult theorizing. It does not sound like a fantasy about love. Moreover, Joyce relates brutality within the home towards children and brutality in the political sphere towards colonial subjects. Hence, when the colonized and humiliated men of *Dubliners* return home, either they become immobilized by their children's expression of grief, like the trapped father of 'A Little Cloud' – 'The wailing of the child pierced the drum of his ear. It was useless, useless! He was a prisoner for life. His arms trembled with anger and suddenly bending to the child's face he shouted:—Stop!' (D 79–80) – or worse, they resort to relief in violence, as the shamed, colonized father does in 'Counterparts': 'The boy uttered a squeal of pain as the stick cut his thigh. He clasped his hands together in the air and his voice shook with fright.—O, pa! he cried. Don't beat me, pa! And I'll ... I'll say a *Hail Mary* for you ... I'll say a *Hail Mary* for you, pa, if you don't beat me' (*D* 94).

6 When he considers modernist fiction, Jean-Michel Rabaté begins with the Freudian position, but builds on it. He concurs that 'modernism is systematically 'haunted' by voices from the past,' and what 'returns is, in a classically Freudian fashion, what has not been processed, accommodated, incorporated into the self by mourning.' In this context, Rabaté then evokes a Derridean perspective: 'Modernism postulates both the necessity and the impossibility of mourning' (xvi).

7 The collection of essays *Modernism and Mourning* begins with the Freudian model, but also draws extensively on the work of Derrida and other theorists. Although it is full of insightful, compelling work, the authors contend only with mourning for the dead. Furthermore, as noted, there are no children mentioned in the text and Derrida's work on the tears of children is not mentioned. The grief of children and its potential suppression are not discussed; the scholars do not explore how it may shape and influence the conduct of adults.

8 For further discussion, see Heaney (12 ff.).

9 Pam Heaney explains that Freud's 'understanding of mourning was influ-

enced by his self-analysis after his father's death.' She notes that 'Freud believed that the task of mourning required the gradual freeing up or withdrawal of psychic energy that had been attached (cathected) to the internal representation of the dead parent so that psychic energy would be available to form new attachments' (11–12).

10 Derrida also references this phenomenon in a response to Catherine Malabou at the conference 'Augustine and Postmodernism: *Confessions* and *Circumfession*,' held at Villanova University in 2001. Derrida differentiates himself from Heidegger in his use of a literary 'I' and claims that he speaks 'of tears and laughter,' since what 'is constant in "Circumfession" is the experience of weeping "with" Augustine, something that Heidegger never pays attention to.' He then asserts that Heidegger would not have read *Circumfession*, because it is literature and thus would have been considered 'inauthentic' (138). At the same conference, in response to Hent de Vries, he clarifies that *Circumfession* is 'not a spiritual exercise'; rather, it is 'just childish exercise' (88).

11 For a discussion of the historical context of this assertion and Woolf's sense of the break with Victorian values see Joyce.

12 For those readers interested in studies on the gender shift, two recent works offer excellent insight into Woolf and war; see Schneider and Phillips.

13 Discussing Ford Madox Ford's *Parade's End,* John Onions argues that 'Ford's success in writing about the war stems precisely from his avoidance of the typical binary structure – war and peace, ironic discrepancy – which underpins First World War fiction' (116). I believe that the collapse of the binary structure of the domestic and military home fronts, the world of the child and the world of the adult, also contributes to defining his fiction.

14 Notably, David Krell foregrounds a time of grieving in his life when he had an unexpected encounter with Derrida, who was able to make sense of his feelings because he works from within a concept of the 'foolish logic to which only children and the mad are susceptible' (58).

15 Elizabeth Barrett Browning's sonnet 'Grief' commands the bereaved: 'Deep-hearted man, express / Grief for thy Dead in silence like to death—/ Most like a monumental statue set / In everlasting watch and moveless woe / Till itself crumble to the dust beneath.' Then she calls the reader to witness the effect of the suppressed grief: 'Touch it; the marble eyelids are not wet: / If it could weep, it could arise and go.' Barrett Browning's sonnet leaves us with a final impression of immobility in the image of the statue: 'moveless woe.' This figure, petrified by suppressed grief, recurs in all of the selected modernist works under discussion. An attempt to identify

a shift into modernism, according to fiction writers' changing ideas about the suppression of grief, will, of course, have many exceptions. For instance, in *In Memoriam*, Tennyson's elegy for his friend, the poet feels reduced by grief to the state of an infant; he stresses the way in which his grief renders him inarticulate: 'So runs my dream: but what am I? / An infant crying in the night: / An infant crying for the light: / And with no language but a cry' (54).

16 Hughes's father was one of seventeen survivors of Gallipoli; as Dwight Eddins records: 'he was unwilling to talk to his son about his war experiences,' and 'thus, it was the silences themselves that embodied for the younger Hughes a traumatic eloquence' (136). Niobe seems to convey something of Hughes's father's silent grief. In one of Hughes's poems, his father cries out through the night as he dreams over and over again of climbing out of the trench in order to bring his children to 'safety' (149).

17 In 1917, reviewing Siegfried Sassoon's war poetry, Edmund Gosse describes the poet as 'finding the age out of joint' (Hynes 191). Barker sees Hamlet as representative of 'incipient modernity' because of his separate and developed interiority in contrast to the more blended public / private self of the Renaissance (27). Eagleton reads him according to a Derridean model as 'pure deferral and diffusion' (72). Also modern, I believe, is Shakespeare's focus on the suppression of grief and its resultant soldiers. Niall Lucy asserts that this is 'why Derrida insists that inheritance always involves "the work of mourning," calling us to remember the others of the past who promised us a future in which others (like us) could come "to be,"' and he specifies '(the reference here, of course, is to Shakespeare's *Hamlet*).' As Lucy explains, Hamlet's engagement with his father's spectre raises questions about 'being and time in general,' and for Derrida these are 'urgently political questions' (*Dictionary* 75, 17).

18 As Susan Letzler Cole puts it: '*Hamlet* is the tragedy of a mourner in a world which provides no context for mourning' (3). What is striking is that the modernist authors in this study describe contemporary fictional worlds that again and again provide no allowance for grieving.

19 For a discussion of Derrida's specific work on *Hamlet*, in terms of madness and in relation to Joyce's texts, see Roughley (12–13).

20 As Derrida writes: 'Words fail us, since all language that would return to the self, to us, would seem indecent, a reflexive discourse that would end up coming back to the stricken community, to its consolation or its mourning' (*WM* 200).

21 For a discussion of Woolf's engagement with Hamlet in terms of gender and

sexuality, see Abel (20, 94).

22 In a cultural history of tears, Lutz notes that 'we know surprisingly little about it,' since 'until recently tears have been remarkably neglected as a subject of investigation.' The lack of sustained work in science results in our understanding of tears coming from 'innumerable poetic, fictional, dramatic, and cinematic representations of the human proclivity to weep' (18–19).

23 Shakespeare, grieving for the death of his son, Hamnet, creates the fictional son, Hamlet, who he has mourning the death of his father. In *Ulysses*, when Stephen Dedalus articulates his theory of *Hamlet*, he speaks of the playwright's dead son as well as entwines his thoughts about the play with his own mother's death, which he still mourns: 'I wept alone' (241–3). In a comparable collapse of time, Derrida, mourning the death of his mother, imagines himself in the position of his children as they suffer his future death: 'I weep like my own children on the edge of my grave' (*C* 41). One can see that Derrida's sense of time here or the relation between the past (grandmother), present (father), and future (children) is fluid. His grief does not turn him to stone; instead, he becomes malleable. The work of mourning requires seeing (at least) double: the moment given to us by the past, what we remember and mourn, is what contains the unknowable promise of the future. Derrida rarely references children; however, when he discusses grief or writes while grieving, the figure of the child often appears.

24 For an exploration of this dynamic, raised in the context of questions of gender and melancholy, see Judith Butler, who explores the way in which aggression breaks the hold of grief. See also Franz Fanon, who concurs that vengeful violence may function as a cure for grief as melancholy.

25 For further study, see Joseph Zornado, who looks at the relationship between 'violent child-rearing practices and how they lead directly to fascistic personality.' He explores this through the work of Adorno and through Horkheimer's ideas on The Authoritarian Personality (77).

26 Carol Shloss argues eloquently that yet another of Joyce's innovations was to interpret his daughter, Lucia's, behaviour according to artistic, rather than prevailing psychological, models. In particular, Shloss notes that 'Victorian gentility' often served to mask 'the barbarity of acts that were supposed to protect children' (316).

27 When Mark Vessey asks Derrida what draws him to the *Confessions*, he replies: 'I was impressed by the number of times in which Augustine refers to his tears.' Derrida then reminds us that he is 'interested only in writers who cry or weep' (Kearney 31).

28 For the First World War fighter, the ideal thing was to be a typical Englishman: 'And to be a typical Englishman meant, of course, that one repressed inner feelings' (Eksteins 184). This suppression was taught at home and appeared as a lesson well learned on the home front. Christopher Tietjens of Ford Madox Ford's *Parade's End* insists, while he is at war: 'I can never go home. I have to go underground' (491). Significantly, it is not the war that makes him yearn to descend, but the wounding done by his family and wife at home.

29 Woolf details here a return to a realm Derrida also thinks of as *writing*, but discusses often under the idea of *différance*, which is a term that has meaning only when written. *Différance* is the time before difference: 'It is therefore a question of drawing back toward a point at which all determined contradictions, in the form of given, factual historical structures, can appear, and appear as relative to this zero point at which determined meaning and nonmeaning come together in their common origin' (*WD* 56).

30 At the same time, according to writing's 'double-movement,' the child suffers a 'blow' at the moment when she learns speech, because with it she is taught to choose and adhere to presence over play, authoritative binary oppositions over writing. Woolf's grief and other aspects of herself become severed when she is taught to be articulate. Yet writing remains a realm of wholeness where the *a* of *différance* can be can be experienced. In his study of Derrida, David Krell defines this kind of sorrow: 'even an affirmed mourning remains profoundly committed to the human body, as the site of its tears, its ache, its dull aphasia, its emptiness' (90). Derrida links a kind of primal aphasia with literature's turn to what Judith Lee calls 'imagining,' specifically in response to the 'unspeakable' in grief (189). Derrida writes: 'Within original aphasia, when the voice of the god or the poet is missing, one must be satisfied with the vicars of speech that are the cry and writing' (*WD* 73). Sorrow's impairment of speech requires the rector to step down and allow a vicar to respond. The vicar cannot deliver his sermons, but he can cry and write.

31 In contrast, Walter Benjamin asks us to see that the First World War silenced its soldiers: 'Was it not noticeable at the end of the war that men returned from the battlefield grown silent – not richer, but poorer in communicable experience?' (84).

32 Likewise, the novelists in this study stand apart from the popular war fiction of the time, in which 'tough minded' characters 'present the view that war taught individuals how to be "proper" men.' Thus, the popular war thrillers by 'Sapper' are praised in a literary review of the time for the description of 'how a boy "is molded into a man."' See Hammond and Towheed 118–21.

33 Derrida stresses that, when reading is mourning practice, it works first and foremost as an activity within, a writing for the writing self: 'Readability bears this mourning: a phrase can be readable, it must be able to become readable, up to a certain point, without the reader, he or she, or any other place of reading, occupying the ultimate position of the addressee' (*WM* 220). Likewise, Ross Chambers believes that 'reading can, and should, be understood as a practice of mourning' (lx).

34 Modernism appeals to Derrida because this kind of writing (and he is speaking specifically of Joyce) encourages active interpretation: 'we must write, we must sign, we must bring about new events with untranslatable marks – and this is the frantic call, the distress of a signature that is asking for a *yes* from the other, the pleading injunction for a counter-signature' (*Ulysses Gramophone* 283). The emotional terms, 'frantic' and 'distress,' are compelling in a study that strives to hear grief at play within fiction. As David Krell suggests, Derrida is like a child; he wants to play because 'play is the disruption of presence' (*WD* 292). Instead of pursuing the presence of truth or justice, Derrida leans more towards a 'Nietzschean *affirmation,* that is the joyous affirmation of a world of signs without fault, without truth, and without origin which is offered to an active interpretation' (*Ulysses Gramophone* 283).

35 In her final book, *1900*, Rebecca West invokes a familial metaphor to write about imperialism: 'In certain times and places it engendered such costly tragedy as the Boer War; in other times and places it abolished such accomplishments as head-splitting by sword. It has resembled parenthood at its most enlightened, and parenthood hostile and perverted' (108–9). Jahan Ramazani identifies a parallel dual movement in the modern elegy: 'The funeral director turns grief into a pathology, a temporary illness that needs to be isolated and cured'; in contrast, the modern elegist 'clutch[es] grief as a necessary and humanizing affect' (17).

36 Focused on *A Portrait of the Artist as a Young Man* and *Ulysses*, Gian Balsamo sees Proust's exploration of personal grief in his fiction as a 'literary parallel to Joyce's depiction of Stephen's introspective life, and more particularly of his impotent mourning' (418). In anticipation of the way in which I read *Finnegans Wake*, according to Balsamo, 'Stephen's tentative adoption of an inarticulate, unrelational, non-signifying voice of incomprehension bears the traces of a poetic agenda, of an aesthetics of grief' (428).

37 Discussing Proust's late decision to include the First World War in *À la recherche du temps perdu*, Rabaté writes that he 'wanted to place Combray on the frontline and therefore moved the location of the village from Normandy to northern France' (11). While Proust is outside my limited scope of British

writers, it is telling, especially when Rabaté identifies the pun in the haunting name of the Guermantes, which 'homophonically suggest[s] that *les guerres mentent* (wars are a lie),' that Proust relocates the site of his childhood, marked by the requirement to suppress his grief, as a front line in a world war (11–12).

38 The word *suppress* was at the forefront during the First World War, as despair set in at mid-war and literary pieces in reaction to the unprecedented death and horror were suppressed under the provisions of the Defence of the Realm Act (Hynes 151).

39 *Derrida Reader* 274. E.M. Forster maintains that the writing and reading of novels are activities centred around acknowledging the perpetually deferred spirit of intimate expression and knowledge; thus, he claims that human intercourse 'is seen to be haunted by a spectre' because we cannot 'understand each other, except in a rough and ready way; we cannot reveal ourselves, even when we want to' (69). As J. Hillis Miller maintains: all a novelist can do is create a 'ghostly present' by means of a 'narrator's ability to resurrect the past not as reality but as verbal image' (*Mrs. Dalloway* 62).

1 Translating the Foreign Language of Childhood Grief: Joseph Conrad's *Under Western Eyes*

1 Critics react to.the 'contorted narratorial procedure,' which embodies 'a kind of struggle with the material to be conveyed' (Fletcher and Bradbury 398).

2 Jakob Lothe, although not focused on grief, explains that Conrad uses the English teacher not only as a 'narrator in the technical sense (as teller of a story) but also as a reflective observer' (266). I will explore the way in which he serves to stress grief's ostensibly foreign nature.

3 It is the *before* that makes the *after* what Niall Lucy calls 'radically unforeseeable'; the usual way of organizing time collapses or, as Hamlet says, 'The time is out of joint.' One has a responsibility to the dead, the living, and the yet to be born (*Dictionary* 114).

4 Conrad, who as a child suffered the loss of his parents, creates what Rising calls the 'furtive paternal function' (26).

5 Josiane Paccaud-Huguet foregrounds his familiarity with *Hamlet* before she explores its role in *Under Western Eyes* from a Lacanian perspective. Albeit reaching a different conclusion, she also reads the novel as an exploration of a failure to perform the rites of mourning (173–7).

6 Meyer discusses the fact that first Conrad's mother, and then his father, suffered drawn-out deaths from tuberculosis of the lungs, which is the same illness that slowly kills James Wait (113).

7 Tightening the bonds between *Under Western Eyes* at one end of the modernist spectrum and Beckett's absurdist plays at the other, Ted Billy compares Conrad's 'dramatization of immobility' to the 'images of paralysis' in Beckett's theatre (66–7).

8 Derrida questions this type of work, for good 'inspiration is the spirit-breath [*souffle*] of life, which will not take dictation.' He asserts that this kind of inspiration: 'would return me to true communication with myself and would give me back speech' (*WD* 179).

9 As Yannick Le Boulicaut explains, 'fear of the unspeakable creates immobilism' in Conrad's fiction and the author finds 'a sort of therapy in the written word' (143–5).

10 Lisa Rado argues that Conrad's 'linguistic pessimism distances *Under Western Eyes* from the modernist tradition' (84). She asserts that Conrad 'question[s] the concept of authorship' in this novel (97). While I agree that the novel is *not* about confession and redemption and the capacity of language to transparently convey one's thoughts and feelings, I do believe that *Under Western Eyes* is about the struggle to articulate grief and childhood so that this suppressed emotion and this hidden self do not haunt one's present conduct in deadly ways. I suggest a different reading whereby Conrad's articulation of suppressed grief, coupled with his conjuring of the wounded child-ghost, is a highly modernist act that contributes to the broken sentences, the fragmented works, of other modernist writers.

11 'Let us begin by letting him speak,' announces Derrida as he mourns for Louis Marin (*WM* 143). Yet Derrida also claims that 'speaking is impossible' when he confronts Paul de Man's death. At the same time, he admits that 'so too would be silence or absence or refusal to share one's sadness' (*Memoires* xvi).

12 Carola Kaplan explores Conrad's response, through the creation of Natalia, to Dostoyevsky's Sonya. Natalia cannot feel a compassionate bond to the murderer, in contrast to Sonya, who is able to find pity within her. Natalia is a paragon of suppression, conveyed by silence.

13 Critics, such as Catherine Rising, have shown that Razumov constructs an identity out of his sensitivity to his plight as the illegitimate child of a royal father and as a child who never knew his mother; however, there is more work to be done in terms of exploring the thesis that one of the key motivations in Razumov's betrayal of Haldin is his attempt to secure his father's love and respect.

14 *Under Western Eyes* legitimizes the bastard child Razumov: as the British teacher quotes from his journal, he offers the lost child a new literary home in English letters. Although the teacher is unaware of the implications,

Conrad encourages the reader to see Razumov's journal as a 'dormant seed' that becomes a disseminating text. As Gayatri Spivak explains, 'within this structural metaphor' of 'the father (the text or meaning)' engendering 'the son or seed (preface or word),' 'Derrida's cry is 'dissemination,' the seed that neither inseminates nor is recovered by the father, but is scattered abroad' (preface xi).

15 Anthony Fothergill writes insightfully of the literary prize Razumov seeks: 'the silver medal had functioned as a metonym for a successful academic life, so its proleptic loss demands a revised narrative' (41). Building on his analysis, I would argue that the revised text its loss demands is a grieving one.

16 As noted, Derrida calls this force of writing *gram* or *différance:* 'The play of differences supposes, in effect, syntheses and referrals which forbid at any moment, or in any sense, that a simple element be present in and of itself, referring only to itself' (*P* 26).

17 Derrida reaches similar conclusions about writing grief: 'The replacement of "absence" by "other" here no doubt indicates that the substitutive value is no longer operative in the couple "absence/ presence" but in the couple "same/ other" that introduces the dimension of mourning' (*WM* 150).

18 Gail Fincham notes that Razumov's diary is composed in Geneva on the Isle of Jean-Jacques Rousseau, and she uses this detail to investigate Conrad's treatment of Enlightenment rationality. She concludes the discussion of the philosophical underpinnings of the novel by arguing that *Under Western Eyes* foregrounds the 'role of compassion or sympathy in balancing rationality' (61). Although outside the scope of this study, I wonder if Conrad's reference to Rousseau in the composition of Razumov's diary was connected to his treatment of children in the novel, in the light of the philosopher's focus in his writings on the child as naturally good and as existing in his own right.

19 Debra Romanick Baldwin traces Conrad's use of the legend of Saint Thekla and concludes: 'In this novel, which begins with a crime of betrayal driven by an abstract idea, it is Tekla who represents the crime's antithesis in her devotion to particular human beings' (155).

2 Childhood Grief as Resident Alien in Jean Rhys's Five Novellas

1 Pierrette Frickey treats Rhys's novels as if they culminate in a kind of symbolic rebirth (535–46). While she imagines the rebirth as achieving a kind of wholeness, I believe Derrida's system works as an intriguing alternative, whereby the wholeness is complemented by articulating the fragment or the

ghost of the lost self (the wounded child), who can never be regained or
integrated, but to whom one may listen and speak. Elgin Mellown reads
Rhys's first four novels as charting a spiritual progress from 'the joy of
childhood' into the ordeals of adult life (106); he even reads the overt
misery of Antoinette as a child as part of the pattern of the 'Rhys heroine':
she has 'a happy childhood in a tropical state of nature' (113). The critic's
blocked ability to record and respond to the intense loneliness and grief of
Antoinette, which dominates the childhood portion of *Wide Sargasso Sea*,
parallels the block that makes critics fail to discuss the son of Tietjens in
Parade's End.

2 In *After Leaving Mr. Mackenzie*, the process of becoming stone cold is repeatedly described; hence, Julia feels 'as if something huge, made of ice, were
breathing on her' (42). Julia's sister speaks to her 'coldly,' which makes her
fearful of receiving the 'cold shoulder' from the rest of her family (54). She
experiences the emotions of melancholy and terror 'like a douche of cold
water' (55). Thus, despite Julia's constant crying, Rhys reveals that as she becomes colder and colder, she moves further and further away from the tropical zone of grief.

3 Helen Carr asserts that Rhys's characters feel 'themselves silenced or unheard' and that she positions herself, the novelist, as having 'the right and
power to speak on their behalf' (6). In a letter, Rhys records advice from
a publisher: 'If you grow hard you will not be able to write'; although surprised, since he was 'supposed to be as flinty as a rock himself,' Rhys admits
'he was right' (*Letters* 176). In 1963 she writes to Francis Wyndham, who is
waiting for the completed manuscript of *Wide Sargasso Sea*, a letter that she
says is 'not personal'; rather, it is 'one of those heart cries.' She explains: 'I
felt I could not go on without talking to somebody even on paper. Telling
someone how I felt.' This direct reference to emotional need apparently
requires a defence, and she states: 'I am not potty you know.' She makes
it clear to him that it is imperative her letter does not go 'unanswered'
(*Letters* 243–5).

4 Rhys describes this return in a letter: 'After "Mackenzie" I married again
and lived in London. Then the West Indies started knocking at my heart.
So – "Voyage in the Dark." That (the knocking) has never stopped'
(*Letters* 171).

5 The novel draws on the twisted affair Rhys had with Ford Madox Ford. The
original title was 'Postures,' but since my focus is on fiction rather than biography, the title *Quartet* is more evocative. The jailed husband is less of a character than Marya's childhood self, who, added to her adult self, forms the
fourth along with Heidler and his wife.

6 Derrida's exploration of the work of mourning in the *Specters of Marx* links haunting and hunting: 'My feeling, then, is that Marx scares himself [*se fait peur*], he himself pursues [*il s'acharne* lui- même] relentlessly someone who almost resembles him to the point that we could mistake one for the other: a brother, a double, thus a diabolical image. A kind of ghost of himself. Whom he would like to distance, distinguish: to *oppose*' (139). Both Derrida and Rhys explore the hate that surfaces when the child is denied.

7 In a letter, Rhys herself tries to suppress emotion in order to be more British: 'You must fill in the gaps yourself. To avoid sentimentality and end on the astringent note so beloved of the Angliche' (*Letters* 35).

8 Proust explores this phenomenon in great detail in *À la recherche du temps perdu*.

9 Kenneth Ramchand describes Rochester as 'a certain kind of mind [trying] to break free and expose its buried emotions and yearnings' (197). He quotes this scene of hiding childhood feelings and describes it as 'suppression' and he refers to him as becoming hardened (202). However, rather than naming parenting or beliefs about child-rearing, he enlists large economic and political structures: 'The force of materialism, social aspiration and the operations of mechanical intellect radically separated from true feeling are features of the dehumanisation of man in many modern societies' (204). Ramchand identifies, but then turns away from, childhood pain. Hence, he concludes that Antoinette's suicide is an attempt to return to the 'warmth and colour and innocence of her childhood world' (205). Rhys has written a childhood for Antoinette in which her mother is cold and rejects her repeatedly. While the tropical garden is colourful, the child's life is grey and sad, as she feels lonely and in jeopardy.

10 In a letter to Selma Vaz Dias about *Wide Sargasso Sea*, Rhys notes, 'I hate to think of them pawing at my book – Not understanding,' and adds, 'I long too for it to be understood' (*Letters* 235).

11 The command, 'Smile Please,' is what Rhys chose to call her unfinished autobiography.

12 Derrida reveals that 'writing structurally carries within itself (counts discounts) the process of its own erasure and annulation, all the while marking what *remains* of this erasure' (*P* 68).

13 One cannot speak of rocking horses as symbolic of a wounded childhood without immediately thinking of D.H. Lawrence's short story 'The Rocking-Horse Winner.' Perhaps Rhys read this story, which contributes to the focus of modernists on childhood grief.

14 Derrida stresses in *Circumfession*, while he dialogues with his child, that he did not have his own sons circumcised (95). The suffering of the father is

not visited upon the children unto the third and fourth generation when the father remembers childhood suffering.

15 Jean Rhys's sense of the hurt child may be autobiographically based. Teresa O'Connor draws on Rhys's 'Black Exercise Book,' a kind of diary, in a study of her fiction. She writes that the 'book is most difficult to follow. For the most part Rhys kept the journal in pencil and apparently often wrote in it while she was drunk. Most of the inclusions are fragmentary, almost incoherent and with virtually no punctuation' (4). It is in this exercise book that Rhys 'mentions beatings a great deal' and 'they seem to have been harsh and most often administered by her mother' (39). Rhys does not write about children being beaten in her fiction; she writes about racism, colonialism, war, and the battle between the sexes. However, these adult crises seem haunted by the beaten child who grieves.

16 Arnold Davidson maintains that this moment of gazing in a looking glass shows the 'two are now sisters again but sisters in sorrow and suffering'; his analysis of doubling reveals 'that Antoinette's childhood tragedies are psychologically as well as symbolically related to her adult ones' (26).

17 In contrast, Gayatri Spivak maintains a dividing line between the black and white characters. Thus, she interprets Christophine as a 'commodified person,' but she does not see Rochester, sold by his own father, as suffering a similar plight ('Three Women's Texts' 185). She imagines Christophine as 'driven out of the story,' although to me, her final lines suggest that her knowledge and power are beyond the literary tradition.

18 While Rhys and Ford use patois to recall and return to a childhood language, Derrida tries to find those absent words by means of writing footnotes, or in the margin, or around childhood photographs; thus, he expresses his 'hope of getting close to the proper language of my life on the screen of circumcision.' On the screen of *Circumfession*, he wants to reflect 'me and the others' (144).

19 As noted, Derrida speaks the same sentence, 'I want to kill myself,' and he wonders if his readers 'see [my / his] tears, today, those of the child' (*C* 38–40).

20 Michael Thorpe highlights Rochester's wounded childhood and the way in which his father sells him; he concludes that it does not take much to 'harden Edward's habit of repressed feeling into cold alienation' (183).

21 Derrida examines this pattern whereby being haunted makes one susceptible to repetition: 'They contaminate each other sometimes in such a troubling manner, since the simulacrum consists precisely in miming the phantom or in simulating the phantasm of the other' (*S* 110). Teresa O'Connor expresses the phenomenon concisely: 'Mirroring this cultural and historical

failure is the betrayal of the child by the parent,' which is 'a failure that the child can neither forgive nor forget. Just as [Daniel] Cosway cannot leave the memory of the hurt done to him by his father, so does Rochester perpetually return to his similar wound' (206).

22 Wally Look Lai asserts that, when Antoinette and Rochester meet, it 'is more than an encounter between two people: it is an encounter between two worlds' (40). In contrast, I find Rhys is at pains to show that, by means of their childhood suffering and suppression, they belong to the same world and speak the same language.

23 Deborah Kloepfer writes in compelling ways about the 'mother-child dyad' in Rhys's fiction, offering a different and rich way of understanding childhood and grief in her work when they are studied as part of a tradition of women's writing: 'Rhys makes explicit connection between maternity and a kind of language that is not language' (81).

3 Grieving the Child of the Shell-Shocked Soldier: Rebecca West's *The Return of the Soldier*

1 *The Return of the Soldier* was extremely popular upon publication right after the war (Glendinning 66). Moreover, 'Shaw was quoted as saying that *The Return of the Soldier* was one of the best stories in the language' (70). Although of evident impact when first published, the novella is rarely taught, has not received a great deal of critical attention, and is mostly now unknown (Schweizer 17). For a summary of recent critical approaches see Bonikowski.

2 Claire Tylee sets the novel within the context of the war and women's consciousness. While she acknowledges the death of the child, she sees the protagonist's two-year-old as representative of 'his hopes for the future' as opposed to being expressive of his own childhood (147).

3 Critics to date show little interest in Chris Baldry's dead child. Ann Norton stresses class issues and love triangles (11–13). Motley Deakin concludes that the story argues for Chris's 'need to return to his real world of social obligation and military duty' (132–3). Notably, Peter Childs argues that the First World War historically brought about a societal change between sexes: 'men were taking the position of children, establishing a role reversal in which women were active and in control, while men were supine, passive and vulnerable' (176). However, he mentions twice yet does not discuss the death of Chris's two-year-old son. Instead, he asserts that the 'narrative's interest lies far less in Chris's condition than in the relationships between the three women' (178).

4 Society intervenes so early – 'on the seventh day,' in Derrida's case – in order to take the baby and, by means of ancient ritual with the promise of a bond with God and society, to cause a 'wounded baby,' one who lacks the ability to record and thus remember this early incision into the body. As Derrida describes it: 'that wound that I have never seen, seen with my own eyes' (*C* 66–8). For readers, this provides a new understanding of Derrida's emphasis on the trace (the mark of absence) in any discussion of philosophy or literature; he describes himself as following 'the traces of blood, the first I remember having seen with my own eyes, outside, since I was and remain blind to that of my seventh or eighth day' (108).

5 Shell shock and returning to a childhood state were often spoken of in tandem, as the following example from 1916 attests: 'Shell Shock! Do they know what it means? Men become like weak children, crying and waving their arms madly, clinging to the nearest man and praying not to be left alone.' (Shephard 39).

6 Focused on class and gender issues, Norton sees Jenny and Kitty initially in the nursery because they are relegated 'to the worlds of motherhood and the continuous "childhood" of a woman's life.' She sees the dead child as a symbol of the patriarchy: 'The male child who lived there – Kitty's and Chris's son – died at age two, but his kingdom of toys is preserved like an emblem of expected masculine occupations' (10).

7 Although she does not credit Rebecca West with consciously constructing her character's suffering, nor does she relate it to Chris's own childhood grief, Elaine Showalter recognizes 'the connections between male hysteria and a whole range of male social obligations.' She sees his cure as sending 'him back into a normality' that is both 'unfeeling and unreal' (*1987: Female Malady* 191, 241).

8 Niall Lucy offers a concise point about postcards or letters for Derrida: 'truth is contextual and therefore always open to postal effects of misattribution, misdirection, mistiming and so forth' (*Dictionary* 100).

9 Derrida addresses in relevant ways the empty sign of the purse and the way in which it expresses the spectral force of Chris: 'an acute thought of mourning' causes an effect 'from the fantastic force of the specter, and from a supplement of force; and the increase becomes fantastic at the very heart of lack' (*WM* 153).

10 Childhood suffering is specifically connected with turning to stone, in West's *The Fountain Overflows*; the child, Rosamund, has an abusive father and she has turned to stone: 'Surely she stammered because stone should not be asked to speak' (167).

11 In his historical survey of soldiers' trauma in the First World War, David
    Carradine writes that in many cases: 'the last thoughts which soldiers enter-
    tained were of their mothers' (211).

12 In *A War of Nerves*, Ben Shephard quotes a prominent First World War psy-
    chiatrist who believed: '[shell shock is] a condition which is essentially child-
    ish and infantile in its nature. Rest in bed and simple encouragement is not
    enough to educate a child. Progressive daily achievement is the only way
    whereby manhood and self-respect can be regained.' Chris has lost his last
    chance at childhood with the cure of his shell shock. The 'infantile' state, so
    defined at this time by being inarticulate, is correlated to the shell-shocked
    soldier who, when 'he attempts to speak he stutters and stammers in the
    most appalling way' (74).

13 For readers interested in a Freudian approach to the story, see Wyatt
    Bonikowski and Misha Kavka. Bonikowski discusses West's desire to distance
    her novel from Freudian theories at the same time as he applies Freud's
    theories to analyse the novel in effective ways. He looks at the death drive
    in Chris, which requires him to face the death of his son and then face his
    own death at war. He looks at the 'repressed passion' and 'sexual excess' of
    Jenny the narrator (530). Misha Kavka also considers Freud's impact
    on West and offers a detailed treatment of the death of the two-year-old son
    and what this means in terms of Chris's grief. Where Kavka and I differ in
    our reading of the story is in the role of Chris's parents and the shift that oc-
    curs in their relationship to *their* son, according to Woolf's sense that mod-
    ernism results on one level from a change in relations between parent and
    child. Kavka concludes that the novel deals with gender relations, with an
    interesting shift occurring between the 'masculine order' and the 'maternal
    body.' For further work on gender, specifically feminism in West's novel, see
    Laura Cowen.

14 First World War psychiatrist Dr Henry Head explains the specific suffering
    of the officer: 'in the British army he has to think of his men as a father
    thinks of his children. It is to a great extent anxiety on behalf of others. It is
    this sense of responsibility which makes so many young officers break down'
    (Shephard 57).

15 Stetz argues that it is only the wine of adult truth that belongs to reality;
    thus, she concludes: 'West's interest lies more in the development of a
    coherent philosophy by which to live than in her protagonist's emotional
    development' (71). Alternatively, I find the emotional development funda-
    mental in the novella. I prefer the synchrony that West and Derrida write of:
    the milk of childhood and the wine of adulthood, neither privileged over
    the other and both contributing to the construction of the self.

16 Victoria Glendinning maintains that the novella 'turns entirely on the partial amnesia of a shell-shocked officer, and the healing significance of parenthood' (65). The significance is explored on every level in the novella; however, West ends *The Return of the Soldier* with parenthood's sickening infection, not cure.

4 Childhood Grief on the Home Front: Ford Madox Ford's *The Good Soldier* and *Parade's End*

1 For readers interested in a Freudian analysis of *The Good Soldier* see Eugene Goodheart, who notes that although there is no evidence that Ford read Freud, nonetheless there has been discussion of how he anticipated and perhaps responded to his theories. Goodheart does not discuss the figure of the child or the role of childhood.

2 For a summary of the debate about *Parade's End*'s being a trilogy versus a tetralogy, see Michela Calderaro, who outlines, in terms important for my approach, that *The Last Post* is an integral final text, since it describes 'both the crisis of discourse and the crisis of the novelist who can no longer find the words with which to express the old world and who is still looking for a new language to represent a new world' (22).

3 In *Circumfession*, when Derrida writes the 'story of [his] stories,' he calls keeping the child / adult bond alive his 'synchrony' (75). In this grieving work, in a final poetic passage he seems to address this child-self directly: 'you the floating toy at high tide and under the moon, you the crossing between these two phantoms of witnesses who will never come down to the same' (315). Concerned, like Ford, with witnessing, Derrida implies that the double perspective of haunting is the source of otherness within the self. The child's play, the 'toy,' acts as a kind of crossroads if one can keep it vivid; this child's perspective is key in Ford's novels, as will be examined in this chapter.

4 The critical tradition surrounding Edward Ashburnham reveals a continuing belief in the dignity and beauty of suppressing emotions. Robert Huntley reads Ashburnham as a 'latter-day feudalist' with an 'active sense of communal responsibility and aristocratic leadership' that is lost in the modern age (175). R.W. Lid concurs that 'the real source of the trouble is the inadequacy of the values and conventions of the characters to a changing and almost necessarily hypocritical society in which they live' (78). Richard Cassell argues: 'Ashburnham is the only one able to meet a real moral test. He is the victim of the three women who surround him and of sheer bad luck' (156). John Meixner sees Ashburnham's wife, Leonora, as a villain

who sees her husband's 'generosities' as a 'wild extravagance' ('Saddest
Story' 73). Peter Childs supports this view: 'The comic absurdity of this state
of affairs is the result of the debasing of old values and the frustration or
perversion of emergent, new ones' (159). Carl Rollyson sees Ashburnham
as 'an innocent' (25). Ashburnham is many things, but innocent he is not.
His generosities are better defined as infidelity: the buying and selling
of young women, including his foster-daughter; prostitution; and gambling
away his estate. Ashburnham continues to seduce into the twenty-first century. It is quite remarkable that he is seen as an old-style hero, in a setting
where modernism is the villain. Ford's contradictory, grieving / good soldier bears closer scrutiny.

5 According to Max Saunders's biography, Ford knew first hand the effects of
a violent father: 'Helen Rossetti, perhaps identified another source of his
childhood terrors in his father's disciplining, when she recalled how her
visits to the Hueffers were made unpleasant by '"old Franz's bullying of the
boys" – something Ford characteristically never complained of' (32).

6 Derrida discovers in the 'experience of this time of reading' the works of
Louis Marin, for whom he mourns, that his friend is 'all the while mobilizing a corpus' (*WM* 161). The link between writing, reading, and being
moved is clear.

7 Saunders reads *The Good Soldier* as involved in exploring 'the interests and
torments of sex' (405). Sondra Stang imagines Edward's suicide as 'the atro-
phy of sexual power through disuse and paralysis,' which is surprising, since
the man conducts many affairs (82).

8 As an antidote to the critical tradition that idealizes Ashburnham, Robert
Green points to the dual conduct of the good soldier: Ford 'renders the
tension between the world of an idealised, romanticised aristocracy and the
reality of debts, mortgages, and marital dishonour' (77–8).

9 In a letter from the front to Lucy Masterman, Ford complains that no one
has been writing to him and he worries about becoming 'a ghost' (*Letters*
75; see also 84). The onslaught of firing guns becomes too much; after a few
lines, his 'hand is shaking badly,' and he signs off with a joke about the guns
popping up 'out of baby's rattles & tea cosy' (75). It is effectively jarring
that in his lonely, frightened letter, near violent death, Ford writes of infants
and home.

10 Writing of Sarah Kofman, Derrida speaks of her conjuring death, 'which
implies both to conjure it up and conjure it away, to summon ghosts and
chase them away, always in the name of life' (*WM* 171). Derrida imagines
Kofman's suicide in an affirming way, which forms a clear contrast to the
function of suicide in Ford's novel. The ghostly child who haunts Kofman is

spoken to, written about, permitted to laugh and offered comfort when crying. Derrida writes that one of the lessons taught by Kofman is that 'this tormented being laughed a lot,' and she laughs 'like a little girl shaken by the
irresistible joy of uncontrollable laughter on the verge of tears, a little girl
whose kept secret does not age' (174). The child's secret is kept as part of
childhood; it does not become absorbed into the adult self or suppressed.

11 Stang mentions him once (111). John Onions refers to Tietjens's son only
   in passing to highlight the character's inability to articulate his feelings;
   moreover, he says that Tietjens 'permits his own character to be blackened
   in order to protect Sylvia' (132). Tietjens hates Sylvia, but loves his son,
   and his goal is to protect him. Despite writing insightfully about Tietjens,
   Onions cannot fully contend with this character or with Ford's thoughts on
   war while eliding the child in the text. Of course this is an easy omission to
   make, since Ford makes the boy a present absence throughout.

12 Derrida feels a comparable return when he is shocked by Sarah Kofman's
   suicide: he 'had to try to relearn everything' and, as he writes the piece, he
   is 'still at it' (*WM* 172).

13 Sebastian Knowles notes the deconstructive trend when the house of
   Tietjens 'search[es] for an heir and end[s] up with a bastard' (208). Like
   Derrida, Ford exposes the ruse of the proper name, which convention sees
   as the mark of individuality when, in fact, it is more significantly a 'linguistic-
   social classification' (*G* 111).

5 Creating a Space for Childhood's Sound Waves: Virginia Woolf's *A Haunted House* and *The Waves*

1 The one exception to this is the narrating child-voice of Antoinette at the
  outset of *Wide Sargasso Sea*. Although Rhys worked on this novel throughout
  her writing life, she did not publish it until 1966; thus, it differs from the
  other four novellas published in the modernist era between the two wars.

2 There have been some key references to Woolf's use of child figures and
  some others to her addressing grief. As noted, in a 1919 book review Ford
  Madox Ford defines Woolf's fiction as articulating the 'unmistakable voice of
  one's childhood' (*Essays* 188). Some critics read Woolf as drawing on a 'childlike consciousness' and as fascinated with Proust's recapture of lost time
  (Goodenough 227; Stevenson 105); others detail her own psychological tri-
  als with grief in response to personal losses (Spilka 2). Most notably, Daniel
  Ferrer identifies Woolf's recall of the 'forgotten past, the child's attitude in
  all its ambivalence, which takes itself into the present and transforms the
  character into a battlefield' (14). Hermione Lee, in her remarkable

biography of Woolf, explains that 'one of the most powerful impulses in her writing' was 'to write not just about childhood but *as if a child*' (23).

3 Karen Schneider argues that 'Woolf traced the roots of war to divisive, adversarial habits of mind – paradigms of difference and opposition of which the male-female dichotomy seemed the most fundamental' (109). Elizabeth Abel also investigates Woolf's anticipation of war in terms of her reading of Freud and her understanding of imposed gender roles (103–7). In the following chapter, I add to this adversarial habit of mind the way in which adults saw and related to children. I believe that this too was explored by Woolf in her fiction as a contributing factor to war.

4 Harvena Richter explores the meaning for Woolf of the moth and concludes that it is 'the very motion of creativity' (209).

5 Anna Snaith notes a break in the either / or categories, as Woolf articulates what seems unspeakable; she maintains that the 'dichotomy between utterance and internal articulation is one of many which free indirect discourse deconstructs' (68).

6 The editors of Derrida's texts of mourning identify a comparable impulse in the philosopher: contending with his sorrow. Derrida feels a 'responsibility, to speak not only *of* but *with* or even *to* the dead'; he expresses a 'desire to tear the fabric of language that would reduce the dead to the living, the other to the same' (Braut and Naas 25).

7 Instead of rigid adherence to structures, Derrida offers 'the movement of *différance*' in order to shake up 'the oppositional concepts that mark our language, such as, to take only a few examples, sensible / intelligible, intuition / signification, nature / culture' (*P* 9).

8 For a discussion of this description of the photographs in terms of gender ideology see Abel (89–94).

9 Woolf's sister, Vanessa Bell, writes in response to *The Waves*, which on one level is an elegy for their brother Thoby, who died as a young man: 'if you wouldn't think me foolish I should say you have found the "lullaby capable of singing him to rest"' (367). Bell's comparison of the novel to a lullaby recognizes that Woolf may compensate for a lack of parental compassion in the world; thus, the novel is partially written for a wounded childhood, in an attempt to compensate for an absent mother. The family, as is well documented in scholarly work, mourned intensely for the premature death of Woolf's mother. Two different recent essays are excellent starting points for readers interested in pursuing the biographical angle of Woolf's experience with grief; see Dalsimer and Dalgarno.

10 Helen Wussow's argument that 'Woolf mocks the self-centred imperialism represented by Percival' requires suppressing Percival's preschool years,

which is easy to do because Woolf never provides any interior monologue for him, and the other children never reference his family (111).

11 Henry Alley uses the term 'omnibus' to characterize Woolf's seemingly disjointed yet encompassing narrative technique in *Mrs. Dalloway*. Its fragmented style, which nonetheless conveys a 'connection between minds,' is relevant to the approach of the pieces in *A Haunted House* as well (401).

12 In *Circumfession,* Derrida offers a scripted and visual correlative for this story. He writes on the left lower margin, 'this dream in me, since always, of another language,' and on the opposite page he has a picture of himself as a child at about age three sitting in a toy automobile (4–5). He provokes the reader to consider the child on the cusp of language acquisition, which means bypassing his early childhood self and all the attendant feelings that were never put into words. The car, a mere toy, is nonetheless a signifier, like an omnibus for moving, for acceleration, for being grown up and going places.

13 Drawing on Derridean theories of reading, Patricia Laurence asserts that Woolf is 'the first woman novelist in Modernity to practice silence rather than speech' (1–11).

14 Karen DeMeester describes Woolf as 'drawing her narratives from the characters' prespeech levels of consciousness' as a way to preserve 'the fragmentation of consciousness that occurs in the aftermath of trauma' (650).

15 One of Derrida's key concepts is the 'mark,' as Niall Lucy explains: 'Derrida's argument turns on the recognition that any "mark" – anything that could be (or is recognised as) a sign, spoken or written, linguistic or otherwise semiotic – must be able to be repeated and thus *re*-marked' (*Debating* 24). Woolf clearly explores similar lines in her story, which re-marks upon the mark.

16 Claire Tylee notes that the 'society which Virginia Woolf describes in *Mrs. Dalloway* is one which suppresses emotion, especially grief' (155). Without developing this idea further, since her focus is on gender norms, Tylee makes a connection between Septimus's repressed 'grief' and his inability to maintain 'the charade' any longer when his wife asks him about having children (163). Woolf makes the idea of an infant trigger the shell-shocked soldier's unravelling; this is relevant to her explorations of childhood, grief, and good soldiers in *The Waves*.

17 Although she treats the absence in terms of desire rather than grief, Elizabeth Abel nonetheless presents a relevant counterpoint to the shell shock of the First World War in the 'tableau of female loss' in Clarissa Dalloway's almost absent childhood (31–2).

18 Suzanne Raitt sees Woolf herself employing such a strategy, for she finds in the diaries 'a history of grief and recovery' (33).

19 Marcus remarks on Percival's 'fall from a donkey' (151); yet in Woolf's novel his fall is from a horse: 'He fell. His horse tripped' (*W* 101). This seems like a petty detail, but if we recall John Hulcoop's detailed research on Woolf's ideas about heroism and her use of horse imagery, it requires a rethinking of Percival as some simple allegorical figure for imperialism. Hulcoop reveals that 'the magnanimous hero on horseback' who appears throughout her writing career, in both masculine and feminine forms, thereby forming 'one of the most powerful symbols in Woolf's work,' is connected to her brother Thoby (for whom this novel is thought to be a 'lullaby') (471).

20 Toril Moi, invoking Derrida, expresses an alternative to this interpretation: 'In her own textual practice, Woolf exposes the way in which language refuses to be pinned down to an underlying essential meaning.' And more precisely for my concerns, she asks: 'For what can this self-identical identity be if all meaning is a ceaseless play of difference, if *absence* as much as presence is the foundation of meaning?' (9).

21 Julia Briggs calls this the 'egotistical stage of the nursery,' which reminds us of the deeply ingrained social belief that children need, for society's sake, to tone down their egoism and the attendant intense emotions that accompany it (76). In contrast, in her memoir of early childhood, Woolf writes: 'I feel that strong emotion must leave its trace' (*MB* 67). 'Trace,' like 'mark,' is another key word for Derrida. Gayatri Spivak details its meaning for him: 'Derrida's trace is the mark of the absence of a presence, an always already absent present, of the lack at the origin that is the condition of thought and experience' (introd. xvii). This has a great deal of resonance for Woolf's sense of strong emotion and the traces of it from childhood to adulthood.

22 Woolf may allude to one of Captain F.S. Brereton's forty-eight novels, entitled *With Shield and Assegai*. Hynes reports that this military surgeon produced a voluble amount of literature all of which was similar and had certain didactic purposes: 'Brereton's villains are there partly to reveal the weakness, the disunity, the softness of England' (44).

23 Kathy Phillips discovers the word *assegais* in Leonard Woolf's *Empire and Commerce*, in which he criticizes the way in which 'irresponsible [European] traders armed with rifles believe it's their right and duty to exploit Africans armed with assegais' (Woolf 353; Phillips 180).

24 Often quoted and discussed is Woolf's diary entry: 'I have an idea that I will invent a new name for my books to supplant "novel." A new—by Virginia Woolf. But what? Elegy?' (III.34). Vanessa Bell comes closest I think to naming this new genre, for certainly in *The Waves* Woolf composes an elegiac lullaby mourning Thoby and the lost possibilities of childhood.

25 As Judith Lee points out, this passage 'calls to mind the bodily destruction evidenced on a battlefield' (188). This is not the first time Woolf has used

this pattern. Earlier, Bernard goes to St Paul's and hears 'one boy's voice,' which 'wails round the dome like some lost and wandering dove,' while beneath it are 'warriors at rest under their old banners' (*W* 190).

6 The 'Laughtears' of the Child Be Longing: James Joyce's *Finnegans Wake*

1 Carol Shloss, through the lens of biography, sees the *Wake* as 'both an expropriation of a child's experience and an act of atonement for it' (391).

2 For a more thorough discussion of Derrida and the way in which he writes about Joyce's funerary statue in *The Post Card*, see McArthur. For a discussion of Joyce's *Finnegans Wake* and Derrida's *Glas*, see Roughley, who explores how, at 'the level of the text's overall structure, Derrida's writing deconstructs the form in which that writing is presented in ways that continue his investigation of such notions as presence, existence, unity, and mimesis as they are articulated in language' (44).

3 Shari Benstock puts Joyce and Derrida in dialogue, for they both: 'raise questions concerning the impulse to write and examine the authority on which writing rests.' She seeks to reveal the 'route (root) of desire that writing traces.' In this context, she quotes from Derrida's *La Carte Postale*: 'Le désir – de cette histoire des postes mondiales n'est peut-être qu'une façon, très enfantine, de pleurer la fin prochaine de notre "correspondance"' (Derrida 74; Benstock 170). Changing the focus from desire to grief, my emphasis will be on the childish, silenced (*enfantine*) way we cry about endings and losses (*pleurer la fin*). Thus, as discussed throughout this study, we write correspondence for the child, since the 'problematic of child language and consciousness is radically signified by *enfant*, the French term for child, and its Latin cognate *infans*, "unspeaking"' (Goodenough, Heberle, and Sokoloff 3).

4 See the letter to Harriet Shaw Weaver in Roland McHugh's *Annotations* (219).

5 Simon Carnell maintains that Joyce's anti-fascist stance reverses other modernist plans to harden the heart and respond with discipline (153). Geert Lernout in his genetic research on the *Wake's* opening finds that 'the first chapter centers from its earliest drafts on the issue of war' (59).

6 When working on Joyce's final text, I draw repeatedly on Roland McHugh's *Annotations to* Finnegans Wake. The *Annotations* match every line and page of the *Wake*, and if I try to document McHugh each time I address a passage from the text, it would be too cumbersome. The reader may assume that, each time I analyse an allusion to the text or offer glosses based on the blend of languages, McHugh's notes supply vital information. I depend throughout on his research, knowledge, and insight.

7 As John Bishop demonstrates, the *Wake* 'impinges everywhere on the amnesic domain of "childhide" (483. 31 [a deeply "hidden" "childhood"])' that has the capacity to rejuvenate the sleeping self (319–20). As Grace Eckley's research supports, the *Wake* is packed full of children's lore in the form of fairy tales, toys, games, contemporary events, and nursery rhymes.

8 Derrida writes a letter to Francine Loreau in response to the death of her husband, Max. He reflects on the dead poet's 'unrelenting desire' as 'the rending cry that separates language from itself at its birth, on the verge of articulation' (*WM* 95). While grieving, Derrida singles out the paradoxical eloquence of the inarticulate infant in the poet's work: the presence of the cry becomes forever absent as language is acquired; yet it is this cry we know and seek to hear.

9 Allyson Booth describes the disorientation of soldiers returning from war in terms of language: 'When veterans returned to England, the language of civilians there seems to have become as inaccessible as the language of the French or Germans must have been at the front.' In reference to *All Quiet on the Western Front*, she discusses the bond between soldiers as being like 'a child listening to the voices of his parents at night' (32). In other words, Joyce's sense in *Finnegans Wake* that language forms bonds as much as it isolates, so that the news may sound to us as confusing as the adult language spoken to a child in a nursery, is not so surprising. Moreover, as we have seen in other novels in this study as well as in the *Wake*, there is a disturbing collapse in the distinction between the home and the home front.

10 Sidney Feshbach identifies the theme of the home as 'unsafe' in Joyce's fiction as a key component of the depiction of Stephen Dedalus as a child in *A Portrait of the Artist as a Young Man* (8–9).

11 Moshe Gold analyses Joyce's use of the myth of Cadmus as a way 'to express the cultural constellation of parenting, violence, law, and the alphabets of his world' (286). Notably for my concerns, Gold believes that Joyce's text was meant to produce 'one specific child: the actual printed book of *Finnegans Wake*' (269). He argues that Shem's use of the 'lifewand' refers to the male sex organ; thus, he 'writes with his penis' (286). While I am less concerned with the production of the child and more focused on the rearing of the child, I find Gold's research, in terms of textual production, confirms my reading of the babbling child figure of the *Wake*. As Gold explains: 'Vico sees the overall meaning of Cadmus as "a grand example of the inarticulateness with which the still infant world laboured to express itself,"' which he sees as Joyce's way of linking 'parenting, violence, law, and the alphabets of his world' as a 'cultural constellation' throughout the 'inarticulate discourse' of the *Wake* (272).

12 For a discussion of Lewis's dread of the label 'womanly,' which can be related in interesting ways to his disgust with a fictional focus on children, see Phillips.

13 Scholarly work on Lewis concentrates on his belief that Joyce was 'obsessed with time and unconcerned with space.' See, for instance, R.J. Schork's essay 'Generic Primer' for a discussion of 'Joyce's hostile critic Wyndham Lewis' (125). See also Luca Crispi's chapter in the same volume, 'Storiella as She Was Wryt' for a precise treatment of the timing of Lewis's and Joyce's literary disagreement. Critics have not yet discussed Joyce's response to the assessment of his 'child-cult.'

14 Schork identifies this allusion to the *Aeneid* in a letter Joyce wrote to Harriet Weaver where, in a discussion of his work on *Finnegans Wake*, he quotes Virgil: 'Though I shall feel like Eneas [*sic*] when invited by Dido to tell his tale *"Infandum regina, iubes renovare doloren." Nevertheless he told it*' (*Letters* III.73). Schork translates: 'You order me, Queen, to make new unutterable sorrow' (137).

15 For a discussion of Babel in Joyce and Derrida, see Alan Roughley, whose work also contains an inclusion of Shari Benstock's and Murray McArthur's thoughts on this subject (37–43). Since none of these writers has discussed the child's role, I add this figure to the discussion.

16 Geoffrey Bennington privileges this kind of grieving. He assigns Derrida's term 'incorporation' to this experience of grief: 'the other remain[s] in me like a foreign body, living dead' (146). Derrida describes this kind of grief in *Circumfession*: he incorporates the language of the child, the ignorant, inarticulate words and letters that belonged to him and that no one can take away. They cannot impose a sacred tongue on him or a national one. The spectral child, like the friends he mourns, are figures he incorporates and maintains as foreign, as other; he does not assimilate or annul them. Instead, he speaks to and with them for they are the *living* dead.

17 For a discussion of the way in which Joyce predates and parallels Freud's theories in 'Mourning and Melancholia' see Gana. The focus of the study is on mania and suicide rather than children's grief. Gana has written an-other excellent article on mourning in *Dubliners*, which argues that 'the figure of prosopopoeia in Joyce's story,' 'The Dead,' functions 'to thwart' the 'Freudian work of mourning' (160). One learns from Gana's work that Joyce was not merely working within the Freudian paradigm; instead, he was offering different, innovative ways of understanding grief's function.

18 Cork is the birthplace of Joyce's father; thus, the oppressive bond between parent and child in this line verges on an autobiographical comment. For a discussion of early Freudian readings of *A Portrait of the Artist as a Young Man* see Troy.

19 As Christine Van Boheemen-Saaf maintains: 'The sole strategy of survival
   for the child deprived of personal speech (and by extension the colonial
   subject invaded by the hegemonic language) is therefore, paradoxically, to
   cling to language, to speech, even if in his state of shattered anxiety the only
   words available are the ones sounding the trauma' (63). In his exploration
   of childhood trauma, Derrida concurs with a concise, haunting confession:
   'I love words too much because I have no language of my own' (*C* 92).

20 Carol Shloss's brilliant study of Lucia Joyce's life adds a tragic dimension
   to what paralysis may have meant to Joyce in the *Wake*: 'Her behavior was
   called "catatonia" – the refusal of gesture – which, in the case of a dancer, is
   an extraordinary form of eloquence' (219).

21 Reading Max Loreau's poetry, then writing to his widow, Derrida explains
   that he 'could feel something in *int* breaking through in these texts,
   around the *inti*mate, the *int*erior, and the po*int*' (*WM* 103). The sensual
   self hears the wounding sound that opens up the self to the voices of those
   lost and unable to respond. Constantly positioning himself as listening to
   those he mourns, Derrida here 'feels' through language's sounds rather
   than thinks about the meaning of words. Essentially, he listens like a pre-
   verbal child: words are sounds, and his return to this previous self who is
   'interior' and 'intimate' allows for the rending and breaking that express
   his grief. David Hayman imagines Joyce's paternal character in the *Wake* in
   comparable terms: 'It seems [he] "hears" with an inner ear' and thus becomes the 'silent collector of oral histories' (258).

22 Rather than establish blame or expose a villain, Joyce's approach seems
   more Derridean, as Peggy Kamuf explains: deconstruction is the work
   by which 'institutions, which are not just linguistic institutions, are
   being opened to the difference or exteriority repressed – forgotten in a
   strong sense – within them' (introd. xvii).

23 Joyce seems more interested in what Niall Lucy sees as the fundamental
   concern of deconstruction, which is 'the will to question' (*Dictionary* 37).
   John Paul Riquelme notes that the end of the childhood phase of *A Portrait
   of the Artist as a Young Man* is Stephen's 'communion with nature and with
   his fellow students' after standing up for himself, when abused by Father
   Dolan, by speaking to the Rector (117). Notably for my purposes, Joyce also
   details how Stephen's father mocks his son by turning his articulation of suffering into a story to amuse other adults.

24 The son being a 'twig of the hider that tanned him' appears in a section
   that Joyce renders personal by recording his initials, 'A.A.' (Joyce's middle
   names, Augustine Aloysius). In this section, which I will look at in detail
   later, A.A. is connected to Aeneas, whom Joyce compares himself to, as they
   both tell tales of 'unutterable sorrow.'

25 Derrida argues for a similar depth in one of Sarah Kofman's books: 'to affirm this truth of life through the symptom of repression, to express the
irrepressible as it is put to the test of repression, to get, in a word, the better
of life, that is to say, of death, giving an account of life: to defeat death by affirming a "hold on the truth of life"' (*WM* 176). Positioning himself here as
'an anguished scholar,' Derrida reaches out to Kofman's truth through her
suffering, through the necessity for her as a child to repress the truth to survive. When he writes in response to Jean-François Lyotard's death, Derrida's
choice of words reminds us that the truth of grief resides underground: 'the
unthinkable itself, in the depths of tears' (*WM* 214).

26 Likewise, at the end of the *Dubliners* story 'Clay,' Joe's grief is assuaged by
drinking: 'his eyes filled up so much with tears that he could not find what
he was looking for and in the end he had to ask his wife to tell him where
the corkscrew was' (102).

27 Joyce turns to the epic tradition and Derrida draws on St Augustine's
Confessions. He refers several times to the occasion when Augustine's
mother, Monica, sees her son 'overcome with grief' and he remains 'silent
and restrain[s] [his] tears' (*C* 20). Derrida quotes Augustine's concern with
grieving as a 'sin' and examines his worry about readers' feeling 'scornful'
in response to his sadness (49–50, 264–5). He quotes Augustine's command
to repress the 'flow' of his tears until his eyes 'were quite dry' (195). When
Derrida first hears of his own mother's pending death, he tries 'in vain not
only to cry but' also 'to stop [himself] from crying' (52–5). Derrida imagines
the *Confessions* as St Augustine's 'immense and finite sponge pregnant like a
memory with all the abandoned or held back tears' (106). While Augustine
uses this sponge to soak up his tears, Derrida clings to it, releasing the grief.
If Augustine's 'babyhood is long since dead,' Derrida will turn around to the
time before this death to the memorial pregnancy full of grief (85).

28 Joyce gives Homer, and thus the epic tradition, a nod in this scene by signalling the *Wake*'s great paternal figure, HCE, in his depiction of Howth Castle
as 'homerigh, castle and earthenhouse' (21.13).

29 Eckley shows Joyce's use of children's games in the episode and records a
wide range of references to grief as part of the game 'Sally Waters' (107).

30 For an understanding of Lucia Joyce's contribution to the Prankquean
episode, see Shloss (273). Relevant to my study is that, at the moment that
Lucia is reunited with her parents after being isolated for months in a mental health institution, Shloss records that she was 'distraught with grief and
beside herself with joy' (272). These are key terms for the Prankquean episode and the *Wake* as a whole.

31 Schork hears an echo of the *Aeneid*'s golden bough in the following line in
the *Wake*: 'let her be peace on the bough' (465.13–14). This is an interesting

possibility, since the golden bough is what allows Aeneas to discover the underworld and address the shades of Dido, fallen warriors, and his father. Joyce's reference to 'peace' here may suggest that peace is achieved through listening to and speaking with the dead, an important aspect of Derrida's mourning work.

32 In the light of Shloss's biographical study of Lucia Joyce, the 'girls' of the *Wake* take on further meaning (425–6). Important for my purposes, she reveals how Joyce and Lucia, parent and child, shared an ability to communicate, through art, what could not be said with words: 'The two communicate with a secret, unarticulated voice.' Moreover, Joyce 'understands the body to be the hieroglyphic of mysterious writing, the dancer's steps to be an alphabet of the inexpressible' (152).

33 Vicki Mahaffey pointed out the overlap between laughter and slaughter to me at the 2002 Joyce conference in Trieste.

34 Translation from the French by Roland McHugh.

35 Derrida quotes in *Circumfession* from his notebook, which quotes from Marvell's poem 'Eyes and Tears.' He anticipates Joyce's understanding of knowledge's relationship to grief: '*How wisely Nature did decree, With the same eyes to weep and see!*' (99).

36 For an elucidatory treatment of the funeral games of the *Wake* as constructed on ancient Irish rituals, see Gibson (134–78).

37 For a thorough discussion of Joyce's treatment of power ranging from Jove to Hitler, both being parts of the construction of HCE as an 'atrocious father,' see Beckman (48–62).

38 For a study of Joyce's references to Rome in the context of fascist aesthetics see Lilly.

39 For a treatment of this section of the *Wake*, which reaches a comparable conclusion – 'Butt is fully as warlike as the father-general he condemns' – see Beckman (121–51). Richard Beckman's analysis looks at children's revenge instead of grief; noting echoes from *Hamlet* in terms of revenge and aggression, he views this episode through the lens of Freud's *Totem and Taboo*. Thus, those interested in childhood aggression in the *Wake* would find this an excellent starting place. He concludes: 'Swearing to Jupiter with a mashy German accent calls up the terrible specter of the Great War and evokes the imperialist fascism that Joyce knew was brewing the next one [...] More than anything else, the father's rudeness and the sons' dread of their dreadful father lead to war itself and to the actual pulling of the trigger' (151).

40 For a discussion of the obscene in Joyce's works preceding *Finnegans Wake*, see Pease.

Bibliography

Abel, Elizabeth. *Virginia Woolf and the Fictions of Psychoanalysis*. Chicago: U of Chicago P, 1989.

Ackerman, Robert J. *Silent Sons: A Book For and About Men*. New York: Simon, 1993.

Alley, Henry. 'Mrs. Dalloway and Three of Its Contemporary Children.' *Papers on Language and Literature* 42.4 (2006): 401–19.

Angier, Carole. *Jean Rhys*. New York: Viking, 1985.

Ariès, Philippe. *Centuries of Childhood: A Social History of Family Life*. Trans. Robert Baldick. New York: Knopf, 1962.

Athill, Diana. *Stet: An Editor's Life*. London: Granta, 2000.

Baldwin, Debra Romanick. 'Politics, Martyrdom and the Legend of Saint Thekla in *Under Western Eyes*.' *Conradiana* 32.2 (2000): 144–57.

Balsamo, Gian. 'Mourning to Death: Love, Altruism, and Stephen Dedalus's Poetry of Grief.' *Literature and Theology* 21.4 (2007): 417–36.

Banfield, Ann. *The Phantom Table: Woolf, Fry, Russell and the Epistemology of Modernism*. Cambridge: Cambridge UP, 2000.

Barker, Francis. *The Tremulous Private Body: Essays on Subjection*. London: Methuen, 1984.

Bazin, Nancy Topping, and Jane Hamovit Lauter. 'Virginia Woolf's Keen Sensitivity to War: Its Roots and Its Impact on Her Novels.' *Virginia Woolf and War: Fiction, Reality, and Myth*. Ed. Mark Hussey. Syracuse: Syracuse UP, 1991.

Beckett, Samuel. *Endgame* and *Act Without Words*. Trans. Beckett. New York: Grove, 1958.

Beckman, Richard. *Joyce's Rare View: The Nature of Things in* Finnegans Wake. Gainesville: UP of Florida, 2007.

– 'Perils of Marriage in *Finnegans Wake*.' *James Joyce Quarterly* 33.1 (1995): 83–99.

Bell, Michael. 'The Metaphysics of Modernism.' *The Cambridge Companion to Modernism*. Ed. Michael Levenson. Cambridge: Cambridge UP, 1999.

Bell, Vanessa. *The Selected Letters of Vanessa Bell*. Ed. Regina Marler. London: Bloomsbury, 1993.

Benjamin, Walter. *Illuminations: Essays and Reflections*. Ed. Hannah Arendt. Trans. Harry Zohn. New York: Harcourt, 1968.

Bennington, Geoffrey. 'Derridabase.' *Jacques Derrida*. Trans. Geoffrey Bennington. Chicago: U of Chicago P, 1993.

Benstock, Shari. 'The Letter of the Law: *La Carte Postale* in *Finnegans Wake*.' *Philological Quarterly* 63 (1984): 163–85.

Bhabha, Homi. *The Location of Culture*. London: Routledge, 1994.

Bonikowski, Wyatt. '*The Return of the Soldier* Brings Death Home.' *Modern Fiction Studies* 51.3 (2005): 513–35.

Booth, Allyson. *Postcards from the Trenches: Negotiating the Space between Modernism and the First World War*. New York and Oxford: Oxford UP, 1996.

Bormanis, John. 'Lilith on the Liffey: Gender, Rebellion, and Anticolonialism in *Finnegans Wake*.' *James Joyce Quarterly* 34.4 (1997): 489–503.

Bowie, Malcolm. *Proust Among the Stars*. New York: Columbia UP, 1998.

Bradbury, Malcolm. *Modernism: A Guide to European Literature, 1890–1930*. Eds. Malcolm Bradbury and James McFarlane. London: Penguin, 1976.

– 'The Denuded Place: War and Form in *Parade's End* and *U.S.A.*' *The First World War in Fiction: A Collection of Critical Essays*. Ed. Holger Klein. London: Macmillan, 1976.

Bradshaw, David. 'The Socio-Political Vision of the Novels.' *The Cambridge Companion to Virginia Woolf*. Ed. Sue Roe and Susan Sellers. Cambridge: Cambridge UP, 2000.

Briggs, Julia. 'The Novels of the 1930s.' *The Cambridge Companion to Virginia Woolf*. Ed. Sue Roe and Susan Sellers. Cambridge: Cambridge UP, 2000.

Brivic, Sheldon. 'Reality as Fetish: The Crime in *Finnegans Wake*.' *James Joyce Quarterly* 34.4 (1997): 449–60.

Browning, Elizabeth Barrett. 'Grief.' *The Poetical Works of Elizabeth Barrett Browning*. Ed. Harriet Waters Preston. Boston: Houghton, 1974.

Burman, Erica. 'The Pedagogics of Post / Modernity: The Address to the Child as Political Subject and Object.' *Children in Culture: Approaches to Childhood*. Ed. Karín Lesnik-Oberstein. London: Macmillan; New York, St. Martin's, 1998.

Butler, Judith. *The Psychic Life of Power*. Stanford: Stanford UP, 1997.

Butler, Samuel. *The Way of All Flesh*. 2nd ed. London: Cape, 1922.

Calderaro, Michela A. *A Silent New World: Ford Madox Ford's* Parade's End. Bologna: Cooperativa Libraria Universitaria Editrice Bologna, 1993.

Cantwell, Mary. 'A Conversation with Jean Rhys.' *Critical Perspectives on Jean Rhys*. Ed. Pierrette Frickey. Washington, D.C.: Three Continents, 1990.

Caputo, John D. *The Prayers and Tears of Jacques Derrida: Religion without Religion*. Bloomington and Indianapolis: Indiana UP, 1997.

– 'Shedding Tears Beyond Being.' *Augustine and Postmodernism:* Confessions *and* Circumfession. Ed. John D. Caputo and Michael Scanlon. Bloomington and Indianapolis: Indiana UP, 2005.

Carabine, Keith. *The Life and the Art: A Study of Conrad's* Under Western Eyes. Amsterdam: Rodopi, 1996.

Caradine, David. 'Death and Grief in Modern Britain.' *Mirrors of Mortality: Studies in the Social History of Death*. Ed. Joachim Whaley. New York: St Martin's, 1981.

Carnell, Simon. '*Finnegans Wake*: "the most formidable anti-fascist book produced between the two wars ... "?' Finnegans Wake: 'teems of times.' Ed. Andrew Treip. Amsterdam: Rodopi, 1994.

Carr, Helen. *Jean Rhys*. Plymouth: Northcote, 1996.

Cassell, Richard A. *Ford Madox Ford: A Study of His Novels*. Baltimore: Johns Hopkins UP, 1961.

Chambers, Ross. *Facing It: Aids Diaries and the Death of the Author*. Ann Arbor: U of Michigan P, 1998.

Chase, Karen, and Michael Levenson. *The Spectacle of Intimacy: A Public Life for the Victorian Family*. Princeton: Princeton UP, 2000.

Cheng, Vincent J. 'English Behaviour and Repression: 'A Call: The Tale of Two Passions.' Ford Madox Ford: A Reappraisal*. Ed. Robert Hampson and Tony Davenport. Amsterdam: Rodopi, 2002.

– *Joyce, Race, and Empire*. Cambridge: Cambridge UP, 1995.

Childs, Peter. *Modernism*. London: Routledge, 2000.

Choy, Wayson. *The Jade Peony*. Vancouver: Douglas & McIntyre, 1995.

Christ, Grace Hyslop. *Healing Children's Grief*. Oxford: Oxford UP, 2000.

Clark, Hilary. '"Legibly depressed": Shame, Mourning, and Melancholia in *Finnegans Wake*.' James Joyce Quarterly 34.4 (1997): 461–71.

Cobley, Evelyn. *Representing War: Form and Ideology in First World War Narratives*. Toronto: U of Toronto P, 1993.

Cole, Susan Letzler. *The Absent One: Mourning Ritual, Tragedy, and the Performance of Ambivalence*. University Park and London: Pennsylvania State UP, 1985.

Conley, Tim. '"Oh me none onsens!": *Finnegans Wake* and the Negation of Meaning.' James Joyce Quarterly 39.2 (2002): 233–49.

Conrad, Joseph. *The Collected Letters of Joseph Conrad*. Ed. Frederick R. Karl and Laurence Davies. 4 vols. Cambridge: Cambridge UP, 1983–90.

– *A Personal Record*. London: Dent, 1919.

– 'The Secret Sharer.' *Twixt Land and Sea.* London: Penguin, 1978.

– *Under Western Eyes* (*UWE*). London: Dent, 1923.

Cowen, Laura. 'The Fine Frenzy of Artistic Vision: Rebecca West's *The Return of the Soldier* as a Feminist Analysis of World War I.' *Centennial Review* 42 (1998): 285–308.

Crane, Stephen. *The Red Badge of Courage.* New York: Bantam, 1983.

Crispi, Luca. 'Storiella as She Was Wryt: *Chapter II.2.' How Joyce Wrote* Finnegans Wake: *A Chapter-by-Chapter Genetic Guide.* Madison: U of Wisconsin P, 2007.

Crispi, Luca, with Sam Slote and Dirk Van Hulle. 'Introduction.' *How Joyce Wrote* Finnegans Wake: *A Chapter-by-Chapter Genetic Guide.* Madison: U of Wisconsin P, 2007.

Cunningham, Michael. *The Hours.* New York: Farrar, Straus and Giroux, 2002.

Dalgarno, Emily. 'Ideology into Fiction: Virginia Woolf's "A Sketch of the Past."' *Novel: A Forum on Fiction* 27.2 (1994): 175–95.

Dalsimer, Katherine. 'The Vicissitudes of Mourning.' *Psychoanalytic Study of the Child* 49 (1994): 394–411.

Davidson, Arnold E. *Jean Rhys.* New York: Ungar, 1985.

Deakin, Motley F. *Rebecca West.* Boston: Hall, 1980.

DeMeester, Karen. 'Trauma and Recovery in Virginia Woolf's *Mrs. Dalloway.' Modern Fiction Studies* 44.3 (1998): 649–73.

Derrida, Jacques. *Acts of Literature* (*L*). Ed. Derek Attridge. New York: Routledge, 1992.

– *Circumfession* (*C*). *Jacques Derrida.* Trans. Geoffrey Bennington. Chicago: U of Chicago P, 1993.

– 'Deconstruction and the Other.' *Dialogues with Contemporary Continental Thinkers.* Ed. Richard Kearney. Manchester: Manchester UP, 1984.

– 'Différance' (*D*). *Speech and Phenomena.* Trans. David B. Alison. Evanston: Northwestern UP, 1973.

– *Dissemination.* Trans. Barbara Johnson. Chicago: U of Chicago P, 1981.

– *Margins of Philosophy* (*MP*). Trans. Alan Bass. Chicago: U of Chicago P, 1982.

– *Memoires for Paul de Man.* Rev. ed. Trans. Cecile Lindsay, Jonathan Culler, Eduardo Cadava, and Peggy Kamuf. New York: Columbia UP, 1989.

– *Of Grammatology.* Trans. Gayatri C. Spivak. Baltimore: Johns Hopkins UP, 1976.

– *Positions* (*P*). Trans. Alan Bass. Chicago: U of Chicago P, 1981.

– *The Post Card: From Socrates to Freud and Beyond.* Trans. Alan Bass. Chicago: U of Chicago P, 1987.

– 'Psyche: Inventions of the Other.' Trans. Catherine Porter. *A Derrida Reader: Between the Blinds.* Ed. Peggy Kamuf. New York: Columbia UP, 1991. 200–20.

– *Specters of Marx: The State of the Debt, the Work of Mourning, and the New International* (*S*). Trans. Peggy Kamuf. New York: Routledge, 1994.

– 'The Time Is Out of Joint.' Trans. Peggy Kamuf. *Deconstruction Is / in*
America. Ed. Anselm Haverkamp. New York: New York UP, 1995.
– 'Two Words for Joyce.' *Post-Structuralist Joyce: Essays from the French*. Ed. Derek
Attridge and Daniel Ferrer. Cambridge: Cambridge UP, 1984.
– 'Tympan' (*T*). Trans. Alan Bass. *A Derrida Reader: Between the Blinds*.
Ed. Peggy Kamuf. New York: Columbia UP, 1991.
– *The Work of Mourning* (*WM*). Ed. Pascale-Anne Brault and Michael Naas.
Chicago: U of Chicago P, 2001.
– *Writing and Difference* (*WD*). Trans. Alan Bass. Chicago: U. of Chicago P, 1978.
de Vries, Hent. 'Instances.' *Augustine and Postmodernism:* Confessions *and*
Circumfession. Ed. John D. Caputo and Michael Scanlon. Bloomington and
Indianapolis: Indiana UP, 2005.
Dick, Susan. 'Literary Realism.' *The Cambridge Companion to Virginia Woolf*.
Ed. Sue Roe and Susan Sellers. Cambridge: Cambridge UP, 2000.
Draine, Betsy. 'Chronotope and Intertext: The Case of Jean Rhys' *Quartet.'*
Influence and Intertextuality in Literary History. Ed. Jay Clayton and Eric
Rothstein. Madison: U of Wisconsin P, 1991.
Dyregrov, Atle. *Grief in Children: A Handbook for Adults*. London: Jessica
Kingsley, 1991.
Eagleton, Terry. *William Shakespeare*. Oxford: Blackwell, 1986.
Eddins, Dwight. 'The Iniquities of the Fathers: Ted Hughes and the Great War.'
World War I and the Cultures of Modernity. Ed. Douglas Mackaman and Michael
Mays. Jackson: UP of Mississippi, 2000.
Eckley, Grace. *Children's Lore in* Finnegans Wake. Syracuse: Syracuse UP, 1985.
Eide, Marian. 'The Language of Flows: Fluidity, Virology, and *Finnegans Wake.'*
James Joyce Quarterly 34.4 (1997): 473–88.
Eksteins, Modris. *Rites of Spring: The Great War and the Birth of the Modern Age*.
Toronto: Lester & Orpen Dennys, 1989.
Emery, Mary Lou. *Jean Rhys at 'World's End': Novels of Colonial and Sexual Exile*.
Austin: U of Texas P, 1990.
Fanon, Franz. *The Wretched of the Earth*. New York: Grove, 1968.
Ferrer, Daniel. *Virginia Woolf and the Language of Madness*. Trans. Geoffrey
Bennington and Rachel Bowlby. London: Routledge, 1990.
Feshbach, Sidney. 'The Magic Lantern of Tradition in *A Portrait of the Artist as
a Young Man.' Joyce Studies Annual 1996*. Ed. Thomas F. Staley. Austin: U of
Texas P, 1996.
Fincham, Gail. '"To make you see": Narration and Focalization in *Under
Western Eyes.' Joseph Conrad: Voice, Sequence, History, Genre*. Ed. Jakob Lothe,
Jeremy Hawthorn, and James Phelan. Columbus: Ohio State UP, 2008.
Findley, Timothy. *The Wars*. Markham, Ont.: Penguin, 1978.

Fletcher, John and Malcolm Bradbury. 'The Introverted Novel.' *Modernism: A Guide to European Literature, 1890–1930*. Ed. Malcolm Bradbury and James McFarlane. London: Penguin, 1976.

Ford, Ford Madox. *A Call: The Tale of Two Passions*. London: Chatto, 1910.

– *Critical Essays*. Ed. Max Saunders and Richard Stang. Manchester: Carcanet, 2002.

– *The Good Soldier* (*GS*). New York: Random, 1989.

– *Letters of Ford Madox Ford*. Ed. Richard M. Ludwig. Princeton: Princeton UP, 1965.

– *Parade's End* (*PE*). New York: Penguin, 1982.

Forster, E.M. *Aspects of the Novel*. Ed. Oliver Stallybrass. London: Penguin, 1962.

Fothergill, Anthony. 'Signs, Interpolations, Meanings: Conrad and the Politics of Utterance.' *Conrad and Theory*. Ed. Andrew Gibson and Robert Hampson. Amsterdam: Rodopi, 1998.

Fraser, Gail. *Interweaving Patterns in the Works of Joseph Conrad*. Ann Arbor: UMI Research P, 1988.

Freud, Sigmund. 'Mourning and Melancholia.' Vol. 14. *The Standard Edition of the Complete Psychological Works of Sigmund Freud*. Ed. James Strachey. London: Hogarth, 1953–74.

Frickey, Pierrette. 'Jean Rhys.' *International Literature in English*. Ed. Robert L. Ross. New York: Garland, 1991.

Friedman, Ellen G. 'Breaking the Master Narrative: Jean Rhys' *Wide Sargasso Sea*.' *Breaking the Sequence: Women's Experimental Fiction*. Ed. Ellen G. Friedman and Miriam Fuchs. Princeton: Princeton UP, 1989.

Froula, Christine. '*Mrs. Dalloway*'s Postwar Elegy: Women, War, and the Art of Mourning.' MODERNISM / *modernity* 9.1 (2002): 125–63.

Gana, Nouri. 'The Poetics of Mourning: The Tropologic of Prosopopoeia in Joyce's "The Dead."' *American Imago* 60.2 (2003): 159–78.

– 'The Vicissitudes of Melancholia in Freud and Joyce.' *James Joyce Quarterly* 44.1 (2006): 95–109.

Gathorne-Hardy, Jonathan. *The Rise and Fall of the British Nanny*. London: Hodder, 1972.

Gardiner, Judith Kegan. 'Rhys Recalls Ford: *Quartet* and *The Good Soldier*.' *Tulsa Studies in Women's Literature* 1 (1982): 67–81.

Gibson, George Cinclair. *Wake Rites: The Ancient Irish Rituals of* Finnegans Wake. Gainesville: UP of Florida, 2005.

Gilbert, Sandra. Preface. *World War I and the Cultures of Modernity*. Ed. Douglas Mackaman and Michael Mays. Jackson: UP of Mississippi, 2000.

Glendinning, Victoria. *Rebecca West: A Life*. New York: Fawcett, 1987.

Gold, Moshe. 'Printing the Dragon's Bite: Joyce's Poetic History of Thoth, Cadmus, and Gutenberg in *Finnegans Wake.' James Joyce Quarterly* 42–3 (2004–6): 269–95.

Goldman, Jane. '"Purple Buttons on her Bodice": Feminist History and Iconography in *The Waves.' Woolf Studies Annual* 2 (1996): 3–25.

Goodenough, Elizabeth N. 'Demons of Wickedness, Angels of Delight.' *Hawthorne and Women: Engendering and Expanding the Hawthorne Tradition.* Ed. John L. Idol Jr and Melinda M. Ponder. Amherst: U of Massachusetts P, 1999.

– Introduction. *Infant Tongues: The Voice of the Child in Literature.* Ed. Elizabeth Goodenough, Mark A. Heberle, and Naomi Sokoloff. Detroit: Wayne State UP, 1994.

– '"We Haven't the Words": The Silence of Children in the Novels of Virginia Woolf.' *Infant Tongues: The Voice of the Child in Literature.* Ed. Elizabeth Goodenough, Mark A. Heberle, and Naomi Sokoloff. Detroit: Wayne State UP, 1994.

Goodheart, Eugene. 'The Art of Ambivalence in *The Good Soldier.' Sewanee Review* 106.4 (1998): 619–30.

Green, Robert. *Ford Madox Ford: Prose and Politics.* Cambridge,: Cambridge UP, 1981.

Gregg, Veronica. 'Symbolic Imagery and Mirroring Techniques in *Wide Sargasso Sea.' Critical Perspectives on Jean Rhys.* Ed. Pierrette Frickey. Washington, D.C.: Three Continents, 1990.

Hammond, Mary, and Shafquat Towheed. *Publishing in the First World War: Essays in Book History.* Houndmills: Palgrave Macmillan, 2007.

Hartman, Geoffrey H. 'Virginia's Web.' *Beyond Formalism: Literary Essays, 1958–1970.* New Haven: Yale UP, 1970.

Haslam, Sara. *Fragmenting Modernism: Ford Madox Ford, the Novel and the Great War.* Manchester: Manchester UP, 2002.

Hayman, David. 'Male Maturity or the *Pub*lic Rise and Private Decline of HC Earwicker: *Chapter II.3.' How Joyce Wrote* Finnegans Wake. Madison: U of Wisconsin P, 2007.

Heaney, Pam. *Children's Grief.* Dunedin, New Zealand: Longacre, 2004.

Heberle, Mark A. Introduction. *Infant Tongues: The Voice of the Child in Literature.* Ed. Elizabeth Goodenough, Mark A. Heberle, and Naomi Sokoloff. Detroit: Wayne State UP, 1994.

Hendrick, H. 'Constructions and Reconstructions of British Childhood: An Interpretive Survey, 1800 to the Present.' *Constructing and Reconstructing Childhood: Contemporary Issues in the Sociological Study of Childhood.* Ed. A. James and A. Prout. London: Falmer, 1990.

Heywood, J.S. *Childhood and Society a Hundred Years Ago*. London: National Children's Home, 1969.

Hofheinz, Thomas C. *Joyce and the Invention of Irish History: Finnegans Wake in Context*. Cambridge: Cambridge UP, 1995.

Holland, John, Ruth Dance, Nic MacManus, and Carole Stitt. *Lost for Words: Loss and Bereavement Awareness Training*. London: Kingsley, 2005.

Homer. *The Iliad*. Trans. Robert Fagles. New York: Penguin, 1990.

Howells, Coral Ann. 'Jean Rhys (1890–1979).' *The Gender of Modernism: A Critical Anthology*. Ed. Bonnie Kime Scott. Bloomington: Indiana UP, 1990.

Hughes, Ted. *Tales from Ovid: Twenty-Four Passages from the* Metamorphoses. London: Faber, 1997.

Hulcoop, John F. 'Percival and the Porpoise: Woolf's Heroic Theme in *The Waves*.' *Twentieth Century Literature* 34. 4 (1988): 468–88.

Huntley, H. Robert. *The Alien Protagonist of Ford Madox Ford*. Chapel Hill: U of North Carolina P, 1970.

Hussey, Mark. 'Living in a War Zone.' *Virginia Woolf and War: Fiction, Reality, and Myth*. Ed. Mark Hussey. Syracuse: Syracuse UP, 1991.

Hynes, Samuel. *The Edwardian Turn of Mind*. Princeton: Princeton UP, 1968.

– 'The Epistemology of *The Good Soldier*.' *Ford Madox Ford: Modern Judgements*. Ed. Richard A. Cassell. London: Macmillan, 1972.

– *A War Imagined: The First World War and English Culture*. London: Bodley, 1990.

Ignatieff, Michael. *Blood and Belonging: Journeys into the New Nationalism*. New York: Penguin, 1993.

JanMohamed, Abdul R. *Manichean Aesthetics: The Politics of Literature in Colonial Africa*. Amherst: U of Massachusetts P, 1983.

Johnson, Barbara. *The Wake of Deconstruction*. Oxford: Blackwell, 1994.

– *A World of Difference*. Baltimore: Johns Hopkins UP, 1987.

Joyce, James. *Dubliners* (*D*). 1914. New ed. Corrected text Robert Scholes with Richard Ellmann. New York: Viking, 1967.

– *Finnegans Wake* (*FW*). London: Faber, 1950.

– *A Portrait of the Artist as a Young Man* (*P*). Ed. Chester G. Anderson. New York: Viking, 1964.

– *Ulysses* (*U*). Ed. Hans Walter Gabler et al. New York: Garland, 1984, 1986.

Joyce, Simon. *The Victorians in the Rearview Mirror*. Athens: Ohio UP, 2007.

Kamuf, Peggy. Introduction. *A Derrida Reader Between the Blinds*. Ed. Peggy Kamuf. New York: Columbia UP, 1991.

Kaplan, Carola M., and Anne B. Simpson, Eds. *Seeing Double: Revisioning Edwardian and Modernist Literature*. London: Macmillan, 1996.

Kappers-den Hollander, Martien. 'A Gloomy Child and Its Devoted Godmother: Jean Rhys, *Barred, Sous Les Verrous* and *In De Strik*.' *Critical*

Perspectives on Jean Rhys. Ed. Pierrette Frickey. Washington, D.C.: Three Continents, 1990.

Kavka, Misha. 'Men in (Shell-) Shock: Masculinity, Trauma, and Psychoanalysis in Rebecca West's *The Return of the Soldier.*' *Studies in Twentieth Century Literature* 22 (1998): 151–71.

Kearney, Richard. Moderator. '*Confessions* and *Circumfession*: A Roundtable Discussion with Jacques Derrida.' *Augustine and Postmodernism:* Confessions *and* Circumfession. Ed. John D. Caputo and Michael J. Scanlon. Bloomington and Indianapolis: Indiana UP, 2005.

Kershner, R.B. *The Twentieth-Century Novel: An Introduction.* Boston: Bedford, 1997.

Kingsbury, Celia Malone. *The Peculiar Sanity of War: Hysteria in the Literature of World War I.* Lubbock: Texas Tech UP, 2002.

Kloepfer, Deborah Kelly. *The Unspeakable Mother: Forbidden Discourse in Jean Rhys and H.D.* Ithaca: Cornell UP, 1989.

Knowles, Sebastian D.G. *A Purgatorial Flame: Seven British Writers in the Second World War.* Philadelphia: U of Pennsylvania P, 1990.

Krell, David Farrell. *The Purest of Bastards: Works of Mourning, Art, and Affirmation in the Thought of Jacques Derrida.* University Park: Pennsylvania UP, 2000.

Kristeva, Julia. *New Maladies of the Soul.* Trans. Ross Guberman. New York: Columbia UP, 1995.

Kumar, Shiv K. *Bergson and the Stream of Consciousness Novel.* London and Glasgow: Blackie, 1962.

Lasdun, Susan. *Making Victorians: The Drummond Children's World, 1827–1832.* Illus. Drummond Children. London: Gollancz, 1983.

Laurence, Patricia Ondek. *The Reading of Silence: Virginia Woolf and the English Tradition.* Stanford: Stanford UP, 1991.

Lauter, Jane Hamovit, and Nancy Topping Bazin. 'Virginia Woolf's Keen Sensitivity to War: Its Roots and Its Impact on Her Novels.' *Virginia Woolf and War: Fiction, Reality, and Myth.* Ed. Mark Hussey. Syracuse: Syracuse UP, 1991.

Le Boulicaut, Yannick. 'Is There Therapy in Speech in Conrad's Works?' *Conradiana* 34.1–2 (2002): 137–46.

Lee, Herminone. *Virginia Woolf.* London: Vintage, 1997.

Lee, Judith. '"This Hideous Shaping and Moulding": War and *The Waves.*' *Virginia Woolf and War: Fiction, Reality, and Myth.* Ed. Mark Hussey. Syracuse: Syracuse UP, 1991.

Le Gallez, Paula. *The Rhys Woman.* London: Macmillan, 1990.

Lernout, Geert. 'The Beginning: *Chapter I.1.*' *How Joyce Wrote* Finnegans Wake. Madison: U of Wisconsin P, 2007.

Levenback, Karen L. *Virginia Woolf and the Great War.* Syracuse: Syracuse UP, 1999.
– 'Virginia Woolf and Returning Soldiers: The Great War and the Reality of
   Survival in *Mrs. Dalloway* and *The Years.' Woolf Studies Annual* 2 (1996): 71–88.
Levenson, Michael. Introduction. *The Cambridge Companion to Modernism.*
   Ed. Michael Levenson. Cambridge: Cambridge UP, 1999.
Levenson, Michael, and Karen Chase. *The Spectacle of Intimacy: A Public Life for
   the Victorian Family.* Princeton: Princeton UP, 2000.
Lewis, C.S. *A Grief Observed.* London: Faber, 1961.
Lewis, Wyndham. *Time and Western Man.* Boston: Beacon, 1957.
Lid, R.W. *Ford Madox Ford: The Essence of his Art.* Berkeley: U of California P, 1964.
Lilly, Amy M. 'Fascist Aesthetics and Formations of Collective Subjectivity in
   Finnegans Wake.' James Joyce Quarterly 36.2 (1999): 107–23.
Longenbach, James. 'Modern Poetry.' *The Cambridge Companion to Modernism.*
   Ed. Michael Levenson. Cambridge: Cambridge UP, 1999.
Look Lai, Wally. 'The Road to Thornfield Hall: An Analysis of *Wide Sargasso
   Sea.' New Beacon Reviews* 1. Ed. John La Rose. London: New Beacon, 1968.
Lothe, Jakob. *Conrad's Narrative Method.* Oxford: Clarendon, 1989.
Lucy, Niall. *Debating Derrida.* Victoria: Melbourne UP, 1995.
– *A Derrida Dictionary.* Malden, Mass.: Blackwell, 2004.
Lutz, Tom. *Crying: The Natural and Cultural History of Tears.* New York: Norton, 1999.
Mahaffey, Vicki. *Reauthorizing Joyce.* Cambridge: Cambridge UP, 1988.
Malabou, Catherine. 'The Form of an "I."' *Augustine and Postmodernism:
   Confessions and* Circumfession. Ed. John D. Caputo and Michael Scanlon.
   Bloomington and Indianapolis: Indiana UP, 2005.
Marcus, Jane. 'Britannia Rules *The Waves.' Decolonizing Tradition: New Views of
   Twentieth-Century 'British' Literary Canons.* Ed. Karen Lawrence. Urbana: U of
   Illinois P, 1992.
– Editor's Introduction. *The Young Rebecca: Writings of Rebecca West, 1911–17.*
   Ed. Jane Marcus. London: Virago, 1982
McArthur, Murray. 'The Example of Joyce: Derrida Reading Joyce.' *James Joyce
   Quarterly* 32.2 (1995): 227–41.
McFarlane, James. *Modernism: A Guide to European Literature, 1890–1930.*
   Ed. Malcolm Bradbury and James McFarlane. London: Penguin, 1976.
McHugh, Roland. *Annotations to* Finnegans Wake. Rev. ed. Baltimore: Johns
   Hopkins UP, 1991.
Meisel, Perry. *The Absent Father: Virginia Woolf and Walter Pater.* New Haven:
   Yale UP, 1980.
Meixner, John A. *Ford Madox Ford's Novels.* Minneapolis: U of Minnesota P, 1962.
– 'The Saddest Story.' *Ford Madox Ford: Modern Judgments.* Ed. Richard A.
   Cassell. London: Macmillan, 1972.

Mellown, Elgin. 'Character and Themes in the Novels of Jean Rhys.' *Critical Perspectives on Jean Rhys*. Ed. Pierrette Frickey. Washington, D.C.: Three Continents, 1990.

Meyer, Bernard C. 'On the Psychogenesis of the *Nigger.*' *Twentieth Century Interpretations of* The Nigger of the Narcissus*: A Collection of Critical Essays*. Ed. John A. Palmer. Englewood Cliffs, N.J.: Prentice, 1969.

Miller, Alice. *For Your Own Good: Hidden Cruelty in Child-rearing and the Roots of Violence*. 3rd ed. Trans. Hildegarde and Hunter Hannum. New York: Farrar, 1983.

Miller, J. Hillis. *The Ethics of Reading: Kant, de Man, Eliot, Trollope, James, and Benjamin*. New York: Columbia UP, 1987.

– '*Mrs. Dalloway*: Repetition as the Raising of the Dead.' *Critical Essays on Virginia Woolf*. Ed. Morris Beja. Boston: Hall, 1985.

Moi, Toril. *Sexual / Textual Politics: Feminist Literary History*. London: Methuen, 1985.

Morse, J. Mitchell. 'Where Terms Begin: Book I, chapter 1.' *A Conceptual Guide to* Finnegans Wake. Ed. Michael H. Begnal and Fritz Senn. University Park: Pennsylvania State UP, 1974.

Moss, Mark. *Manliness and Militarism: Educating Young Boys in Ontario for War*. Oxford: Oxford UP, 2001.

Muir, Edwin. Review. *Virginia Woolf: The Critical Heritage*. Ed. Robin Majumdar and Allen McLaurin. London and Boston: Routledge, 1975.

Naipaul, V.S. 'Without a Dog's Chance.' *Critical Perspectives on Jean Rhys*. Ed. Pierrette Frickey. Washington, D.C.: Three Continents, 1990.

Nebeker, Helen. *Jean Rhys: Woman in Passage*. Montreal: Eden, 1981.

Norris, Margot. *The Decentered Universe of* Finnegans Wake. Baltimore: Johns Hopkins UP, 1976.

– *Joyce's Web: The Social Unraveling of Modernism*. Austin: U of Texas P, 1992.

Norton, Ann V. *Paradoxical Feminism: The Novels of Rebecca West*. Lanham: International Scholars, 2000.

O'Connor, Teresa. *Jean Rhys: The West Indian Novels*. New York: New York UP, 1986.

Onions, John. *English Fiction and Drama of the Great War, 1918–1939*. London: Macmillan, 1990.

Orel, Harold. *The Literary Achievement of Rebecca West*. London: Macmillan, 1986.

Paccaud-Huguet, Josiane. '*Under Western Eyes* and *Hamlet:* Where Angels Fear to Tread.' *Conradiana* 26.2–3 (1994): 169–86.

Painter, George D. *Marcel Proust: A Bibliography*. 1959–65. London: Random, 1996.

Pease, Allison. 'The Mastery of Form: Beardsley and Joyce.' *Modernism, Mass Culture, and the Aesthetics of Obscenity*. Cambridge: Cambridge UP, 2000.

Pennells, Margaret, and Susan Smith. *The Forgotten Mourners*. London: Kingsley, 1996.

Phillips, Kathy J. *Manipulating Masculinity: War and Gender in Modern British and American Literature*. New York: Macmillan, 2006.

– *Virginia Woolf Against Empire*. Knoxville: U of Tennessee P, 1994.

Plante, David. 'Jean Rhys: A Remembrance.' *Paris Review* 76 (1979): 238–84.

Poole, Roger. *The Unknown Virginia Woolf*. Cambridge: Cambridge UP, 1978.

Potter, Jane. *Boys in Khaki, Girls in Print: Women's Literary Responses to the Great War, 1914–1918*. Oxford: Clarendon, 2005.

Proust, Marcel. *Against Sainte-Beuve and Other Essays*. Trans. John Sturrock. New York: Penguin, 1988.

– *Remembrance of Things Past*. Vol. 1. Trans. C.K. Scott Moncrieff and Terence Kilmartin. London: Chatto, 1981.

Rabaté, Jean-Michel. *The Ghosts of Modernity*. Gainesville: UP of Florida, 1996.

– 'Lapsus ex machine.' *Post-Structuralist Joyce: Essays from the French*. Ed. Derek Attridge and Daniel Ferrer. Cambridge: Cambridge UP, 1984.

Rado, Lisa. 'Walking Through Phantoms: Irony, Scepticism, and Razumov's Self-Delusion in *Under Western Eyes*.' *Conradiana* 24.2 (1992): 83–99.

Rae, Patricia, ed. *Modernism and Mourning*. Lewisburg: Bucknell UP, 2007.

Raitt, Suzanne. 'Virginia Woolf's Early Novels.' *The Cambridge Companion to Virginia Woolf*. Ed. Sue Roe and Susan Sellers. Cambridge: Cambridge UP, 2000.

Ramazani, Jahan. *Poetry of Mourning: The Modern Elegy from Hardy to Heany*. Chicago: U of Chicago P, 1994.

Ramchand, Kenneth. '*Wide Sargasso Sea*.' *Critical Perspectives on Jean Rhys*. Ed. Pierrette Frickey. Washington, D.C.: Three Continents, 1990.

Rasula, Jed. '*Finnegans Wake* and the Character of the Letter.' *James Joyce Quarterly* 34.4 (1997): 517–30.

Rhys, Jean. *After Leaving Mr. Mackenzie (ALMM)*.London: Penguin, 1971.

– *Good Morning, Midnight (GMM)*. London: Penguin, 1969.

– *The Left Bank and Other Stories*. Pref. Ford Madox Ford. Freeport: Books for Libraries, 1970.

– *The Letters of Jean Rhys*. Ed. Francis Wyndham and Diana Melly. New York: Viking, 1984

– *Quartet (Q)*. London: Penguin, 1973.

– *Smile Please: An Unfinished Autobiography (S)*. Foreword Diana Athill. Berkeley: Creative Arts, 1979.

– *Tales of the Wide Caribbean: A New Collection of Short Stories.* Selected and introd. by Kenneth Ramchand. London: Heinemann Educational, n.d.
– *Voyage in the Dark (V).* London: Penguin, 1969.
– *Wide Sargasso Sea (WSS).* London: Penguin, 1968.
Richter, Harvena. 'Hunting the Moth: Virginia Woolf and the Creative Imagination.' *Critical Essays on Virginia Woolf.* Ed. Morris Beja. Boston: Hall, 1985.
Rickard, John S. *Joyce's Book of Memory: The Mnemotechnic of* Ulysses. Durham: Duke UP, 1999.
– *Virginia Woolf: The Inward Voyage.* Princeton: Princeton UP, 1970.
Riquelme, John Paul. '*Stephen Hero, Dubliners,* and *A Portrait of the Artist as a Young Man*: Styles of Realism and Fantasy.' *The Cambridge Companion to James Joyce.* Ed. Derek Attridge. Cambridge: Cambridge UP, 1990.
Rising, Catherine. 'Raskolnikov and Razumov: From Passive to Active Subjectivity in *Under Western Eyes.*' *Conradiana* 33.1 (2001): 24–39.
Rollyson, Carl. *The Literary Legacy of Rebecca West.* San Francisco: International Scholars, 1998.
Romanick, Debra. 'Victorious Wretch? The Puzzle of Haldin's Name in *Under Western Eyes.*' *Conradiana* 30.1 (1998): 44–52.
Rose, Lionel. *The Erosion of Childhood: Child Oppression in Britain, 1860–1918.* London: Routledge, 1991.
Roughley, Alan. *Reading Derrida Reading Joyce.* Gainesville: UP of Florida, 1999.
Saunders, Max. *Ford Madox Ford: A Dual Life.* 2 vols. Oxford: Oxford UP, 1996.
Schiesari, Juliana. *The Gendering of Melancholia: Feminism, Psychoanalysis, and the Symbolics of Loss in Renaissance Literature.* Ithaca: Cornell UP, 1992.
Schneider, Karen. *Loving Arms: British Women Writing the Second World War.* Lexington: UP of Kentucky, 1997.
Schork, R.J. 'Genetic Primer: Chapter I.6.' *How Joyce Wrote* Finnegans Wake: *A Chapter-by-Chapter Genetic Guide.* Madison:U of Wisconsin P, 2007.
– *Greek and Hellenic Culture in Joyce.* Gainesville: UP of Florida, 1998.
– *Latin and Roman Culture in Joyce.* Gainesville: UP of Florida, 1997.
Schweizer, Bernard. *Rebecca West: Heroism, Rebellion, and the Female Epic.* Westport: Greenwood, 2002.
Scott, Bonnie Kime. *Refiguring Modernism.* 2 vols. Bloomington: Indiana UP, 1995.
Seymour Yapp, C. *Children's Nursing: Lectures to Probationers.* London: Poor Law Publications, 1924.
Shakespeare, William. *Hamlet.* Ed. Harold Jenkins. London: Methuen, 1982.
Shay, Jonathan. *Achilles in Vietnam: Combat Trauma and the Undoing of Character.* New York: Simon, 1994.
Shelley, Percy Bysshe. 'Ozymandias.' *The Norton Anthology of English Literature.* Gen. ed. M.H. Abrams. 6th ed. Vol. 2. New York: Norton, 1996.

Shephard, Ben. *A War of Nerves.* London: Cape, 2000.

Sheppard, Richard. 'The Crisis of Language.' *Modernism: A Guide to European Literature, 1890–1930.* Ed. Malcolm Bradbury and James McFarlane. London: Penguin, 1976.

Shloss, Carol Loeb. *Lucia Joyce: To Dance in the* Wake. New York: Farrar, 2003.

Showalter, Elaine. *'Mrs. Dalloway.' Virginia Woolf: Introductions to the Major Works.* Ed. Julia Briggs. London: Virago, 1994.

– *The Female Malady: Women, Madness and English Culture, 1830–1980.* New York: Pantheon, 1985. London: Virago, 1987.

Slote, Sam. 'Needles in the Camel's Eye Concerning A Time of the "Collide-orscape."' Finnegans Wake*: 'teems of times.'* Ed. Andrew Treip. Amsterdam: Rodopi, 1994.

Smith, Susan Bennett. 'Reinventing Grief Work: Virginia Woolf's Feminist Representations of Mourning in *Mrs. Dalloway* and *To the Lighthouse.' Twentieth Century Literature* 41.4 (1995): 310–27.

Snaith, Anna. *Virginia Woolf: Public and Private Negotiations.* London: Macmillan, 2000.

Snitow, Ann Barr. *Ford Madox Ford and the Voice of Uncertainty.* Baton Rouge: Louisiana State UP, 1984.

Sokoloff, Naomi. 'Introduction.' *Infant Tongues: The Voice of the Child in Literature.* Ed. Elizabeth Goodenough, Mark A. Heberle, and Naomi Sokoloff. Detroit: Wayne State UP, 1994.

Spilka, Mark. *Virginia Woolf's Quarrel with Grieving.* Lincoln: U of Nebraska P, 1980.

Spivak, Gayatri Chakravorty. 'Three Women's Texts and a Critique of Imperialism.' *The Feminist Reader: Essays in Gender and the Politics of Literary Criticism.* Ed. Catherine Belsey and Jane Moore. London: Macmillan, 1989.

Stang, Sondra. *Ford Madox Ford.* New York: Ungar, 1977.

Steppe, Wolfhard. 'The Merry Greeks (with a Farewell to *epicleti*).' *James Joyce Quarterly* 32.3–4 (1995): 597–617.

Stetz, Margaret Diane. 'Drinking "the Wine of Truth": Philosophical Change in West's *The Return of the Soldier.' Arizona Quarterly* 43.1 (1987): 63–78.

– 'Rebecca West's Criticism: Alliance, Tradition, and Modernism.' *Rereading Modernism: New Directions in Feminist Criticism.* Ed. Lisa Rado. New York: Garland, 1994.

Stewart, Garrett. 'Catching the Stylistic D/rift: Sound Defects in Woolf's *The Waves.' English Literary History* 54 (1987): 421–61.

Stevenson, Randall. *Modernist Fiction: An Introduction.* New York: Harvester, 1992.

Strachey, Lytton. *Eminent Victorians.* New York: Garden City, n.d.

Strange, Julie-Marie. *Death, Grief and Poverty in Britain, 1870–1914.* Cambridge: Cambridge UP, 2005.

Taylor, Charles. *Sources of the Self: The Making of the Modern Identity.* Cambridge, Mass.: Harvard UP, 1989.

Tennyson, Alfred, Lord. *In Memoriam 54. The Norton Anthology of English Literature.* Gen. ed. M.H. Abrams. 6th ed. Vol 2. New York: Norton, 1996.

Thornton, Sara. 'The Vanity of Childhood: Constructing, Deconstructing, and Destroying the Child in the Novel of the 1840s.' *Children in Culture: Approaches to Childhood.* Ed. Karín Lesnik-Oberstein. London: Macmillan; New York, St Martin's, 1998.

Thorpe, Michael. '"The Other Side": *Wide Sargasso Sea* and *Jane Eyre.' Critical Perspectives on Jean Rhys.* Ed. Pierrette Frickey. Washington, D.C.: Three Continents, 1990.

Tiffin, Helen. 'Mirror and Mask: Colonial Motifs in the Novels of Jean Rhys.' *World Literature Written in English* 17 (1978): 328–41.

Treip, Andrew. '"As Per Periodicity": Vico, Freud and the Serial Awakening of Book III Chapter 4.' Finnegans Wake: *'teems of times.'* Ed. Andrew Treip. Amsterdam: Rodopi, 1994.

– 'Lost Histereve: Vichian Soundings and Reverberations in the Genesis of *Finnegans Wake* II.4.' *James Joyce Quarterly* 32.3–4 (1995): 641–57.

Troy, Michele K. 'Two Very Different Portraits: Anglo-American and German Reception of Joyce's *A Portrait of the Artist as a Young Man.' James Joyce Quarterly* 35.1 (1997): 37–58.

Tylee, Claire M. *The Great War and Women's Consciousness: Images of Militarism and Womanhood in Women's Writings, 1914–64.* London: Macmillan, 1990.

Urwin, C., and E. Sharland. 'From Bodies to Minds in Childcare Literature: Advice to Parents in Inter-War Britain.' *In the Name of the Child: Health and Welfare, 1880–1940.* London: Routledge, 1992.

Usui, Masami. 'The Female Victims of the War in *Mrs. Dalloway.' Virginia Woolf and War: Fiction, Reality, and Myth.* Ed. Mark Hussey. Syracuse: Syracuse UP, 1991.

Van Boheemen-Saaf, Christine. *Joyce, Derrida, Lacan, and the Trauma of History.* Cambridge: Cambridge UP, 1999.

Virgil. *The Aeneid.* Trans. Robert Fitzgerald. New York: Random, 1983.

Watkin, William. *On Mourning: Theories of Loss in Modern Literature.* Edinburgh: Edinburgh UP, 2004.

Webb, Nancy Boyd. *Helping Bereaved Children.* 2nd ed. New York: Guilford, 2002.

Weiss, Timothy. *Fairy Tale and Romance in the Works of Ford Madox Ford.* Lanham: UP of America, 1984.

West, C. *How to Nurse Sick Children*. London: Longman, 1854.

West, Rebecca. Review of *The Good Soldier. Ford Madox Ford: The Critical Heritage*. Ed. Frank MacShane. London: Routledge, 1972.

– *The Court and the Castle: Some Treatments of a Recurrent Theme*. New Haven: Yale UP, 1957.

– *The Fountain Overflows*. London: Virago, 1984.

– *The Judge*. London: Hutchinson, 1922.

– *1900*. New York: Viking, 1982.

– *The Return of the Soldier (RS)*. London: Penguin, 1998.

– *The Young Rebecca: Writings of Rebecca West, 1911–1917*. Ed. Jane Marcus. London: Virago, 1982.

White, Franklin A. 'Children's Hospitals.' *The Evolution of Hospitals in Britain*. Ed. F.N.L. Poynter. London: Pitman Medical, 1964.

Wilde, Oscar. *The Happy Prince and Other Tales*. New York: Knopf, 1995.

Williams, Trevor L. '"Brothers of the great white lodge": Joyce and the Critique of Imperialism.' *James Joyce Quarterly* 33.3 (1996): 377–97.

Williams, William Carlos. '*Parade's End* (1951).' *Ford Madox Ford: Modern Judgments*. Ed. Richard A. Cassell. London: Macmillan, 1972.

Winter, Jay. *Sites of Memory, Sites of Mourning: The Great War in European Cultural History*. Cambridge: Cambridge UP, 1995.

Woolf, Virginia. *The Diary of Virginia Woolf*. Ed. Anne Olivier Bell and Andrew McNeillie. 3 vols. London: Hogarth, 1977–84.

– *The Essays of Virginia Woolf*. Vol. 3. Ed. Andrew McNeillie. London: Hogarth, 1988.

– *A Haunted House and Other Stories (HH)*. New York: Penguin, 1973.

– *Moments of Being (MB)*. Ed. Jeanne Schulkind. 2nd ed. London: Hogarth, 1985.

– *Mrs. Dalloway*. London: Grafton, 1976.

– *Roger Fry: A Biography*. London: Hogarth, 1940.

– *A Room of One's Own; Three Guineas*. Ed. Morag Shiach. Oxford: Oxford UP, 1992.

– *To the Lighthouse*. Ed. Stella McNichol. Introd. and notes Hermione Lee. London: Penguin, 1992.

– *The Waves (W)*. London: Panther, 1977.

Wussow, Helen. *The Nightmare of History: The Fictions of Virginia Woolf and D.H. Lawrence*. Bethlehem: Lehigh UP. London: Associated UP, 1998.

Zornado, Joseph. *Inventing the Child: Culture, Ideology, and the Story of Childhood*. New York: Garland, 2001.

Zwerdling, Alex. '*Mrs. Dalloway* and the Social System.' *Critical Essays on Virginia Woolf*. Ed. Morris Beja. Boston: Hall, 1985.

Index